MARCO⊕POLO

KT-239-095

PARIS

Sighteeing Highlights

The world-famous Louvre. Notre-Dame. Champs-Elysées and the Eiffel Tower. Arc de Triomphe and the enchanting Place des Vosges – if you don't have weeks to spend in Paris, you face some tough choices. We present the sights you should not miss!

Do You Feel Like...

... special places in Paris for flying high and seeing far in the urban jungle, new trends, exotic and fascinating things from all over the world, biking or romantic moments? Discover Paris just the way you like it.

SEEING FAR

TREND-SPOTTING

WORLD CULTURES

FIT & FUN

ROMANCE

BACKGROUND

ENJOY PARIS

Erotic with diamanté: the Bluebell Girls in the Lido de Paris

Très parisien: legendary Brasserie La Coupole

PRICE CLASSES
Restaurants
(set meal without drinks)
€€€€	over €100
€€€	€50 – 100
€€	€30 – 50
€	€15 – 30

Hotels (double room without breakfast)
€€€€	over €350
€€€	€200 – 350
€€	€130 – 200
€	up to €130

TOURS

SIGHTS FROM A TO Z

One can spend weeks in the Louvre

PRACTICAL INFORMATION

BACKGROUND

France's capital and economic centre, multicultural metropolis, capital of superlatives, the real art of living and poesie – find out about this world city.

Facts

Population and Politics

Tempting scenes, scents and sounds are associated with the name of Paris. The multicultural city is considered the embodiment of the wide world and is one of the most popular destinations for city breaks.

Paris is the **capital of the French Republic**, the seat of the president, of the **government** and of both chambers of the French parliament – the National Assembly and the Senate. in spite of all attempts of decentralization, Paris determines what France thinks, who has political influence and what is in fashion. Today one in five French citizens live in the capital; this is where the economy and the art scene get their impulses, and the zeitgeist its European touch. Paris charms visitors with its inimitable elegance and wonderful peculiarities, with historic continuity and unending change.

Metropolis and world city

France's capital is situated in the centre of the fertile **Parisian basin**. Seven hills rise in the historic centre, of which the highest is the 129-m/423-ft Butte de Montmartre. Outside the city the rivers Marne and Oise flow into the Seine. Just like the ship in the Parisian coat of arms Paris is moored in the Seine: *fluctuat nec mergitur* – tossed about but unsinkable. Whereas during the Middle Ages merchant ships from all over Europe dropped anchor in Paris, today the Seine is a peaceful transport artery for cruise boats and barges. Settlement began on the river islands of Île de la Cité and Île St-Louis, where the Seine was easy to cross. As the ground rose on the southern bank to Montagne Ste-Geneviève – today's Quartier Latin – the left bank was just as free from flooding as the right bank of the Seine. Therefore Roman Lutetia was founded on the rive gauche; from the Middle Ages trade developed on the rive droite north of the Seine.

Ship in the city coat of arms

2.2 million people live in the »**Ville de Paris**«, which at 105.4 sq km/41 sq mi has only one fifteenth of the surface area of Greater London. This makes Paris the most densely populated capital in Europe. The suburbs – »**banlieues**« – skirt the city in two concentric circles. The inner circle is formed by the three **départements** Hauts-de-Seine, Val-de-Marne and Seine-Saint-Denis. The départements of Seine-et-Marne, Essone, Val d'Oise and Yvelines, which still have a rural character, make up the outer circle. Together the eight départements form the Île-de-France region; with an area of 12,012 sq km/4638 sq mi and some twelve million inhabitants it is Europe's third-largest conurbation.

A European mega metropolis

The Fontaine des Fleuves on Place de la Concorde

▶ Ville de Paris
Capital of the Republic of France

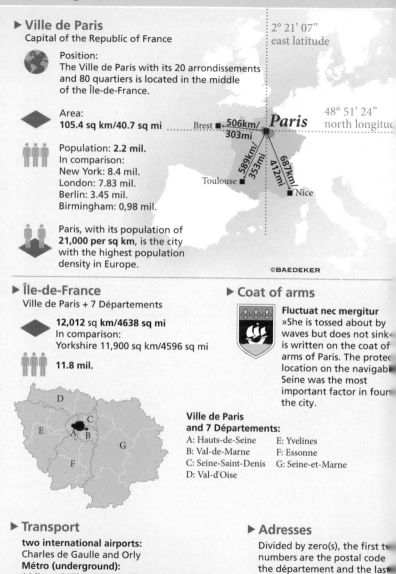

Position:
The Ville de Paris with its 20 arrondissements and 80 quartiers is located in the middle of the Île-de-France.

Area:
105.4 sq km/40.7 sq mi

Population: **2.2 mil.**
In comparison:
New York: 8.4 mil.
London: 7.83 mil.
Berlin: 3.45 mil.
Birmingham: 0,98 mil.

Paris, with its population of **21,000 per sq km**, is the city with the highest population density in Europe.

2° 21' 07"
east latitude

Paris

48° 51' 24"
north longitud

Brest ■ **506km/303mi**

589km/353mi

687km/412mi

Toulouse ■

■ Nice

©BAEDEKER

▶ Île-de-France
Ville de Paris + 7 Départements

12,012 sq km/**4638 sq mi**
In comparison:
Yorkshire 11,900 sq km/4596 sq mi

11.8 mil.

**Ville de Paris
and 7 Départements:**
A: Hauts-de-Seine   E: Yvelines
B: Val-de-Marne   F: Essonne
C: Seine-Saint-Denis G: Seine-et-Marne
D: Val-d'Oise

▶ Coat of arms

Fluctuat nec mergitur
»She is tossed about by waves but does not sink« is written on the coat of arms of Paris. The protec location on the navigabl Seine was the most important factor in foun the city.

▶ Transport
two international airports:
Charles de Gaulle and Orly
Métro (underground):
14 lines, 217km/130mi rail network, 300 stations
RER (metrorail):
5 lines, 587km/352mi rail network, 246 stations
Tram:
8 lines; funicular (Montmartre)

▶ Adresses

Divided by zero(s), the first tw numbers are the postal code the département and the las number(s) stand for the **arrondissement**.

 75001 1st arrondisser (Paris)

Economy

Île de France: richest region in France, GDP per capita: 46,980 Euros.
593,000 businesses produce 29% of the French GDP.
Paris: known for international banks and insurance companies, haute couture, luxury goods, media.
Port de Paris: second largest European inland harbour after Duisburg-Ruhrort, turnover: 22.6 mil. tons (2012).

GDP compared to Europe
in billions of Euros

Germany
2773
2146 France

EU total: 17,960

▶ Climate

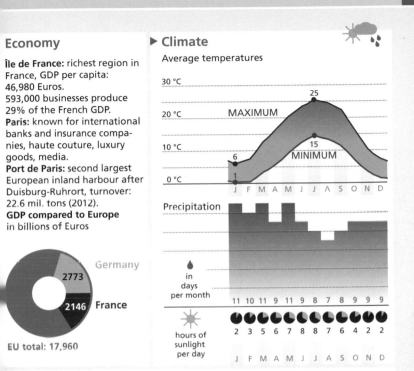

Average temperatures

30 °C

25

20 °C MAXIMUM

10 °C 6 15 MINIMUM

0 °C 1

J F M A M J J A S O N D

Precipitation

in days per month

11 10 11 9 11 9 8 7 8 9 9 9

hours of sunlight per day

2 3 5 6 7 8 8 7 6 4 2 2

J F M A M J J A S O N D

Stronghold of gourmets

Paris is considered to be the city of gourmets, which can be seen in the fact that it has more three-star chefs than all of Britain. Anyone who gets a star in the Guide Michelin is taken up into the Olympus of the best gastronomy. Tokyo has the largest number of stars worldwide (247).

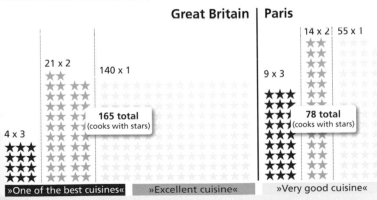

Great Britain | Paris

Great Britain:
4 x 3
21 x 2
140 x 1
165 total (cooks with stars)

Paris:
9 x 3
14 x 2
55 x 1
78 total (cooks with stars)

»One of the best cuisines« »Excellent cuisine« »Very good cuisine«

**Two
»conseils«
for the city**

Paris has been both commune and département since 1977. Every six years the Parisians elect a city council of 163 members, the **Conseil de Paris**, which chooses the mayor (maire) and, in its function as the **Conseil Général**, is responsible for the département. In 2014 the Socialist Anne Hidalgo was elected as Paris's first female mayor and successor to Bertrand Delanoë. The head of the département is the Préfet de Paris, presently Daniel Canepa, who is appointed by the government, functions as prefect of the Île-de-France region and presides over the regional council (Conseil Régional). The police force is headed by a police prefect.

**Arrondisse-
ments and
quartiers**

The Département Ville de Paris consists of **20 arrondissements** (districts); each of those is divided in turn into **four quartiers** (quarters). The layout of the arrondissements resembles a spiral that starts from Louvre (1st arr.) and twice coils itself clockwise around the historic centre of Île de la Cité to the 20th arr. at Place de la Nation. The last two digits of the postcode indicated the arrondissement. The traditional quartiers derive their names from villages such as La Villette, Belleville and Chaillot that have been incorporated into the city, from churches such as St-Germain-des-Prés, from buildings such as Les Halles and Opéra, or from historical characteristics such as the Quartier Latin. »**Faubourgs**« – meaning literally »outside the castle« – are suburbs that were usually named after the nearest village – Montmartre, for example, was the suburb in the direction of the village Montmartre.

**Multicultural
Paris**

Paris, which covers only 2% of the territory of France, attracts workers from all over the country. Nearly one sixth of the population of France live in the Paris area; approximately two thirds of Parisians hail from elsewhere. Each French region is represented by its own segment of the population. Half of the 3.3 million foreigners in France live in Île-de-France, most of them in Clichy and Seine-Saint-Denis. In Paris, a city that has attracted a large number of immigrants for centuries, the proportion of citizens originating abroad is nearly 18%, rising to 26–35% in the 2nd, 10th, 18th and 19th arrondissements. Paris is regarded as an important cultural hub of sub-Saharan Africa. The 13th arrondissement harbours **Europe's biggest Chinatown**. Belleville and Goutte d'Or demonstrate, for the most part, how Christians, Jews and Muslims can live together peacefully. They are connected not just by faith but by origin – almost all of them coming the former French colonies in North Africa.

**Christians,
Jews and
Muslims**

Paris is the seat of an archbishop and has well over 100 Catholic parishes. Moreover, there are several dozen Protestant churches, over 20 Greek and Russian Orthodox churches and a Jewish congregation with approximately 220,000 members, 70% of whom are Sephardic

Multicultural Paris

Jews of North African origin. Three large mosques (mosquées-cathédrales) cater for the now second-largest religious group, the Muslims. They include the oldest mosque in France, built in 1922.

After Brussels, Paris is in second place in the world when it comes to the headquarters of international organisations. The three best-known are UNESCO (since 1946), the secretariat of the Organization for Economic Cooperation and Development (OECD) and INTER-POL, the European body formed by national criminal investigation departments. The European Space Agency (ESA), the International Chamber of Commerce and the International Energy Agency (iea) also operate out of Paris.

International organizations

Economy

Biotechnology and the automotive industry, aeronautics, IT and media, retail and various services: this broad-based mix of industries make Paris and the Île-de-France the strongest regional economy in Europe, a fact reflected in the gross national product, which currently stands at around €555 billion per year, even exceeding that of countries such as Sweden or Belgium.

Almost all French companies and a high percentage of the world's largest corporations have offices in Greater Paris. This concentration of corporate activity makes Paris the leading European labour market, which employs some 3.5 million people including more than half of all French managers.

Centre of the French economy

Welcome to Everyday Life

Experience what Paris is like away from the hordes of tourists, encounter completely »normal« people or meet the locals privately – here are some tips:

THE PARIS OF THE PARISIANS

Out of love for their city locals volunteer to show visitors their own Parisian neighbourhoods, including markets, cafés, theatres, galleries, plus other favourite places of the Seine metropolis. And the best thing about the tour is that it's free!

Paris Greeters, *2–3-hour city walks for max. 6 people in French or English, booking two weeks in advance. By way of thanks, the »Parisien d'un Jour, Parisien toujours« association is always grateful for donations from satisfied customers. www.parisiendunjour.fr*

PARIS AT WORK

A look into the printing works of »Le Parisien« or the silversmiths/workshop of Christofle, driving a train in the simulator at SNCF or get an impression of the pharmaceutical industry at Sanofi-Aventis: every year the Département Seine-Saint-Denis organizes around 500 factory or plant tours.

www.tourisme93.com/visites/ 8-entreprises-et-services

ARTISANS IN ACTION

Art Déco cabinet makers, the art of gilding, watchmakers, felt and textile works, lithography, miniature enamel painting – up-close insights into the working world of Paris are also provided by the **Journées des Métiers d'Art**, by which in all odd-numbered years in April, hundreds of artisans in the capital open up their workshops to visitors.

www.journeesdesmetiersdart.com

ACCOMMODATION AND FOOD

With the advent of Web 2.0 Parisian hoteliers have got some completion on their hands, in the shape of an Internet phenomenon that has been growing at lightning speed across the globe, namely **social networks** that offer accommodation ranging from charming mini-rooms to designer apartments.
www.airnbn.com, www.housetrip.com www.9flats.com

An alternative is »**Echange de maison**«, private house-swaps arranged according to the motto »I'll stay at your place and you can stay at mine«. These are very common in France and there are tens of thousands of possibilities in Greater Paris alone.
www.trocmaison.com
www.echange-maison.net
www.haustauschferien.com

Or perhaps you'd like to enjoy an evening meal with a Parisian family. For €65 per head your host will prepare a delicious meal full of specialities – also an excellent opportunity to make new friends!
www.voulezvousdiner.com

City districts

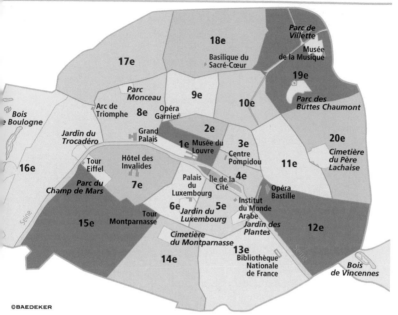

18e
Parc de Villette
Basilique du Sacré-Cœur
Musée de la Musique
17e
19e
Parc Monceau
9e
10e
Parc des Buttes Chaumont
Arc de Triomphe
8e
Opéra Garnier
Bois de Boulogne
2e
Jardin du Trocadéro
Grand Palais
1e Musée du Louvre
3e
Centre Pompidou
20e
Cimetière du Père Lachaise
Tour Eiffel
Hôtel des Invalides
11e
16e
Parc du Champ de Mars
7e
Palais du Luxembourg
Île de la Cité
4e
Opéra Bastille
Institut du Monde Arabe
6e Jardin du Luxembourg
5e
15e
Tour Montparnasse
Jardin des Plantes
12e
Cimetière du Montparnasse
13e
14e
Bibliothèque Nationale de France
Bois de Vincennes
Seine

©BAEDEKER

Multinational orientation exhibition site

The economy in the Greater Paris area is very internationally oriented, with multinational corporations accounting for 15% of the workforce and rising. Besides the new **MICT** (media, information and communication technology), the emphasis is on biotechnology and nanotechnology as well as classic industrial fields such as the two export heavyweights, the **automotive and aerospace industries**. Each year in June, the latter stages the world's leading aviation and aerospace exhibition at Le Bourget with the Salon International de l'Aéronautique et de l'Espace (SIAE). Other important sectors are the consumer goods and cosmetics industries. Innovative **technologies of the future** such as in the field of renewable energies are promoted in the Paris area by nine »Pôles de compétitivité« (competitiveness clusters), partnerships based around a specific theme, some of which collaborate internationally (as in the aerospace industry). 80,000 researchers and an annual R & D expenditure of up to 20 billion euros make Paris one of Europe's leading research locations, whose reputation was built primarily on the large scientific facility of CEA Saclay, which was established in 1945 to focus mainly on nuclear and particle physics and now has more than 6000 employees.

While industrial production is concentrated in the outer suburbs, and La Défense in the west of the city has become the preserve of global company headquarters, the city itself is characterized predominantly by **small and medium-sized businesses** that have left their mark on the various neighbourhoods. Thus, makers of furniture and instruments are to this day based in Faubourg St-Antoine (11th–12th arr.). Faubourg St-Honoré is the home of haute couture, and on Place Vendôme and Rue de la Paix you will find the city's most expensive jewellers. Luxury labels are concentrated in the streets around Opéra Garnier, while publishers and bookstores have established themselves in the district around the Théâtre de l'Odéon. Rue du Paradis is synonymous in Paris for crystal ware, and the Sentier neighbourhood is where you get cheap textiles from China.

Crafts industries and luxury labels

Since 1923 trade fairs have taken place at Porte de Versailles, where the **Parc des Expositions** with its 44 meeting rooms, three auditoria and eight halls covering over 200,000 m2 is the largest of the dozen or so Paris exhibition spaces. This is also where the highlight of the calendar of 100 trade fairs and 1000 congresses is held, the Salon de l'Agriculture (www.salon-agriculture.com). Founded in 1964, the **Agricultural Fair** in February/March has been the undisputed crowd puller, with around 650,000 visitors. In addition to farm machinery and local products, the »largest farm in France« shows off 4500 animals: lambs, pigs, poultry and cows. »Caresser les culs des vaches« (patting cows on the behind) is highly political and is considered in France to be a measure of the down-to-earthness of a president. Jacques Chirac was a master of the discipline, while Nicolas Sarkozy learned it only slowly – the Parisians murmur that he prefers doing it to women.

Trade fairs and congresses

More than 33 million tourists visit Paris each year and get the cash registers ringing. Numerically, the British take first place among the foreign visitor contingent (1.9 million), followed by Americans (1.5 million) and Spanish (1.1 million). With 1 million visitors each, the Germans share fifth place with the Italians. Coming on strong are guests from the Middle East (400,000). The most popular attraction of the Seine metropolis is Notre Dame with 13.6 million annual visitors, followed by Sacré Coeur (10.5 million), the Louvre (8.3 million) and Eiffel Tower (7.1 million). Besides the Louvre the most popular museums are the Centre Pompidou (3.1 million) and the Musée d' Orsay (2.9 million).

Tourism

Creation of a World City

From island village in the Seine to the vibrant capital of the Grande Nation: the history of France, whose fate is determined to this day in the city on the Seine, is mirrored in the eventful past of Paris.

Five small islands in the Seine, three of which were joined to the banks as the water level sank, are the origin of today's city. In Bercy archaeologists discovered Neolithic jewellery and everyday items from around 4000 BC. In the 3rd century BC Celtic Parisii built their huts on Île de la Cité and called their main settlement Lucotesia or »louk-teih« (the »place of swamps«). The Celts lived by fishing and levied tolls at this important crossing point of trade routes.

Early period

FROM ANCIENT LUTETIA TO ROYAL CAPITAL

52 BC	Roman colonial town Lutetia
AD 508	Paris becomes the capital of the Merovingian kingdom
Mid-11th century	Royal residence in Paris

From 52 BC, after the conquest of Gaul by Julius Caesar, the Roman colony of Lutetia Parisiorum developed mainly on the left bank of the Seine with a linear pattern of streets that is evident in the city centre to this day. Town houses, theatres, Roman baths and temples were built, as building material was plentiful: lime, sandstone and sand on the left, gypsum on the right bank of the Seine. Dionysius, the »Apostle of Gaul« and first bishop of Paris, preached the Christian message around AD 250, was beheaded in AD 280 and buried in St-Denis, the future burial place of French kings. In the 4th century the name Civitas Parisiorum was mentioned for the first time.

Roman rule

The peaceful coexistence of Gauls and Romans ended in the late 5th century when the Merovingians under Clovis I drove out the Romans, subjugated the Alemanni, defeated the other Germanic tribal chieftains and created a unified kingdom. In 508 they made Paris their capital and converted the Roman government palace on the Île de la Cité into a Merovingian stronghold.

Merovingians 6th century

King Henri IV gave his capital Paris a new appearance

Carolingians Under the Carolingian dynasty, the main political focus of France shifted to the east. Paris, which already had more than 20,000 residents around AD 800, lost its political status but boomed as a trading centre. The wealth of the city attracted the Vikings, who looted Paris several times – until Count Odo from the Robertian dynasty defended the city successfully in AD 885.

Capetians After the death of Louis V, the last Carolingian, the »dux francorum« **(987–1328)** **Hugo Capet**, was elected king in 987. Paris profited from its new role as royal residence and quickly expanded on both banks of the Seine. River trade prospered due to the monopoly on the Seine held by Parisian boatmen and the new quays at Place de la Grève. The sprawling city gained a first ring of defences between 1190 and 1210 under King Philippe Auguste II. The wall with the Louvre fortification enclosed Île de la Cité with the royal palace and cathedral; La Ville, the settlement of craftsmen and merchants on the north bank; and the Université, a centre of learning with a cathedral school on the south bank.

The reign of **King Louis IX** (1226–70) was the most glittering period that Paris had yet seen. Louis established an efficient administration and a supreme royal court (parliament) and allowed the capital's citizens to maintain their own police force instead of the royal guards. Louis, the »Saint«, amassed a precious collection of relics, for which he built the chapel royal Ste-Chapelle on Île de la Cité. In 1257 Canon Robert de Sorbon founded a college for penniless theology students, the future Sorbonne.

NEW GLORY FOR THE EMBATTLED CAPITAL

1419–31	English occupation of Paris
1572	Murder of Huguenots in the St Bartholomew's Day massacre
Around 1600	Far-reaching urban development under Henri IV

House of When the Capetian dynasty died out, both Philippe VI of Valois, **Valois** nephew of King Philippe IV, and his grandson, the King Edward III **(1328–1498)** of England, claimed the French throne, which lead to the outbreak of the Hundred Years' War between England and France (1337–1453). Famines, epidemics and occupation by the English, who were not driven out of France once and for all until 1453 by Charles VII, drastically reduced the population and greatly held back the development of the city.

Etienne In 1358, Etienne Marcel, who as »Prévôt des Marchands« was the **Marcel** representative of the most important guilds, took advantage of the captivity of King Jean II (John the Good) by the English to seize control of the city government. Although this first citizens' revolt was put down violently by Charles V, Dauphin de France, in view of the struggles for power between the estates of the realm and rivalries between the citizens and the king, Charles V (the Wise) moved not into the palace on Île de la Cité but into the fortified Louvre when he ascended the throne in 1364.

Only in 1527 under François I did Paris again officially become the site of the royal residence. The city owed to François I its Renaissance Hôtel de Ville, the first banks, the stock exchange, the new Louvre building and the Collège de France. In the marsh (marais) on the right bank of the Seine the aristocracy built their houses. In the second half of the 16th century the city and the country were full of religious unrest. In Paris, the religious conflicts between Ignatius of Loyola, the founder of the Society of Jesus in Montmartre, and the Protestant reformer Jean Calvin, who both lived intermittently in the city, escalated into the massacre of St Bartholomew's Day. In the night of 23–24 August 1572, the leaders of the Protestant confederates and 3000 fellow believers were murdered.

House of Orléans-Angoulême (1498–1589)

Stability did not return until 1589, when Henri IV (1589–1610; ►picture p. 22) ascended the throne and guaranteed limited freedom of worship to Protestants under the Edict of Nantes in 1598. He radically redeveloped the centre of the city, which now had a population of 400,000. Besides great royal projects, buildings for the citizens were constructed. Streets were straightened, widened and surfaced; Pont-Neuf was completed and given pavements; Place des Vosges – then called Place Royal – was laid out, and the Louvre and the Tuileries Palace were extended.

House of Bourbon (1589–1792), Henri IV of France

After the assassination of Henri IV, the Grand Siècle of the city began in the reign of Louis XIII (1610–40). Cardinal Richelieu, First Minister from 1624, established a firm ministerial government that was independent of the nobility; he founded the Académie Française in 1635 and made Paris a centre of the Counter-Reformation and of absolutism. In the archbishopric that was created in 1622, 60 new monasteries were founded and 20 churches with mag-

> **MARCO POLO TIP**
>
> ! »*Good King Henry*«   **Insider Tip**
>
> …otherwise known as Henry of Navarre (Henri IV), can be found in Desmond Seward's »The First Bourbon« (2013). Famous for having had 60 mistresses, Henry's deeds (► p. 57) ensured him a coveted place in French history. To mark the 400th anniversary of his death in 2010, Jo Baier directed the epic movie »Henry of Navarre« based on Heinrich Mann's historical novels about the king. The film »La Reine Margot« was about Henry's first wife Margaret of Valois, based on the novel by Alexandre Dumas and directed by Patrice Chéreau.

nificent domes were built. During the minority of Louis XIV, Cardinal Mazarin ruled the country. He fought against the rebellious nobility of the »Fronde« and in 1661 founded the Collège des Quatre Nations, the future Institut de France.

Louis XIV, The Sun King (1643–1715) After the death of Cardinal Mazarin, Louis XIV, who had come of age, took sole control of government in 1661. With the help of a standing army, centralized administration, a dependent legislature and judiciary, a planned economy and the Catholic established church – the Edict of Fontainebleau (1685) prohibited Protestant religious practice – he realized the idea of an absolute ruler by the grace of God. Although the king moved his residence from the Louvre into the newly built Baroque palace of Versailles in response to the resistance of the Parisian citizens and nobility to his absolutist rule, the city continued to expand as the economic centre of the nation. The Tuileries Garden took on its present shape; the Champs-Elysées, Place Louis-le-Grand (Place Vendôme), Place des Victoires, Hôtel, Les Invalides and the Louvre colonnade were built. The Sun King's love of building, the immense costs of the court and his numerous wars ruined public finances, which the experiments of the Controller General of Finances John Law (1716–20) failed to repair.

REVOLUTION AND EMPIRE

1789	Storming of the Bastille
1792	First Republic
1804	Coronation of Napoleon as emperor
1848	Street fighting in Paris

From Louis XV to the French Revolution During the long reign of Louis XV (1715–74), despotism became more and more oppressive; even parliament was abolished in 1771. Paris was further embellished with the Ecole Militaire, the Mint, Place de la Concorde and the church of St Geneviève (Panthéon), but the vast majority of the 500,000 residents lived in poverty. Criticism was voiced in the salons of the Enlightenment; on the streets, popular displeasure grew.

The French Revolution (▶MARCO POLO Insight p. 178) On 14 July 1789, the people of Paris stormed the Bastille, which as the state prison was the symbol of absolutist oppression, and on 5 October 1789, Louis XVI was forced to return with his family to the Tuileries Palace in Paris. At first the French Revolution was supported by liberal forces from all levels of society. After the Declaration of the Rights of Man on 26 Aug 1789, the National Assembly worked out a constitution in 1790 to establish a constitutional monarchy. However, the attempted escape of the royal family intensified internal differences

The Storming of the Bastille (lithograph c. 1840)

between the main parties (Girondins and Montagnards) and the political clubs of the Jacobins (Cordeliers and Feuillants) and led to the storming of the Tuileries. On 21 September 1792, the National Convention abolished the monarchy and proclaimed a republic. On 21 January 1793 Louis XVI died by the guillotine, an instrument of execution that was to be busily employed on Place de la Révolution (Place de la Concorde since 1795) for several years. The increasingly violent riots of the masses, the reign of terror of the Committee of Public Safety and the threat of the royalist alliance abroad plunged Paris into political turmoil and social hardship.

General Napoleon Bonaparte came to power by a coup in the summer of 1799. He implemented the achievements of the revolution in political and administrative terms, established the French civil code (Code Napoléon), the division of France into départements and the position of prefect of police. Napoleon I was crowned emperor in Notre-Dame in 1804. Paris owes to him the Arc de Triomphe, the harmonious appearance of Rue de Rivoli and the extension of the Louvre, which from 1793 became a public museum that he filled with the spoils of war. **Napoleon I (1799–1815)**

The Restoration after the Congress of Vienna in 1814–15 lent political influence to the upper middle classes. After the intermezzo of Louis XVIII (1814–24) and Charles X (1824–30), the July Revolution of 1830 led to the reign of the »Citizen King« Louis-Philippe, who held power until 1848 and promoted capitalism without restraint. France's first railway line, from Paris to St-Germain-en-Laye, was inaugurated in 1837; in 1834 gas light illuminated the boulevards of the city, which had been surfaced with asphalt. Under Prime Minister Thiers Paris was given a new ring of defences between 1841 and 1845. **Restoration and Revolutions**

Industrialization exacerbated class conflict. The slums in the outskirts were a stark contrast to the glittering city centre. A cholera epidemic claimed 20,000 victims in the overpopulated quarters of the old part of the city in 1831. In February 1848, the unrest erupted into street fighting, but within a few months the middle classes had put down the uprising of the Parisian proletariat and established the Second Republic. **Second Republic**

Haussmann's Legacy

No other government transformed Paris so completely as the one of Napoleon III and his prefect Baron Georges-Eugène Haussmann. Between 1852 and 1870 the Second Empire invested more than 2.5 billion gold francs in the renovation of the city – a scheme that became a model for urban projects worldwide.

▶ **Rebuilding schemes planned by Haussmann**

— streets

▪▪▪ peripheral railway with 27 stations

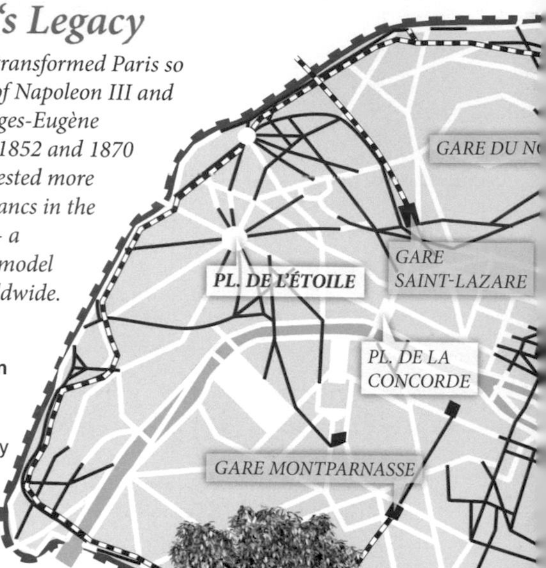

GARE DU N[O]

PL. DE L'ÉTOILE

GARE SAINT-LAZARE

PL. DE LA CONCORDE

GARE MONTPARNASSE

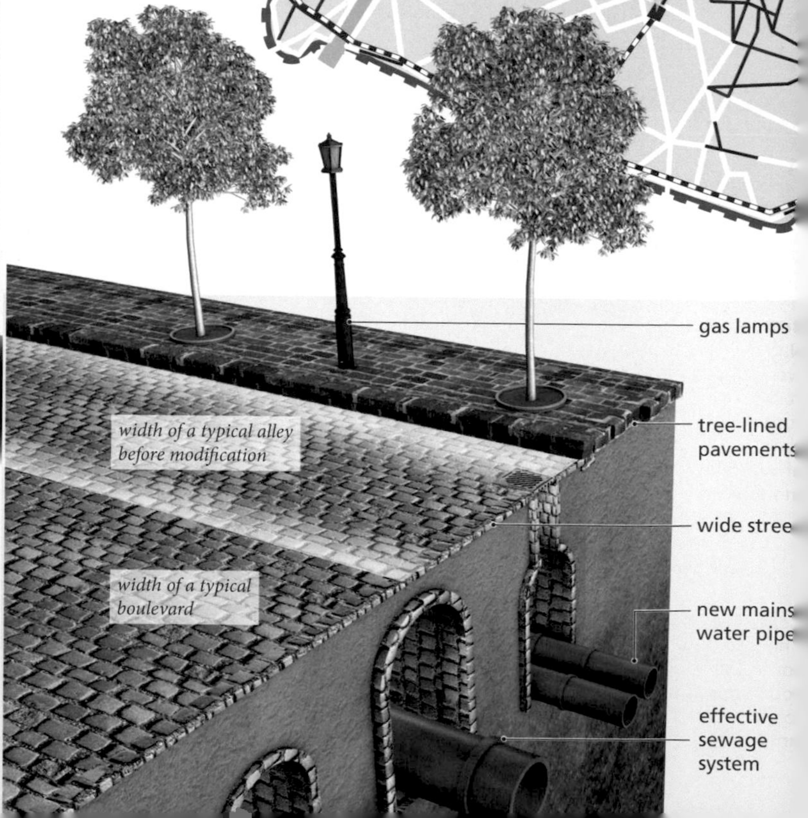

gas lamps

tree-lined pavements

wide stree[t]

width of a typical alley before modification

width of a typical boulevard

new mains water pipe

effective sewage system

©BAEDEKER

▶ The end of medieval Paris
Haussmann's first task was the completion of the Louvre and the demolition of the working class district that reached right up to the palace. After that, almost the entire medieval fabric of the Île de la Cité disappeared, and the island was linked to both banks of the Seine by a north-south axis.

Population growth
Between 1850 and 1870 the population grew by almost 70%.

| 1850 | 1,200,000 |
| 1870 | 2,000,000 |

▶ Two urban hubs
As the focal point of the western Rive Droite, Haussmann laid out the star-shaped Place de l'Étoile around the Arc de Triomphe, from where twelve boulevards fanned out across the city. Its eastern counterpart was the much less grand Place de la Nation, which was created in the middle of a working-class district.

25,000 houses were demolished

40,000 newly built houses

of which **30,000** were directly connected to the mains water supply.

▶road boulevards
Narrow, winding alleyways were replaced by broad, straight roads with uninter-rupted views and uniform facades, which almost always finished at a major monument or building.

Repayment
The 2.5 billion francs required for the scheme, which the city took up in the form of bank loans, were not fully repaid until 1929.

▶ Parisian sewage system
The world's most modern sewage system picked up and transported the waste beneath the boulevards, an investment in the future from which Paris still benefits.

Length of sewage after the transformation
560.6km/348,6mi

Length of sewage before Haussmann
107.4km/66.1mi

INTO THE MODERN AGE

1851	Second Empire under Napoleon III
1852–70	Remodelling of Paris under Baron Haussmann
1855, 1867, 1889, 1900	World exhibitions in Paris
1871	Uprising: the »Paris Commune«

Second Empire
After a coup Louis Napoleon Bonaparte, a nephew of Napoleon I, was crowned emperor of the Second Empire as Napoleon III in December 1851. By 1870 the population of the metropolis had grown to 2 million. Paris was rapidly remodelled by the city planning of Prefect Baron Georges Haussmann. Boulevards laid out to create long perspective views may have destroyed the medieval face of the city, but they made Paris a fashionable metropolis. At the same time the new boulevards served to control revolts better and to facilitate the movements of military forces. Napoleon III had Bois de Boulogne and Bois de Vincennes remodelled as public parks and provided the city with covered markets, railway stations and a sewage system (" Baedeker Special p. 28). Impressive monumental buildings such as the opera house by Charles Garnier and shopping arcades in iron and glass were erected. New districts were created beyond the old customs border of 1785 Paris was divided into 20 semi-autonomous arrondissements. It became the most modern city of its time, as the world exhibitions of 1855, 1867, 1889 and 1900 demonstrated.

»Beaver« Haussmann in action

Franco-Prussian War
The defeat at Sedan and the capture of Napoleon III brought an end to the Second Empire. A provisional government proclaimed the Third Republic in the city hall of Paris on 4 September 1870, but could not prevent the siege and occupation of Paris by German forces on 28 January 1871. From March to May 1871 the Communist and Socialist labour force formed the »Paris Commune« and rebelled against the middle-class monarchist National Assembly. Government troops quelled the workers' revolt mercilessly.

BELLE EPOQUE TO WORLD WAR II

1870–1940	Third Republic
14 June 1940	German troops occupy Paris
26 August 1944	General Charles de Gaulle enters Paris

Belle Epoque (1871–1914)
While France was losing its role of political leadership in Europe, Paris glittered in the splendour of the Belle Epoque between 1871 and 1914. In addition to opulent department stores and other temples of the business world, spectacular buildings such as the Eiffel Tower

(built in 1889 and the world's tallest building until 1930), the Grand Palais and Petit Palais (1900), Pont Alexandre III, the basilica of Sacré-Cœur (1900) and the Métro between Maillot and Vincennes (1900) were landmarks of city planning.

Victory over the German Reich, expressed in the Treaty of Versailles of 1919, made France a great power again. The Roaring Twenties with Paris as the centre of fashion and art deco design, as base for a thriving bohemian literary scene and the leading proponents of modern art, came to an abrupt end with the advent of the Great Depression. The development of the city, which now had three million inhabitants, stagnated. On the other hand, political conflict culminated in demonstrations, strikes and street fighting. The presidents of the republic, Millerand (1920–24), Gaston Doumergue (1924–31), Paul Doumer (1931–32) and Albert Lebrun (1932–40) could not prevent the polarization of the party system towards radical groups. From 1936 to 1938 the Popular Front of Socialists and Communists took power under Léon Blum and Chautemps.

Between the world wars

On 14 June 1940, German troops occupied Paris. The government of the unoccupied remaining part of France had withdrawn to Vichy under the command of Marshal Pétain. The nation was torn between opposites, with occupied and unoccupied zones, the Résistance and collaboration. General Charles de Gaulle organized resistance from London and Algiers. This escalated into open rebellion in the summer of 1944, when the Allies reached the Seine. General von Chol-

Vichy Regime and Résistance (1940–44)

General de Gaulle with members of the Résistance on Champs-Elysées on 26 August 1944 titz, the German governor of Paris, refused to carry out Hitler's order to destroy the city. On 26 August 1944, General de Gaulle marched his troops into Paris and led a provisional government until the National Assembly proclaimed a new constitution on 13 October 1946.

DE GAULLE TO MITTERAND

1946–58	Fourth Republic
Since 1958	Fifth Republic
1968	Student revolt

Fourth Republic (1946–58) The post-war years brought an unstable Fourth Republic, reconstruction on the home front and conflicts with the colonies, which were converted into the Union Française. At the same time France broke with the Soviet Union, turned towards Western Europe and reconciled itself with Germany in the Paris Agreements of 1954..

Fifth Republic (since 1958), For the majority of the French people General de Gaulle, who had long since bowed out of politics, still had the unifying authority to end the state crisis of 1958. He was appointed head of government with extraordinary powers, and a constitution with far-reaching responsibilities for the president was enacted. Thanks to the pro-business policy of the de Gaulle administration, France made the breakthrough to become a modern industrial society. The office quarter La Défense, the exhibition hall CNIT, the UNESCO building and the Radio France building represented France's economic strength in the early 1960s. The change from living space to offices and increasing rents drove many Parisians out of the city to the outlying residential areas; the number of inhabitants dropped to 2 million. In 1962 the author André Malraux, as minister of education and cultural affairs, enacted a law for the protection of historic buildings and monuments, which did not, however, prevent the demolition of Les Halles and the evacuation of the central market to Rungis in 1969.

Student revolts in 1968 In May 1968 student unrest in protest against the cultural, educational and social policies of de Gaulle shook France, with workers joining the revolts often in wildcat strikes. Despite this, the Gaullists were confirmed in government when elections were brought forward. Nevertheless, de Gaulle resigned in April 1969 after a lost referendum concerning regionalization.

President Pompidou (1969–74) De Gaulle's successor Georges Pompidou cultivated grand presidential gestures in the urban development of Paris. The old covered markets (Les Halles) were replaced by the Forum des Halles above a huge

Métro intersection in 1969. Nearby, the Centre Pompidou cultural complex was inaugurated in 1977 after having taken eight years to build. In the same year the city got its first mayor to be elected by the people, Jacques Chirac (▶Famous Personalities). Previously, a prefect appointed by the government had headed the administration.

After Valéry Giscard d'Estaing's term of office, the presidential elections of 1981 produced the first Socialist head of state, François Mitterrand. For 14 years he carried out the duties of his office with almost monarchical authority, created more grand building schemes for Paris, succeeded in abolishing the death penalty and became a powerful force in the integration of Europe. The main emphasis of his prestigious building projects was on culture. In 1986, the science and technology museum Cité des Sciences et de l'Industrie in Parc de la Villette was inaugurated, and Gare d'Orsay was transformed into a museum of 19th-century art. Opened in 1988, the Institut du Monde Arabe, an Arab cultural centre, was created as a forum for reconciliation and understanding between France and its former colonies.

President Mitterrand (1981–95)

PARIS TODAY

2001	Bertrand Delanoë becomes mayor of Paris
2005, 2007, 2009	Major unrest in the Parisian suburbs
2008	Nicolas Sarkozy becomes president
2012	François Hollande becomes president
2014	Anne Hidalgo replaced Delanoë as the city's first female mayor

Many of the cultural monuments commissioned by Mitterrand were completed in time for the 200th anniversary of the French Revolution in 1989: the big glass pyramid in the forecourt of the Louvre, the Paris Opera on Place de la Bastille, the Grande Arche in La Défense and the ministry of finance in Bercy. In 1992 the Disneyland amusement park opened in Chessy near Paris. Since 1991 the banks of the Seine between the Eiffel Tower and the Île Saint-Louis as well as the Cathedral of Notre Dame have been on the UNESCO World Heritage List, and since 2012 the banks along this stretch of the river have been car free.

Paris today

In the north of Paris the Cité de la Musique, which was designed by Christian de Portzamparc, opened in 1995, and as the last of his great monuments François Mitterrand inaugurated the new National Library in the eastern quarter of Tolbiac in the same year. The renovation of the Centre Pompidou was finished for the millennium and after almost two decades of construction work the renovation of the Louvre to the largest art museum in the world was completed.

Two spectacular museums were opened in 2006: Jean Nouvel's glass palace housing the ethnological Musée du Quai Branly and the renovated Orangerie with Claude Monet's Water Lilies. The famous Impressionist collection of the Musée d'Orsay was redesigned in 2011, and in 2015 Jean Nouvel's futuristic Philharmonie de Paris concert hall opened in La Villette.

Flashpoint Banlieue buildings La péripherique , the ring road around Paris, has become a demarcation line separating the wonderful world of luxury and fashion from a no man's land of drab blocks of flats with squares full of litter and blighted opportunities. In the concrete jungles of the more rundown banlieues, the proportion of immigrants is extremely high, in some communities with up to two thirds of the residents coming from Africa. On 27 October 2005 two teenagers died in the Paris suburb of Clichy-sous-Bois while on the run from the police, an incident that triggered weeks of serious riots, initially contained within the greater Paris area but then spread to a further 300 communities across the country. The root cause of the riots were the deteriorating living conditions in the »exclusion zone« at the gates of the city, with high unemployment and increasing violence, poverty and discrimination. For the first time since the war in Algeria, a state of emergency was imposed in France, an official acknowledgment of the failure of integration policies. The then Interior Minister Sarkozy was full of rhetoric, talking of a decisive crackdown, but as president in 2007 he announced the creation of more social programmes. But nothing very much has happened so far, and even so long after the riots Paris still doesn't have its trouble spots under control, discrimination has continued and it's only a matter of time before the next riots break out..

At the 1995 presidential elections, France got its first neogaullist president for 21 years in the shape of the long-serving Mayor of Paris, Jacques Chirac. He won again in 2002, but then quit office prematurely in 2007 (▶Famous Personalities). In 2001 Tunisian-born Bertrand Delanoë was elected Mayor of Paris, becoming the first socialist in 100 years to hold the office. In the 2008 municipal elections the openly

Parcours in no man's land

The world of cinema has also addressed the growing crime rate in the suburbs of the Seine metropolis. With his 2004 movie Banlieue 13 (English: District 13), which is set in in a crime-ridden walled ghetto in the year 2010, Luc Besson introduced the subject to the big screen and at the same time created a cinematic tribute to a sport that had its origins between the concrete high-rises of Paris: parcours. Elegant and daring at the same time, the »traceur« overcomes the obstacles he encounters on the direct route from A to B: benches and flower beds, rubbish bins, walls, even high-rise buildings and the canyons between them.

gay mayor, who had won the hearts of the Parisians with unusual schemes such as »Paris Plage« and the introduction of Vélib (the city's large-scale public bicycle hiring scheme) was reconfirmed for a second term in office until March 2014, when Spanish-born socialist Anne Hidalgo won the mayoral elections, becoming the first female Mayor of Paris.

On 16 May 2007, in the Elysée Palace, Chirac relinquished his office to the new French President Nicolas Sarkozy. In the regional elections of 2010 Sarkozy's UMP party the suffered a major defeat, with the Socialists victorious in almost every region. With Sarkozy weakened by the Bettencourt Affair and the euro crisis, his Socialist challenger François Hollande achieved a narrow victory in the second round of voting on 6th May 2012. Having entered the race under the motto »France Forte«, Sarkozy is thus far the first incumbent French president not to be elected to a second term in office. Seventeen years after François Mitterrand, Hollande is the second Socialist to lead the Grande Nation. The economist, who once taught at the elite Sciences Po (Paris Institute of Political Studies), is considered a pragmatist. In the runoff he won 51.6% of the vote, with Sarkozy on 8.3%. The performance of Marine La Pen of the right-wing Front National came as a shock to many people: she achieved 17.9% of the vote in the first round in April, and

The highest office of state

François Hollande is the second Socialist to lead the Grande Nation

in June managed to get her party back into parliament. The Liberal François Bayrou received 9.1% of the vote, while 2.3% voted for the Green candidate Eva Joly in the first round. The Socialists also won an absolute majority in the election for the National Assembly (Assemblée Nationale) in June 2012.

In April 2014 Anne Hidalgo was elected the first female mayor of Paris.

Arts and Culture

The Beauty on the Seine

Where is it still possible to find ruins of Ancient Rome? Who made Paris the most modern city of its time? Where does the term mansard come from? And how did François Mitterrand immortalize his terms of office in the metropolis on the Seine? Read on!

THE ORIGINS OF LUTETIA

After the conquest of Gaul by the Romans, the Seine islands that had been settled by Celts took on a new look. On the left bank the Roman colonial town Lutetia Parisiorum evolved with a linear pattern of streets. The Roman forum was situated between today's Boulevard St Michel, Rue Saint Jacques and Rue Cujas. It had a temple on a podium, colonnades with rows of shops, as well as a basilica, which served as a courtroom, trading centre and covered market. On the outskirts of the town, entertainment for the people was provided in the amphitheatre Arènes de Lutèce.

Roman heritage

In the Merovingian kingdom, churches were modelled on the ancient basilicas that served various secular purposes. They had a longitudinal ground plan, mostly facing east to the sunrise as the symbol of resurrection, a nave and lower side aisles. An enormous church with a vestibule, west-work and double aisles was built on Île de la Cité in the 6th century in honour of St Stephen, but only the foundations remain of it today – under the forecourt Notre-Dame cathedral. The impressive Abbey of St Denis was built in 775 over the sepulchre of St Dionysius.

The first basilicas

GOTHIC: GOD IS THE LIGHT

The choir of the abbey church of St Denis, consecrated in 1144, in which Abbot Suger of St Denis was involved in the design, is considered to be the birthplace of the Gothic style that quickly established itself across France and Europe. The masons of the age were excited by Abbot Suger's notion that »God is the light«, and the massive Romanesque architectural style was replaced by a skeletal method of construction that allowed light to flood in, though the term Gothic

Birthplace of Gothic

Guimard's Métro entrances in Art nouveau style remind of the year 1900 when the story of the Métro started

Sublime Gothic architecture: Notre-Dame

was only applied later after the Florentine Giorgio Vasari had derogatorily described it as the «style of the Goths«. In the Gothic style of architecture, the load-bearing wall gives way to vast windows; rosettes on the west façade and transepts symbolize the worship of the Virgin Mary as a mystic rose. In a cross-ribbed vault the ribs bear the weight of the roof and transfer it to the supporting structure of the pillars and columns, while from the outside the buttresses and flying buttresses provide support for the walls. Slender clustered columns combined with pointed arches permit a less restricted interior space and a higher vault.

The western part of Notre-Dame Cathedral, which was built from 1163 to 1240, was given a façade of two towers with a rose window between them and a gallery with statues of the biblical kings of Judaea. At first the interior of this galleried basilica with a nave and double aisles had a four-part early Gothic elevation with arcades of round pillars, a gallery and windows on two levels. From 1225 these two window storeys were combined to create large clerestory windows in the High Gothic style. Since 1246 the rose windows in the »style rayonnant« have taken up the whole breadth of the north and south façades of the transept.

The two-storey former palace chapel Ste-Chapelle is considered a miracle of filigree tracery, stained glass and light; it was built from 1245 to 1248 by Louis IX with all the characteristic features of the High Gothic period. The richly decorated Flamboyant style of the 15th century, featuring the flame-like tracery, vaulting springing from columns and pendants hanging from the vaults can be admired in St-Merri, St-Germain-l'Auxerrois, St-Severin and St-Etienne-du-Mont.

In 1190 the northern part of Paris was enclosed within a circular wall. The ring of defences was completed in the south in 1210. It was reinforced to the west with the fortified Louvre; to the east the massive bulwark of the Bastille protected the city. Under Etienne Marcel, the royal provost of the merchants, Paris became the biggest stronghold in the kingdom – just 60km/37mi away from the nearest English military base. In the 14th century the Conciergerie was built with spacious Gothic halls and the Tour de L'Horloge. The whole range of late Gothic decoration can be seen on the hôtel of the archbishops of Sens, which was built from 1474 to 1519, and that of the abbots of Cluny.

Mighty bulwarks

Book illumination, stained glass and painted panels offered a further field of activity for Parisian artisans. The crude realism of the Parisian painting schools did not change into a graceful courtly style until the 15th century. At first the artists set their motifs in a supernatural world, usually without background depth, until Jean Fouquet (1420–80), court painter of Louis XI who had contacts artistic developments in Italy, combined verisimilitude with a feeling for decoration. Sculptors were busy with architectural details such as gargoyles, buttress ornamentations, portal sculptures, church statues, pillar statues, reliefs and church furnishings including baptismal fonts, pulpits, rood screens, carved altars and tombs. Notre-Dame has particularly extensive sculptural decoration.

Painting and sculpture

PARIS IN THE RENAISSANCE AND MANNERIST PERIODS

France had no contact with Italian Renaissance art until the Italian wars under François I. Jean Clouet and his son François worked as court painters for François I. They specialized in pencil portraits, which were often copied on canvas. In 1530 Florentine artists, first of all Rosso Fiorentino, then Primaticcio and Niccoló dell' Abate, were brought by the king to decorate his palace at Fontainebleau. At this time in Italy the classical style of ancient art had already given way to mannered, i.e. exaggeratedly artificial and unnatural forms. Sharp contrasts of light and shade, daring foreshortening and the graphic representation of an object from below as well as unnatural lighting effects were used by the painters of the school of Fontainebleau, whose masterpiece was the Gallery of François I in the château of Fontainebleau. Jean Goujon and Antoine Caron continued to work in the Mannerist style for Catherine de' Medici, producing decorations for festive processions and stage settings.

Italian Influences

As a sculptor, Jean Goujon carved the bas-reliefs of the Fontaine des Innocents (1547–49) and the caryatids of the Louvre façade. Jean

Stained glass windows and tomb art

Cousin le Jeune created the stained glass windows in St Gervais-St Protais, which are rich in colours and figures; magnificent stained glass windows adorn the church St Etienne-du-Mont with its imposing rood screen (1521–35). In the 16th century, Germain Pilon extended the spectrum of funerary art by constructing temple-like mausoleums. The royal tombs in the basilica St Denis feature deceased monarchs both in worldly splendour and as undressed corpses.

Mannerist decoration   The church of St-Eustache, started in 1532 and repeatedly restored, is the most important sacred building of the 16th century with its mixture of late Gothic and Mannerist styles. The leading architects of the time – Pierre Lescot (1515–87), Baptiste Androuet Du Cerceau (1560–1602) and Philibert Delorme (1517–70) – designed royal palaces with steep-pitched roofs and attic storeys and embellished them with intertwined and ribbon-like ornaments.

THE SPLENDOUR OF THE GRAND SIÈCLE AND ROCOCO

Urban landmarks   Under Henri IV the Grand Siècle, as the 17th century is often called in Paris, opened with new landmarks in the city: Pont Neuf over the Seine and Place Royale (now Place des Vosges; 1605–12), which is surrounded by arcades. With their masonry of stone and brick, Place Dauphine and Hôpital St Louis are typical of the Louis XIII style. Plaster and horizontal lines enliven the façade of Hôtel de Sully (1624–40). Salomon de Brosse combined Italian and French forms in his design for the Palais du Luxembourg. In the Marais district, city palaces for the nobility, known as hôtels, were built by the architects François Mansart, Delamair and Le Muet, mostly with three wings on a U-shaped plan, with a courtyard and garden.

Louis XIV style   The architects working for the Sun King not only created the epoch-making palace at Versailles in the Louis XIV style, with its forecourt and geometrical gardens from 1661, but also demonstrated their skills in Paris: Jules Hardouin-Mansart built the Hôtel des Invalides, designed Place Vendôme and Place des Victoires, built the Hôtel Conti and enlarged the attics with the creation of the mansard that was named after him. Le Vau designed the churches St Louis-en-l'Île and St Sulpice, built Hôtel Lambert and the Collège des Quatre Nations. Jacques Lemercier set city planning trends with the churches of the Sorbonne and Val-de-Grâce, which have mighty domes, as well as with his Palais Cardinal. Between 1667 and 1674, Perrault decorated the Louvre with a colonnade of paired columns with niches in the walls for statue. Gabriel designed the Ecole Militaire and the expansive Place de la Concorde together with broad avenues such as the future Champs-Elysées.

Living quarters were equipped with exquisite furnishings in the Regence style (1715–23). During the Louis XV style that followed (up to 1774), in 1735 Boffrand and others decorated the interiors of the Hôtel de Soubise with exuberant, delicately naturalistic features such as interlaced ornaments and rocaille shells. Lepautre faced his palace and hotel buildings in neoclassical style with Corinthian capitals, heavy cornices and entablatures in a classical vein. Functional forms are typical of the façades of the apartments that were built along Rue du Faubourg St-Denis from 1719. Typical of the Louis XVI style are such decorative forms such as swags, ties and vase motifs.

Louis XV style

In the field of painting in the 17th century, the three brothers Antoine, Louis and Mathieu Le Nain produced portraits, religious themes and rustic scenes in a strongly realistic style. Georges de la Tour was fond of cleverly illuminated night scenes, Philippe de Champaigne was a popular portrait painter and Jacques Callot was a master of fantastic and sarcastic etchings. Nicolas Poussin, who spent most of his working life in Italy, supplied the French court with paintings in which harmony of forms and simplicity of composition testified to his studies of the ancient world. Claude Gellée, called Le Lorrain, reflected the emotional world in landscapes. Charles Lebrun concentrated on the great presentation of historical and religious events. Pierre Mignard was skilled in small formats and produced the

Religious themes, landscape paintings and portraits

Diana Leaving her Bath, erotic masterpiece of François Boucher (1742)

mignardes that are named after him in an elegant realistic style. In the 18th century, Antoine Watteau captivated his contemporaries with courtly milieu scenes, Jean-Honoré Fragonard celebrated joie de vivre and sensual pleasures in his pictures and François Boucher created lascivious, sophisticated nude paintings. Jean-Baptiste Siméon Chardin painted middle-class daily life.

Court sculptors

Pierre Puget, François Girardon and Antoine Coyzevox were the most important court sculptors of the 17th century. They carved garden sculptures, monuments, portrait busts and tombs. In the 18th century the Coustou family of sculptors made religious works and allegorical figures for the royal palaces and gardens. Jean-Baptiste Lemoyne, rector of the academy of arts from 1798, specialized in portrait busts. His pupil Jean-Baptiste Pigalle created tombs and memorials in a monumental style with a good deal of pathos in addition to lifelike portrait busts.

THE ANCIENT WORLD AS A MODEL

Mixture of styles of the Empire period

Empire Influenced by the imperial ideas of the age of Napoleon, known as the Empire period, mixtures of styles – elements from ancient Egypt, the Orient and classical antiquity – were dominant in

Grand and Petit Palais where built for the world exhibition in 1900

furniture, interior design, arts and crafts. The Arc de Triomphe du Carrousel (1806–8) by Percier and Fontaine is a typical example of the adoption of ancient Roman architecture at that time.

In the late 18th and early 19th centuries, the neoclassical style reverted to the austere architectural vocabulary of the Greek and Roman ancient world in reaction to the playful decorative forms of the Baroque period. This resulted in clearly structured design, for buildings such as opera houses, museums and city halls, as well as in residential and villa architecture.

Clear classical forms

The Panthéon, which was built by Soufflot from 1764 to 1790, is a church with a cross-shaped ground plan, a Corinthian portico, barrel vaults in the transepts and a colonnaded tambour dome. The façade of St Sulpice church by Servandoni and Chalgrin, completed in 1777, is adorned by a sequence of the classical order of columns. The Madeleine church, built by Vignon and Huvé between 1806 and 1842, has the form of a windowless Roman Corinthian peristyle temple with three skylights.

On the former Place de l'Étoile, J. F. Chalgrin's Arc de Triomphe, completed in 1836, represented a conspicuous feature of urban planning on the Louvre – Concorde – Champs-Elysées axis. François Rude, who also designed the memorial to Marshal Michel Ney, carved the reliefs. In the field of painting Jacques Louis David represented republican patriotic ideals in the style of the ancient world. Jean Auguste Ingres was the master of a cool, sober style of painting portraits, nudes and historical allegories. In the works of the Romantic painters Théodore Géricault and Eugène Delacroix colour gained more life of its own and determined the dynamics of form.

19TH CENTURY: TOWARDS THE MODERN AGE

Under Napoleon III and his prefect Baron Georges Eugène Haussmann, Paris underwent changes that determine its character to this day (►MARCO POLO Insight p.28). The city presented itself as a metropolis that was modern but conscious of its history during the world exhibitions of 1855, 1867, 1878, 1889 and 1900 – the Eiffel Tower, which has become the symbol of Paris, is a reminder of the world exhibition of 1889.

Radical city planning

In the second half of the 19th century Historicism as a reaction to the neoclassical style took its impulses from the ideas and values of great epochs of the past, using forms that ranged from Gothic to Renaissance and Baroque. The most magnificent example of this »Belle Epoque style« is the opera house by Charles Garnier with its extravagant mixture of Renaissance and Baroque. The Grand Palais and

Magnificent Historicism

Petit Palais, the railway stations Est, Nord and Orsay, the national library and the department store Le Printemps were given a Historicist appearance. After being gutted by fire in 1871, the Hôtel de Ville was rebuilt in neo-Renaissance style. In church architecture the domed neo-Romanesque and Byzantine Sacré-Coeur (1876–1910) on Montmartre set creative trends.

Realism At the suggestion of Théodore Rousseau, in 1847 the landscape painters Daubigny, Corot, Troyon and Dupré, the »Barbizon school« settled in the village of the same name in the forest of Fontainebleau in order to capture on canvas the atmosphere of natural motifs by painting outdoors. From 1850 Gustave Courbet proclaimed painting to be a mirror of »only real and really existing things«. He, Honoré Daumier and François Millet represented socially involved, critical Realism, which was intended to rouse the well-to-do middle classes from their complacency. In sculpture, exponents of Realism such as Carpeaux, Rodin, Dalou, Bourdelle and Maillol worked in styles that ranged from lively and expressive to quiet and restrained.

Fontaines Wallace It is to Sir Richard Wallace, a francophile Englishman, that the Paris owes its typical traditional green cast iron drinking fountains. The wealthy Londoner had made the French capital his new home. After the destruction of 1870–1 Wallace designed a robust and yet elegant drinking fountain for Paris that was also cheap to produce. Inspired by the art of the Renaissance, the 2.7-m high fountains enabled the populace to quench their thirst for free. The allegories of kindness, compassion, moderation and simplicity around the base bear a cupola adorned with dolphins. The first of the Wallace fountains, of which there are still 108 in place today, was inaugurated in the autumn of 1872 on the Boulevard de la Villette. The crowd was enthusiastic. »Pleurer comme une fontaine Wallace« they say on the Seine when someone sheds bitter tears. And the Parisians love their fountains to this day – something that would have pleased Sir Richard no end.

Impression-ism Impressionism was born on 15 April 1874, when a group of painters opened an exhibition in Paris, in the studio of the photographer Nadar. It included the painting Impression, soleil levant (Impression, Sunrise) by the young Claude Monet, which shows the harbour of Le Havre in early morning mist. When a journalist in his review of the exhibition disdainfully called the painters »Impressionists« following Monet's painting, the new art movement had found its name. In answer to academic studio painting its representatives, including Claude Monet, Camille Pissarro, Auguste Renoir and Alfred Sisley, put their faith in plein air painting in order to transform nature as a subjective impression into a world of colour and light and to capture

Auguste Renoir painted *Bal at Moulin de la Galette* in 1876

transient objects such as clouds, fog or rays of light in atmospheric paintings. When the group disbanded after its last joint exhibition in 1886, only Georges Seurat and Paul Signac as pointillists still clung to the technique of applying colours in dots or small dabs.

At the end of the 19th century, Art Nouveau reacted against Historicism with natural, fluid forms and an ornamental play of lines. The unmistakeable Parisian Métro entrances were designed by Hector Guimard in plant-like glass latticework on Boulevard St-Michel (" picture p. 36), Place des Abbesses and Place Dauphine; his residential buildings such as Castel Béranger at 14, Rue de la Fontaine and his tulip-shaped lamps are just as unmistakeable. René Lalique used floral and insect motifs in his jewellery creations.

Art Nouveau

In the late 19th century Symbolism, fraught with meaning, followed as a countermovement to Impressionism. Odile Redon and Gustave Moreau were among its devotees; an impressive exhibition of Moreau's complete works can be seen in his Parisian private house.

Symbolism

Taking Gauguin's painting style, which breaks away from colours and form, as a starting point, the Parisian group of artists called Les Nabis

Nabis

(the prophets) including Pierre Bonnard, Paul Sérusier, Eduard Vuillard and Félix Vallotton developed a flat decorative painting style between 1888 and 1905.

20TH CENTURY: STAGE OF WORLD ART

Photography   The photographer Eugène Atget observed everyday events in the streets of the vibrant metropolis. Edouard Boubat, Izis and Brassaï captured the night life, Jacques-Henri Lartigue the hustle and bustle of the 1920s, Henri Cartier-Bresson and Willy Ronis produced picturesque views of the city; Robert Doisneau took poetic snapshots of the pulsating city (" Baedeker Special p.50).

Poster art   Guillaume-Sulpice Garvani illustrated the life of the poor with black-and-white posters; Jules Chéret was the first to use coloured lithographs, the medium in which Toulouse-Lautrec put revues, cabaret shows and theatres in the spotlight. Alphonse Mucha, who came from Prague to Paris in 1887, covered his posters with ornamental decorative motifs in Art Nouveau style.

Picasso's *Demoiselles d'Avignon* is a key work of Cubism

When in 1905 pictures in which the »colours exploded like dynamite cartridges« were displayed in public, the critic Louis Vauxcelles described the paintings of Henri Matisse, Maurice de Vlaminck and André Derain as the works of »Fauves« (wild beasts) and so named this manner of painting in dynamic colours and forms.

Fauvism

In Paris, Georges Rouault and Chaim Soutine are considered the most important representatives of the European-wide Expressionist movement. They took existential questions and social tensions as the subject of their works at the beginning of the 20th century.

Expression-ism

The late work of Cézanne, who created his artistic depictions of nature through geometric shapes, and the influence of African sculpture led Pablo Picasso and Georges Braque in about 1907 to the Cubist style of representation. They reduced the motif of a painting to its many-facetted component parts and abolished the illusion of space in favour of a grouping and ordering of individual elements on the surface of the painting as Picasso did in *Desmoiselles d'Avignon*.which he painted in 1907 From 1912 onwards, synthetic Cubism integrated particles of reality such as pieces of wood and paper scraps into works of art.

Cubism

Functionalism was the dominant movement in architecture after the First World War. In Paris the bridges of Eugène Freyssinet were built; the airship hangars of Orly were constructed from 1916 to 1924 as spans of pre-stressed concrete and the church Notre-Dame in Raincy was built between 1922 and 1925 by Auguste Perret with windows made of concrete glass elements.

Functionalism

The poet Guillaume Apollinaire coined the term in 1917 and the writer André Breton provided the programme with his Manifesto of Surrealism in 1924: everyday experiences, spontaneous acts, dream sequences and interpretations of psychology were turned into works of art beyond logical evaluation by astonishing combinations. Max Ernst, Yves Tanguy, Joan Miró, Salvador Dalí, Hans Arp, André Masson, Man Ray, Marcel Duchamp and Francis Picabia were the most prominent exponents of Surrealism.

Surrealism

Constructivism, which was brought to Paris by exiled Russian artists, developed into a constructive-abstract trend, which in 1931 on the initiative of the Belgian painter, sculptor and architect Georges Vantongerloo led to the creation of the Abstraction-Création group. This artists' association, which existed until 1937, also included Gabo, Pevsner, Mondrian, Doesburg, Lissitzky, Kupka, Kandinsky, Baumeister, and Herbin. In its non-representational style, more significance was generally accorded to colour than to form.

Abstraction-Création

Ieoh Ming Pei's glass pyramid stands in Cour Napoléon over the main entance of the Louvre

Ecole de Paris, Informel

Different movements of abstract painting joined together in the Ecole de Paris from the Second World War until about 1960. The painting style called Informel rejected fixed rules of composition and made it possible to realize impulsive colour rhythms, paint spots and trickles. Antoni Tàpies talked of the »significance of shapelessness«. Painting as a spontaneously performed act was also the concern of Tachism in the 1950s and early 1960s (the term is derived from the French word »tache«, meaning »stain«) with artists such as Georges Mathieu and Jean Fautrier. One proponent of Informel, Jean Dubuffet, devoted himself to the forms of expression of mentally disordered, children and amateur painters in order to enrich the professional intent of style with spontaneous creative sources in Art Brut (unspoilt art).

Nouveau Réalisme

Parallel to the Anglo-American Pop Art the artists of the Nouveau Réalisme movement took a critical and positive approach to the everyday world, as in the blue sponge reliefs of Yves Klein, the accumulations of shaving brushes in the works of Arman, or the compacted automobiles, discarded metal, or rubbish of César. Jean Tinguely with his kinetic scrap metal objects and Niki de Saint-Phalle with her imaginative figures created the Stravinsky Fountain in front of the Centre Pompidou.

From the mid-1960s, five satellite towns sprung up around Paris: Marne-la-Vallée and Cergy-Pontoise to the north of the Seine and Melun-Sénart, Evry and Saint-Quentin-en-Yvelines to the south. They have since become synonymous with architectural experiments and social tensions. In Marne-la-Vallée in 1982, the Catalan architect Ricardo Bofill in 1982 created the residential complex of Palacio d'Abraxas studded with architectural quotations. Opposite stands El Teatro, a surrealist apartment tower with 600 apartments on 19 floors. Since 1985 the landmark of Noisy-le-Grand has been the vast residential complex of Arènes de Picasso designed by Manolo Nuñez-Yanowsky. The futuristic cathedral of Evry was built according to the designs of Mario Botta in 1988–95.

Villes Nouvelles

From the 1960s many government building contracts were awarded to international architectural firms. Paul Andreu was the chief architect of Charles de Gaulle airport. The Pompidou Centre, inaugurated in 1977, was the work of the British architect Richard Rogers and the Italian Renzo Piano. In the La Défense quarter, tower blocks of steel and glass flank the Grande Arche, which was designed by the Danish architect Johan Otto von Spreckelsen. In 1986 the Italian Gae Aulenti was responsible for the conversion of Gare d'Orsay into a museum of 19th-century art. The Opéra de la Bastille, which opened in 1989, was designed by Uruguay-born Carlos Ott. That same year the glass pyramid in the Louvre's courtyard was created by the US-Chinese Ieoh Ming Pei. The massive Bibliothèque Nationale de France François Mitterrand was designed by Dominique Perrault and opened in 1995. Completed in 1997, the fortress-like Finance Ministry building in Bercy was the work of the Chilean Borja Huidobroas. Pritzker-Prize winner Jean Nouvel designed the Fondation Cartier in 1994, the Musée du Quai Branly in 2006, and in 2011 took on the new Philharmonie de Paris in the La Villette culture and science park that was conceived by Bernard Tschumi in 1984–89. However, there is a price to pay for the capital's glamour, with the maintenance costs for Mitterand's presidential »grand projets« continuing to weigh heavily on the state coffers.

Ambitious projects

? MARCO ◉ POLO INSIGHT

France's Zero Meridian

In Paris 135 bronze medallions mark the course of the zero meridian, which remained valid in France until Greenwich became the internationally agreed location in 1884. Since then Paris has been situated at a longitude of 2° 21' 07'' east. In 1995 the Dutch concept artist Jan Dibbet plotted the path of the old zero meridian with beer-mat sized »Arago medallions«, complete with N and S pointers, which were set into streets, pavements and buildings. The bronze plaques are a tribute to the physicist and human rights activist François Arago, who championed the final abolition of slavery in France.

START OF THE 21ST CENTURY: GRAND PARIS

Global city   In order that Paris can adapt to the requirements of 21st century, in 2007 President Nicolas Sarkozy launched the »Grand Paris« project, which extends beyond the historical city limits beyond the historical city limits – Paris needs its suburbs to progress after all. The ambitious goal of the president was to make the capital region a dynamic, attractive and radiant »Global City«, which could contribute to the growth of the entire country and make it pre-eminent in the fields of economy, innovation and knowledge.

The Grand Paris project is founded on eight geographical areas. Dominated as it is by aviation and logistics, Roissy-Villepinte, first of all, is intended as the gateway for international trade and a showcase French talent. Le Bourget should be expanded as far as the northern edge of the city. Paris-Saclay, home of the Synchrotron Soleil particle collider, is to be transformed into the French Silicon Valley and get a huge new campus university as well as seven new engineering colleges. A further €5 billion will be invested in the Vallée des Biotech, which is to extend south from Paris to Evry and Saclev. Le Havre on the Seine estuary will be expanded as the port of Paris, and La Défense will be revived as a financial and business centre through the construction of 300,000 m2 of office space and the extension of the RER line E. By 2015, La Défense includes 75 skyscrapers, including five with a height of over 300m/1000ft.

The centre of Paris is be the showcase for France's creative potential, and as the hub of the creative industries is to reflect the diversity of this sector. However, this will also involve creating around the Cité Descartes in the east of Paris a centre of excellence for the construction and development of a »sustainable city« which will bring together new environmental technologies, methods of construction, city services and the ecological and mobility industries. Finally, the Grand Paris project will also include a groundbreaking transport concept involving a fully automated, high-speed métro system with 50 stations and trains running day and at night along its 150 km double loop every 80 seconds. Construction commenced in 2013 and is scheduled for completion in 2023.

Future cul-   To alleviate the notorious lack of space, Sarkozy committed legally to
ture venue- the construction of at least 7000 new homes per year. And new sky-
sand writer scrapers for offices are destined to be constructed within the Périphérique. But before architects, city planners and politicians can build their beloved »gratteciels«, they must not only get the approval of the populace at large but also overturn a law banning the construction of skyscrapers in the city centre that was passed a good 40 years ago. That was the response in the 1970s to eyesores such as the 210-m/689ft high Tour Montparnasse, or the »big black monster« as

La Défense, a showpiece of modern architecture

it's known as locally. Since then, no building in the city centre can exceed a height of 37m/121ft. While many Grand Paris projects for the core city are still on the drawing board and waiting to be implemented, others have already begun. These mainly include new cultural sites. The Philharmonie de Paris at the Parc de la Villette was completed 2015 according to plans by Jean Nouvel. In 2009, Nouvel was also charged with the regeneration of the Seine island of Seguin in Boulougne Billancourt, 2 km away. On the site where Renault built its cars until 2005, an art and eco-city with exhibition hall, galleries, artists' studios, concert halls, multiplex cinema and a centre for digital art is due to be completed by 2020. Solar fields, wind turbines, a hydro power plant and the use of geothermal energy will provide a largely sustainable energy supply.

Famous People

HONORÉ DE BALZAC (1799–1850)

Balzac, who was born in Tours, is considered the pioneer of socio-   **Author**
logical Realism in the modern novel. In contrast to the Romantic
style of his time he portrayed characters caught in the interplay of
social forces and personal passions: the blind paternal love of Père
Goriot, for instance, the jealous cousin Bette or the stingy Père Gran-
det. His major work, »Comédie Humaine«, which was written from
1829, is a panorama of French society from the French Revolution to
the Restoration in more than 40 volumes. Balzac's complete works
comprise almost 90 novels and novellas, 30 short stories and five
stage plays. His mother's side of the family owned a lucrative business
trading cloth in the Marais – and Balzac, who lived in Paris from
1814, grew up in a world in which money played an important part.
Failures as a businessman, risky speculations and a lavish life style
necessitated his vast literary output, which was to ruin his health.
Night after night he worked on his books for hours, always hoping to
be able to pay off his mountain of debt. Inspired by blind optimism
and love for the Polish Countess Evelina Hanska-Rzewuska, he
plunged into new debt and bought a wonderful house in a side street
of the Champs-Elysées. Marked by illness, he moved there after his
wedding to Madame Hanska – and died from exhaustion three
months later at the age of 51.

SIMONE DE BEAUVOIR (1908–86)

Simone de Beauvoir's encounter with Jean-Paul Sartre shaped her life   **Author**
– at first as his fellow student, later as his companion for life. De Beauvoir was born in Paris, studied phi-
losophy and worked as a teacher in
Marseille, Rouen and Paris until
1943, before devoting herself completely to writing. In 1954 she received the Prix Goncourt for her
novel Les Mandarins. Simone de
Beauvoir combined her moral philosophical theories about individual
freedom and responsibility according to Sartre's existentialism with social and political commitment. With
her seminal treatise The Second Sex

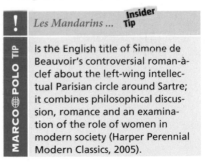

!   *Les Mandarins ...*   **Insider Tip**

MARCO POLO TIP

Is the English title of Simone de
Beauvoir's controversial roman-à-
clef about the left-wing intellectual Parisian circle around Sartre;
it combines philosophical discussion, romance and an examina-
tion of the role of women in
modern society (Harper Perennial
Modern Classics, 2005).

(2 volumes, 1949), which was prohibited by the Catholic church, she
became the leading theoretician of the women's movement. De Beau-

Balzac is buried at Père Lachaise cemetery

Capturing the Moment

The photographer Robert Doisneau bequeathed a very special chronicle of Paris with his black and white photography. His insightful snapshots came to epitomize the atmosphere of life on the Seine.

A snapshot in black and white: people walking past the town hall, a man sitting at bistro table, and in the centre of the image a couple kisses, casually and yet passionately. »Le Baiser de l' Hôtel de Ville« (The Kiss by the Town Hall, 1950) by Robert Doisneau is probably the most iconic snapshot from the city of love, reproduced a million times as postcards and posters. For such moments Doisneau waited for hours, hidden in the crowd, incognito to the actors in his Parisian scenes. He often created images in his mind before pressing the shutter, and sometimes he would help the process along a bit – the couple in the »The Kiss«, for instance, were actually posing.

»Today it is considered the height of ineptitude to speak of patience, and yet there is no other way to catch the moment«. He called his camera the »time cutting machine«, photography a »tool with which one plucks out a picture from the stream of everyday life that can be held up as evidence of the existence of one's own world«.

His own world and era began in 1912 in the shabby Paris suburb of Gentilly. Here Doisneau became well acquainted with poverty, something he spent the first three decades of his life struggling to escape from. His tool was a Rolleiflex camera. He graduated from the Ecole Estienne in 1928 with diplomas lithography and engraving,

and began taking photographs a year later. His first photographic story was published in 1932, and in 1934 he got a job as a working photographer for Renault, which he gave up five years later to work freelance. As a photographer for the Résistance, he documented the occupation and liberation of Paris and got to know Charles Rado, the founder of the photo agency Rapho, who represented him from 1949.

But the photographing flaneur Doisneau always remained faithful to the milieu of the little man and the grey landscape of the Paris banlieues. The glossy photos he took for Vogue, Paris Match and other magazines provided him with a living, but the residents of the suburbs and life in the streets of Paris remained his passion. He peered into the viewfinder with great thought, his visual ruminations making him friends among intellectuals. After World War II came success and recognition. In 1949, Doisneau created a sensation with the volume »La Banlieue de Paris«. In 1951 came his first international exhibition at the Museum of Modern Art in New York. When Doisneau died in 1994, he left his personal chronicle of the city consisting of 325,000 negatives.

Small gestures

»Les Parisiens sont tel qu'il sont« is the title of one of his early pho-

For almost half a century Robert Doisneau portrayed the small scenes of Paris life

tographic books: Parisians, just as they are. That might as well be the motto for all of his work, which humorously and poetically portrays half a century of Parisian life. Doisneau documented life in Les Halles, depicted the little bistros around the corner, the cabarets on the Boulevard de Clichy, the sadness of satellite towns and captured those little gestures that tell so much. In »Le petit balcon« (1953) a dancer sits on the floor of a cabaret, her limp arm resting on the knee of an elderly gentleman. In »The Last Waltz of July 14« (1949) a couple dances in a world of their own in a spooky street. Even if the Paris immortalized by Doisneau's photographs is now long gone, you might still discover such scenes and hear Doisneau say: »Paris is a theatre for which the admission price is the passing of time«.

www.robert-doisneau.com

voir saw the passive role of the woman on a sexual, social and intellectual level as a product of a patriarchal society and demanded change with the emancipatory goal of self-realization for women.

GEORGES BIZET (1838–1875)

Composer   Georges Bizet is France's most famous opera composer of the Romantic period. His contemporaries regarded this bright boy from a Parisian musical family as a child prodigy – his father was already a composer, his mother the sister of the then renowned singing teacher François Delsarte. Just two weeks before his 10th birthday Bizet passed the entrance exam for the Paris Conservatory of Music. He wrote his first symphony at the age of 16 as a piece of homework, which then ended up in the archives. Only in 1935 was the score rediscovered and at once celebrated as an early masterpiece of the gifted composer. In 1869 he married Geneviève Halévy, the daughter of his music teacher at the conservatory. On their sixth wedding anniversary Bizet died suddenly of a heart attack. His premature death at the age of 36 meant that he didn't live to see the success of the work he had completed just that same year, based on a novel by Prosper Mérimée: Carmen. Having received a muted response by his contemporaries, the opera was praised enthusiastically by composers such as Brahms, Tchaikovsky and Debussy, and is today one of the most popular works in the entire operatic canon.

JACQUES CHIRAC (BORN 1932)

Politician   Only rarely in recent history has a politician been so popular with the French as Jacques Chirac, who dominated the politics of the country for five decades. Chirac's career began when he was elected deputy for his home Corrèze département. In 1977 he founded the »Rassemblement pour la République« (RPR), a party which committed itself to the ideas of former president Charles de Gaulle. In the same year, Chirac was elected Mayor of Paris, a post he held until 1995 and from 1986 to 1988 in conjunction with his role as Prime Minister under President François Mitterrand. The ambitious and charismatic Chirac, whom Georges Pompidou had once nicknamed »Le Bulldozer«, succeeded in winning France's highest office of state only in 1995 – his third attempt after 1981 and 1988. At his re-election in 2002, with just 19.9% of the vote Chirac suffered the worst election result of any incumbent French President, while the right-wing populist Jean-Marie Le Pen celebrated his result (16.86%) as a victory. In advance of the 2007 presidential election, Chirac, whose love affair had repeatedly made headlines, announced in a televised address that he would be retiring from politics. In 2009, the political warhorse garnered very different headlines when he became the first leader in modern France ordered to stand trial. The accusation was that as Mayor of Paris he had given fake jobs to friends in the party. In December 2011, Chirac was convicted of embezzling public funds, abuse of trust and illegal conflict of interest, and sentenced to two years' probation. Whether that will damage his reputation? Alain Juppé, a close confidant who was sentenced in 2004 on similar charges to 14 months in prison and a one year ban from politics, has long been rehabilitated and has been Mayor of Bordeaux since 2006.

HENRI IV (1553–1610)

»Paris is well worth a Mass« was the explanation given by the Huguenot leader Henry of Navarre for his conversion to Catholicism in 1593. As Henri IV (► picture p. 23) he was just about to become the first Bourbon king of France. Just after Henry married his first wife, the Catholic Princess Marguerite de Valois on 18 August 1572, the years of religious wars escalated into the massacre of St Bartholomew's Day against the Huguenots on 23–24 August. In 1598 the monarch finally managed to guarantee religious peace in the Edict of Nantes, conceding to the Huguenots the freedom to pursue their religion, granting them social and political equality and renewing a Gallic Catholicism that was independent of Rome. Henri IV succeeded in mastering the crisis of the French state, balancing public finances, opening his country economically by improving traffic routes and giving the capital Paris a new appearance. His wish that every peasant of his kingdom should have a chicken in his pot on Sunday is legendary. The colonization of Canada also began during his reign – Québec was founded in 1608. Henri IV was assassinated in 1610.

French King

NAPOLEON I (1769–1821)

In 1784 the son of a lawyer from Corsica began his training as an officer in the Parisian military school; he was lieutenant at the outbreak of the revolution; in 1793 he took Toulon, which was occupied by the British; he was promoted to general, put down a Royalist uprising in 1795 and by doing so he saved the French Directory, the moderate civil government. In appreciation of this Napoleon Bonaparte was made commander-in-chief of the »Army of Italy«; on 9 November 1799 he dissolved parliament at the head of his troops and made himself »First Consul«, head of state with a constitution tailored to his own wishes and a feigned representation of the people. On the basis

First emperor of France

of a general referendum he became consul for life in 1802, and in 1804 the first emperor of the French as Napoleon I. The traditional enmity between France and England prompted him to wage wars on the coalition, which was headed by Great Britain; he subjugated Austria and Prussia in these wars. He occupied Portugal and Spain in order to force the Britain to its knees by the Continental System – the first full economic war in history. By declaring war on Russia, which opposed the Continental System, he strove for mastery of the whole of Europe. The failure of the invasion of Russia, defeat in the Battle of Leipzig (1813) and the occupation of Paris by the allies forced Napoleon to abdicate in 1814 and go into exile on the island of Elba. In 1815 he tried to regain power in the famous »Hundred Days«; however, his army was defeated at Waterloo once and for all. Napoleon himself was banished to the island of St Helena, where he died in 1821. His mortal remains were transported to Paris and buried in the Dôme des Invalides in 1840. »I have helped revolution to gain a foothold«, Napoleon claimed, and indeed, his balancing of public finances through a new currency and a regular tax system, his administrative reform, his educational reform, his concordat with the pope and his famous Code Civil (Napoleonic Code), the first French civil code of law of 1804, safeguarded France's civil society and justify the great fame of the little Corsican to this day.

YVES SAINT LAURENT (1936–2008)

Fashion
designer

He had himself photographed in the nude on a velvet pillow for his perfume, was the first to dress women in tuxedos and he created a stir all his life with avant-garde fashion, innovative scents and unusual advertising ideas. Like no one else, Yves Saint Laurent liberated French fashion from its corset post 1945. His maxim was: »Fashion is fleeting, style forever«. Thus, the Parisian designer didn't choose to shock the public with garish, gaudy creations, but won them over with perfect tailoring in the guise of avant-garde. This single-minded, gentle son of a cinema chain operator began his career in the fashion house of Christian Dior, where he took over as head designer after the death of Dior in 1957. In 1960 Laurent was drafted into the Algerian war, but suffered a nervous breakdown after only a few days. The consequences of »rehabilitation« in a psychiatric clinic included life-long drug addiction and legal battles with Dior, which ended with a victory for YSL and the capital to start his own fashion house. From 1962 he created classics such as the completely straight-cut jacket and the Norman coat to go with a short, tight skirt. He invented the trouser suit for women and also made fashion accessible to the less well heeled. In 1966 Yves Saint Laurent was the first couturier to come out with a line of ready-to-wear fashion that was given the label »Rive Gauche«. »I know that I have advanced the cause of fashion and opened to women a hitherto forbidden universe« said Laurent, as he bowed out of the fashion world in January 2002 with a final show in Paris. Laurent died in 2008 after a long illness, reportedly of a brain tumour – though persistent rumours say it was AIDS. Shortly before his death, he had joined in a same sex civil union with his long time partner Pierre Bergé. Alongside his unique creations, to which

the Metropolitan Museum of Art in New York had devoted a solo exhibition even during YSL's lifetime, the audience-shy fashion designer bequeathed a fine art collection. Its sale realised 374 million euros, which provided the capital for two foundations, one of which goes to supporting AIDS research and the other to the fashion designer's museum.

ENJOY PARIS

What's trendy in Paris? Where's there to go in the evening? Where can you eat particularly well, have the best shopping? What can you do with children, which hotels are recommended and how do you book the most important events in advance?

Accommodation

Bonne nuit!

Hip, classy or budget? In the capital of light and fashion, the hotel industry has mastered the art of performance, the perfect seduction, the theatrical show with plush and pageantry, tradition and trend – and everything très parisien.

Even if the economic crisis may have caused tourist numbers to fall in some places, Paris is booming. The number of overnight stays has been increasing for years, and growth is expected to continue. In 2013, the Parisian hoteliers could feel more than satisfied about the more than 36 million overnight stays at an occupancy rate of almost 80 percent, and that despite the soaring room prices – still less than in London but almost 50% more than in Berlin.

Paris is booming

Paris has a lot of visitors – not only in the high season for tourism and when major events such as the fashion fair and the Tour de France are held. This makes it essential to book a room in good time. The **facilities** of French hotels were **reclassified in 2011**: alongside the 1–4-star and the 4-star luxury categories there is now the »Palace« category for establishments exceeding the 5-star level. At least until the next review in 2016, 12 hotels in Paris bear this new distinction, including the George V, the Plaza Athénée and the Ritz. Booking through a travel agency or online portals such as www.hotels.com or www.booking.com it is often possible to save time and money. Most hotels require written confirmation by email or letter and a credit card number or deposit. The rates can vary greatly depending on the season and online deals, the prices are usually for a double room without breakfast.

Book well in advance

ACCOMMODATION WEBSITES
Hotels
www.paris.hotelguide.net
www.paris.org/Hotels/OR/
www.parishotels.com
www.hotelsparis.net
www.paris-france-hotels.net

Bed and Breakfast
www.chambre-ville.com
www.hotelqualiteparis.fr
www.authenticbandb.com
www.bed-and-breakfast-in-paris.com
www.parisbandb.com
www.airbnb.co.uk

Jewel of the luxury category: the elegant Hotel Shangri-La in the former city palace of Prince Roland Bonaparte, a great nephew of Napoléon

Hotels, B&B's and Hostels

Where to stay

1. Crillon
2. Four Seasons George V
3. Lancaster
4. Mandarin Oriental Paris
5. Pavillon de la Reine
6. Ritz
7. Shangri-La Hotel
8. Bellechasse
9. Ferrandi
10. Gabriel
11. L'Hôtel
12. Lutetia
13. Mathi's Elysées
14. Pavillon des Lettres
15. Le Petit Moulin
16. Thoumieux
17. 7 Eiffel
18. Amour
19. Apostrophe Hôtel
20. Hostellerie du Ma

With Charm and Character

Since the turn of the millennium the Paris hotel market has been rapidly evolving. Venerable establishments have been feeling the competition from smaller boutique hotels that have responded to trend-conscious travellers with personal service and personalised décor.

The **boutique hotels** of Paris are luxury establishments with less than 50 rooms, which bear the signature of famous designers. Among the finest such accommodation on the Seine is the last home of Oscar Wilde, which is simply called **L' Hôtel**. »Give me the luxuries and I can dispense with the necessities« wrote Wilde, who after spending two years in Reading prison for homosexuality, in 1897 left England and went into exile in Paris. Photos in the lobby recall the sharp-witted writer who, though penniless, was allowed to stay in room 16. In a frame above the reception desk hangs a reminder from the hotel to settle the bill – when Wilde died in November 1900 he had left behind an unpaid bill over 26,430 francs. Jacques Garcia converted the Second Empire mansion into an elegant and discrete hotel with retro chic. From the Michelin-starred restaurant there are views into the courtyard garden, and there's a pool and steam room in the basement (► p 72).

In the Marais, fashion designer **Christian Lacroix** has transformed an old bakery into the tiny **romantic hotel Le Petit Moulin**. Behind the listed facade Lacroix created a mix of fashion and theatre, a blend of styles, colours and patterns. Each of the 17 rooms is itself a work of great creativity with large-patterned fabrics in bright colours, ethnic objects, XXL sized engravings and drawings by the designer (►p. 72).

Andrée Putmann has designed two hotels in Paris: Pershing Hall, which opened in 2001, and **Le Mathi's**, for which the designer chose the theme of »Boudoir«. The grande dame of French design employs a style mix of rigour and flowing lines, with lots of brass and gold, restrained black, mosaic and chandeliers, a touch of Art Déco, a pinch of Empire. In the 23 rooms, she reveals her penchant for colour and exciting contrasts, for example in the treatment of the walls – deep blue in one room, covered in reddish-brown brocade in another. Ornate beds made of metal or plain leather-covered couches make for a relaxing night. It isn't easy to get a table in the restaurant because it's currently one of the most popular establishments in Paris, with celebrities like Roman Polanski and Vogue editor Emmanuelle Alt indulging in the classic French cuisine. VIPs from the worlds of politics, fashion and show business congregate in the nostalgic Mathis Bar (► p. 172.

While the Paris boutique hotels like to wallow in an abundance of

Star designer Jacques Garcia gave the L' Hôtel its special touch

colours, forms and traditions, the **design hotels** have a cooler, more trendy look: steel instead of soft wood, black leather instead of glowing fabrics, minimalism instead of opulence. Innovative high-tech materials and latest technologies are just as much a part of their décor as modern art on the walls and creative cuisine from the kitchen. Such cool, contemporary chic is the hallmark of the **Hotel Gabriel**. The Zen atmosphere of its light-flooded rooms is intended to detox the guest, with relaxing sleep, healthy food, relaxation teas, light and sound programmes, massage and spa treatments (▶ p. 72).

India Mahdavi is a master of the »Global chic« that she has brought to the **Hotel Thoumieux** in the shape of a bold mix of patterns and materials, wallpaper with floral ornaments, marble-topped tables and graphically patterned carpets, combined with a leo print carpet, a red chair and a gilded mirror. Just as exclusive and unique as the 15 spacious rooms is the cuisine of Jean-François Piège, who has banished the sommelier and menu both from his brasserie on the ground floor and his starred restaurant on the top floor and replaced them with his surprise »Les Règles du Jeu«, daily creations from produce purchased at the market (▶ p. 72).

In the 20th arrondissement the **Mama Shelter** is a moderately priced option styled by **Philippe Starck**. Facilities include Mac computers in every room and guests can take pictures of themselves using »Photo Booth«, which will then be posted on public screens around the hotel. Running the kitchen is Alain Senderens, who has returned his three stars in order to try something new. Now he prepares creative »Comfort Food« which is served on long tables. The home-smoked salmon comes with wasabi cream and the grilled Angus steak is marinated according to one of grandmother's recipes. A cheaper alternative is the Mama Pizza with arugula, mozzarella and pistachios for €14 in the hotel's pizzeria (► p. 76).

That inexpensive no longer just applies to cheap chain hotels around the periphery but also to stylish

Nice atmosphere, reasonably priced and delicious: »Mama's« Pizzeria

and trendy places in the heart of town is demonstrated by the **Gat'folies** close to the opera house: 38 budget rooms with bohemian flair, inspired by the Folies Bergères. A good deal for lovers is a night in a double room with champagne, fruit, breakfast and late checkout for €120 (► p. 76).

In Paris' first literature hotel, **Le Pavillon des Lettres**, each of the 26 rooms pays homage to the work of

the author or poet after which it is named – from Hans Christian Anderson to Emile Zola. To this end, the Parisian interior designer Didier Benderli hasn't only used evocative colours, furniture and fabrics but also quotes on the walls that reflect the imagery of the night, poetry and dreams (► p.72).

The first Parisian hotel to be built in Art Nouveau style was the **Lutetia**. Designed by Louis-Charles Boileau, it celebrated its centenary in 2010. Various prestigious literary awards such as the Prix Médicia, the Prix Antonin Carême and the readers' prize of *Elle* magazine are awarded at the Lutetia, and literary Saturdays and reading lounges for literature fans regularly form part of the programme. The Literary Suite has its own library, and works by contemporary artists such as Arman, César and Thierry Bisch are displayed in the lobby. In the »Le Paris« restaurant star chef Philippe Renard spoils guests with the best that the capital has to offer (► p. 72).

Finally, the **Apostrophe Hôtel** is the first »poem hotel«► in Paris. The design of the 16 uniquely decorated rooms was conceived by Sandrine Alouf around the subject the imprint left by man through the centuries. Each room has a different theme – alluded to on the curtains and headboards – ranging from calligraphy and typesetting to newspapers, books and posters. The facade features the imaginary shadows of trees created by Catherine Feff (► p. 73).

Mother Nature was at hand when it came to fitting out the rooms of the €€€ **Hidden Hotel** (http://hidden-hotel.com). Softwood divides the living space from the washing area dominated by slate and marble, and hidden by airy linen drapes the coco-mat beds occupy their own secret alcove. The healthy breakfast provides sustainable vitality. Two seals of quality attest to the **environmental friendliness** of an establishment: »La clé du concierge« and »La clé verte«. Among the establishments to have been awarded these is the € **Solarhotel**, which has organic breakfasts and solar panels on the facade (www.solarhotel.fr). The first hotel in France to be given the European Eco-label was the €€€ **Premier Regent's Garden** in Paris (www.hotel-regents-paris.com).

Green hotels

To provide their guests with holistic wellbeing, many hotels have created a **spa** or **wellness centre**, often in collaboration **renowned cosmetic brands**. At the Plaza Athénée it is Dior that sets the tone (www.plaza-athenee-paris.com), while at the Hotel Renaissance Vendôme there is a branch of the posh Geneva After the Rain spa. Nuxe products are used in the wellness centre at the Square (www.hotelsquare.com). Luxury hotels such as the Shangri-La or Mandarin Oriental leave nothing to be desired in their wonderful spa areas.

Hotel spas

Hotel residences that combine the freedom of a **holiday flat with the service of a hotel** are on the rise. As well as the large chains Residhome, Suitehotel, Fousse, Citéa and Citadines there are several small-scale providers that operate aparthotels with an individual atmosphere. Our recommendation: €€€ La Maison Saint-Germain (158, Boulevard Saint-Germain, www.maison-saint-germain.com).

Hotel residences

Insider Tip

For young people there are 32 hostels with over 5500 beds in the Paris area. During the long summer holidays accommodation in student halls of residence is also available.

Youth hotels and youth hostels

❶ Accueil des Jeunes de France (AJF), www.hihostels.com.
Halls of residence: CISP (www.cisp.fr), CROUS (www.crous-paris.fr) and the Maison des Mines in Rue St-Jacques (www.maisondesmines.com).

A low-cost alternative to the hotel is the B & B – more than 600 Parisians have now opened up their houses to guests. Many of them subscribe to the **Hôtes Qualité Paris** quality charter introduced by the Tourist Board in 2008. Very popular are the non-commercial offers of private rooms, such as those offered by community-marketplaces such as Airbnb (▶ p. 19).

Bed & Breakfast

The capital's only campsite is situated in the middle of the Bois de Boulogne and was modernized in 2012 (2, Allée du Bord de l'Eau, 16th arr., www.campingparis.fr).

Camping

Recommended hotels

Legendary grand hotels, new boutique hotels or inexpensive, simple establishments and private accommodation with a special flair and authentic charm – Paris has everything.

PRICE CATEGORIES
€€€€ more than €400
€€€ €200–€350
€€ €130–€200 €
€ up to €130
Double room per night not including breakfast

FAMOUS LUXURY HOTELS

❶ Crillon €€€€
10, Place de la Concorde (8th arr.)
Tel. 01 44 71 15 01
www.crillon.com
Double room from €550
147 rooms and suites in the style of Louis XV in this hotel that belongs to the Taittinger champagne dynasty. The Leonard Bernstein Suite complete with roof terrace looks out over the Place de la Concorde. Chandeliers, mirrors and marble vie for attention in the grand Les Ambassadeurs restaurant. The wood-panelled ►L'Obé► and the bar are favourite haunts of the art and fashion scene. One of the most romantic places to enjoy afternoon tea is the winter garden decorated in purple and gold. CLOSED UNTIL 2015.

❷ Four Seasons George V €€€€
31, Avenue George V (8th arr.)
Tel. 01 49 52 70 00,
www.fourseasons.com/paris
Double room from €890
Grand luxury hotel with 245 rooms and suites in the style of Louis XVI. Allow yourself to be pampered with massage and aromatherapy in the elegant spa. Eric Briffard's Le Cinq restaurant has two Michelin stars. The balcony of the romantic honeymoon suite has a direct view of the Eiffel Tower.

❸ Lancaster €€€€
7, Rue de Berri (8th arr.)
Tel. 01 40 76 40 18,
www.hotel-lancaster.fr
Double room from €480
Greta Garbo, Clark Gable and Marlene Dietrich, who had suite no. 45 for three years, knew that there is no finer place to stay near the Champs-Elysées than the Lancaster. 57 delightful rooms surrounding a magical Zen garden. Michel Troisgros is in charge at the Michelin-starred La Table restaurant.

❹ Mandarin Oriental Paris €€€€
251, Rue St-Honoré (1st arr.)
Tel. 01 70 98 78 88,
www.mandarinoriental.com/paris
Double room from €790
Star violinist Vanessa Mae performed at the opening of this luxurious and modern 5-star hotel with its 99 rooms and 39 suites in the autumn of 2011. With silk and embroidered taffeta, dark wood, pale colours and chrome, the Parisian architects Sybille de Margerie, Patrick Jouin and Sanjit Manku skillfully combined tradi-

tional and modern styles. Responsible for the Asian-inspired cuisine is the two-star chef Thierry Marx, who studied in Thailand, Hong Kong and Japan. The spa is heaven on earth.

❺ Pavillon de la Reine €€€€
28, Place des Vosges
(3rd arr.)
Tel. 01 40 29 19 19
www.pavillon-de-la-reine.com
Double room from €420
Louis XIII had this enchanting palais converted into a residence for his queen, Anne of Austria. The old wooden beams of the ceilings and the antique furnishings are a reminder of the heyday of the Marais in the 17th century.

❻ Ritz €€€€
15, Place Vendôme (1st arr.)
Tel. 01 43 16 30 30,
www.ritz.com
Double room from €XXX
»If someone is in Paris and doesn't stay at the Ritz, there is only one excuse: that he can't afford it«, wrote Ernest Hemingway,

who lived here for years. And Coco Chanel lodged for almost four decades in a suite at the Ritz. The grand hotel reopened in 2015 after extensive renovation.

❼ Shangri-La Hotel €€€€   *Insider Tip*
10, Avenue d'Iéna (16th arr.)
Tel. 01 80 27 19 35,
www.shangri-la.com
Double room from €800
▶ picture p. 62
In 2011, the city palais built at the Trocadéro in 1896 for Prince Roland Bonaparte was transformed into an elegant and intimate jewel of luxury. Half of the 101 rooms and suites, some done out in opulent Empire style and some in modern luxury, overlook the Eiffel Tower. Eastern and western influences complement each other at the La Bauhinia, Phillippe Labbé serves up modern and fresh interpretations of French classics at the L'Abeille, while the Shang Palace serves Cantonese haute cuisine (▶ p. 115). The gorgeous Chi Spa with its 16-m pool provides pure pampering

Luxury living in the terrace suite at the Mandarin Oriental Paris

HOTELS €200–€350

Insider Tip

❽ Bellechasse €€€/€€
8, Rue de Bellechasse (7th arr.)
Tel. 01 45 50 22 31
www. lebellechasse.com, 34 rooms.
Here at the Bellechasse Christian Lacroix has combined neoclassical aesthetics of the 19th century with sensual and contemporary design. Excellent sound proofing!

❾ Ferrandi €€€
92, Rue du Cherche-Midi (6th arr.)
Tel. 01 42 22 97 40, 42 rooms.
www.hotel-ferrandi-paris.com
Mahogany furniture, wood panelling and crystal chandeliers, a cosy open fire and soft four-poster beds – occupying a fine 19th-century palais and renovated in 2010 the Ferrandi is very popular.

❿ Gabriel €€€
25, Rue du Grand Prieuré (11th arr.), Tel. 01 47 00 13 38
www. gabrielparismarais.com
The first Parisian »Detox« hotel relies on tranquil white, soft light and relaxation under the rain shower (▶ p. 67).

⓫ L'Hôtel €€€/€€€€
13, Rue des Beaux-Arts (8th arr.)
Tel. 01 44 41 99 00
www.l-hotel.com
Red velvet and golden tassels, marble, brass and cameo lockets – 20 rooms and suites, some in Art Déco, some in the style of Napoleon III and some modern (▶ p. 66).

⓬ Lutetia €€€
45, Boulevard Raspail (6th arr.)
Tel. 01 49 54 46 46
www.lutetia-paris.com, 230 rooms.
Even Henri Matisse, Antoine de St-Exupéry and Charles de Gaulle appreciated the discreet luxury of this fine establishment (▶ p. 68).

⓭ Mathi's Elysées €€€
3, Rue Ponthieu (8th arr.)
Tel. 01 53 76 01 62
www.paris-hotel-mathis.com
Silk taffeta curtains, antique furniture, indian cabochon tiles in the bathroom and soft light from pleated lampshades: the 23 rooms are a sensual and intoxicating creation in neo-baroque, the restaurant and bar a trendy gathering ground for the Parisian elite (▶ p. 66).

⓮ Pavillon des Lettres €€€
12, Rue des Sausaies (8th arr.)
Tel. 01 49 24 26 26
www.pavillondeslettres.com
26 rooms = 26 letters and authors that leave their mark on the atmosphere of the rooms (▶ p. 148).

⓯ Le Petit Moulin €€€/€€€€
29/31, Rue du Poitou (3rd arr.)
Tel. 01 42 74 10 10
www.paris-hotel-petitmoulin.com
17 gems of rooms done out by Christian Lacroix in brightly-opulent pop chic in the heart of the Marais (▶ p. 66)

⓰ Thoumieux €€€
79, Rue Saint-Dominique (7th arr.)
Tel. 01 47 05 49 75
www.thoumieux.fr
Neo-Art Déco hotel with one of the trendiest restaurants in the capital (▶ p. 87)

For romantics: the magical 7 Eiffel boutique hotel

⑰ 7 Eiffel €€€
17 bis, Rue Amélie
(7th arr.)
Tel. 01 45 55 10 01
www.hotel-7eiffel-paris.com
Boutique hotel beautifully renovated in 2010 with 36 rooms, roof
terrace and charming bar in the
heart of the vibrant 7th arrondissement. The Eiffel Tower is just
around the corner, as is the Rue
Clerc zone with its nice little gourmet shops, restaurants and patis-
series. Wholesome breakfast and
very friendly service.

HOTELS €130–€200
⑱ Amour €€
8, Rue Navarin (9th arr.)
Tel. 01 48 78 31 80
www.hotelamourparis.fr
Walls in purple, deep blue or
black, huge white beds and nude
photography by Terry Richardson
– this hotel for sensual hours in
the city of love is hip and a trendy
place to stay for the style conscious, who instead of telephone
and television will find Kiehl's toi-
letries and iPod chargers. The in-
crowd comes to dine on beef car-
paccio and burgundy in the leafy
courtyard.

⑲ Apostrophe Hôtel €€ *Insider Tip*
3, Rue Chevreuse (6th arr.)
Tel. 01 56 54 31 3
http://apostrophe-hotel.com/hotel
In the heart of the literary district
of Montparnasse each of the 16
rooms tells its own story (▶ p. 68).

⑳ Hostellerie du Marais €€
30, Rue de Turenne (3rd arr.)

Tel. 01 42 72 73 47
www.hostelleriedumarais.com
In the heart of the Marais, just a stone's throw from the Picasso Museum. Breakfast is served in the 17th-century vaulted cellar.

㉑ Hotel des Grandes Ecoles €€
75, Rue Cardinal Lemoine (5th arr.)
Tel. 01 43 26 79 23
www.hotel-grandes-ecoles.com
Charming country house-style establishment dating from the turn of the 20th century, around the corner from the Pantheon and the Sorbonne. Most of the 51 quiet rooms overlook the park with old trees and rhododendrons. Breakfast is served on the terrace in summer.

㉒ Le Sainte-Beuve €€
9, Rue Sainte-Beuve (6th arr.)
Tel. 01 45 48 20 07
www.hotelsaintebeuveparis.fr
In a side street of Boulevard du Montparnasse, with rooms tastefully decorated in white and pastel shades.

Insider Tip

㉓ Marais Bastille €€
36, Boulevard Richard Lenoir (11th arr.)
Tel. 01 48 05 75 00
www. maraisbastille.com
This Best Western Hotel lies in the heart of the Marais, just around the corner from the Picasso Museum and Place des Vosges, brasseries, bistros and small antique shops. It has 37 bright and spacious rooms, and a foyer adorned in contemporary works by Arnaud Franc. Lovely staff and delicious breakfast buffet.

㉔ Place du Louvre €€
21, Rue des Prètres-Saint-Germain-l'Auxerrois (1st arr.)
Tel. 01 42 33 78 68,
20 rooms
www.paris-hotel-place-du-louvre.com
Mondrian, Miro or would you prefer Picasso? The rooms are named after famous painters and decorated with pictures by the masters. The Louvre is just outside – tickets can be procured on request.

㉕ Secret de Paris €€/€€€
2, Rue de Parme (9th arr.)
Tel. 01 53 16 33 33,
29 rooms.
www.hotel-design-secret-de-paris.com
This friendly boutique hotel in the Trinité interprets the top sights of Paris in six discreet themes – bed down in the ambience of the Eiffel Tower, Musee d'Orsay or Moulin Rouge!

㉖ Sèvres Saint-Germain €€
22, Rue Saint-Placide (6th arr.)
Tel. 01 45 48 10 67
www.sevres-saint-germain.com
Charming little hotel with 30 attractive rooms in a 17th-century city palais in the heart of Saint-Germain; good breakfast and friendly service.

UNDER €130
㉗ Beaumarchais €
3, Rue Oberkampf (11th arr.)
Tel. 01 53 36 86 86
www.hotelbeaumarchais.com
Simple, bright, budget rooms in the trendy area around the Rue Oberkampf

Contemporary art adorns the Hotel Marais Bastille

㉘ Hotel de Nesle €
7, Rue de Nesle (6th arr.)
Tel. 01 43 54 62 41
www. hoteldenesleparis.com
Molière, Notre-Dame or Abélard &
Héloise – 20 themed rooms, a ro
mantic garden with sun terrace
and a Moroccan steam room –
and all in the heart of Saint-Germain-des-Prés!

㉙ Nouvel Hotel € Insider Tip
24, Avenue de Bel Air (12th arr.)
Note: telephone bookings
only???.
Tel. 01 43 43 01 81
www.nouvel-hotel-paris.com
With great attention to detail
Claude und Danielle Marillier have

transformed this former boarding
school for girls near Place de la
Nation into a romantic place to
stay. Breakfast is taken in the
beautiful garden – there is direct
access to the green oasis. They
also have large family rooms.

㉚ Eldorado €
18, Rue des Dames (17th arr.)
Tel. 01 45 22 35 21
www.eldoradohotel.fr
Attractive little hotel at the foot of
Montmartre. All 39 rooms are in-
dividually furnished with memen-
tos from Africa and Asia. Away
from the hustle and bustle enjoy
an aperitif in the courtyard of Bistrot des Dames and enjoy the at-

mosphere of the young and trendy Batignolles district.

③ 29 Lepic €
29, Rue Lepic (18th arr.)
Tel. 0156 555004
www.29lepic.com, 38 rooms
Hotel in the heart of old Montmartre renovated in 2012, with nice little restaurants and cafés close at hand. Each of the five floors is done out in a different colour.

㉜ Gat' Folies €/€€
14, Rue Geoffroy Marie (9th arr.)
Tel. 01 44 83 67 15
www.gatrooms.fr
Coolly styled hotel at the top end of the budget category, with 38 single and double rooms. A healthy breakfast for a good start to the day (▶ p. 68).

㉝ Mama Shelter €/€€
109, Rue de Bagnolet (20. Arr.)
Tel. 01 43 48 48 48
www.mamashelter.com, 172 rooms
Ultra modern 3-star hotel with iMac computers. Both communicative and casual, it was voted top business hotel in 2011 (▶ p. 68).

BED & BREAKFAST
㉞ Une Chambre à Montmartre €€
18, Rue Gabrielle (18th arr.)
Tel. 06 82 84 65 28
www.chambre-montmartre.com
From your room you can gaze at the Eiffel Tower, from the shower

The Musée d'Orsay was the inspiration for the suite at the Hotel Secret de Pari

at Sacré Cœur, and at breakfast in the garden you can hear the birds: this chambre d'hôte designed by Claire Maubert is a delightful gem full of charm and style.

㉟ Les Toits de Paris € *Insider Tip*
25, Rue de l'Abbé Groult (15th arr.)
Tel. 06 60 57 92 05
www.chambrehotesparis.fr
A cosy, typically Parisian loft (20 m2), a full French breakfast and attentive hosts who will put together tailor-made tours on request – here above the rooftops of Paris along the Rive Gauche, the city's special joie de vivre is within your grasp.

YOUTH HOSTELS AND YOUTH HOTELS
Mije
Tel. 01 42 74 23 45
www.mije.com
The three youth hostels Fauconnier, Fourcy und Maubuisson are all located in the Marais, housed in 17th-century former city palaces of the aristocracy with leafy courtyards. Guests can have dinner at the restaurant at 6, Rue Fourcy for €10.50.

㊱ Fauconnier €
11, Rue du Fauconnier (4th arr.)
Métro: Pont-Marie, Saint-Paul

㊲ Fourcy €
6, Rue de Fourcy (4th arr.)
Métro: Saint-Paul

㊳ Maubuisson €
12, Rue des Barres (4th arr.)
Métro: Hôtel de Ville

㊴ St. Christopher's Inn €
159, Rue de Crimée (19th arr.)
Tel. 01 40 34 34 40
www.st-christophers.co.uk
Double rooms or dorms with up to 6 beds, complimentary breakfast and 6-euro dinner: Opened in 2011, this St. Christopher's Inn shows that cheap can also be good.

㊵ OOPS! Hostel €
50, Avenue des Gobelins (13rd arr.)
Tel. 01 47 07 47 00
http://oops-paris.com
Fun with style - trendy and modern budget hotel for young people. Small but clean rooms, Vélib station just outside the door.

Children in Paris

Excitement, Fun and Play

Young adventurers can take a boat ride through Paris, encounter Mickey Mouse and Asterix in theme parks or learn how to paint like Picasso and Monet.

Children under five years old travel free on the bus and in the Métro, and those between five and ten pay half price. Child rates and family tickets are also available for museums and other attractions. Many museums grant **free admission for young visitors up to the age of 18** and lay on specially organized **exhibitions, courses and holiday programmes** for children. They include the ▶Louvre, the ▶Musée d'Orsay, the ▶Musée du Quai Branly, the ▶Musée Jacquemart André, the ▶Centre Pompidou with a ▶Galerie des Enfants▶ and ▶La Villette with its Cité des Enfants and the Cité de la Musique with music by everyone from Wagner to Pink Floyd. The Tok-Tok studio in the ▶Palais de Tokyo offers everything from birthday parties to art courses and story times.

Reductions and children's programmes

The view of the city from above is always impressive – from the Eiffel Tower and Arc de Triomphe, Notre-Dame and Sacré-Cœur. Bus tours with the open-topped l'Open Tour, Big Bus or Cars Rouges and a cruise on the Seine are fun for children. A visit to the Ferme Georges-Ville farm in the **Bois de ▶Vincennes**, with calves, pigs, sheep and goats, is very reasonably priced, in addition to which Vincennes has a zoo and large playground in the Parc Floral. Almost all Paris parks have a puppet theatre and play araes; some of them, like the Jardin des Halles, have adventure playgrounds. In the Parc des Buttes-Chaumont, the **Guignol de Paris** presents Punch and Judy shows for young and old on Wed, Sat and Sun at 4.45pm (www.guignol-paris. com). In the ▶**Bois de Boulogne** visitors can rent bicycles with child seats and cycle around the lakes (▶p. 191). Anyone good on a skateboard or inliners can show off his/her skills on the terrace of the **Trocadéro**. Between Christmas and New Year a municipal carrousel is erected at the Trocadéro, providing free rides for children. In the ▶**Jardin du Luxembourg** model boats can be hired for sailing on the round pond.

Fun time

The theme parks around the city guarantee lots of fun and adventure, most notably ▶**Disneyland** and the **Asterixpark**. Like in the UK, France has all-day schooling. Except for the holidays, therefore, children's programmes and children's theatre performances only take place on Wed, Sat and Sun afternoon. Many museums run an »Atel-

Take the kids to Paris? Mais oui!

ier d'Enfants«, a children's workshop, in which they paint and play under pedagogical guidance. The **Cité des Sciences et de l'Industrie** of La ▶Villette is especially popular. Here offspring can play with buttons and levers and discover science for themselves through their own experiments. After La Villette you can also take them on a boat trip (▶Paris Canal, p. 194). In the **Grevin wax museum** children will encounter Spiderman, music stars and footballing legends (▶ p. 117), in the **Musée de la Poupée** there is a doll's doctor and doll courses for children aged four and over (▶ p. 133). The highlight of **Choco Story** is of course the chocolate tasting (▶ p. 133). A visit to the **circus** is always an experience (▶ p. 251). Punch and Judy shows, carrousel, hall of mirrors and the Phenix Jr circus are all part of the **Jardin d'Acclimation** in the ▶Bois de Boulogne, reached aboard a small colourful train that departs from Porte Maillot.

Musée en Herbe
The Musée en Herbe between the Louvre and Les Halles features a **child-friendly art exhibition with creative workshops** on Picasso, Leonardo da Vinci, Monet, Chagall, Keith Haring and Niki de Saint Phalle.
❶ 21, Rue Hérold, 1st arr., daily 10am–7pm, Thur till 9pm, one-hour children's tours from age 5 at 11am, 2pm, 3pm, 4pm and 7pm, children €10, adults €6; 2–4 year-olds half-hour tour at 10.30am and 1.30pm, children €6, parents free, www.musee-en-herbe.com

Like in a fairy tale
On a **one-hour boat ride**, the dwarves Lila and Philou get children involved in Paris with songs and anecdotes, questions and stories – simply magical.
❶ Croisière Enchantée, Bateaux Parisiens, www.bateauxparisiens.com/croisiere-promenade-paris/croisiere-enchantee.html; daily at 3.45pm from Tour Eiffel jetty, from €12 per person

River Café
So that parents can dine in peace on this **romantic restaurant ship** on the Seine, on Sat and Sun from 1pm–3.15pm they put on a **children's programme** including masking garlands, magic workshops, face painting and fishing. The children's menu with burger, fries and Nutella crêpe costs €14.
River Café: 146 Quai de Stalingrad, Issy-les-Moulineaux
Tel. 01 40 93 50 20, Métro: Issy-Val de Seine, www.lerivercafe.net

INFORMATION AND CHILDREN'S HOSPITAL
Kiosques Paris-Jeunes
14, Rue François Miron (4th arr.)
www.jeunes.paris.fr
Métro: Hôtel de Ville, St-Paul, Pont Marie

101, Quai Branly (15th arr.)
Métro: Bir-Hakeim
Information about sport and culture

Hôpital Necker-Enfants Malades
149–151, Rue de Sèvres

(15th arr.), tel. 01 44 49 40 00
www.necker.fr

BABYSITTER
Au Paradis des Petits
Tel. 01 43 65 58 58
www.auparadisdespetits.com

LARGE ANIMALS FOR LIT-TLE SCALLYWAGS
Ferme Georges-Ville
A real farm in the middle of Paris
▶Vincennes p. 343

Grande Galerie de l'Evolution
Travelling the world through jungle, desert and steppe ▶ p. 225

Parc des Félins **Insider Tip**
Domaine de la Fortelle, Nesles
www.parc-des-felins.com
52 km/32 mi southeast of Paris
May, June and Sept daily 10am–5pm, July and Aug daily 9.30am–7.30pm, Nov to April Tue–Sun 10am–5pm, children aged 4–9 €10, over 10s/adults €16.50
Lions, tigers, snow leopards and cheetahs can be admired in their large enclosures in this 60-hectare wildlife park – or up-close on a 20-minute tour aboard the panorama train.

Parc Zoologique de Thoiry
Parc et Château de Thoiry, Thoiry
Tel. 01 34 87 53 76
www.thoiry.net
56 km/35 mi west of Paris

Daily 10am–5pm, July and Aug till 6pm, closed Dec and Jan, children €21, adults €27.50
Elephants, lions, giraffes, wolves, hippos, rhinos and zebras inhabit this 150-ha safari park surrounding a château, where children are guided around by Tulu the monkey.

FUN PARKS
Disneyland
▶ p. 207

Parc Asterix
30 km/19 mi north of Paris
Mid-April to beginning of Nov daily 10am–6pm and for the Gallic Nights at the end of Oct 7pm–11pm.
Shuttle Bus from the Louvre, departure 8.45pm, return 6.30pm
3–11 year-olds €33, 12s and over €44
www.parcasterix.tr.
Six magical worlds from the ancient Appian Way and the Gallic village of invincible friends Asterix and Obelix to a Roman town, involving time-travel through 1000 years of Gallic history

Playmobil Fun Park
12 km/7 mi south of Paris
22/24 Allée des Jachères, Fresnes
Tue–Sun 10am–6pm
www.playmobil.fr, from age 3 €2
Twelve fun Playmobil-themed worlds in XXL

Entertainment

Long Nights

Paris knows how to turn night into day. The choice is overwhelming, the sound global. And this is true not only for music. Cinema, cabaret and theatre, opera, ballet or nightclub – there is something for everyone.

After nightfall the metropolis on the Seine looks just as glamorous and spectacular as it does by day. To start with there is the **atmospheric illumination** of 180 magnificent buildings, bridges and churches (above all: Tour Eiffel) that make Paris by night such a magical, romantic place. And those not content with strolling along the banks of the Seine or indulging the mood in one of the many Parisian cafés and restaurants until late at night, can find an endless variety of entertainment.

Into the early morning

Paris at night is a vibrant concoction of party districts, which differ significantly in character and the kinds of people they attract.
VIPs, celebrities and politicians meet in the bars and nightclubs **around the Champs-Élysées** and the Palais Royal, where strict bouncers ensure that they can keep themselves to themselves. At the Butte **Montmartre**, the red light district exists alongside a lively avant-garde scene. In the studenty **Quartier Latin**, bars, snack bars and restaurants of every category stand cheek by jowl along the old, winding streets, which are bustling even on weekdays. **Saint-Germain-des-Prés** is famous for its jazz clubs, while the **Bastille** district throbs to the sound of modern dance. Further north, in and around **Rue Oberkampf**, a variety of bars, cafés and clubs have also established themselves. **Belleville** and the streets adjacent to **Canal Saint-Martin**, meanwhile, promise a vibrant subculture and alternative venues.

Hip spots

Le dernier métro is not only the title of a classic film by François Truffaut, but also the display that comes up in the **Métro** when, at around 12.15–12.30am, the last trains leave the centre for their respective terminus destinations. The time in between until the Métro starts up again at around 5.30am is covered by the »Noctilien« night buses (www.noctilien.fr). Only on Saturdays does the Métro run until 2.15am.

Geting around

Details of events can be found in the city magazines *Pariscope* (www.pariscope.com) and *L'Officiel des Spectacles* (www.offi.fr).

Information

Trendy place to go: Café Charbon in Rue Oberkampf

»*Laissez-nous danser!*«

The Parisians' enthusiasm for jazz is legendary, and with its love for rock and pop tout Paris goes wild in clubs and bars until the early hours of the morning. And in the summer the locals take to the Guinguettes on the Seine and Marne, dancing in waltz time to soulful songs. The French chanson is what made Maurice Chevalier, Edith Piaf and Yves Montand famous. Today's chart-toppers include Patrick Bruel, Patricia Kaas and Zaz

Now more than ever, it's jazz, rock and pop that set the tone in the capital. They influence fashion and dominate the Parisian clubs. Even before the Second World War, Paris was a stronghold of jazz, where Josephine Baker held the world in awe with her nude dances to "Negro music" and Stéphane Grappelli played European jazz with Django Reinhardt at the Hot Club. In the 1950s, the city on the Seine was considered *the* **jazz metropolis**. And it wasn't only French stars such as Juliette Greco and Barbara and Boris Vian that were worshipped here. Also American jazz greats like Miles Davis, Billie Holiday and Count Basie appeared in the clubs of Saint-Germain-des-Prés in front of enraptured audiences and then stayed in the capital – sometimes even for years. Interest subsided with the advent of disco music, until a renaissance began in the mid-1980s. Today fans of blues, swing and New Orleans can find what they're looking for in the many jazz clubs of the capital. For an exceptional jazz evening you can even hop aboard the Melody Blues which lays on a jazz dinner on the Seine every Wednesday evening, departing from Pont de Bercy (www.melody blues.com).

Happiness in Three-Quarter Time

When France introduced the work-free Sunday in 1906, one music venue after another opened up along the Marne and the whole of Paris crowded onto steam trains to dance in time with the **musette** on the river. The atmosphere of gay abandon was undoubtedly enhanced by some of the illustrious company that also frequented the venues: pimps, prostitutes, thieves and other crooks who had been condemned to living outside a 30-km radius of the city. Of the nearly 200 **guinguettes** that once surrounded the metropolis like a necklace of excursion venues, only about a dozen now remain. However, with the rise of Paris East, dancing on the river has become très branché – and established itself right in the new heart of the capital, where, in the shadow of the National Library they now dance the night away on music boats on the Seine (www.culture-guinguette.com).

Dancing the **tango** is now also very trendy. In summer you can practise your vals and milonga on the banks of the Seine in the open air (▶MARCO POLO Insider Tip p. 220).

Of Love and Sorrow

The first time a chanson was sung at a state funeral was on 16 July 1857. It was Les souvenirs du peuple, a song glorifying Napoleon I. The man being carried to his grave had reclaimed the song from the political propaganda it had been associated with ever since the French Revolution: **Pierre-Jean de Beranger**. The funeral demonstrated just what passions the chanson could arouse in Parisians: the rulers of the Second Republic had to hold the populace at bay with 20,000 soldiers because they feared a revolt.

Song and rebellion in France have always gone hand in hand. In the mid-17th century, supporters of the Fronde, the uprising of the Paris Parliament, chanted their songs on the Pont Neuf. The slogans of the French Revolution and the spirit of the Paris Commune are conveyed most vividly in songs, which are contained to this day in the booklet Amis de la Commune de Paris. Among many other forgotten songs it includes famous works such as the national anthem **La Marseillaise** or the song of the working class, L'Internationale. But it wasn't until the free thinker Pierre-Jean de Beranger produced his five volumes of songs that the popular chanson was born. His melodies instantly caught on with the populace. All major chansonniers of the 19th century were connected to 500 singing groups of the Paris workers, artisans and petty bourgeoisie. When Louis Napoleon had almost all **sociétiés chantantes** closed down in 1853, there

The »Sparrow of Paris«: Edith Piaf

began the period of the café-concerts, where songs were sung for fun with little in the way of literary or political pretensions.

That changed in 1881 when **Le Chat Noir cabaret** opened on the Butte de Montmartre. Here Aristide Bruant sang of social misery and of crooks and whores, and even became the star of snobs who took his insults as a joke. The singer wore his trademark black coat, black boots, broad-brimmed black hat and red scarf – immortalised in the posters by Toulouse-Lautrec that made Bruant world famous. With her long, black gloves Yvette Guilbert could be seen on stage for one hour a day at the »Concert Parisien«, after which she sang in more elegant salons.

In around 1900 the scene on Montmartre changed as cabaret began facing increased competition from music halls like the **Olympia**, which opened in 1893. At the same time, revues with stars such as Mistinguett, Josephine Baker and **Maurice Chevalier** were produced in opulently ornate theatres. The man with tuxedo and straw hat, who made it from Parisian poverty to the big stage, was a celebrated entertainer right up until the 1960s. The artist who rose to become the icon of the French chanson also came from modest circumstances: the »**Little Sparrow**« **Edith Piaf** (1915–63). Her life was beset with car accidents, illness and drugs and yet she still succeeded in capturing people's hearts again and again: in 1953 she sang the revolutionary song Ça ira, and in 1960 her signature Non, je ne regrette rien topped the French charts for seven weeks. Edith Piaf died in 1963 at the age of only 47, but even among the existentialists of the 1960s, who would meet up in the cafés of Saint-Germain-des-Prés dressed entirely in black, the chanson remained alive, questioning having and being, telling of love, sorrow and issues that were no longer private but had become political once again. Georges Brassens, Maxime Le Forestier and Re-naud became the musical voice of the 1968-ers. The crooners Michel Sardou, Gilbert Bécaud, Charles Aznavours and Yves Montand held up a mirror to yearning, while Julien Clerc, Véronique Sanson and Johnny Halliday sang themselves melodiously into the hearts of the youth. Kaas gave the chanson fresh impetus with borrowings from jazz, pop and fado. That the genre remains as alive as ever is demonstrated by Karimouche, Alizée and Cali with their sensitive, cheeky and rousing lyrics.

Celebrated shooting star of the chanson skies is Isabelle Geoffrey, alias **Zaz**, who like Edith Piaf began as a street musician. With her guitar, double bass and powerful voice she impressed passers by in Montmartre before storming the international charts in 2011 with her hit Je veux.

Anyone interested in learning more about the history of chanson should take a look at the exhibition in the **Hall de la Chanson** in Parc de la Villette (www.lehall.com).

Shooting star Zaz mixes her chansons with gypsy jazz, swing and pop

Hip Spots, clubs, revues and chanson stages
▶map p. 108/109

A night out in Paris can be expensive. Depending on the venue, the day of the week and what's on, entry to nightclubs costs between €10 and €30. Many places are closed in August. Clothing is all-important. Anyone not considered chic, hip or elegant enough has no chance of getting past the strict bouncers of the more trendy clubs.

JAZZCLUBS
❶ Au Duc des Lombards   *Inside Tip*
42, Rue des Lombards (1st arr.)
Tel. 01 42 33 22 88
www.ducdeslombards.com
Métro: Châtelet-Les Halles
This pleasant jazz club, in which John Coltrane, Charlie Parker and Lester Young have performed, offers all genres from free jazz to hardbop. Free jam sessions Fri and Sat from midnight. TSF broadcasts from the jazz club every Monday from 7pm.

❷ Caveau de la Huchette
▶ MARCO POLO Insider Tip p. 300

❸ New Morning
7-9, Rue des Petites Écuries (10th arr.), Tel. 01 45 23 51 41
www.newmorning.com
Métro: Château d'Eau
You have to decide for yourself whether this former factory with space for 600 people is the best jazz club in the city. But the fact remains that almost all the top names in jazz have performed at the »Niou« at some time or another including Miles Davis, Chet Baker, Oscar Petersen and Terry Callier. Even today you can go there to hear famous music greats or up and coming talents like Erik Truffaz and Julien Lourau.

❹ Le Petit Journal Montparnasse   *Insider Tip*
13, Rue du Commandant Mouchotte (14th arr.)
Tel. 01 4 21 56 70, http://petit-journalmontparnasse.com
Métro: Montparnasse
Big bands and gospel choirs alternate on this big stage, the acoustics are brilliant and the atmosphere too: wood-panelled walls and a 10-m long bar. In summer from 6.30pm jazz pianist Philippe Bas accompanies your aperitif on the terrace.

❺ Le Petit Journal St-Michel
71, Boulevard St-Michel (5th arr.)
Tel. 01 43 26 28 59
www.petitjournalsaintmichel.abcsalles.com
Métro: Luxemburg
To go with your dinner you can have New Orleans swing, bebop, blues or dixie.

❻ Sunset-Sunside
60, Rue des Lombards (1st arr.)
Tel. 01 40 26 46 60
www.sunset-sunside.com
Métro: Châtelet-Les Halles
All jazz styles post 1940 resound in this vaulted cellar with Métro tiles and old photos. Gigs by talented newcomers as well as well-known bands.

Paris is a jazz stronghold

ROCK UND POP

7 Le Bataclan
50, Boulevard Voltaire (11th arr.)
Tel. 01 47 00 39 12
www.le-bataclan-com
Métro: Oberkampf
The venue of the 11th arr ever since the middle of the 19th century, at which world famous acts including Jane Birkin, Gossip, David Guetta and Michael Youn have performed.

8 La Flèche d'Or
102, Rue de Bagnolet (20. Arr.)
Tel. 01 44 64 01 02
www.flechedor.fr
Métro: Gambetta
In a former station opposite the Mama Shelter hotel (▶ p. 76) this music club presents three or four concerts nightly, with everything from independent rock to chanson.

Insider Tip

9 Le Nouveau Casino
109, Rue Oberkampf (11th arr.)

Tel. 01 43 75 57 40
www.nouveaucasino.net Métro: Parmentier
Live music in baroque surroundings with an unusual programme ranging from pop to deep house to rock.

10 Olympia
28, Boulevard des Capucines
Tel. 08 92 68 33 68
www.olympiahall.com
Métro: Madeleine, Opéra
Edith Piaf, Gilbert Bécaud, Patricia Kaas, Frank Sinatra and the Beatles have all performed here. Since 2000 the famous concert hall has resided a few steps away from its original location.

11 Point Éphémère
200, Quai de Valmy (10th arr.)
Tel. 01 40 34 02 48
www.pointephemere.org
Métro: Jaurès, Louis-Blanc
Culture thrives in this old warehouse by the Canal St-Martin: ex-

hibitions, bar-restaurant and concert stage, which combines electro, jazz and rock. Several times a month Parisians dance until dawn to the sounds of *Kill the DJ*.

⑫ **Zénith**
211, Avenue Jean-Jaurès
(19th arr.)
Tel. 01 42 40 60 00
www.zenith-paris.com
Métro: Porte de Pantin
James Blunt, Carmina Burana or Rock meets Classic – the most important concert hall for rock, pop, musicals and varietés has 6400 seats.

GUINGUETTES
⑬ **Batofar**
▶ MARCO POLO Insider Tip p. 319

⑭ **Chez Gégène**
162, Quai de Polangis, Allée des Guinguettes, Jointville-le-Pont
Tel. 01 48 83 29 43
www.chez-gegene.fr
The walls in this guinguette, which opened in 1895 and was frequented by stars of screen and stage feature some amusing artwork. The comedian Bovril even immortalized the dance club in a song that became the French leisure anthem: *À Joinville-le-Pont*.

⑮ **La Dame de Canton**
11, Quai François-Mauriac
Tel. 01 53 61 08 49
www.damedecanton.com
Métro: Quai de la Gare
Gypsy jazz, chanson and salsa feature on board this Chinese junk; there is a DJ in action at weekends.

⑯ **La Guinguette à Roland** Insider Tip
103, Chemin du Contre-Halage
Champigny-sur-Marne
Tel. 01 47 06 00 91
Like his partner Christine and his waiter Claude, Roland Vigue wears the togs of the canotiers, the ferrymen: straw boater, striped shirt and dark sailor trousers. The dance music is also traditional: musette and other melodies that Corinne Rousselet plays on her accordion.

⑰ **L'Île du Martin-Pêcheur**
41, Quai du Victor Hugo
Champigny-sur-Marne
Tel. 01 49 83 03 02
www.guinguette.fr
Colourful lights illuminate the patio tables on an island in the Marne, while a two-man band plays twist, boogie-woogie, java and Chabadabada from the new wave film classic *A Man and a Woman*.

TANGO
www.tango-argentin.fr
Provides a good overview of the »Milongas«, the Parisian tango clubs

⑱ **Casa del Tango**
11, Allée Darius Milhaud (19th arr.)
Tel. 01 40 40 73 60
www.lacasadeltango.net
Métro: Ourcq
Tango courses, balls and concerts

HIP, BARS
AND NIGHTCLUBS
⑲ **Le Back Up**
18, Rue de la Croix Nivert
(15th arr.), tel. 01 47 83 26 17
www.lebackup.com

Métro: Cambronne
More than 1000 people can dance together at this enormous club and slake their thirst at the 20-m long bar.

㉔ Le Balajo
9, Rue de Lappe (11th arr.)
Tel. 01 47 00 07 87, www.balajo.fr
Métro: Bastille
Legendary dance hall, in which they dance to the waltz musette on Mon and Thur 2pm–7pm and to rock 'n' roll, salsa and bachata on Tue–Sat evenings.

! *Shaken or stirred?* **Insider Tip**

MARCO POLO TIP

Colin Peter Field, head bartender at the iconic **㉑ Hemingway Bar** in the legendary Hotel Ritz Paris has been honoured by Forbes Magazine as the »Best Bartender in the World«. In his book Le Ritz Paris, une histoire de cocktails: la simplicité comme credo (Editions de la Martinière 2011), Field tells when, where and by whom the true classics were created and how to properly prepare a dry martini, a »honey frost« or the »Singapore sling«. Supermodel Kate Moss, who wrote the foreword, prefers the »French 76« made with vodka, lime juice and champagne.

㉒ Le Baron
6, Avenue Marceau (8th arr.)
Tel. 01 47 20 04 01
www.clublebaron.com
Métro: Alma-Marceau
Comfortable armchairs, subdued lighting and a large wing next to the dance floor – this villa is very vogue. Stars, models, politicians and partygoers.

㉓ Café Charbon
109, Rue Oberkampf (11th arr.)
Tel. 01 43 57 55 13
www.lecafecharbon.com
Métro: Parmentier
Mojito, Cuba libre and caipirinha, with tapas, burgers and salads – both indoors and outdoors this former coal merchant's is always jam-packed. Live music evenings and at weekends.

㉔ Café de l'Industrie
16, Rue Saint-Sabin (11th arr.)
Tel. 01 47 00 13 53
Métro: Bréguet-Sabin
A popular pub done out in colonial style, for those who want a reasonable bite to eat before they go out on the town.

㉕ Chez Moune
54, Rue Jean-Baptiste-Pigalle (9th arr.) Tel. 01 45 26 64 64
http://chezmoune.fr
Métro: Pigalle
A young, style- and fashion-conscious clientele dances at this trendy nightclub at the foot of the Butte de Montmartre.

㉖ Harry's New York Bar
5, Rue Daunou (2nd arr.)
Tel. 01 42 61 71 14
www. harrysbar.fr

Métro: Opéra
Hemingway and Scott Fitzgerald, Zazie and Quentin Tarantino have all quaffed their whisky at Harry's New York Bar, where the ►Bloody Mary► was invented in 1921.

㉗ Madam
128, Rue de la Boëtie (8th arr.)
Tel. 01 53 76 02 11
www.le-madam.abcsalles.com
Métro: George V
House is »hip«, so »tout Paris« descends on this little club to dance until the small hours.

㉘ Pau Brasil **Insider Tip**
32, Rue de Tilsitt (17th arr.)
Tel. 01 53 57 77 66
www.paubrasil.fr
Métro: Charles de Gaulle – Etoile
Caipirinha and capoeira, cabaret, dance and champagne with dinner: this place rocks with South American joie de vivre.

㉙ Le Saint
7, Rue Saint-Séverin (5th arr.)
Tel. 01 43 25 50 04
www.lesaintdisco.com
Métro: Saint Michel
In this vaulted cellar from the 13th century they dance the night away to rock and soul from the 1950s to the 1970s.

㉚ Six Seven
65, Rue Pierre Charron (8th arr.)
Tel. 01 58 56 20 51
www.sixsevenclub.com
Métro: George V
The parties that this nightclub on the Champs-Elysées regularly organizes for women are considered the hottest events for female revellers – but men are also welcome.

Feathers, rhinestones and much eroticism: the Bluebell Girls at the Lido de Paris

REVUE THEATRE
㉛ Crazy Horse
12, Avenue Georges V. (8th arr.)
Tel. 01 47 23 32 32
www.lecrazyhorseparis.com
Métro: Alma-Marceau
Grace, beauty, humour and fantasy – the beautiful girls have been the hallmark of the aesthetic erotic show for more than 60 years. By the way, Charles Aznavour began his career here.

㉜ Folies Bergère
32, Rue Richer (9th arr.)
Tel. 01 44 79 98 90
www.foliesbergere.com
Métro: Cadet
Alternating cheeky vaudeville shows in Paris's oldest vaudeville theatre, opened in 1867.

㉝ Lido de Paris
116, Avenue des Champs-Elysées (8th arr.)
Tel. 01 40 76 56 10

The Moulin Rouge was birthplace of the French »can-can«

www.lido.fr
Métro: George V
Elaborate laser effects and a classic programme featuring the famous Bluebell Girls: the giant hall has been full ever since 1946. Before a performance you can take a look behind the scenes of the famous cabaret establishment with the »L'Envers du décor du Lido« tour.

㉔ Moulin Rouge
▶ Pigalle, p. 294

CHANSON HALLS
㉟ Bobino
20, Rue de la Gaîté (9th arr.)
Tel. 01 43 27 75 75
www.bobino.fr
Métro: Edgar-Quinet
Modern concert hall with 850 seats, which also features chanson and varieté in the programme.

㊱ La Java
105, Rue du Faubourg-du-Temple (10th arr.), tel. 01 42 02 20 52
www.la-java.fr
Métro: Belleville, Goncourt
The place where Edith Piaf sang and Django Reinhardt played his jazz is today a venue for world music, rock, electro and chanson.

㊲ Le Limonaire `Insider Tip`
18, Cité Bergère (9th arr.)
Tel. 01 45 22 33 33
www.limonaire.free.fr
Métro: Grands Boulevards
Hearty stews, large tankards of beer and dedicated singers: Noel Tartier's pub has been one of the city's most discerning chanson venues for more than 20 years.

㊳ Les Trois Baudets
64, Boulevard de Clichy (18th arr.)
Tel. 01 442 62 33 33
www.lestroisbaudets.com
Métro: Blanche
Venue specializing in new French chanson; also opens up for a young audience on Sun at 3pm

㊴ Le Vieux Belleville
15, Rue des Envierges (20. Arr.)
Tel. 01 44 62 92 66
www.le-vieux-belleville.com
Métro: Pyrénées
While the accordion player does tunes by Edith Piaf, the host serves classics such as »Coq au Vin«.

THEATRE, OPERA AND BALLET

Paris has nearly 140 theatres, which offer nightly French classics and contemporary comedies, light entertainment and avant-garde experiment, vaudeville and boulevard theatre, one man shows, dancing and poetry. Highlights for Paris visitors with a good knowledge of French are the classics of the **Comédie Française** and the innovative productions of **Bouffes du Nord**.

Theatre

Aida, Faust or Lulu – the repertoire of the **Opéra de la Bastille** is fantastic. Ballet performances and guest appearances are mainly staged in the **Opéra Garnier**. Closely linked with the Opera Garnier is the name of **Roland Petit** who died in 2011 at the age of 87. He had started dancing there as a nine-year-old and was ballet director for six months in the 1970s. He then moved to the Paris Casino but remained attached to the Opera Garnier throughout his life. For them, he created eleven choreographies, including Notre Dame de Paris, Le Rendezvous and Le Jeune homme et la mort. Operas and operettas are also staged at the **Opéra Comique** and **Théatre des Champs-Elysées**. Well-known concert halls for classical music are the **Salle Gaveau** and the **Salle Pleyel**. Mega concerts from the likes of David Guetta, Patricia Kaas and Michel Sardou usually take place at the **Olympia** (► p 88), the **Zénith** (► p 89) and the **Palais Omnisports** in Bercy (► p 188). As a stage for new music, the **Gaîté Lyrique** with a concert hall for 800 people was completed on the edge of the Marais district in 2011. The first concerts in the **Philharmonie de Paris**, built according to plans by Jean Nouvel in the Parc de la Villette, took place in January 2015. All major churches such as Notre-Dame, Sainte-Chapelle or Madeleine are famous for their organ concerts and chamber music recitals. At least twice a month the centre for contemporary music, **Centre Musical Fleury Goutte d' Or – Barbara**, enables new bands to have their first experience of the stage (www.fgo-barbara.fr).

Opera, ballet and concerts

CINEMA

Cinema is a real passion for the Parisians, who queue up on Fridays and Saturdays to see the latest films. Even back in the 1920s Paris witnessed the creation of artistically important films such as Man Ray's *Le retour à la raison*, Fernand Léger's *Ballet méchanique* and *Un chien andalou* by Luis Buñuel and Salvador Dalí. After Hitler's rise to power in Germany, many leading lights of the film studios in Berlin went into exile in and via Paris, including Fritz Lang, Billy Wilder and Max Ophüls. They took the atmosphere of René Clair's poetic images of Paris – *July 14, Bastille Day, Under the Roofs of Paris* – to

World-class movie metropolis

No chance without booking in advance: the ballet performances at the Théatre de la Ville are usually booked out months in advance

Hollywood, where comedies romanticizing the city such as Minelli's *An American in Paris* were produced. Many other films are set in Paris, from early works such as Marcel Carné's *Children of Paradise* of (1942) to Catherine Deneuve as *Belle de Jour* (1973), *The last Métro* (1981), *Amélie* (2001) and *Hunting and Gathering* (2007) to the subtle love story *Paris* (2008) by Cédric Klapisch and Woody Allen's romantic homage to the Seine metropolis *Midnight in Paris*, which came out in 2011. The most important publication for young film critics is the Parisian movie magazine **Cahiers du Cinéma**. The city was and remains a source of inspiration and place of work for some of the greatest French directors, who have included Claude Chabrol, Jean-Luc Godard, Eric Rohmer, François Truffaut and Guillaume Canet.

Paradise for film buffs

Almost 400 cinema screens, a third of them independent, show a good 500 films each week. Those staying longer in the city should take a look at the retrospectives that, for example, the Accatone, Champo or the cinémathèques dedicate to directors, actors or periods in the history of the cinema. At the beginning of July the Seine metropolis celebrates its cinematic heritage for two weeks during the »Paris Cinéma« festival. On one day in the week – usually Monday or Wednesday – ticket prices are reduced by up to 30%. The cinema programme can be found in the city magazines *Pariscope* and L'Officiel des Spectacles as well as at www.allocine.fr.

THEATRE, OPERA AND BALLET

Bouffes du Nord
37 bis, Boulevard de la Chapelle (10th arr.)
Tel. 01 46 07 34 50
www.bouffesdunord.com
Métro: La Chapelle
Poems by Nietzsche, letters from Kafka to his father or Molière's comedy *The Bourgeois Gentleman* – Olivier Mantei and Olivier Poubelle have big shoes to fill: from 1974 to 2010 Peter Brook, one of the greatest directors of world theatre, was in charge here.

Cartoucherie de Vincennes
▶ Vincennes, p. 343

Comédie Française
▶ p. 288

Gaïté Lyrique
3 bis, Rue Papin (3rd arr.)
Tel. 01 53 01 51 51
www.gaite-lyrique.net
Métro: Réaumur-Sébastopol, Arts et Métiers
New culture centre for digital art and contemporary music.

Opéra Bastille
▶ Bastille, p. 181

Opéra Comique
5, Rue Favart (2nd arr.)
Tel. 01 47 42 57 50
www.opera-comique.com
Métro: Richelieu-Drouot
Where Georges Bizet's *Carmen* was first performed in 1875, today you can see French operas and operettas by Debussy, Offenbach and Ravel.

Opéra-Garnier
▶ p. 73, 215

! *On horseback ..* **Insider Tip**

MARCO ⊕ POLO TIP

... the Zingaro equestrian show carries you away into in an amazingly colourful fairytale world – an unforgettable experience for the whole family (entrance: 176, Avenue Jean-Jaurès, Aubervilliers; Métro: Fort d'Aubervilliers, tel. 01 48 39 18 03, www.bartabas.fr/Zingaro).

Philharmonie de Paris
▶ p. 340

Salle Gaveau
45, Rue La Boëtie (8th arr.)
Tel. 01 45 63 20 30
www.sallegaveau.com
Métro: Saint-Augustin
The Salle Gaveau frequently hosts world stars such as Anna Netrebko, Rolando Villazón and Erwin Schrott.

MARCO ● POLO TIP

! *Grand picture palace* Insider Tip

With its Art Nouveau façade, Neo-baroque décor and giant screen for an audience of 2650, the Grand Rex, which opened in 1932, is the most beautiful cinema in Paris. In the humorous, 50-minute journey of discovery *Les Etoiles du Rex*, films and movie stars come to life with re-enacted scenes and special effects (1, Boulevard Poissonière, 2nd arr., tel. *08 92 68 05 96; www.le grandrex.com; tour: Wed–Sun 10am–7pm).

Salle Pleyel
252, Faubourg St-Honoré (8th arr.)
Tel. 01 45 61 53 00
www.sallepleyel.fr
Métro: Charles de Gaulle - Etoile
This Art Déco concert hall seats almost 1,000 people. There are performances not just of Bruckner, Mozart and Brahms but also jazz and chanson.

Théâtre de la Huchette
▶ MARCO POLO Insider Tip S. 300

Théâtre National de Chaillot
▶ p. 284

Théâtre des Champs-Elysées
15, Avenue Montaigne (8th arr.)
Tel. 01 49 52 50 50
www.theatrechampselysees.fr
Métro: Franklin-Roosevelt
Mozart's *Magic Flute*, Andrea Bocelli and guest performances by the St Petersburg Ballet – this elegant theatre has everything from Baroque to Modern and is also where the Orchestre National de France is based.

Théâtre National de l'Odéon (Théâtre de l'Europe)
2, Rue Corneille (6th arr.)
Tel. 01 44 85 40 40, Métro: Odéon www.theatre-odeon.fr
Second stage of the Comédie Française which does modern productions of classical works such as Molière's comedies and Dumas's *The Lady of the Camellias*.

Théâtre de la Ville Paris
2, Place du Châtelet (4th arr.)
Tel. 01 42 74 22 77
www.theatredelaville-paris.com
Métro: Châtelet
Modern dance and classical music are the focus of this City theatre under the direction of Emmanuel Demarcy-Mota. Their other venue is the Théâtre des Abbesses (31, Rue des Abbesses, 18th arr., tel. 01 48 87 54 42).

ADVANCE TICKET SALES
Tickets online
www.ticketnet.fr
www.theatreonline.com
www.viator.com/paris-shows
en.parisinfo.com

FNAC
www.fnactickets.com
Tel. *08 92 68 36 22 Forum des Halles, 1–7, Rue
Pierre Lescot (1st arr.)
Mon–Sat 10am–7.30pm
74, Av. des Champs-Elysées
Métro: George V, daily 10am–11.45pm, Sun from noon

Last Minute Kiosque Théâtre
15, Place de la Madeleine (8th arr.), Métro: Madeleine
Esplanade de la Tour Montparnasse (14th arr.), Métro:

Montparnasse-Bienvenue
Tue–Sat 12.30–8pm, Sun till 4pm

CINEMAS
Champo
51, Rue des Ecoles (5th arr.)
Tel. 01 43 54 51 60
www.lechampo.com
Film festivals and retrospectives
from Orson Welles to Polanski

Forum des Images
▶ S. 202

La Géode
▶ S. 339

Max Linder Panorama
24, Boulevard Poissonière
(9th arr.)
Tel. 08 92 68 50 52
http://maxlinder.cine.allocine.fr
Modern cinema with cool design
and seating for 700. The visitor's
book includes Serge Gainsbourg,
Sting and Wim Wenders, who
premiered his film *Until the End
of the World* here.

MK2
14, Quai de Seine und
7, Quai de la Loire Canal de
l'Ourcq (19th arr.)
www.mk2.com
Current films, retrospectives and
festivals. Situated opposite each
other, the two cinemas are connected by an electric mini-ferry
across the canal

La Pagode *Insider Tip*
57 bis, Rue de Babylone
(7th arr.)
Tel. 08 92 89 28 92
www.etoile-cinemas.com
Cinema dating from 1896 where
some legendary films have had
their premiere. Today the programme is dominated by sophisticated auteur films.

Food and Drink

L'art de vivre

... means enjoying something in style, and in France that always includes good food. In 2010 UNESCO even put French
cuisine on the World Heritage list, and the best place to discover it is of course Paris. Nowhere else in the world can you
find such a concentration of starred restaurants, trendy experimental kitchens and legendary traditional eateries.

Paris regards itself as the gourmet capital of the world, and justifi-
ably so. Veritable artists are at work in the kitchens of the gourmet
temples serving **haute cuisine**. The atmospheric **brasseries** and
little **bistros**, which are like a second home for many locals, provide
authentic Parisian food. Those who prefer can embark on a **culinary world tour** and in Asian and African restaurants sample the
cuisine of former French colonies or the gastronomic heritage of
immigrants from other parts of France. Of course French wine is
part of the dining experience. Or you can always try a glass of
draught beer: the 0.2 l glass is known as a »demi« a half-litre as a
»véritable« and a litre as »formidable«. »Très parisien« are the many
street cafés. This is where you can immerse yourself in Parisian
life, see and be seen, celebrate the joy of life, chat, hotly debate –
and of course flirt.

Gourmet capital of the world

Parisians like to take their time when eating, but breakfast is usually
over and done with quickly. A large »bol«, a porcelain bowl with hot
chocolate or milk coffee, together with a »tartine beurré«, an often
toasted half baguette with jam, which is dunked into the coffee, »ça
suffit« – is enough. If you have your »**petit déjeuner**« in a café, it will
consist of coffee, tea or chocolate with a croissant or brioche and a
glass of orange juice. Most hotels also offer muesli, cheese, ham, yo-
ghurt and a boiled egg for breakfast. Lunch (**déjeuner**) is served in
restaurants between noon and 2.30pm either as a fixed menu with
starter, main course and dessert or à la carte. Cheaper options are the
»**plat du jour**«, the dish of the day with coffee, or a »**formule**« consisting of a main course and choice of starter or dessert. At lunchtime, French women like to choose one of the substantial salads from
the menu. Dinner (**dîner**) is more substantial and more expensive
than the corresponding lunchtime menu. You get a complimentary
carafe d'eau (carafe of tap water) plus a basket of freshly cut bread or
baguette. It is recommended to **book a table** for **dinner**.

Three meals of the day

A celebration of the traditional Parisian lifestyle:
Brasserie Bofinger

Typical Parisian Dishes

When the Parisians go to their favourite bistro to celebrate the impor-
tant moments in life, classics of French cuisine including delicious spe-
cialties from all parts of the country are always included.

Soupe à l'oignon: traders and customers in the market halls of Paris
enjoyed a nice hot onion soup as
long ago as the 18th century. To
prepare it onion rings are browned
with garlic in butter, dusted with
flour and then cooked until soft in
white wine and broth. On top of
the filled bowls of soup come
toasted slices of white bread,
which are sprinkled with grated
cheese and baked until the cheese
has melted. Bon appetit!

Coq au vin is a national dish. Allow the chicken to rest 24 to 36
hours in a marinade of celery, carrot onion and garlic, herbs and
Pinot Noir before searing it, dusted
it with flour and then stewing for
1.5 hours stewing. Bacon and
mushrooms are added shortly before the end. Voilà!

Steak au poivre: Some like it hot,
and lots of pepper is the most important thing for a Parisian pepper
steak, which is served with pommes
frites and sautéed mushrooms. The
raw steak is coated in coarsely
ground pepper and then fried in
clarified butter – »saignant« (rare),
»à point« (medium) or »bien cuit«
(well done). For the jus, Cognac
and red wine is added to the juices,
the mixture then reduced and refined with double cream before a
final seasoning of more fresh pepper. Parfait!

Bœuf bourguignon: It wasn't just Inspector Maigret who loved this stew, in the comedy drama Julie & Julia Meryl Streep also raved about bœuf bourguignon. The secret lies in the long cooking time. On a low flame the beef, bacon, shallots, garlic and carrot stew for hours in a full-bodied red burgundy.

Langouste à la Parisienne: In December, the fish stalls in the capital are piled high with large baskets of oysters, crab and Atlantic lobster. The latter are the traditional feast of Parisians at Christmas time or New Year. To prepare »Langouste à la parisienne« the lobster is cooked very briefly in fish stock. Once the shell has turned red from the cooking, the animal is taken out and placed on a plate garnished with cold cauliflower, carrots, green beans, asparagus and mayonnaise. It tastes best together with champagne.

The liqueur **Grand Marnier** comes from a suburb of Versailles. It was first created by Alexandre Marnier-Lapostolle in 1880, from a blend of Cognac brandy, distilled essence of bitter orange and sugar. Grand Marnier is a vital ingredient of **crêpes Suzette**, wafer-thin pancakes that are drizzled with the liqueur and then flambéed. The pancakes probably got their name at the end of the 19th century from a pretty actress from the Comédie Française named Suzette, for whom the cook at the neighbouring Marivaux restaurant delivered them specially, while they were still hot.

The World of the Head Chefs

Paris is the culinary capital of Europe and in common with several other world cities has its very own Michelin guide. Since 2008 the editor in chief of the French editions has been the German restaurateur Juliane Caspar, the first woman and first non-French national to occupy the position. Mon Dieu – the ranks of the master chefs were horrified.

Gault Millau gave him the title of »Chef of the Century«, and over the course of his career he has notched up a total of 28 Michelin stars: **Joël Robuchon**, France's most highly decorated chef. The undisputed ruler of haute cuisine started out as a pastry chef in his native city of Poitiers. After his apprenticeship, the 19-year-old moved to Paris where he honed his skills at the Hotel Brittany, the Harmony-Lafayette and aboard a restaurant ship, before launching out on his own, ultimately opening 19 restaurants all over the world and returning to Paris in 2010 (▶ L'Atelier, p. 106).

Three-star chef **Alain Ducasse** adapted an idea first developed by British star chef Jamie Olivier a decade ago, but instead of supporting unemployed youth with no prospects from the suburbs, Ducasse helps women with no chance in the jobs market and trains them up in the kitchen. »15 Women with a Future« is the name of the ambitious project launched by this successful star cook, food writer and gastro entrepreneur, which began in 2010. After a nine-month crash course in the kitchen the women are given a certificate of apprenticeship. But the young cooks, most

3-star chef Alain Ducasse focuses on the essential ingredients.

of them migrants, are then retained. Those who have learned to turn a plate into a work of art are taken on in one of Ducase's Paris restaurants: »Le Plaza Athénée«, »Aux Lyonnais«, »Rech«, »Relais Plaza«, »Benoit«, »Cour Jardin« or »Le Jules Verne« on the second level of the Eiffel Tower (▸p. 107).

Alain Passard learned cooking from his Breton grandmother. As a child one of his favourite dishes was »fricassée de coquillages« (mussel fricassee), and just like his »Mamie« prepared it in butter sauce, he now tries to emulate his childhood passions in the earthy-elegant ambience of »L'Arpege«. But he has long since given up on the meat dishes, for which he once received his three Michelin stars: Alain Passard is now a staunch vegetarian and uses vegetables exclusively from his own garden. Guests will still find poultry and fish dishes on the menu, but the main emphasis is now vegetables, so beautifully prepared that Passard has so far successfully defended all of his three stars (▸ p. 106).

Another successful Breton chef is **Christian Le Squer**, who has brought from his home the love of simple produce rooted in the region. His passion for cooking was sparked by a fisherman, who took him out on his crab boat for two weeks when he was 14 years old and introduced him to the Breton seafood pantry on the high seas. Even today, after the hotel school and renowned haute cuisine establishments such as Lucas Carton, Taillevent, the Opéra and the Ritz, Le Squer's cuisine is refreshingly straightforward (▸ p. 1077).

Grilled Racan pigeon on green Puy lentils, or would you prefer mullet with smoked aubergine in lemon confit? For the finest cuisine prepared by a woman, look no further than the young **Hélène Darroze**, who easily manages to hold her own in this male-dominated world. »I grew up right next to the stove of my grandfather in the region of Les Landes« explains Hélène, who learned her cooking with Alain Ducasse before opening up her own award-winning restaurant in Rue d'Assas (▸ p. 107).

Pierre Gagnaire is considered to have been at the forefront of the fusion movement, which revolutionized the art of cooking around the turn of the millennium. His artfully devised ten-course taster menu is a feast for the senses, whereby the sea urchin jelly rests on a melange of red mullet and squid, the parsley is smoked and the bread is baked with seaweed (▸ p. 110).

The restaurant of **Erich Fréchon** in the Hôtel Le Bristol used to be called »Sarkozy's canteen«. It wasn't just any old head of government who stopped off at this 5-star establishment, but the president of France himself often walked briskly from the Palais de L'Elysée to the gourmet temple, which gained its three Michelin stars in 2009 on account of Fréchon's uniquely innovative cuisine (▸ p. 107).

Brasseries and Bistros

Nothing embodies the Parisian way of life quite so much as »le bistrot«. Small, cosy, with an intimate atmosphere, it gladdens the Parisian's heart. A bistro lives to the rhythm of its district, but the soul of the bistro is the patron whom everyone in the district knows and who treats his guests as if they were at his own home.

In the morning Parisians will stop for a quick coffee and croissant at the **bistro**, for lunch they'll have the dish of the day there with colleagues, and after work meet up for an apéritif with friends and later for dîner. On the menu are time-honoured dishes, which may be less refined than those in a restaurant, but are certainly no less tasty. Everything is homemade and is served up in decent-sized portions. But top chefs have also discovered the bistro, where they offer their creations at more reasonable prices. Thus in 2005, starred chef Alain Ducasse took over the **Bistro Benoit**, which celebrated its 100th birthday in 2012. From his Michelin-starred kitchen come roasted quail, saddle of rabbit with herb stuffing and hen pheasant with duck foie gras and cep mushroom pie (▶ p.110).

David Rathegeber, who cooked for Ducasse for 12 years, now runs the **Bistro de l'Assiette**. The bright dining room with simple wooden tables is a successful blend of Modern and Art Déco, the seasonally adjusted menu both down to earth and refined – try the guinea fowl on caramelized sauerkraut, pheasant terrine with truffles and the airy chocolate soufflé (▶ p.110). The **Bistro Jadis** also serves haute

cuisine at very reasonable prices. Under the direction of Gagnaire's pupil Guillaume Delage gastronomic delights such as red mullet with wasabi and lamb with sweet potato purée are served (▶ p. 114).

At the **Bistrot du Peintre**, the food is like the »Jadis« of yore. This is the oldest eatery in the Bastille district, and it has retained its original furnishings from 1902 with lots of brass, decorative lamps and Art Nouveau nymphs. The fact that the patron comes from the Auvergne is reflected in the menu, which as well as dishes from the volcanic landscape of that part of France also features specialities from other regions (▶ p. 111).

Paris owes its world-famous **brasseries** to refugees from the eastern region of Alsace. After Alsace-Lorraine fell to the German Empire in 1871, many Alsatian refugees settled in the French capital and opened up brewery restaurants just like they had in their homeland, the »**Brasseries**«. Beer was on tap in the spacious bars and wines like Riesling, Silvaner und Gewürztraminer were brought to the table in clay jugs. To this day, menus are dominated by hearty dishes such as sauerkraut, braised pork shoulder and, in months with

A Paris institution: Brasserie Lipp

names containing the letter R, enormous seafood platters. Among the most glamorous brasseries dating from the Belle Epoque era is the **Bofinger**, which is a listed building. In 1864 the young Alsatian Frédéric Bofinger became the first person in Paris to serve draught beer here. The sweet blond beer was an immediate hit, but it was news of his sauerkraut dishes in particular, including the creamy »choucroute de la mer« with salmon, monkfish and lobster, that spread most rapidly. Today Georges Belondrade also spoils his guests with with tender lemon zander and slow-cooked leg of lamb. Since 1919 the jewel of the dining room has been the ornate glass dome made by the workshop of Néret and Royer (▶ p. 111).

Léon Fargue's cheerful yellow tiles and floral *Belle Epoque* ceramics, ceiling paintings with African motifs and subtly tilted wall mirrors decorate the **Brasserie Lipp**. Soon after its opening in 1880, well-known artists and writers started congregating at the brasserie run by Léonard Lipp and his wife Elise. Even politics was made at the Lipp – in 1965 General de Gaulle organized a public reconciliation lunch between the feuding Valéry Giscard d'Estaing and Georges Pompidou. It was at the Lipp that everyone from Picasso to Yves Saint Laurent and François Mitterrand dined, where Jean-Paul Gaultier, Madonna and Bill Clinton were guests. The sauerkraut with smoked sausage, bacon and potatoes and the extremely delicate millefeuilles are a must (▶ p. 114).

It is said that »governments are formed at the Lipp and dismantled again at **La Coupole**«. Construction of the largest Parisian brasserie commenced in 1927. For the interior Paul Solvet chose to have 33 hand-painted columns, mosaic floors, Art Déco lamps, padded niches and the central painted dome. In the basement where Joséphine Baker once performed they now dance the Salsa. The fact that the smart Montparnasse venue still attracts artists was evident at cinemas in 2007: in the film adaptation of Anna Gavalda's bestseller *Hunting and Gathering* Audrey Tatou celebrated the happiness of true friendship by having crêpes at La Coupole (▶ p. 112).

Recommended restaurants

Whether starred restaurants, Art Déco temples with artistic tradition or simple bistros serving French regional specialities – Paris promises divine culinary experiences both for lunch and dinner.

PRICE CATEGORY

€€€€	more than €100
€€€	€50–€100
€€	€30–€50
€	€15–€30

Menu without drinks

FAMOUS GOURMET TEMPLES

❶ Alain Ducasse au Plaza Athénée €€€€
23–27, Av. de Montaigne (8th arr.)
Tel. 01 53 67 65 00
www.alain-ducasse.com
Daily except Thur and Fri, dinner only Sat & Sun, closed mid-July to Mid Aug
Glittering chandeliers and high stucco ceilings adorn the domain of three-star chef Alain Ducasse. Together with his new head chef Christophe Saintage, in 2011 he elevated haute cuisine to a concept that focuses on pure ingredients: lobster with potatoes, duck with white turnips, sea bream with fennel (menu €360, ► p. 102).

❷ L'Ambroisie €€€€
9, Place des Vosges (4th arr.)
Tel. 01 42 78 51 45, www.ambroisie-placedesvosges.com
Closed Sun, Mon and 1–21 Aug.
Bernhard Pacaud, who received his three Michelin stars in 1986, is today supported in the kitchen by his son Mathieu. Located under the arcades of the magical Place des Vosges, the restaurant is luxurious but still modest (menu from €190).

❸ L'Arpège €€€€
84, Rue de Varenne (7th arr.)
Tel. 01 47 05 09 06
Closed Sat and Sun.
www.alain-passard.com
Three-star chef Alain Passard devotes himself entirely to the vegetables that he cultivates in his own kitchen garden (menu: lunch €120, dinner €340 ► p.103).

❹ L'Atelier €€€€
133, Champs-Elysées (8th arr.)
Tel. 01 47 23 75 75
www.joel-robuchon.net

> **MARCO POLO TIP !** Insider Tip
>
> *High Bonnet..*
>
> ... a Novel of Epicurean Adventures. The story recounted by Idwal Jones is delicious and light like a soufflé. With lots of humour he tells of the most important things in life: love, friendship and good food. Our hero Jean-Marie would actually like to go to sea, but then fortune takes the young man to the Paris of the 1930s and to the gourmet temple Faisan d'Or, where high society, petty and serious crooks and lots of masters in the art of living wine and dine, and where true love awaits. While reading you can almost taste the divine dishes (Modern Library Food 2001).

Like in a sushi bar you can sit at the bar at Joël Robuchon's place and savour his culinary works of art (menu découverte €150, ▶ p. 82).

❺ Epicure €€€€ / €€€
112, Rue du Faubourg
Saint-Honoré (8th arr.)
Tel. 01 53 43 43 00
www.lebristolparis.com
Crystal chandeliers, open fireplace and marble floor – Erich Fréchon's restaurant at the Hôtel Le Bristol was newly done out in bright colours by Pierre-Yves Rochon in 2012 (menu from €180, ▶ p. 103)

❻ Le Grand Véfour €€€€
17, Rue de Beaujolais (1st arr.)
Tel. 01 42 96 56 27
www.grand-vefour.com
Closed Sat, Sun and Aug.
Guy Martin's two-star cuisine is served up in regal décor under the arcades of the Palais Royal. Napoleon dined with Josephine at the table in the middle on the right (menu: lunch €88, dinner €268)

❼ Le Jules Verne €€€€
Tour Eiffel (7th arr.)
Tel. 01 45 55 61 44
www.lejulesverne-paris.com
Here Paris really does lie at your feet. The interior is done out in subtle black and mauve tones, so as not to distract diners from the breathtaking view from the second floor of the Eiffel Tower (menu: lunch €165, dinner €200, ▶ p. 103).

❿ Laurent €€€€
41, Avenue Gabriel (8th arr.)
Tel. 01 42 25 00 39
www.le-laurent.com

! The art of cooking *Insider Tip*

MARCO POLO TIP

Michelin has honoured him with one star, Gault Millau named him Chef of the Year 2010: William Ledeuil. The founder of the refined, Far Eastern **❽ Zé Kitchen Galerie** (4, Rue des Grands Augustins, 6th arr., tel. 01 44 32 00 32, www.ze-kitchengalerie, closed Fri, Sat lunch and Sun, AAAA) opened a second restaurant in 2011, the **❾ Kitchen Galerie Bis** (25, Rue des Grands Augustins, 6th arr., tel. 01 46 33 00 85, http://kitchen-galeriebis.com, closed Sun and Mon, AAA) where he also inventively transforms non-French dishes with spices, herbs and fruit from Japan, Thailand and Vietnam. He reveals his best recipes in his cookbook Ze Kitchen Galerie (Editions de La Martinière 2011).

Closed Sat lunch and Sun.
In this rotunda restaurant decorated with columns, stucco and fine fabrics, chef Alain Pégouret cooks dishes with a southern touch. 100-year-old chestnut trees provide shade on the terrace (menu from €185).

⓫ Ledoyen €€€€
1, Avenue Dutuit, Carré des Champs-Elysées (8th arr.)
Tel. 01 53 05 10 01
www.ledoyen.com
Closed Sun and Mon lunch.
Christian Le Squer's restaurant for Paris' high society promises the finest cuisine and a sensational wine list (menu: lunch €150, dinner from €220, ▶ p. 103).

⓬ Hélène Darroze €€€€/€€€
4 Rue d'Assas (6th arr.)

Restaurants, Cafés and Entertainment

Restaurants
1. Alain Ducasse
2. L'Ambroisie
3. L'Arpège
4. L'Atelier
5. Epicure
6. Le Grand Véfour
7. Le Jules Verne
8. Zé Kitchen Galerie
9. Kitchen Galerie Bis
10. Laurent
11. Ledoyen
12. Hélène Darroze
13. Pierre Gagnaire
14. Alcazar
15. Benoit
16. L'Ecaille de la Fontaine
17. Le Train Bleu
18. L'Assiette
19. Le Bistrot du Peintre
20. Bofinger
21. Bouillon Racine
22. Le Comptoir du Relais
23. La Coupole
24. Le Dôme
25. Le Drouant
26. L'Epi Dupin
27. Le Fermette Marbeuf
28. Chez Françoise
29. Frenchie
30. Le Grand Café des Capucines
31. La Grande Cascade
32. Jadis
33. Lipp
34. Le Petit Zinc
35. Ambassade d'Auvergne
36. La Bonne Franquette
37. Chartier
38. Le Monteverde
39. Playtime
40. Hiramatsu
41. Mansouria
42. Chamarré Montmartre
43. Shang Palace

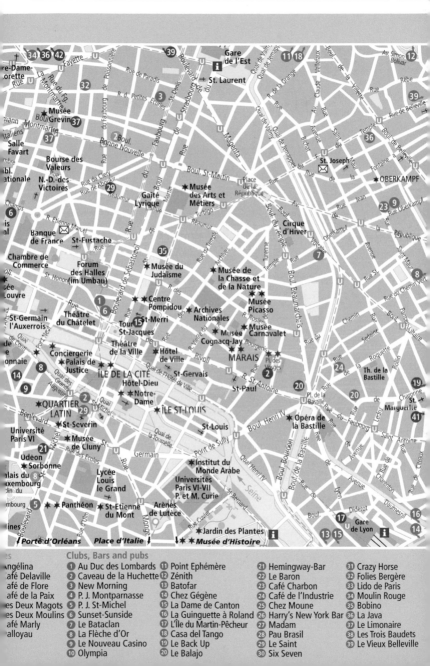

Tel. 01 42 22 00 11
www.helenedarroze.com
closed Sun and Mon.
Sommelière Céline recommends top vintages from the excellent wine cellar to go with each course. To finish off try the vintage Francis Darroze Armagnac (menu: lunch €52, dinner €125, ▶ p. 103).

⑬ Pierre Gagnaire €€€€
6, Rue Balzac (8th arr.)
Tel. 01 58 36 12 50
www.pierre-gagnaire.com
Forget all the good intentions: the 5-course Grand Dessert alone makes the indulgence worth it. And before that perhaps a suprême de poularde macérée au lait d'amande, a poularde poached in almond milk? Whatever you go for, Pierre Gagnaire's cuisine is as flawlessly perfect as the snow-white table linen (menu: lunch €90, dinner €225/260 ▶ p. 103).

TRADITIONAL RESTAURANTS AND MODERN CUISINE

⑭ Alcazar €€€
62, Rue Mazarine (6th arr.)
Tel. 01 53 10 19 99
www.alcazar.fr
Top designer Sir Terence Conran transformed this former revue theatre into a chic restaurant. Before the meal have a gin fizz at the Mezzanine Bar. Light strawberry muffins are baked for Sunday lunch. Regular readings and cabaret.

⑮ Benoit €€€
20, Rue Saint-Martin (4th arr.)
Tel. 01 72 25 76
www.benoit-paris.com
Michelin-starred establishment from Alain Ducasse, for lovers of the finest French cuisine, ▶ p. 84

⑯ L'Ecaille de la Fontaine €€€
15, Rue Gaillon (2nd arr.)
Tel. 01 47 42 02 99
www.la-fontaine-gaillon.com
Gérard Dépardieu's bistro and restaurant Fontaine Gaillon are an ideal place to indulge in the sound of the sea right in the middle of Paris. Freshly caught Breton oysters, prawns, crabs and whelks together with a tangy white wine – pure delight! In 2010 the passionate entertainer, chef and bon viveur Dépardieu also opened up »Le Bien Décidé«, another wine bistro at 117, Rue du Cherche Midi in the 6th arr..

⑰ Le Train Bleu €€€   **Insider Tip**
20, Boulevard Diderot
Gare de Lyon, 1. Stock (12th arr.)
Tel. 01 43 43 09 06
www.le-train-bleu.com
This beautiful station restaurant is in the Gare de Lyon, which dates from 1900. The name comes from the legendary ▶Blue Train▶ that connected Paris with the Côte d'Azur from 1922 to 1960. The restaurant serves specialities from Lyon beneath wonderful ceiling paintings that depict a train journey.

⑱ L'Assiette €€
181, Rue du Château (14th arr.)
Tel. 01 43 22 64 86
www.restaurant-lassiette.com
David Rathgeber has his roots in authentic French cuisine ▶ p. 104.

⑲ Le Bistrot du Peintre
€€ / €
116, Avenue Ledru Rollin
(11th arr.)
Tel. 01 44 00 34 39
www.bistrodupeintre.com
The »bistro of the painter« is an
Art Nouveau jewel in the heart of
the Bastoche, the trendy district of
the Paris »in scene« ▶ p. 104.

⑳ Bofinger €€
3, Rue de la Bastille (3rd arr.)
Tel. 01 42 72 87 82
tgl. bis 1.00 Uhr
www.bofingerparis.com
The seafood platter with oysters,
shrimp, whelks and mussels is
more than enough for two
▶ p. 105.

㉑ Bouillon Racine €€
3, Rue Racine (6th arr.)
Tel. 01 44 32 15 60
www.bouillon-racine.com
Art Nouveau bistro dating from
1906, where the foie gras is fla-
voured with Breton Guérande salt
and served on fig compote. The
homemade chocolate ice cream
with 72% Valrhona chocolate is
to die for.

㉒ Le Comptoir du **Insider Tip**
Relais €€ /€€€
9, Carrefour de l'Odéon (6th arr.)
Tel. 01 44 27 07 97
www.hotel-paris-relais-
saint-germain.com
Yves Camdeborde learned his
trade at the Hotel Crillon, and today runs this pleasant bistro in the
heart of Saint-Germain. For lunch,
guests are spoiled with delicious
traditional appetizers made from
market-fresh ingredients, and in
the evening there is a very fine
5-course menu.

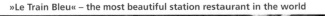

»Le Train Bleu« – the most beautiful station restaurant in the world

For seafood fans: Le Dôme

㉓ La Coupole €€
102, Boulevard du Montparnasse
(14th arr.), tel. 01 43 20 14 20
www.flobrasseries.com/
coupoleparis
Baked foie gras with figs or would
you prefer filet steak flambéed in
Cognac? For dessert you should
definitely try a cream puff filled
with mocca and doused with
chocolate sauce ▶ p. 105.

㉔ Le Dôme €€ Insider Tip
108, Boulevard du Montparnasse
(14th arr.), tel. 01 42 63 48 18
Closed Mon
http://exclusiverestaurants.com
This romantic Art Déco style seafood restaurant has always been
the best place for oysters! Franck
Graux serves them together with
aromatic bread and butter made
from unpasteurized milk – even
after midnight.

㉕ Le Drouant €€
18, Place Gaillon (2nd arr.)
Tel. 01 42 65 15 16
Closed Sat and Sun
www.drouant.com
Because of the reputation of this
1930s style restaurant, it's the
place where the jury convenes for
the annual Prix Goncourt literature
prize. And head chef Antoine
Westermann has also considered
the youngsters by creating a delicious children's menu for €15.

㉖ L'Epi Dupin €€
11, Rue Dupin (6th arr.)
Tel. 01 42 22 64 56
www.epidupin.com
Haute cuisine at moderate prices
is served by François Pasteau,
Erwan Lévêque and Florent Mavit
at the ten tables of their fine bistro in Saint-Germain-des-Prés
(closed Sat, Sun and Mon lunch).

㉗ Le Fermette Marbeuf €€
5, Rue Marbeuf (8th arr.)
Tel. 01 42 86 00 88
www.fermettemarbeuf.com
Emil Hurté designed this beautiful
restaurant in Art Nouveau style in
1898. Today guests can savour
hot oysters in champagne sauce,
Burgundy snails and a light soufflé
with Grand Marnier.

㉘ Chez Françoise €€ Insider Tip
Aérogare des Invalides (7th arr.)
Tel. 01 47 05 49 03
http://chezfrancoise.com
Excellent traditional fare has been
served in the large dining room
for more than 40 years. The wines
and the prices are very decent.
Daily except Sun from 8.30pm live
jazz and blues.

㉙ Frenchie €€
5, Rue du Nil (5th arr.)
Tel. 01 40 39 96 19
Mon–Fri. 7pm–10.30pm.
www.frenchie-restaurant.com
The name gives it away: in this little restaurant they cook à la française: foie gras, Basque pork belly with beetroot, smoked mackerel with wild spinach and honey with summer truffle or hazelnut tart for dessert.

㉚ Le Grand Café des Capucines €€
4, Boulevard des Capucines
(9th arr.), Tel. 01 43 12 19 00
www.legrandcafe.com

It was here on 28 December 1895, together with their cinematographer, that the Lumière brothers staged the first public screening of a film. Our tip: duck breast with strawberries and olive polenta.

㉛ La Grande Cascade €€
Allée de Longchamp,
Bois de Boulogne (16th arr.)
Tel. 01 45 27 33 51
www.grandecascade.com
A real delight from both a visual and culinary perspective. Glass roof, bars and ceilings in Empire style. The porcini mushroom tart and macaroni with truffles are delicious.

Always popular: the Art Déco brasserie La Coupole with busy waiters, bright wood panelling and snow-white tablecloths

㉜ Jadis €€
208, Rue de la Croix Nivert
(15th arr.), tel. 01 45 57 73 20
www.bistrot-jadis.com
Also to take away: wild boar
terrine with pistachios and prunes
(▶ p. 104)

㉝ Lipp €€
151, Boulevard St-Germain
(6th arr.), tel. 01 45 48 53 91
www.groupe-bertrand.com/
lipp.php
Every one of France's well-known
politicians, writers and journalists
has probably dined here at least
once (▶ p. 105).

㉞ Le Petit Zinc €€ Insider Tip
11, Rue Saint Benoît (6th arr.)
Tel. 01 42 86 61 00
www.petit-zinc.com
Lovely art nouveau interior and
top-quality food: Breton oysters,
snail ravioli and pheasant with
celery mousse.

㉟ Ambassade d'Auvergne €€
22, Rue du Grenier St-Lazare
(3rd arr.), tel. 01 42 72 31 22
www.ambassade-auvergne.com
Authentic cuisine featuring calves
head, duck breast and spicy goat's
cheese from the Massif Central.

㊱ La Bonne Franquette €
2, Rue des Saules (18th arr.)
Tel. 01 42 52 02 42
www.labonnefranquette.com
"Love, eat, drink and sing« is the
motto of this atmospheric restaurant in Montmartre. Fresh French
bistro cuisine, a leafy terrace, 150
wines and regular live appearances by French musicians.

㊲ Chartier €
7, Rue du Faubourg-
Montmartre (9th arr.)
Tel. 01 47 70 86 29
www.restaurant-chartier.com
Nimble waiters in white aprons,
black waistcoats and bow ties
have been serving hearty fare in
this large old-style restaurant since
1896: French stews, blanquette of
veal and black pudding. As many
as 20 waiters daily serve up 1500
meals in rapid succession – three
courses in 45 minutes. Despite
this there are still long queues to
get in, but it's well worth the
wait! Sit on the terrace and indulge in a popular Parisian pas-
time: people-watching.

㊳ Le Monteverdi €
5–7, Rue Guisarde (6th arr.)
Tel. 01 42 34 55 90, closed Sun
www.lemonteverdi.com
Delightful place, with a mixture of
French and Italian cuisine – we
recommend spaghetti with clams
or the juicy steak Robespierre.
Classic melodies emanate from
the piano, after all Claudio Mon-
teverdi is a direct descendant of
the famous composer.

㊴ Playtime €
5, Rue des Petits Hôtels (10th arr.)
Tel. 01 44 79 03 98
Closed Sat and Sun.
Just around the corner from the
Gare de l'Est, Jean-Michel
Rassinoux and Viveka Sandklef
conjure up such delights as cori-
ander risotto with escalope of veal
at very reasonable prices. The
name of the restaurant is an homage to Jacques Tati's film set in
Paris.

Straight out of China: the Shang Palace with hardwood chairs, mahogany panelling and columns of jade

FROM AROUND THE WORLD

The French capital is also a cultural melting pot when it comes to cooking.

40 Hiramatsu €€
52, Rue de Longchamp (16th arr.)
Tel. 01 56 81 08 80
www.hiramatsu.co.jp/fr
Closed Sun and Mon.
The very best in Japanese food is served to a maximum of 18 diners; with more than 10,000 bottles the wine cellar is also superb.

41 Mansouria €€
11, Rue Faidherbe (11th arr.)
Tel. 01 43 71 00 16
www.mansouria.fr
Closed Fri and Sun.
In this Moroccan restaurant run by Fatéma Hal, the braised lamb with couscous is a feast for the senses.

42 Chamarré Montmartre €€€/€€
52, Rue Lamarck (18th arr.)
Tel. 01 42 55 05 42
www.chamarre-montmartre.com
Almost all dishes contain fish or seafood. The Mauritian head chef Antoine Heerah learned his trade with Alain Passard. Great treat for the kids: the children's dish.

43 Shang Palace €€€/€€ Insider Tip
Hotel Shangri-La
10, Avenue d'Iéna (16th arr.)
Tel. 01 53 67 19 92
Since 2011 Frank Xu has spoiled guests at the Shang Palace with Cantonese haute cuisine, which is characterized by its mild flavours. Refined creations with salmon, jellyfish and abalone tickle the western palate.

CAFÉ CULTURE
Cafés are bastions of the traditional French lifestyle, whereby the transition to bistro is easy.

❶ Angélina
226, Rue de Rivoli (1st arr.)
Tel.0142608200
Coco Chanel and Audrey Hepburn enjoyed taking a break from the all the hustle and bustle in this Belle Epoque salon under the arcades of the Rue de Rivoli. Today it's the fashion scene that congregates here to enjoy Angélina's famous »chocolat chaud africain« with plenty of whipped cream from the silver tray. Cake tip: the »Mont Blanc«.

❷ Café Delaville
34, Boulevard Bonne Nouvelle
(10th arr), tel. 01 48 24 48 09
www.delavillecafe.com
The mix of modern and Art Déco, combined with fragrant coffee, appetizers or grilled sirloin steak, make this café popular place in the Grands Boulevards. DJs play Thur–Sat, on Sunday there's brunch on the terrace.

❸ Café de Flore
172, Boulevard Saint-Germain
(6th arr.), Tel. 01 45 48 55 26
www.cafedeflore.fr
Jean-Paul Sartre was a regular guest in this literary café, and his partner Simone de Beauvoir is said to have worked on her novel *The Second Sex* here. In November, the literary Prix de Flore is awarded to promising young authors. The drinks list as as impressive as the interior, the menu offers a fine selection of small dishes.

Sartre and Picasso liked to come to Café de Flore.

❹ Café de la Paix
▶ MARCO POLO Insider Tip p. 215

❺ Café Les Deux Magots
6, Place de St-Germain-des-Prés
(6th arr.), tel. 01 45 48 55 25
www.lesdeuxmagots.fr
André Gide, Paul Eluard, Jean-Paul
Sartre and Albert Camus were
among the regulars at this famous
terrace café, which opened in
1881. The prestigious literary Prix
des Deux Magots has been awarded here since 1933. The dinner
menu combines classic French with
international fish and meat dishes.
During the day, there are excellent
sandwiches, toasts and salads to
satisfy your hunger (▶ p. 308).

❻ Café Les Deux Moulins
▶ MARCO POLO Insider Tip p. 293

❼ Café Marly
▶ MARCO POLO Insider Tip p. 228

❽ Dalloyau *Insider Tip*
101, Rue du Faubourg St-Honoré
(1st arr.), seven further outlets in
Paris, www.dalloyau.fr
Baking at its best since 1682 – not
just to take home but also in the
attached salon de thé. The millefeuilles consisting of very fine puff
pastry with pastry cream and icing
have achieved cult status and
there's also the »La Réligieuse de
Rêve«, a really divine chocolate
gâteau.

TO GET YOUR TEETH INTO

They create their colourful macaroons, eclairs, millefeuilles, tartes *Pâtissiers*
and timbales like haute couture: the legendary pâtissiers of Paris.
Stars of the profession include **Arnaud Larher** with his sensational
raspberry torte (53, Rue Caulain-Court, www.arnaud-larher.com),
Arnaud Delmontel with his summer light rhubarb-meringue gâteau
(39, Rue des Martyrs, www.arnaud-delmontel.com) and **Jacques
Genin** with the best caramel eclairs in the capital (33, Rue de
Turenne, http://jacquesgenin.fr). Wonderfully creamy and crispy at
the same time are the millefeuilles du dimanche made by Philippe
Conticini at his **Pâtisserie des Rêves** (93, Rue du Bac, www.lapatis-
seriedesreves.com).
The irresistible little **macaroons** made from almond flour even existed back in the Middle Ages, and it is said that Marie Antoinette
herself loved the light and airy meringue confections, with their
cream fillings. The round sandwich creations have about the same
diameter as a 2-euro coin – and can easily cost that much. They come
in more than 40 flavours, from coffee, caramel and rose extract to
raspberry reduction, cassis and mousse au chocolat, baked in the elegant pâtisseries of **Pierre Hermé** (72, Rue Bonaparte, www.pierre-
herme.com) and **Ladurée** (18, Rue Royale, www.laduree.fr). Beautifully packaged in colourful boxes, they make a popular gift in Paris
when you're invited to dinner.

Holidays · Festivals · Events

To the Rhythm of the Capital

Throughout the year, the Paris events calendar is packed. The city offers something for everyone. Events and festivals are a great opportunity to get to know the capital city. Many events organized by the city administration can be visited free of charge. If one were to ask the French, however, there is one event that outshines all others: the celebration of the Quartorze Juillet, the 14th of July.

National Holiday

On the eve of the National Holiday, the Bals Populaires, the immensely popular folk balls, are held in the city's fire stations, with dancing from nine o'clock in the evening to four in the morning. At ten in the morning trumpets and bugles on the Champs-Elysées announce the arrival of the President of the Republic. To drum rolls, the armed forces march in step along the most beautiful avenue in the world; helicopters and jet fighters are put through their paces above the heads of tout Paris. Then the military parade makes way for free concerts on the Champs de Mars, where from 5pm stars like Julian Perretta, Bénabarand Yannick Noah perform until the grand finale: the fireworks display at the Eiffel Tower, a stunning explosion of colour in the Paris night sky, which has a different theme every year.

New Year's

The only time the tower looks as colourful as that is at New Year's, which is celebrated in Paris without any of the loud bangs you might hear in other major European cities. Instead, having met up with friends for dinner on New Year's Eve, people congregate at the Eiffel Tower in time for the spectacular laser show at midnight, when everyone wishes each other »Bonne Année« with a glass of champagne.

Fête de la Musique

Finally, one of the capital's main annual events is one that is also celebrated across the country: the Fête de la Musique on 21 June. The entire city rocks with street music on squares, roads that are closed to traffic only for this day and along the banks of the canals; with live acts in clubs and bars, free concerts in parks and on open-air stages, and an exuberant zest for life.

Information

The weekly »what's on« magazines *L'Officiel des Spectacles* and *Pariscope* (www.pariscope.fr) are published on Wednesday. In addition, for information about the latest trends, meeting places and theme nights you can consult *Paris Capitale* (www.leclubparis.com/paris-travelguide.asp) and *Nova* (www.novaplanet.com).

Grand finale of the national holiday: the fireworks on 14 July

Events calendar

PUBLIC HOLIDAYS
1 January (jour de l'an), Easter
Monday, Ascension Day
1 May (fête du travail)
8 May (fête de l'armistice de 1945)
14 July (fête nationale)
15 August (Assomption)
1 November (Toussaint)
11 November
   (fête de l'armistice 1918)
25 December (Noël)

EVENTS IN JANUARY
Prix d'Amérique
Horse racing at the Hippodrome
de ▶Vincennes on the last Sunday

Haute Couture
International fashion show with
top designers like Karl Lagerfeld,
Diego della Valle and Sarah Bur-
ton (www.modeaparis.com)

FEBRUARY
Chinese New Year
At the beginning of February Paris's Chinese community rings in
the New Year with two processions: the first one runs through
the Marais (Hôtel de Ville, Rue du
Temple, Rue Turbigo, Rue du Renard und Rue Beaubourg), and
the second makes its way through
Chinatown (Avenue d'Ivry, Avenue de Choisy, Place d'Italie, Rue
de Tolbiac).

**Salon International de
l'agriculture**
This agricultural fair breaks all at-
tendance records and presidents
have to show how down to earth
they are by patting the bulls.
(www.salon-agriculture.com)

MARCH
Carnaval de Paris
Exuberance like in Rio: carnival on
the Seine (www.carnavaldeparis.
org)

**Prix du Président de la
République**
Horse-racing at the Hippodrome
d'Auteuil on Palm Sunday

Salon des Indépendants
Spring exhibition of fine art in the
Grand Palais (www.artistes-
independants.fr)

Bose Blue Note Festival
Top event with international jazz
stars performing all over Paris
(www.bosebluenotefestival.com)

Festival Chorus
Big music festival with festival village in front of the Grande Arche
in La Défense (www.festival-
chorus.fr)

Banlieues Bleues
Jazz, blues and funk from newcomers and big names performing
45 concerts in St-Denis (www.
banlieuesbleues.org).

Paris Fashion Week
Seven days, more than 90 prêt-à-
porter shows with big names including Dior, Chanel and Louis
Vuitton (www.modeaparis.com)

APRIL
Paris Marathon
on the last Sunday; start at 9am
on the Champs-Elysées

Twice a year top designers like Karl Lagerfeld present the latest trends of the fashion world during Paris Fashion Week

Villette Sonique
Indie Festival in Parc de la Villette (www.villettesonique.com)

MAY
French Open
International tennis tournament (www.rolandgarros.com)

Festival de L'Île-de-France
Concerts, visits (until July, www.festival-idf.fr)

La Nuit des Musées
The »Long Night of the Museums« on a Saturday in the middle of May only ends at around 1am (http://nuitdesmusees.culture.fr)

Portes Ouvertes
Open days organized by galleries and artists in Belleville, followed by Père Lachaise (May), Ménilmontant (Sept) and Montmartre (Nov/Dec) (www.parisgratuit.com/ateliers.html)

Festival du Jazz de Saint-Germain-des-Prés
New talents, shows and encounters with artists in the heart of Saint-Germain, the cradle of Paris Jazz (www.festivaljazz saintgermainparis.com)

Rencontre Chorégraphique Internationale St-Denis
Renowned ballet festival with international stars (www.rencontreschoregraphiques.com)

JUNE

La Fête de la Musique
Concerts and balls all over Paris on 21 June (http://fetedelamusique.culture.fr)

Festival du Marais
Theatre and music in the Marais (until July, http://festival dumarais.org)

Paris Jazz Festival
Jazz festival in the Parc Floral de
Paris with international stars (until
July)

Designer's Days
Shop window for contemporary
design (www.designersdays.com)

**Marché de Fiertés
(Gay Pride)**
Big gay parade (http://marche.
inter-lgbt.org)

JULY
Fête nationale
National holiday on 14 July
(quatorze juillet ▶ p. 119).

Festival Estival de Paris
Summer festival until September
with classical and contemporary
music

Haute Couture
International fashion show
with all the Paris top designers
(www.modeaparis.com)

Quartier d'Eté
Classical, jazz, theatre, circus
(www.quartierdete.com)

Tour de France
The Tour's final race to the finish
line on the Champs-Elysées (www.
letour.fr)

AUGUST
Rock en Seine
Bands like Oasis, Radiohead, Mor-
rissey and The Prodigy have performed at this famous rock festival at the Domaine St-Cloud
(www.rockenseine.com).

Paris Quartier d'Été
Open-air music, dance, performance and street-art by 150 artists from around the world
(www.quartierdete.com).

Jazz à la Villette
Open-air festival in the Par de la
Villette with artists such as Archie
Shepp, Aldo Romano and Macy
Gray (www.jazzalavillette.com).

SEPTEMBER
Salon d'Automne
Autumn art exhibition in the
Grand Palais

Journées du Patrimoine
▶ p. 287

Biennale de Paris
Exhibitions and installations by
young artists in all disciplines of
fine art (every even year, until Nov,
http://biennaledeparis.org)

**Festival International
de Danse**
Ballet festival with stars from
around the world (until mid-
December)

Festival d'Automne
Autumn festival: modern music,
jazz, theatre, folklore (until December, www.festival-automne.
com)

Paris Fashion Week
International prêt-à-porter shows
(www.modeaparis.com)

Techno Parade
With more than half a million
Techno fans this Paris parade is
one of the world's largest music

processions (www.technoparade.fr).

OCTOBER
La Nuit Blanche
Paris all-night cultural happening from 7pm to 7am: readings, concerts and various performances by international artists at over 30 venues in the city

Vendanges de Montmartre
First Saturday in October. Wine festival in Montmartre with music, dance and a procession; wine sales on the street.

Prix de l'Arc de Triomphe
Horse race at the Hippodrome de Longchamp

Les Puces du Design
Design classics and the finest junk from the 1950s to the 1990s (www.pucesdudesign.com).

NOVEMBER
11. November
Military ceremony at the Arc de Triomphe to commemorate the anniversary of the Armistice of 1918

Mois de la Photo
35 photography exhibitions in Paris (www.parisphoto.fr)

For the 14th July national holiday, foreign soldiers also take part in the military parades along the Champs-Elysées

DECEMBER
Festival des Inrocks
Top acts from the independent music scene (www.lesinrocks.com)

Semaine du Fooding
The latest hype on gourmet heaven (www.lefooding.com).

Museums

Unsurpassed Treasures

In Paris and the Île-de-France is there such a huge number of exciting museums that the choice is difficult – and each rainy day can be perfectly planned.

Museums are usually closed on either Monday or Tuesday, and on Thursday many are open until 9pm. Every first Sunday of the month admission to the **state museums** is free; for EU citizens under 26 years of age admission is always free. In the **museums of the Ville de Paris** admission to the permanent collections is free. However, you should allow plenty of time for a museum visit – there are often very long queues, especially for special exhibitions. It is therefore recommended to order tickets in advance online.

Discounts, rest days and admission tickets

You can also obtain individual tickets for selected museums such as the Louvre or the Musée Grévin from the Tourist Information Office. The museums are less crowded during the week and especially in the morning there's a better chance of not having to push your way through throngs of people as you go round the museum – this is particularly true for the enormously popular Louvre, Quai d'Orsay and Quai Branly museums.

The **Pass l a Colline des Musées** (www.lacollinedesmusees.fr) offers discounted admission to the four museums dedicated to contemporary art on the Chaillot hill between the Seine and the Trocadéro: the Cité de l'Architecture et du Patrimoine, the Musée d'Art Moderne de la Ville de Paris, the Musée du Quai Branly and the Palais du Tokyo. With the pass, you pay the full price for the first museum, the next two admissions are cheaper and the visit to the fourth museum is free. The pass, which is available for download on the website, is valid for five days and there is no set order to the visits.

For the »Nuit Blanche« at the beginning of October, everything revolves around art. A whole night long extraordinary works of art, performances and installations are presented in the open-air at unusual venues. In addition, some museums stay open until midnight. Each May Paris celebrates **»La Longue Nuit des Musées«** (Long Night of Museums) with approximately 230 free events, which are advertised on the official website arranged by arrondissement (www.nuitdesmusees.culture.fr) – that helps with the planning! Again, be there on time and do not take on too much – the rush is enormous!

Insider Tip

Luxury in the style of Louis XV is illustrated by the Blue Salon in the Musée Carnavalet, the museum of the history of Paris in the heart of the Marais

Paris Museums

Direct access to the permanent exhibitions of 60 museums, sights and monuments in Paris and its environs is provided by the **Paris Museum Pass**, which is valid for either 2, 4 or 6 days (costing €39, €54 and €69 respectively). It can be ordered online as well as purchased direct from the FNAC and the Office de Tourisme de Paris (www.parismuseumpass.com).

HISTORY / CULTURAL HISTORY

Cité Nationale de l'Histoire de l'Immigration
▶Bercy, p. 190

Cité de la Mode et du Design
▶Tolbiac, Docks en Seine, p. 320

Musée Carnavalet
▶p. 262

Musée d'Art et d'Histoire de la Ville de Saint-Denis
22 bis, Rue Gabriel Péri, St-Denis
Métro: Saint-Denis, Bus: 156 (from Porte de la Chapelle), adults €5,
Mon, Wed, Fri 10am–5.30pm, Thur till 8pm, Sat and Sun 2pm–6.30pm, www.musee-saint-denis.fr
The Carmelite monastery displays items belonging to the order, exhibits from the Paris Commune of 1871, caricatures by Daumier as well as modern art. Don't miss the »Garden of the Five Senses«!

Musée d'Art et d'Histoire du Judaisme
▶Marais, p. 250

Musée de la Mode et du Textile
▶ p. 286

Musée de la Parfumerie
▶p. 216

Musée de la Poste
34, Bd. de Vaugirard (15th arr.)
Métro: Montparnasse-Bienvenue, Pasteur, Mon–Sat 10am–6pm, adults €5, www. ladresse musee-delaposte.com
History of the postal service and philately on five floors

Musée de l'Histoire de France
▶Marais, Hôtel de Rohan-Soubise

Musée de l'Histoire de Paris
▶Musée Carnavalet

Musée de l'Homme
▶Palais de Chaillot

Musée des Arts Décoratifs
▶Rue de Rivoli, p. 301

Musée des Collections Historiques de la Préfecture de Police
4, Rue de la Montagne Sainte-Geneviève (5th arr.)
Métro: Maubert-Mutualité
Mon–Fri 9am–5pm, Sat10am–5pm,
www.prefecture-police-paris.interieur.gouv.fr
admission free

In the Police Museum more than 2000 objects document assassinations, revolutions and criminal cases that made the headlines.

Musée du Quai Branly
▶p. 269

Musée National de la Légion d'Honneur et des Ordres de Chevalerie
Hôtel de Salm, 2, Rue de la Légion d'honneur (7th arr.)
Métro: Solférino, Gare d'Orsay
Wed–Sun 1pm–6pm
www.legiondhonneur.fr
admission and audio guide free
Documents and medals of chivalric orders from the Middle Ages to today's medals of honour

Le Théâtre-Musée des Capucines
39, Boulevard des Capucines (9th arr.), Métro: Opéra
Mon–Sat 9am–6pm
www.fragonard.com, admission free
Just around the corner from his Musée du Parfum (p. 216) Fragonard also converted a theatre dating from the 1930s into a museum, where you admire old recipes and precious flacons as well as buy the company's famous perfumes.

Pavillon de l'Arsenal
21, Boulevard Morland (4th arr.)
Métro-Station: Sully Morland
Tue–Sat 10.30am–6.30pm, Sun 11am–7pm
www.pavillon-arsenal.com
admission free
City history and current urban schemes as well as a 40 m2 mod-

el of the capital at a scale of 1:2000.

ART AND ARCHAEOLOGY
Centre Pompidou
▶p. 196

Ecole Nationale Supérieure des Beaux Arts
14, Rue Bonaparte (6th arr.),
Métro: Saint-Germain-des-Prés
Tue–Sun 1pm–7pm
(except Aug), adults €4
Collections of the 17th-century Royal Academy of Art and the Ecole des Beaux Arts

Espace Dalí
▶Montmartre, p. 253

Fondation Cartier
▶Montparnasse, p. 260

Fondation Le Corbusier
Villa La Roche
10, Square du Docteur Blanche (16th arr.)
Métro: Jasmin, Porte d'Auteuil
www.fondationlecorbusier.asso.fr
Mon 1.30pm–6pm, Tue–Thu 10am–6pm, Fr and Sat 10am–5pm
Groups by appointment, tel. 01 42 88 75 72, admission free
Completed by Le Corbusier in 1925, Villa La Roche is typical of the experimental architecture of the 1920s and today houses a gallery of Cubist painting.

Grand Palais
▶p. 190

Jeu de Paume
▶Tuileries, p. 327

Le 104

104, Rue d'Aubervilliers (19th arr.)
Métro: Stalingrad, www.104.fr
Since 2008 this former fire station
has been a hot house for all art
forms – with studios, exhibition
spaces, bookshop and café.

Louvre

▶ p. 226

Manufacture Royale des Gobelins

Gallery: Tue–Sun 11am–6pm, free
admission last Sun in month,
manufactory tours Tue–Thur 1pm
and during holidays also 3pm.
Advance ticket sales: www.fnac.fr,
ticket office: Galerie des Gobelins
adults €6; manufactory €11, during exhibitions €9, www.
mobiliernational.culture.gouv.fr
They've been weaving tapestries
here for more than 400 years.

Founded in 1607 by Henri IV, during the reign of the Sun King Louis XIV the manufactory was responsible for the interiors of the
palaces. Even today French embassies are done out with their
tapestries and rugs.

Musée Baccarat

11, Place des Etats-Unis (16th arr.)
Metro: Iéna, www.baccarat.fr
Daily except Tue and Sun 10am–
6pm, adults €5, under 18s free
Precious Baccarat crystal glass
from 1828 to the present day

Musée Bourdelle

18, Rue Antoine-Bourdelle
(15th arr.), Métro: Montparnasse-
Bienvenue, Falguière
Tue–Sun 10am–6pm
www.bourdelle-paris.fr
Sculptures by Antoine Bourdelle, a
pupil of Rodin

Monet's *Water Lilies* in the Orangerie

Musée Bouilhet-Christofle
9, Rue Royale (8th arr.)
Métro: Madeleine, www.
christofle.com, admission free
At the headquarters of the company more than 2000 pieces of exquisite silverware illustrate the work of the silversmith to Napoléon III.

Musée Hébert
85, Rue du Cherche-Midi
Métro: Sèvres-Babylone, Vaneau
Presently closed for renovation
www.rmn.fr/Musee-Hebert
In the Hôtel de Montmorency you can see works by the portrait painter Ernest Hébert (1817–1908).

Musée Nissim de Camondo
63, Rue de Monceau (8th arr.)
Métro: Villiers, Monceau
Tue–Sun 10.30am–5.30pm,
Thur till 9pm
www.lesartsdecoratifs.fr/francais/nissim-de-camondo, adults €7.50
Comte Moïse de Camondo donated furniture, tapestries and Rococo porcelain from the second half of the 18th century and named the collection after his son Nissim, who fell in 1917.

Musée Cernuschi
7, Avenue Vélasquez (8th arr.)
Métro: Villiers, Monceau
Tue–Sun 10am–6pm
www.cernuschi.paris.fr
Permanent exhibition free,
Special exhibitions adults €7
Chinese art from the 14th century to the present day

Musée Cognacq-Jay
▶Marais, Hôtel de Donon, p. 251

Musée Dapper
50, Rue Paul Valéry (16th arr.)
Métro: Etoile
Daily except Tue and Thur 11am–7pm
www.dapper.com.fr, adults €6
Pre-colonial African art

Musée Jacquemart André
▶ p. 270

Musée d'Art Moderne de la Ville de Paris
▶Palais de Tokyo, p. 286

Musée de la Vie Romantique
▶Montmartre, p. 257

Musée de l'Orangerie
▶Tuileries, p. 327

Musée d'Orsay
▶ p. 263

Musée de Montmartre
▶Montmartre, p. 255

Musée National Delacroix
▶Saint-Germain-des-Prés, p. 309

Musée Guimet
6, Place d'Iéna (16th Arr.)
Métro: Iéna, Trocadéro
Wed–Mon 10am–6pm
www.guimet.fr
Adults €7.50, under 18s free
The foundation stone for the largest museum of Asian art in Europe was laid in 1889 by the industrialist Emile Guimet, who donated his collection to Paris. The more than 50,000 objects from 17 Asian countries include the world's largest collection from Nepal and Tibet, the finest Chinese porcelain from the Han to the Tang dynas-

The Palais de Tokyo is dedicated to current artistic trends

ties, Buddhist reliefs from the Amaravati School (1st–3rd centuries) and sculptures from Gandhara (1st–6th centuries), as well as monuments from Hadda, which were brought to Paris from Afghanistan in around 1920. The second floor is devoted to writers from Song to the Qing dynasties and Chinese painting. From Japan come the copies of the 23 statues of the Toji Temple in Kyoto. On Thur afternoon there is a traditional tea ceremony in the Japanese garden, and courses in Asian art are held on Sat.

Musée National Jean-Jacques Henner
43, Avenue de Villiers (17th arr.) Métro: Malesherbes, Wagram Daily except Tue 11am–6pm

http://musee-henner.fr, adults €5 Works of the Alsatian painter Jean-Jacques Henner (1829–1905)

Musée Maillol
▶Saint-Germain-des-Prés, p. 312

Musée Marmottan Monet
▶Bois de Boulogne, S. 193

Musée Moreau   .
14, Rue de la Rochefoucault (9th arr.), Métro: Trinité Tue, Wed, Thur 10am–12.45pm, 2pm–5.15pm, Fri–Sun 10am–5.15pm, www.musee-moreau.fr adults €6.50, under 18s free The home and studio of the Symbolist artist Gustave Moreau (1826–98) is now a museum containing 8000 paintings and drawings.

Musée National d'Art Moderne
▶Centre Pompidou, p. 198

Musée du Quai Branly
▶ p. 269

Musée Picasso
▶ p. 272

Musée Rodin
▶ p. 273

Musée Zadkine
100 bis, Rue d'Assas (6th arr.)
Métro: Vavin, Notre Dame des Champs, Port-Royal
Tue–Sun 10am–6pm
www.zadkine.paris.fr
Permanent exhibition admission free
Works by the Franco-Russian sculptor Ossip Zadkine (1890–1967) and his wife Valentine Prax (1897–1981) are on display in the garden as well as in the house and studio renovated in 2012.

LITERATURE, MUSIC AND FILM
Cité de la Musique
▶La Villette, p. 340

Maison Honoré de Balzac
47, Rue Raynouard (16th arr.)
Métro: Passy, Muette
Tue–Sun 10am–6pm;
library Tue–Sun 10am–6pm
www.paris.fr/loisirs/musees-expos/maison-de-balzac
Permanent exhibition admission free
The home of the writer Honoré de Balzac (▶Famous People) with manuscripts, documents and a library of works by and about Balzac

Maison Victor Hugo
▶Place des Vosges, p. 298

Musée de la Musique
▶La Villette, p. 340

Musée des Lettres et Manuscrits
222, Boulevard Saint-Germain (7th arr.), Métro: St Thomas d'Aquin
Tue–Sun 10am–7pm,
Thur till 9.30pm, adults €7
www.museedeslettres.fr
This museum brings together everything that gave voice to literary France – a total of 70,000 letters, sketches, first editions and even an »Enigma« decoding machine.

Musée Edith Piaf
▶Belleville, p. 186

Salon Chopin
Bibliothèque Polonaise de Paris
6, Quai d'Orléans (4th arr.).
Métro: Pont-Marie, adults €5
Tours Tue–Fri 2pm, 3pm,
4pm and 5pm on request,
tel. 01 55 42 83 85, www.biblio theque-polonaise-paris-shlp.fr

Tender devotion:
The Kiss at the
Musée Rodin

In 2009, the Polish Library, which owns memorabilia from Frédéric Chopin, had the last Paris apartment of the composer reconstructed from a watercolour by T. Kwiatkowsk.

MILITARY
Musée de la Marine
▶Palais de Chaillot, p. 283

Musée de l'Armée
▶Invalides, p. 223

NATURE AND TECHNOLOGY
Cité des Sciences
▶La Villette, p. 337

Musée Curie
11, Rue Pierre et Marie Curie (5th arr.), RER: B, Tue–Fri 10am–6pm, closed Aug http://curie.fr , admission free The Radium Institute, originally under the direction of the Nobel Prize winner Marie Curie (1903 physics, 1912 chemistry), opened here in 1914. In the museum, which was restored in 2012, visitors can see her pipettes, lab coats and instruments.

Musée de la Chasse
▶Marais, Hôtel Guénégaud, p. 250

Musée de l'Air et de l'Espace
Aéroport de Paris - Le Bourget BP 173, Métro: line 7 to La Courneuve, then bus 152 Daily except Mon April–Oct 10am–6pm, Nov–March 10am–5pm, www.museeairespace.fr Permanent exhibition admission free

Animations €7, €12, €15 Flight simulator, Spitfire, Boeing 747, Concorde, Dakota and a Super Frelon helicopter – the Aviation Museum is an experience for the whole family.

Musée des Arts et Métiers
▶Place de la République, p. 296

Muséum National d'Histoire Naturelle
▶Jardin des Plantes, p. 225

Palais de la Découverte
▶Grand Palais, p. 213

OTHER
Musée de la Contrefaçon
16, Rue de la Faisanderie (16th arr.) Métro: Porte Dauphine Tue–Sun 2pm–5.30pm, closed Sat and Sun in Aug www.pariserve.tm.fr/culture/musee/contrefacon.htm, adults €4 Chanel No.5, Louis Vuitton bags and bronze sculptures by Rodin – the museum displays more than 300 counterfeits of perfumes, fashion items and cars.

Musée de la Poupée
Impasse Berthaud (4th arr.) Metro: Rambuteau, adults €8 Tue–Sat 10am–6pm www.museedelapoupeeparis.com Everything from delicate 19th-century porcelain dolls to Barbie and Asterix. The owners, Guido and Samy Odin, have a surgery for broken dolls and even run courses in doll making.

Musée de la Publicité
▶Louvre, p. 243

Meet George Clooney and Brad Pitt at the Musée Grevin!

Musée de la vie romantique
▶Montmartre, p. 255

Musée du Vin
Rue des Eaux (16th arr.)
Caveau des Echansons
Métro: Passy
Tue–Sun 10am–6pm
www.museeduvinparis.com
Admission plus glass of wine €11
After visiting the exhibition in the medieval cellars of Passy Abbey, try the local wines.

Musée Grevin
10, Boulevard Montmartre
(9th arr.), Métro: Montmartre
Mon–Fri 10am–6.30pm (last admission: 5.30pm), Sat–Sun 10am–7pm (last admission: 6pm), July and Aug from 9am
www.grevin.com, adults 22 €, children aged 14 and under €15
With more than 300 figures, this wax museum will lead you through eras and events not restricted to Paris, from Napoleon to Sarkozy, from Einstein to Marilyn Monroe, Sebastian Loeb and Brad Pitt.

Choco Story Le Musée Gourmand du Chocolat
20, Boulevard Bonne Nouvelle
(10th Arr.)
Métro: Bonne Nouvelle
Tours daily 10.30am–5.30pm
www.museeduchocolat.fr
Adults €9, children aged 12 and under €6
Black, white, from milk, with or without nuts, melted or crunchy – on three floors this private museum belonging to the Belgian Van-Belle family reveals the 4000-year cultural history of cacao and chocolate – with a taster at the end of course.

Shopping

Elegant, Feminine and Stylish

Paris is one of the best cities in the world for shopping. For the fashion conscious, both haute couture and avant-garde collections are to be found. Antiques, gourmet products and exclusive perfumes are also much sought-after.

It is important to know that January and July in Paris are the months of the »**soldes**«, the sales, when the prices of seasonal fashion items are reduced by up to 70%. Even outside that time there are stores that sell at reduced prices, some of them permanently. In the case of these »soldes permanents« the goods are usually last season's fashion or items with small defects. **Rue d'Alésia** in the 14th arrondissement is the street of the »stocks«, in which stock items and collections from the previous year are sold considerably cheaper. The term »dégriffés« refers to greatly reduced brand products, while »fripes« are second-hand articles. Most shops are open Mon–Sat from 9am to 7pm; smaller shops are often closed on Monday. The large department stores open later one day a week, closing on Fri or Sat usually only at around 9pm. At certain times such as during Advent shops are also open on Sundays from 1pm–6pm. In the Marais and along the Canal St-Martin many small boutiques also open up on Sundays. Many stores along the Champs-Elysées are open 365 days a year. Note: in July and August most of the owner-operated small shops are closed – that's when the Parisians enjoy their summer holidays by the seaside.

Shopping tips

The famous **couturiers** and the most impressive shop-window displays are in Rue du Faubourg-St-Honoré and between Avenue Montaigne and the Champs-Elysées. **Avant-garde** fashion has made its home around Place des Victoires. There are good fashion boutiques in St-Germain-des-Prés and between Rue des Rosiers and Place des Vosges in the Marais. To buy the finest **shoes**, go to Rue de Grenelle, Rue de Cherche-Midi and Rue de Rennes; the most expensive **jewellery** is on Place Vendôme and in Rue de la Paix. The best place for **crystal glass**, **porcelain** and **silver** is Rue du Paradis; for fabrics, tablecloths, cushions and vases try the area around Place de la Madeleine. There is a concentration of high-class antique shops in St-Germain-des-Prés, and of art galleries and bookshops around Rue de Seine. Those interested in furniture should go to Rue du Faubourg-St-Antoine. The best **gourmet food shops** can be found close to Place de la Madeleine.

Parisian chic has that certain something

Parisian Chic

Dior, Chanel or Yves Saint Laurent, who doesn't know them, these big names of the Paris fashion world that stand for exclusivity and wealth? But the fashion world is in a state of flux, and young creative talents from Paris are successfully adopting a different approach to the glamorous fashion houses.

The fascination and reputation of French fashion goes back to the 17th century. Louis XIV had managed to dress the nobility throughout Europe in justaucorps, culottes and allonge wigs. And the fashion of the Rococo era with those sweeping crinolines, constricting corsets and powdered wigs was »created« at the French court. The museum at the Palais Galliera provides a lively and interesting account of the history of French fashion (▶ p.286). Anyone looking for the current trends in Paris should step inside the luxury fashion houses along Avenue Montaigne, Rue du Faubourg St-Honoré and Boulevard de la Madeleine.

Haute couture or prêt-à-porter?

The Englishman Charles Frédérick Worth founded haute couture in Paris in around 1850, by which he replaced the individual dress with the model, introduced the collection and had his dresses paraded by a mannequin, namely his wife Marie. 1868 saw the establishment of the »Chambre Syndicale de la Couture Française«, which drew up the strict statutes regulating the rights and obligations of the fashion houses. Worth influenced the development of international fashion for more that 30 years, from

the crinoline to the cul de Paris. After the First World War, Coco Chanel encountered a new generation of women that had been totally transformed. For working women tight skirts were no more practical than elaborate long hairdos. For Coco Chanel, »Real elegance requires unimpeded freedom of movement«. Her shirtwaist dresses and jersey ensembles with straight jacket and pullover had a massive influence on women's fashion of the 1920s. In 1921 she brought out »Chanel No. 5« and so began the era of »designer fragrances«. Clear freshness and a colourless crystal cube with white label underlined the simple elegance of the fragrance, which became the best-selling perfume in the world. Since 2009, the face of Chanel No. 5 has been Amélie star Audrey Tautou, who also played the title roll in the film biography *Coco Before Chanel*.

When Christian Dior presented his first collection in 1947, it created a sensation. In contrast to the dreary wartime styles we now had the elegant "calyx line", otherwise referred to as the "New Look". "A dress by Dior" – this dream of many women of the post-war period became a symbol of all that was desirable and prohibitively expensive. To dress fashionably became a matter of prestige, and rich

Fashion by Chanel was and remains the epitome of elegance

private clients, royalty and movie stars became the financial mainstay of French haute couture. In 1952 Hubert de Givenchy suddenly became known worldwide when he designed the wardrobe for Audrey Hepburn in Billy Wilder's film *Sabrina*. She also wore dresses by Givenchy in the cult movie *Breakfast at Tiffany's*.

But exclusive haute couture meant nothing to the youth of the 1960s. In London, fashion designers came up with unconventional ideas. Above all there was Mary Quant, who promoted the miniskirt and with boutique fashion led people away from the exclusivity of tailor-made haute couture. In response, the Parisian couturiers began designing youthful, ready-to-wear collections. In 1965, the first »Salon du Prêt-à-Porter« was held in Paris, and in 1973 the "Chambre Syndicale du Prêt-à-porter des Couturiers et Créateurs de Mode" was established. New fashion designers arrived on the scene: Louis Féraud presented his first collection in 1960 and two years later Yves Saint Laurent ventured the leap towards independence with his »Rive Gauche« ready-to-wear brand (▶ Famous Persons).

A decade later Jean-Paul Gaultier combined the tutu with gym shoes and sent women from the street out onto the catwalk – since 2012 the darling of Madonna has also been creative director of Coca-Cola light. Christian Lacroix also operates under the maxim of »anything goes«. This master of mixing combines elements that are apparent opposites but which ultimately harmonize (▶ p. 130). In order to reach even more customers, the creative elite now designs cheap fashion for department stores and mail order catalogues. Even Chanel's icon Karl Lagerfeld has discovered the masses. In 2004 the native of Hamburg with his trademark ponytail designed the first collection for H & M, and since 2012 his new labels »Karl« and »Kollektion Karl Lagerfeld Paris« have been available.

Young creative types have increasingly been drawn from the extensive west of Paris to the east of the city and the Canal St-Martin. The aura around new labels comes alive there in the secluded alleyways and squares like Sainte Marthe – time to discover the idiosyncratic style of that particular neighbourhood!

Exclusive Club

For more than 150 years its haute couture shows have made Paris the fashion capital of the world. Whether a fashion house is allowed to call itself »Haute Couture« is decided by the »Chambre Syndicale de la Couture Française«, the body which sets the rules by which the designers are required to re-apply every year.

▶ **How do you become haute couture?**

1 Only on recommendation.
All haute couture houses belong to a guild. New members can only be accepted on the recommendation of existing members.

2 Headquarters in Paris

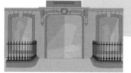

3 Minimum number of employees
The fashion house has to operate an atelier with at least 25 full-time employees

4 Unique designs are required
A fashion designer must demonstrate at least 35 hand-sewn items

©BAEDEKER

From the catwalk to the shops

▶ **Haute Couture**
Exclusive designer fashion with handmade fitted clothes in the highest price category.

▶ **Prêt-à-porter**
Fashion which reacts to new mark◆ and fashion impulses and is preser◆ during Paris Fashion Week

5 **Creations for every occasion**
Different looks for day and evening wear are required

▶ **www.modeaparis.com**
fashion shows and premieres (Féderation française de la Couture et du Prêt-à-Porter)

6 **Presentation is obligatory**
The members present their collections to the press twice a year at the seasonal haute couture shows.

9 **The designer**
is now called a:

Grand Couturier

8 **The fashion label**
bears the title:

Maison de Couture

7 **The creation**
receives the legally protected name:

Haute Couture

From the catalogue and online
Selected items find their way into catalogues or online shops like www.net-a-porter.com

▶ Fashion events:

PARIS FASHION WEEK
March und Sept/October

PARIS HAUTE COUTURE
January and July

LONDON FASHION WEEK
February/March and Sept

ALTAROMA FASHION WEEK
January and September

MILANO MODA
January and September

BERLIN MERCEDES-BENZ FASHION WEEK
January and July

NEW YORK FASHION WEEK
February and September

Nostalgia with a Glass Ceiling

Walter Benjamin regarded them as »the most important architecture of the 20th century«, »as phantasmagoria of a utopian goal«; Louis Aragon called them »human aquariums« and »large glass coffins«; while Julio Cortázar described them as »false sky made of stucco and dirty skylights«: these are the arcades of Paris.

The first arcades appeared at the end of the 18th century, and the heyday of the covered shopping street was between 1800 and 1860. Noise, dirt and stench were becoming ever more rife along the narrow, unpaved roads of the capital. At the same time the invention of the iron girder enabled the construction of long glass roofs with light flooding into the street below. Those were the days when clever speculators realised the kind of economic advantages that could accrue in a part of the city – near the Palais Royal – where both commerce and entertainment were already flourishing. The era also saw the emergence of those strolling

In the Galerie Vivienne you'll find antiquarian books at Jousseaume

loafer types, who would be safe here from the dirt and the noise of the gutter and the ravages of nature, and whose movements, as Benjamin wrote in his Arcades Project, »were determined by the pace of a snail«.

The German Francophile poet Heinrich Heine walked in amazement along the first arcades of the metropolis on the Seine »gazing upwards with my glasses at the end of my nose«. In the end, well over 100 grand shopping malls with restaurants and tearooms came into a glamorous existence in 1st, 2nd, and 9th arrondissements. Then a sharp decline set in. From 1853 under Baron Haussmann, the Prefect of Paris, boulevards with broad pavements and electric lighting were laid out, along which the first large department stores were erected. The covered streets degenerated into mere passageways, to shortcuts between the boulevards: dark and dirty places with drug dealers and prostitutes. But for several years now, the 16 carefully restored arcades in particular have been experiencing a wonderful Renaissance.

The good old days

Among the most visited and most beautiful arcades is the 176-m long and only 3-m wide Galerie Vivi-

The Passage Jouffroy is a great place to browse and discover

enne at Rue des Petits-Champs No. 4 (2nd arr.; www.galerie-vivienne. com) including haute couture by Ana Quasoar, creations by Jean-Paul Gaultier, the antiquarian bookshop Jousseaume, the A priori Thé tearoom and the family wine merchant's Legrand Filles et Fils, where you get delicious snacks to accompany the tasting of their excellent wines.

The neighbouring Galerie Colbert, which also dates from 1826, is an architectural masterpiece with neoclassical mosaic flooring, wooden reliefs, pointed arches in Empire style and a glass roof with an enormous cupola – today it belongs to the National Library. Other jewels include the Galerie Véro-Dodat in the Les Halles district with its black and white tiles, wood panelling on the walls and mirrors between the shop fronts, as well as the neoclassical three-storey Passage du Grand Cerf (2nd arr.). The popular Passage Jouffroy starts by the Musée Grévin on Boulevard Montmartre. Here you can find the only shop in the country specializing in walking sticks: the Segas brothers' assortment ranges from hiking sticks for 100 euros to Spanish makes with tortoiseshell and silver handle for 8000 euros and their folding ebony stick for 14,000 euros. The Pain d'Epices toyshop is a paradise for handmade dolls, teddy bears and other traditional toys. Opposite, the Hôtel Chopin has 37 tiny rooms that are full of charm. In the Passage des Panoramas (www.passagedespanoramas.fr) opened in 1799 the theatre restaurant »Les Troubadours« is hidden between the philately and coin dealers. .

Fashion, perfume and gourmet shops

In France most goods and services are subject to 19.6% value added tax/VAT (Taxe sur la Valeur Ajoutée/TVA). Citizens of countries that do not belong to the European Union can claim a VAT refund on leaving the country if they get the appropriate certificate when purchasing in shops that display the »Tax Free« sign. The reduced rate of 5.5 % is for items like food.

ANTIQUES
Carré Rive Gauche Insider Tip
Over 120 dealers and art galleries on the left bank of the Seine between Quai Voltaire, Rue du Bac, Rue de l'Université and Rue des Saints-Pères sell furniture in the Louis XV style, sculptures, tapestries and art from the Far East. The galleries have open days in early summer: »Cinq jours de l'Object Extraordinaire«.

Place des Vosges
Antique shops and galleries under the arcades, ▶ p. 297

Village Saint-Paul
Small items of furniture, pictures and jewellery in the ▶Marais, p. 248

Le Louvre des Antiquaires
2, Place du Palais-Royal (1st arr.)
www.louvre-antiquaires.com
Métro: Palais-Royal
Tue–Sun 11am–7pm
(except July and Aug).
250 antique dealers on three floors sell pricey furniture and art of all periods and styles.

Le Village Suisse
78, Avenue de Suffren (15th arr.)
Métro: La Motte-Picquet
Thur–Mon 10.30am–7pm
www.levillagesuisseparis.com

Ever since 1920 there have been around 150 dealers in the shadow of the Eiffel Tower selling art and furniture in the upper price bracket.

Hôtel des Ventes Drouot Richelieu
9, Rue Drouot (9th arr.)
Métro: Richelieu-Drouot, Le Peletier
Mon–Sat 11am–6pm
Auctions from 2pm
www.drouot.com
One of the oldest auction houses in the world with 21 rooms

BOOKS, CDS
Bouquinistes
▶Seine, p. 317

FNAC
Forum des Halles 1
Rue Pierre-Lescot (1st arr.)
www.fnac.com
France's largest retail chain for books and media is also the largest national ticket agent, with branches at the airport and on the Champs-Elyseés, among other places.

Shakespeare & Company
▶Quartier Latin, p. 300

Virgin Megastore
52–60, Avenue des Champs-

Elysées (8th arr.); open daily
till midnight; branches at the
Louvre and Grands Boulevards
Huge stock of all kinds of music

GOURMET FOOD SHOPS & WINES
Les Caves Taillevent
199, Rue du Faubourg St-Honoré
(8th arr.)
www.taillevent.com
Sat 10.30am–6pm open tasting of
the fine wines of the house with
head sommelier Brice Mancelet.

Chocolatiers and pâtissiers
▶ p. 117

Debauve et Gallais
30, Rue des Sts-Pères (7th arr.)
33, Rue Vivienne (2nd arr.)
www.debauve-et-gallais.com
Purveyor of the very finest
pralinés since 1800

Fauchon *Insider Tip*
26, Pl. de la Madeleine
(8th arr.)
www.fauchon.fr
Gourmet temple with divine
chocolates, champagne, foie gras,
wine cellar and tea room

Fromagerie Alléosse
13, Rue Poncelet (17th arr.)
www.fromage-alleosse.com
200 varieties of the best cow's,
sheep's and goat's raw milk
cheese, matured in four cellars
downtown

Izraël
30, Rue François Miron (4th arr.)
Exotic spices and spirits
from around the world

Eric Kayser
10, Rue de l'Ancienne Comédie
(6th arr.)
and a further 15 shops
www.maison-kayser.com
Parisian master baker. Try the
apricot bread with pistachios

Nina's Paris
29, rue Danielle Casanova
(1st arr.), www.ninastea.com
Fine teas, infused with 100%
natural flavours – the fragrances
for the Marie-Antoinette tea come
from the Potager du Roi at Versailles

Patrick Roger
108, Boulevard
Saint-Germain (6th Arr.)
www.patrickroger.com
Chocolate shop with truffle
dreams and gourmet chocolates

Poilâne
▶MARCO POLO Insight ▶ p. 311.

DESIGN AND LIFESTYLE
Carrousel du Louvre
99, Rue de Rivoli (1st arr.)
www.carrouseldulouvre.com
Underground shopping centre
adjacent to the Louvre, featuring
45 designer outlets including
Esprit, L'Occitane and Apple

Christofle
24, Rue de la Paix (2nd arr.)
www.christofle.com
Exclusive tableware and
fine silver cutlery

Colette
213, Rue St-Honoré (1st arr.)
www.colette.fr
The latest designer fashion and

furnishings. The mineral water bar in the basement has 80 kinds of water.

Le 66
66, Avenue des Champs-Elysées
www.le66.fr
1200 m2 concept store with functional ambience, well-stocked trendy bookstore and clothing from 130 hot labels covering 2 floors

FLEA MARKETS (MARCHES AUX PUCES)
Marché aux Puces de Saint-Ouen
Avenue de la Porte de Clignancourt (18th arr.)
Métro: Porte de Clignancourt
Sat, Sun and Mon 9am–6pm
Huge market near a social flashpoint: in addition to new wares there's a plenty of second-hand junk, stolen goods and counterfeit items. Watch out for pickpockets!

Marché aux Puces de la Place d'Aligre
Place d'Aligre (12th arr.)
Métro: Ledru-Rollin
Tue–Sat 8am–1pm and 4pm–7.30pm, Sun 8am–1pm
80 stands for market traders

Insider Tip
Marché de Saint-Denis
Rue Gabriel Péri
Thur, Fri and Sun 8am–1pm
Métro: Basilique de Saint-Denis
Situated on Place du Marché Saint-Denis
between the Stade de France and the basilica of Saint-Denis, one of the largest markets in the Paris region makes for a colourful hustle

and bustle with more than 300 stalls. On the square and in the covered market halls Caribbean delights compete with Arab spices, Indian fabrics and delicious products from all over France.

MODERN ART GALLERIES
▶Marais, artists and creative types, p. 251

Alain Blondel
128, Rue Vieille du Temple (3rd arr.), www.galerie-blondel.com
Figurative art by about 30 painters and sculptors

Espace Durand-Dessert
28, Rue de Lappe (11th arr.)
www.espacelmdd.com
European avant-garde, including Merz and Tosani

Agathe Gaillard
3, Rue du Pont-Louis-Philippe (4th arr.)
www.agathegaillard.com
The oldest photography gallery in Paris; Kertesz, Cartier-Bresson and Edouard Boubar all had exhibitions here.

Magnum Gallery
▶ Saint-Germain-des-Prés, p. 310

DEPARTMENT STORES
Bazar de l'Hôtel de Ville
52–64, Rue de Rivoli (4th arr.)
www.bhv.fr
Temple of consumerism for every need

Galeries Lafayette
40, Bd. Haussmann (9th arr.)
www.galerieslafayette.com

Chanel, Dior, Prada and YSL – the most magnificent Art Nouveau department store is a stronghold of fashion and luxury with a sensational perfumery. 150 designers are represented in the shoe department alone. At 3pm on Fridays the latest trends of the fashion metropolis are introduced. From the top floor you can enjoy a panoramic view of Paris. The chocolates from the Pierre Hermé boutique are irresistible.

Grand Bazar
33, Rue des Sèvres

www.brandbazar.fr
The atmosphere might be reminiscent of Aldi, but the selection makes a fashionista's heart beat faster: Manoush, See by Chloé, Antik Batik, Nolita, Anonymous and other trendy designers are significantly less expensive here than elsewhere.

Le Printemps
64, Bd. Haussmann
(9th arr.)
www.printemps.com
High fashion and selected perfumes beneath the enormous

Luxury department store with Europe's largest perfumery: Les Galeries Lafayette

Belle-Epoque glass dome. Book your own personal shopper, who will assist you with individual advice. After your shopping order a little something in the brasserie under the dome, in the Ladurée tea house or on the leafy terrace of the Deli-Cieux with its views over Paris.

WOMEN'S FASHION
Agnès B.
13, rue de Marseille (10th arr.)
http://europe.agnesb.fr/fr
Classical and timeless fashion, accessories, jewellery and beauty products for all the family

Insider Tip
Akris
49, Avenue Montaigne (8th arr.)
Her Royal Highness Princess Charlène of Monaco is also an enthusiastic fan of the discreet outfits by Albert Kriemler.

Vanessa Bruno
12, Rue de Castiglione
www.vanessabruno.com
Vanessa's father is the founder of the Emmanuelle Khan fashion house. Her own label is Scandinavian-style simplicity but very feminine and still affordable.

Barbara Bui
23, Rue Etienne-Marcel
(1st arr.)
www.barbarabui.com
Reasonably priced second collections by a sought-after designer, who loves the feminine look and contrasts: minimalist, romantic and aggressive

Chanel
31, Rue Chambon (1st arr.)
42, Avenue Montaigne (8th arr.)
www.chanel.com
Timeless chic, perfected by Karl Lagerfeld since 1983

Paris Fashion boutiques are sinfully good – and outrageously expensive

Christian Dior
30, Avenue Montaigne
(8th arr.)
www.dior.com
Gorgeous dresses

Jean Paul Gaultier
44, Avenue George V (8th arr.)
and 6, Rue Vivienne (2nd arr.)
www. jeanpaulgaultier.com
Gaultier's blazers are perfectly
cut

Griff Troc
17, Bd. de Courcelles and
119, Bd. Malesherbes (8th arr.)
www.griff-troc.fr
Bargains from Chanel, Lacroix,
Prada, Kenzo und YSL

Hermès
42, Avenue George V (8th arr.)
www.hermes.com
World famous silk scarves and
extraordinary and refined fashion
collections by Christophe Lemaire.

Christian Lacroix
73, Rue du Faubourg St-Honoré
(6th arr.), www.christian-lacroix.fr
The neo-romantic designer loves
the colours of Provence.

Isabel Marant
1, Rue Jacob (6th arr.)
www.isabelmarant.tm.fr
Starting with knitwear and jerseys,
Isabel Marant won the hearts of
the Parisians and today sells her
collection in ten flagship stores
and 450 boutiques around the
world.

Merci!
111, Bd. Beaumarchais (3rd arr.)
www.merci-merci.com

Vintage and designer fashion by
Isabel Marant, Stella McCartney
und YSL – the net proceeds are
donated to needy children.

> **!** *Models up close* **Insider Tip**
>
> **MARCO ⊕ POLO TIP**
>
> Once a month in the tea salon at
> the Hôtel Bristol top models min-
> gle with the guests to show off
> the latest collections (Thés à la
> mode de l'Hôtel Bristol, 112, Rue
> du Faubourg St-Honoré, 8th arr.,
> www.hotel-bristol.com, 3.30pm–
> 5pm, €55).

Réciproque
89 and 95, Rue de la Pompe
(16th arr.), www.reciproque.fr
Large, 700m2 luxury outlet with
clothes by a great couturiers

Rue d'Alésia
Stock items in the 14th arr. by
Cacharel (No. 114), Sonya
Rykiel (No. 64), Dorotennis
(No. 74), Regina Rubens (No. 88)
and Daniel Hechter (No. 92) at
half price

Sonja Rykiel
175, Boulevard Saint-Germain
(6th arr.), www.soniarykiel.fr
Chic outfits for fashion-conscious
women in the flagship store of
the »Queen of Knitwear«

YSL
32, Rue du Faubourg Saint-
Honore (8.Arr.), www.ysl.com
Stefano Pilati, the Milanese head
of design at Yves Saint Laurent, is
always reinterpreting the term
»Exotic«.

MEN'S FASHION
Saint James
66, Rue de Rennes (6th arr.)
www.saint-james.fr
Maritime inspired smart casual
fashion for him and her

L'Eclaireur
3, Rue des Rosiers (4th arr.)
www.leclaireur.com
Designer fashion by Giorgio Brato,
Martin Margiela and Laura B.

Stock B
114, Rue de Turenne (3rd arr.)
www.stock-b.fr
Top-class men's fashion at factory
prices

FOR CHILDREN
Catimini
15, Rue Tronchet (8th arr.)
www.catimini.com
Imaginative clothes for children
and a place to play for toddlers.
Seven branches around Paris.

La Maison des Natalys
76, Rue de Seine (6th arr.)
www.natalys.fr
Delicate pastel colours, pure natural fabrics and cute cuddly toys for
new-born babies to three-year-
olds

Du Pareil au Même
7, Rue Saint-Placide (6th arr.)
www.dpam.fr
16 branches
From rompers for babies to jeans
for teenagers, all of it at attractive
prices

LEATHER AND SHOES
Rodolphe Menudier
14, Rue de Castiglione (1st arr.)
www.rodolphemenudier.com
Extravagant, feminine shoes

Robert Clergerie _Insider Tip_
5, Rue du Cherche-
Midi (6th arr.)
www.robertclergerie.fr
The selection is like the shop:
classic, elegant and beautiful.

Stéphane Kélian
13 bis, Rue Grenelle (7th arr.)
www.stephane-kelian.fr
Distinctive footwear by a popular
designer

Christian Louboutin
38–40, Rue de Grenelle (7th arr.)
www.christianlouboutin.com
Movie stars and models love the
outrageously expensive high heels
with red lacquered soles.

Louis Vuitton
22, Avenue Montaigne (8th arr.)
and 40 Boulevard Haussmann
(9th arr.), www.louisvuitton.com
Life as a journey – accompanied
by luxury luggage, chic prêt-à-porter and accessories

MARKETS
Boulevard Raspail
(6th arr.), Métro: Rennes
Sat 8am–2pm
In Paris there are three markets
for health food and organic produce: Batignoles, Brancusi and
this one, perhaps the most attractive.

Marché aux Fleurs
►Marché aux Oiseaux, p. 219

Marché de Belleville
►MARCO POLO Insider Tip, p. 186

Marché International de Rungis

Mon–Fri noon–3pm
Bus: 216 (Denfert-Rochereau),
185 (Porte d'Italie)
SNCF: from Gare d'Austerlitz
to Pont-de-Rungis
www.rungisinternational.com
Since the demolition of Les Halles
in 1969 the »belly of Paris« has
been in the southern suburb of
Rungis, which supplies Parisians
with fruit and vegetables, meat,
fish and selected delicatessen.

Marché Saint-Pierre

Place Saint-Pierre
(18th arr.)
Métro: Anvers
Tue–Sat 9.30am–6pm
www.marchesaintpierre.com/
Fabric emporium with every imaginable kind of fabric spread over
six floors

PERFUMERIES
Fragonard
▶ p. 216

Galeries Lafayette and Printemps
▶Department stores, p. 144

Jean Patou
5, Rue de Castiglione
www.jeanpatou.com
The inventor of the tennis skirt –
in 1921 Suzanne Lenglen played
at Wimbledon for the first time in
a dress by JP – also created fine

! Wellness at Guerlain   Insider Tip

MARCO ⊕ POLO TIP

For more than 160 years this fami-
ly-owned company has been creating its seductive and exclusive perfumes such as »Misouko« and »Vol
de Nuit«. In 1939, Guerlain opened
the world's first Institut de Beauté
on the main floor of their town
house on the Champs-Elysées. After a gentle facelift by Maxime
d'Angeac and Andrée Putman, today it presents itself as an elegant
spa for purists, which banishes any
hints of fatigue with excellent
massages (68, Champs-Elysées, 8th
arr., tel. 01 45 62 11 21, www.guer-
lainspa.com).

fragrances such as »Mille« and
»Un Amour de Patou«. »Joy« was
once the second best-selling perfume in the world – after »Chanel
No. 5«.

JEWELLERY
▶**Place Vendôme**
Cartier, Van Cleef & Arpels,
Boucheron, Bulgari and Rolex –
the best and most expensive
jewellers

Cartier
13, Rue de la Paix (2nd arr.)
www.cartier.com
Headquarters of the renowned
jeweller founded in 1847, with
branches in Avenue Montaigne
and on Place Vendôme

Sightseeing

Conquer the City!

The Seine metropolis is a complete work of art, so crammed full of attractions and in such a constant state of flux that it can make you dizzy. And yet it has its peaceful and quiet sides, with plenty of hidden nooks and secluded squares. So why not do the same as all the famous people who have succumbed to the charms of the French capital: go with the flow and become a flaneur!

Classic sightseeing often results in stress: in a rush to tick off all the most famous sights you can end up waiting for hours in queues and taking holiday snaps while forgetting to look behind the scenes. Forget about wanting to see everything – Parisians don't even manage that in an entire lifetime. Each one of the 20 Paris arrondissements has its own character that is waiting to be discovered, and there is no better place to study the Parisian way of life than in the café or park. Guided themed tours with native Parisians convey authentic impressions. Those who are a bit more sporty can discover the city while jogging or standing on a Segway. France may have discovered its love for sustainable tourism late, but then all the more intensively, and so in Paris there aren't just organic markets and eco-hotels, vegan restaurants and Fairtrade products, but also a varied range of experiences that can leave a lasting impression. In parts

Insider Tip

Scenic flights

Those looking for a real buzz should take to the skies: between 9am and 7pm in the Parc André Citroën, the Air de Paris helium balloon rises into the sky tethered to a 150-m long cable and provides unforgettable views across the city. Flight time approx. 10 mins (Entelsat Parc André Citroën, 2, Rue de la Montagne-de-la-Fage, 15th arr., Métro: Balard, Javel, André-Citroën, adults €10–12, children €6–10, www.ballondeparis. com). 45-minute long helicopter tours over Paris in a Bell 407 take off from the Hélioport at Le Bourget airport (€290 per person, www.candle-light-dinner.info).

where there are still no cycle routes, bus lanes and taxis are at your disposal; on Sundays the road along the bank of the Canal St-Martin is transformed into a »Voie Verte«, a green promenade for cyclists and pedestrians. Those who like the great outdoors also have the option of two hiking trails that cross Paris from north to south and west to east – a total of 174 km/108 mi of marked paths making up this »randonnée« in the city. If you want to see Paris from above, the best vantage points are the Eiffel Tower, Arc de Triomphe and Tour Montparnasse, with good views also to be had from the dome of Sacre Coeur.

In love on the Champs-Elysées

Getting Around Sustainably

Under the Mayor Bertrand Delanoë Paris transformed itself more than ever before. »Durabilité«, sustainability, is the new watchword, which has also had its impact on tourism and ensured that now, alongside the Métro, bus and Bateaux Mouches, a varied range of sightseeing options has emerged that not only protects the environment, but also opens up completely new perspectives on the metropolis.

The famous flagship project of the green, environmentally friendly Paris is the public bike hire system known as **Vélib**, which was introduced in 2007 and today has 1200 stations with a total of 20,600 **robust city bikes** complete with seven gears and handle bar basket. Hiring one is very easy – at least once your credit/debit card has been accepted. Once this has been achieved, the bike can be removed from the stand using a four-digit secret code that you set yourself, and later returned to any station in the city area. Each time you use one you need to pay a deposit of 150 euros, which in the event of the bicycle not being returned within the allotted time will be charged to your account. Those wanting to rent out a bike for longer or more often should take out a monthly or annual subscription – online or at the Service Point of the City Administration at 29, Rue de Rivoli.

A relaxed bike ride and discovering attractions in the process: those wanting the services of a guide should book a **Fat Tire Bike Tour** – it simply isn't possible to have a more laid-back bike ride! Also absolutely emission-free are the **Segways** that roll through Paris, two-wheeled scooters that are still powered with electricity from the plug but in the future will have hydrogen-fuelled batteries.

In the south of Paris, the **T3 electric tram**, extended in 2012, zooms almost without any sound at all along the old Boulevards des Maréchaux – quickly, safely and with no emissions. Along the tram route there is little in the way of sights to stop off at, but it does provide an up-close look at Parisian daily life. Get off at the Porte de Versailles and plunge headlong into the Paris trade fair bustle, or stay seated until the Georges Brassens stop, where you can visit **Parc Georges Brassens**, which was created in 1975 on the site of the Vaugirad stud. Here you can discover French culinary and medicinal herbs along a nature trail, take in one of the regular exhibitions in the former riding arena and even take part in the demonstrations in the apiary! Nearly twice as big as that one is the **Parc Montsouris**, a beautiful English-style landscaped park with secretive paths and sculptures. The **Cité Universitaire** is a somewhat unusual place, for here every house is built in the traditional style of a different country – nestled in a 30-ha/75-acre park. Young choreographers stage their works at the Théâtre de la Cité.

Paris now also has a municipally-run option for **on the water**, alongside all the numerous commercial operators: the **Voguéo hydrofoil**, which since 2013 has offered a regular service on the Seine between Pont de Suresnes and Vitry, thereby traversing the city from west to east.

Since 2012, electric cars have also been available in Paris: through **Autolib** a total of 3000 Blue Cars can be picked up from 1120 stations in the urban area, with an average of 6 vehicles per station. They are powered by a lithium-metal-polymer battery, have a range of 250 km/155 mi and are equipped with GPS. The vehicles have to be recharged after a maximum of eight hours.

Hybrid limousines are another environmentally friendly option: EcoVisit uses them to introduce the green side of Paris on a two-hour tour, which takes in for example the first office building in the world to be lit exclusively with LED lighting. And of course in the sphere of **sustainable tourism** there's also an option for romantics: enjoying the city to the sound of horses' hooves on a **carriage ride** offered by Paris Calèches, who will pick you up at the Eiffel Tower.

On your bike! – with the municipal Vélib bikes

ADRESSES

Segway Tours
Tel. 01 56 58 10 54
http://citysegwaytours.com
daily 4- and 5-hour tours as well as night tours with the 2-wheeled scooters, starting off at the Eiffel Tower; 4-hour tour from €85.

Fat Tire Bike Tour
24, Rue Edgar Faure
(15th arr.)
Tel. 01 56 58 10 54
http://fattirebiketours.com
4-hour daytime tour from 28 €

Vélib
Tel. 01 30 79 79 30
www.velib.paris.fr
Municipal bike rental system with stations in Paris and the Île-de-France. 24-hr subscription €1.70

in addition to the tariff for the number of hours used, so 2 hours for example would cost €1.70 standing charge + €7 usage. You can subscribe in advance online.

Voguéo
www.vogueo.fr
Municipal Seine boat service operating three lines:
Vitry-sur-Seine–Invalides,
Tour Eiffel–Austerlitz and
Suresnes–Musée d'Orsay

Autolib
www.autolib-paris.fr
The municipal electric cars basic cost €10 for 24 hours, €15 per week with additional rental cost of €7 for the first half hour and €8 for each subsequent half hour.

Touring the city the environmentally friendly way – by Segway

Ecovisit
www.ecovisitparis.com
Guided city tours with a green
theme in hybrid vehicles

Paris Calèches
www.pariscaleches.com
Wed–Sun 10am–7pm
Excursions in a nostalgic horse-
drawn carriage lasting from 30
min up to 2 hours, €140 per hour
– with champagne, red roses and
macarons from Ladurée on
request.

www.rollers-coquillages.org
Meeting point: Place de la Bastille
Every Sunday from 2.30pm a
great throng of Parisians zooms
through the city for 3 hours –
with the police on hand.

CITY WALKS
The Paris of the Parisians
► p. 19

Art Walk – Art Process
52, Rue Sedaine
(11th arr.)
Tel. 01 47 00 90 8
http://art-process.com
Métro: Voltaire
Insider tours through the art
metropolis

Awesome Guide
La Tuilerie, 71130 Clessy
Tel. 063 11 45 13
http://awesome-guide.com
Themed city tours

Les Promenades Urbaines
5 bis, Rue des Haudriettes
(3rd arr.)
Tel. 01 49 51 95 82
www.promenades-urbaines.com

Architects, town planners or
Parisian residents run tours
through their district three times a
month.

Paris Go
34, rue de l'Arcade
(8th arr.)
Tel. 01 53 30 74 40
www.parisgo.fr
Métro: Havre-Caumartin
Social gatherings and themed
tours of the capital, plus free MP3
tours

Paris Par Rues Méconnues
2/4, Square du Nouveau Belleville
(20. Arr.)
Tel. 01 42 79 81 71
http://paris-prm.com
Barbès, Belleville, Bercy – sightseeing by the people for the
people

Paris Walks
www.walkparis.com
Martin O'Grady offers
customized walking tours.

BUS TOURS
Paris Vision
214, Rue de Rivoli (1st arr.)
Tel. 01 44 55 60 00, http://fr.paris-
vision.com, Métro: Tuileries
Strolling in the Marais, Paris by
night, trips to Disneyland and
Versailles, or for €52 a 5-hour city
tour including Seine cruise – so
you can avoid the long queues in
front of the »Iron Lady«.

Cityrama
2, Rue des Pyramides
Tel. 01 44 55 61 00
www. pariscityrama.com
Métro: Louvre-Rivoli

MARCO ⊕ POLO TIP

! *Cast off!* **Insider Tip**

The 2-hour dinner cruise on the Seine aboard the historic vessel »Le Calife« promises and unforgettable evening. Cruise together with Captain Nicolas Gailledrat from Quai Malaquais adjacent to the Pont des Arts past the Seine islands to the Eiffel Tower and back. In the kitchen Dadi conjures up delicious 3-course menus: the Menu Gourmet costs €49 , the Menu Gastronomique €67. It is necessary to book at least eight days in advance (Métro: Louvre-Rivoli, Tel. 01 43 54 50 04, www.calife.com)

Hop-on-Hop-off- tours in open-topped double-decker bus and boat

Balabus
Tel. 08 36 68 77 14
http://www.ratp.fr/en/ratp/r_61597/visit-paris/
On Sunday and public holiday afternoons from 15 April to 30 Dec the Balabus connects the most important sights with 50 stops on the route from Puteaux to La Défense and Gare de Lyon.

Montmartrobus
Also offered by the RATP is the Montmartrobus, a really relaxed way of discovering the famous butte and its environs. Place Pigalle to Place du Tertre, 7.30am–12.50am, complete circuit approx. 15 minutes.

Cars Rouges
17, Quai de Grenelle (15th arr.)
Tel. 01 53 95 39 53, adults €29

www.carsrouges.com
Red double-decker buses, which operate daily from 9.30am–7pm between the Eiffel Tower and Notre Dame. Journey time 2 hours 15 minutes, departure: every 10 minutes in summer, every 20 minutes in winter.

Paris L'Open Tour
13, Rue Auber (9th arr.)
Tel. 01 42 66 56 56
www.parisopentour.com
Day ticket €31, 2 days €34
Open-topped double-deckers operate hop-on/hop-off tours along four routes with 50 stops.

Not a Tourist Destination Tours
32, Rue Pastourelle (3rd arr.)
Tel. 01 71 50 97 97
www.notatouristdestination.com
Themed guided tours for children, teenagers, shopaholics and night owls – all tours €110.

WATERBUS AND CRUISES (SEINE AND CANALS)
Batobus
Port de la Bourdonnais (7th arr.)
Tel.*0825 05 01 01
www.batobus.com
April /May, Sept/Oct daily 10am–7pm, June–Aug till 9.30pm, Nov–March 10.30am–4.30pm the waterbus runs every 15–30 minutes between Tour Eiffel, Musée d'Orsay, St-Germain-des-Prés, Notre-Dame, Hôtel de Ville, Louvre, Champs-Elysées and Jardin des Plantes. Tickets for 1, 2 or 5 days – day ticket from €15 per adult, 2 days €18 available in advance online.

Bateaux Mouches

Tel. 01 42 25 96 10
www.bateaux-mouches.fr
Cruise trips from Port de la
Conférence/Pont de l'Alma
April–Sept 10.15am–11pm,
otherwise till 9pm. For more than
60 years poets, romantics, lovers
and the simply curious have been
exploring Paris from these restaurant and cruise boats – 1 hour 10
minute tour
Adults €12.50, children €5.50.

Bateaux Vedettes du Pont-Neuf

Square du Vert-Galant (1st arr.)
Tel. 01 46 33 98 38
www.vedettesdupontneuf.com
Métro: Pont-Neuf
Daily 10.30am–8pm. One-hour
cruise to the Eiffel Tower, dinner
cruise and excursion along the
Canal St-Martin. Departure from
next to Pont Neuf. One-hour
cruise adults €13, children €7

Canauxrama

13, Quai de la Loire (19th arr.)
Tel. 01 42 39 15 00
www.canauxrama.com
Cruises on the Canal St-Martin,
the Canal St-Denis, on the Seine
and the Marne leaving from the
jetties in the Bassin de la Villette
and the Port de l'Arsenal. 2.5-
hour cruise along the Canal St-
Martin adults €16, children €8.50.

Paris Canal

Tel. 01 42 40 96 97
www.pariscanal.com
Setting off at 9.30am the boat
takes 3 hours to cruise from the
Musée d'Orsay along the Seine
and the Canal St-Martin to Parc
de la Villette, with the return journey leaving at 2.30pm (adults
€19, children €12–16). They also
offer cruises along the Canal de
l'Ourq, Canal Saint-Denis and the
Marne.

Bateaux restaurants de la Marina de Paris

Marina de Paris, Bercy
Tel. 01 43 43 40 30
www.marina-de-paris.com
Métro: Assemblée Nationale,
Solférino, RER: Musée d'Orsay
Lunch and dinner cruises on the
Seine from Quai Anatole France at
Port de Solférino to the Statue of
Liberty. If you want to avoid long
queues at the Musée d'Orsay,
from Fri–Sun you can book lunch
on the Seine with a visit to the
museum included in the price (departure 12.45pm, duration 1 hour
15 min, from €36); daily dinner
cruises at 6.45 and 9.15pm, from
€65.

TOURS

A tour by tour bus will highlight Paris's most important attractions. But it's more exciting to explore the city on foot. Here are some suggestions with tips for some nice walks and excursions hat you'll never forget

Tours Through Paris

Two walks through the centre either side of the Seine reveal the whole essence of Paris – emblematic, magnificent and charming

Tour 1   Royal Paris
This tour traces the city's history and encounters many highlights of metropolis on the Seine.
▶page 165

Tour 2   Rive Gauche: artists and scholars
The left bank of the Seine has for centuries been at the heart of the city's intellectual life
▶page 167

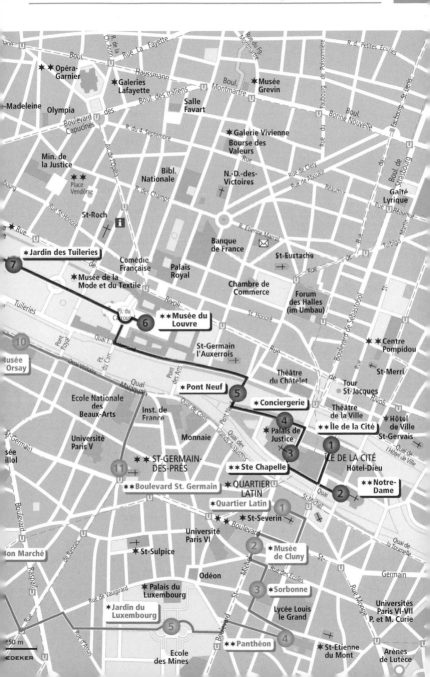

Rue La Fayette

Boul.
★★ Opéra-
Garnier
Haussmann

★ Galeries
Lafayette
Boul. des Italiens

★ Musée
Grevin

Salle
Favart

Olympia

Boulevard
Capucines

★ Galerie Vivienne
Bourse des
Valeurs

Min. de
la Justice

Bibl.
Nationale

N.-D.-des-
Victoires

Place
Vendôme

St-Roch

Banque
de France

St-Eustache

★ Jardin des Tuileries

Comédie
Française

Palais
Royal

Chambre de
Commerce

Forum
des Halles
(im Umbau)

★ Musée de la
Mode et du Textile

★★ Musée du
Louvre

Tuileries

★★ Centre
Pompidou

St-Merri

Musée
Orsay

St-Germain
l'Auxerrois

Théâtre
du Châtelet

Tour
St-Jacques

Ecole Nationale
des
Beaux-Arts

★ Pont Neuf

Inst.
France

★ Conciergerie

Théâtre
de la Ville

★ Hôtel
de Ville
St-Gervais

Université
Paris V

Monnaie

★ Palais de
Justice

★★ Île de la Cité

★★ ST-GERMAIN-
DES-PRÉS

ÎLE DE LA CITÉ
Hôtel-Dieu

★★ Ste Chapelle

★★ Boulevard St. Germain

QUARTIER
LATIN

★★ Notre-
Dame

★ Quartier Latin

Bon Marché

★★ St-Severin

Université
Paris VI

★ St-Sulpice

★ Musée
de Cluny

Odéon

★ Sorbonne

★ Palais du
Luxembourg

Lycée Louis
le Grand

★ Jardin du
Luxembourg

Universités
Paris VI-VII
P. et M. Curie

★★ Panthéon

★ St-Etienne
du Mont

Ecole
des Mines

Arènes
de Lutèce

250 m

EDEKER

Tours Through Paris

A shopping tour through the city or following in the footsteps of the French Revolution

©BAEDEKER

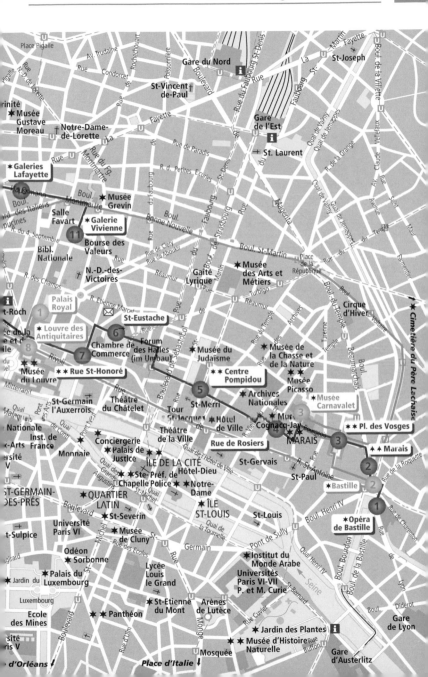

Getting Around in Paris

In this age of Eurostar and cheap flights a day trip to Paris is possible, of course. But in order to take in the most important sights, to have time for shopping and to enjoy a little of the Parisian »savoir vivre«., you should plan in at least three days. The best way to do this is **on foot**. Paris is an inviting city for strolling around – and everywhere there are places to rest and watch the world go by: countless pavement cafés, the quays alongside the Seine, romantic corners and secluded gardens. In the centre, everything is much closer together than many visitors might at first expect. Almost all sights can also be reached quickly and easily by **Métro**. But it's best not to find yourself alone in the tunnel labyrinth of the Métro late at night – take a bus or a taxi instead. A car is unnecessary in Paris. There are traffic snarl-ups everywhere, parking spaces are extremely scarce and for those caught parking illegally the fines are exorbitant. Instead you can take a Vélib, a public rented bicycle, easily procured by credit card from one of 1200 bicycle stations across the city. And one of the nicest ways of seeing Paris is by taking a cruise along the River Seine.

A boat trip on the Seine is always an event

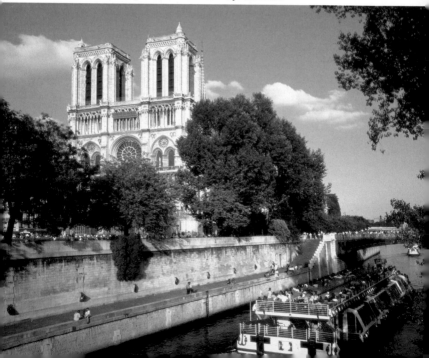

Royal Paris   Tour 1

Start and finish: from Île de la Cité to Place Vendôme
Duration: 1 day

This walk traces the history of Paris and at the same time encounters many of the city's highlights, including a first impression from the tower of the venerable Notre-Dame cathedral.

Starting point is the Cité Métro station on ❶ **∗∗Île de la Cité**, the geographic as well as historic centre of Paris. This was the heart of ancient Lutetia and the birthplace of the French royal power. The island is also the location of the world famous crowd-puller, the Gothic ❷**∗∗cathedral of Notre-Dame**. To avoid too much congestion you should start out early and aim to be in the cathedral by 9am. Make sure you also go up the tower, take a walk in the church garden and visit the crypt of Notre-Dame. To the north of the cathedral a plaque at 10, Rue Chanoinesse recalls two famous lovers, Abélard and Héloïse/Pierre Trimouillat [Ed: CHECK: I think only plaque to Trimouillat at this address??). The island's second highlight is the two-storey ❸**∗∗Sainte-Chapelle** with its amazing stained glass windows. The ❹**∗Conciergerie** was where Danton, Robespierre and Marie-Antoinette were held captive during the French Revolution, before being led to the guillotine. Another Parisian gem is the little Flower Market on the Île de la Cité, which on Sundays is transformed into a bird market. Now you deserve a little break: the little Quai-Quai seafood restaurant at the westernmost tip of the island does delicious tuna ratatouille, garlic lobster and grilled calamari on fennel complete with a view over the Seine (74, Quai des Orfèvres, Tel. 01 46 33 69 75, www.quaiquai-restaurant.com, AA).

Highlights of Tour 1

▶ **Île de la Cité**
with Notre-Dame Cathedral and Ste-Chapelle

▶ **Louvre**
the world's biggest art museum

▶ **Champs-Elysées**
shopping and champagne

▶ **Arc de Triomphe**
magnificent views from the top

Cross the oldest and probably most beautiful of the bridges over the Seine with the misleading name of ❺ **∗Pont Neuf** to the right bank (rive droîte), passing the bouquinistes, the antiquarian booksellers of Quai du Louvre, who sell old tomes and arty postcards.

The Louvre, the world's biggest art museum, is a must

The **❻** ✳✳**Louvre**; once the royal palace, has been a repository for the art of all eras and cultures since 1793. It is better to save a detailed visit to the world's biggest art museum for another day – today enjoy its architectural highlights such as the Lescot façade, the colonnade by Perrault and the enormous glass pyramid by I.M. Pei., beneath which, next to the Louvre information centre, you will find a shopping centre including an Apple store and a branch of Starbucks.

Beyond the Carrousel du Louvre triumphal arch is the **❼** ✳**Jardin des Tuileries**. Men meet up here to play boule, children bounce on the trampolines or ride on the vintage carousel. Anyone wanting to rest the legs can take one of the easy chairs surrounding the pool. Or you can fortify yourself with a p'tit noir and pain choc on the terrace of Café Renard in the shade of old chestnut trees before visiting the **❾** ✳**Orangerie** where Monet's eight murals of water lilies are not to be missed. A few steps further on, the traffic zooms around **❿** ✳✳**Place de la Concorde**. Next to the souvenir stalls horse-drawn carriages await. Climb aboard and take a ride along the much celebrated **⓫** ✳✳**Champs-Elysées**, elegant boulevard and the shop window of the Grande Nation. Get of at No. 99 where a glass of champagne on the terrace of ✳**Fouquet's** is part and parcel of the Parisian savoir vivre. Finally we climb the 284 steps of the steep spiral staircase to the viewing platform on top of the **⓭** ✳✳**Arc de Triomphe**, which Napoleon had erected in honour of his victorious armies. Gaze along the twelve avenues that fan out from the arch, and from historic Paris in the east to the gleaming business district of ✳**La Défense** in the west.

Rive Gauche: Artists and Scholars Tour 2

Start and finish: St-Michel
Duration: at least 3 hours

The left bank of the Seine has been the home of intellectuals for centuries. It was the cradle of Paris's university; Symbolists and Dadaists painted here; Sartre and Beauvoir debated with kindred spirits in the literary cafés of Saint-Germain-des-Prés.

The tour starts at the Métro station Saint-Michel, where, outside the summer months, you are in the midst of the student bustle of the ❶ *** Quartier Latin**. In the ❷ *** palace of the bishops of Cluny**, today an impressive museum of the Middle Ages, the ruins of Roman baths testify to the ancient origins of Paris. The ❸ *** Sorbonne**, which is situated to the south, was founded as long ago as the mid-13th century. If it's lunchtime already you can join students and professors and eat at the »Polidor« restaurant at 46, Rue Monsieur-le-Prince, which has been on the go since 1845 and serves such typical dishes as confit de canard, rognons (kidney) and steak tartare. Walk along Rue Cujas to the ❹ ****Panthéon**, the last resting place of famous French citizens such as Voltaire, Victor Hugo and Marie Curie. Afterwards have a rest from sightseeing in Paris's most beautiful park, ❺ *** Jardin de Luxembourg** with its idyllic corners, the hidden Fontaine de Medici and games of chess in the open air. Thus recovered you'll be fit for some power shopping à la Paris. In the oldest Parisian department store of *** Bon Marché** the Maitres d'Hôtes can read your wishes from your lips and the in-house delivery service will bring your purchases to the hotel, while in the luxury delicatessen department »Grande Epicerie de Paris« you procure some typical treats for a picnic in the sculpture garden of the picnic in the sculpture garden of the ****Musée Rodin**. There you relax next to shining bronze copy of Rodin's »Penseur«, standing out against the blue sky. Behind rises the ❾ *** church of Les Invalides** under whose resplendent dome Napoleon found his last resting place. Now take a stroll through the park to the mag-

Highlights of Tour 2

- **Lively Quartier Latin**

- **Panthéon**
  Mausoleum of the Grande Nation

- **Musée Rodin**
  Picnic next to th scupltures

- **Church of Les Invalides**
  With the tomb of Napoleon I

- **Musée d'Orsay**
  Treasure trove of Impressionist art

- **Saint-Germain-des-Prés**
  Meeting place of literary greats

Art galleries, jazz clubs, cafés and design shops – whatever you are looking for, you will find it in Saint-Germain-des-Prés

nificent ⑩ *Pont Alexandre III and then along the banks of the Seine to the ⑪ **Musée d'Orsay, whose collection of Impressionist paintings is an absolute must for art lovers. In oder to avoid a long queue you should definitiely buy your tickets in advance. The tour around the arty Rive Gauche ends along the main artery of the district, the ⑫ **Boulevard de Saint-Germain-des-Prés, Here, overlooking the Eglise Saint-Germain-des-Prés, three brasseries became the meeting place of the intellectual scene: »Café de Flore«, »Les Deux Magots« and »Brasserie Lipp«, where Ernest Hemingway loved the beer and the potato salad. Do as he did and have yourself a hearty meal. Bon appétit!

Tour 3 Fashionable Rendezvous and Glamorous Shopping

Start and finish: Place de la Bastille to Bourse Métro-Station
Duration: at least 5 hours

This walk is recommended for a wonderful afternoon of strolling around, people-watching and shopping. It leads from the Marais district past trendy shops and chic boutiques to the magnificent department stores and shopping arcades along Boulevard Haussmann.

The shopping tour begins at ❶ *Opéra de la Bastille, a boldly designed landmark that helped spark a revival in the fortunes of eastern Paris. To the west of Place de la Bastille is the ❷ **Marais, once the abode the residence of the aristocrats, then home to Jewish immigrants and now a lively gay community. Many of the fine aristocratic palaces have been beautifully restored and opened to visitors as museums. The nicest ones surround the magical ❸ ****Place des Vosges** with art galleries and cafés under the arcades. At No. 15 is Damman Frères, one of the best tea merchants in the city. Inspector Maigret liked to dine at »Ma Bourgogne« next door (No. 19, ► tip p. 298).

Around the corner lies ❹ ***Rue des Rosiers**, the heart of the Jewish quarter with its small synagogues, kosher restaurants and bakeries, and Hebrew bookshops. It is a quiet place on Sabbath (Saturday), but the area buzzes on Sundays until late at night. Expensive boutiques, art galleries and shops for gays, too, have now established themselves in the former ghetto. Rue Rambuteau leads directly to the famous »culture factory« of the ❺ ****Centre Pompidou**, whose forecourt is an open-air stage for street artists. Continuing through Les Halles, where the city's ancient market halls once stood next to ❽ **St Eustache church** and where a brand new Forum des Halles shopping centre is due to be completed at the by 2016, it is not far to the legendary fashion street of ❼ ****Rue du Faubourg St-Honoré**. Besides the luxury stores of John Galliano (No. 384), Tommy Hilfiger (No. 368) and Hugo Boss (No. 372), there are plenty of accessories boutiques ranging from Chopard (No. 420) to Longchamp (No. 75). Do not miss No. 213: even Karl Lagerfeld rates the Colette concept store with its mineral water bar as a pioneer of avant-garde upscale fashion and lifestyle.

If the budget allows, turn right at Rue de Castiglione to arrive at ❾ ****Place Vendôme** where in 1838 Christofle Charvet opened the world's first specialist shop for bespoke shirts. Rue de la Paix, which is lined by upmarket boutiques, then leads directly to the splendid ❿ ***Opéra Garnier**. Marvel at the magnificent venue from the terrace of the ***Café de la Paix**, where a

Highlights of Tour 3

► **Place des Vosges**
The heart of the Marais

► **Centre Pompidou**
»Culture factory«

► **Rue St-Honoré**
Designer fashion

► **Place Vendôme**
Luxury shopping

► **Boulevard Haussmann**
Elegant Belle Epoque consumer temples

designer tart will provide you with the energy required for the last leg of this shopping marathon: the stroll through department stores and arcades of the Belle Epoque on the Boulevard Haussmann. The shopping list includes Au Printemps, the ⓫ ***Les Galeries Lafayette**, and the ⓬ ***Galerie Vivienne** near the Bourse Métro station.

Tour 4 # In the Footsteps of the French Revolution

Start and destination: Palais Royal to Place de la Concorde
Duration: at least 5 hours

No popular uprising has changed the world has as much as the French Revolution, and after a revolt of the citizens no city has changed its appearance so much as Paris. For the journey through Paris in the years 1789 to 1794 it's best to rent a Vélib bicycle. But all the destinations can also be reached by Métro.

The French Revolution began in the ❶ **Palais Royal** (Métro: Louvre). In 1784 Louis Philippe d'Orléans opened the former residence of the Sun King to traders and farmers, and it wasn't long before the palace was transformed into a popular recreation and entertainment venue – aided by the fact that the police did not have any access. The Jacobins regularly met up in the Café du Foy under the arcades. And this was where, on 13 July 1789, a young journalist named Camille Desmoulins jumped on the table and urged guests to take up arms and storm the Bastille. Shortly thereafter the National Guard moved in and stormed the café, which later became the literary meeting place »Chez Bignon« but no longer exists.

But the rebels were already on their way to the ❷ * **Bastille** and 14 July 1789 they successfully stormed the state prison, whose location is today marked by the **Colonne de Juillet**. Take a leisurely stroll through the streets to the east of Place de la Bastille and discover the charm of the erstwhile »Bastoche« quarter, which was rediscovered by bohemians in the 1980s. Paintings, models and contemporary documents on the storming of the Bastille, as well as busts and portraits of Louis XVI, Marie-Antoinette and Robespierre are on display at the ❸ * **Musée Carnavalet** in the Marais district to the northeast of Place des Vosges. Then deposit your Vélib at the station outside the Chemin-Vert metro station and take the Métro to the Ecole Militaire station at ❹ **Champs de Mars**. The stormy upheavals of 1789 were followed by the moderate phase of the Revolution. Good harvests, a new electoral law and the Declaration of the Rights of Man calmed the people, who in 1790 marked the anniversary of the storming of the Bastille with a »Federation Day« on the Champs de Mars together er with 60,000 National Guardsmen.

Today, the Champ de Mars is a popular place for large and small events. The French love picnicking here, with the view of the ❺ ** **Eiffel Tower**. Do as they do! Just a few steps north of the city's main landmark at Quai Branly you can borrow another Vélib and **cycle along the Seine** back to the year 1791, when France received a new constitution based on a sovereign nation with equal representation chosen by the people, abolishing feudalism. The king was horrified and hatched plans for himself and his family to escape from the palace they had occupied since being forced to relocate from Versailles to Paris: the Tuileries. The site of the royal city palace, which was destroyed in the 1871 uprising of the Paris Commune, is now taken up by the beautiful ❻ *Jardin des Tuileries. The royal family's attempt to flee got them only as far as Varennes near the Belgian border, where they were arrested on 21 July 1791. Their return to the Tuileries was a major event in Paris, with the curious even climbing on the roofs to get a better view of the spectacle. But the renewed house arrest for the ruling family would no longer satisfy the people. On 10 August 1792 insurgents stormed the palace. Louis XVI, Marie Antoinette and their children were brought to the temple prison on Rue du Temple in the Marais. On 21 September 1792 the King was formally

Highlights of Tour 4

► **Bastille**
Entertainment district with a past

► **Musée Carnavalet**
The city's history

► **Picnic by the Eiffel Tower**

► **Tuileries**
A green open space full of history

► **Louvre des Antiquaires**
The finest French antiques

deposed and a republic proclaimed. Nine weeks later, the trial of the king took place in the erstwhile royal riding school; today a plaque in the ❼ **Rue de Rivoli** marks the site of the Salle de Manège, which was destroyed in 1803.

For those who would now like some exquisite shopping, the ❾ * **Louvre des Antiquaires** shopping arcade contains 250 shops selling all kinds of antique items – furniture, fabrics, silverware, textiles and paintings. On the morning of 21 January 1793 the French ruler, who had initially embraced the goals of the Revolution was beheaded on the then Place de la Révolution under his civil name of Louis Capet by the executioner Charles Henri Sanson. On 16 October of the same year, his wife Marie Antoinette was guillotined on the same square, now known as ❿ **Place de la Concorde**. However, it wasn't just the hated nobles and aristocrats who ended up losing their heads here, but also Danton, Robespierre and even Joseph Ignace Guillotin, inventor of the notorious killing machine. The Revolution devoured its children. In 1795 – much to the regret of the populace – the beheadings were stopped, and Paris's largest square reverted to its original name and the one it still bears to day: Unity Square.

Trips

It takes barely half an hour on the suburban train RER C from Paris to ▶ Versailles, the magnificent palace of Louis XIV, which like the basilica of ▶ Saint-Denis about 10km/6mi north of Paris is a UNESCO World Heritage site. ▶ Disneyland Paris in Marne-La-Vallée 30km/20mi to the east provides a journey into a magical fairytale world. And there are many more excursion destinations besides.

* Meudon

Illustrious artists, politicians and musicians made their home 9km/6mi southwest of Paris in **Meudon** high above the Seine. The poets Ronsard, Balzac and Céline lived here, and in 1841 Wagner composed *The Flying Dutchman* in Meudon. From 1929 to 1941 Hans Arp and Sophie Taeuber lived in the studio they designed themselves, which was has been transformed into a **museum** by the **Fondation Arp** and in 2012 was equipped with a library devoted to works about Arp, Taeuber and their artistic epoch. Auguste Rodin spent the last 20 years of his life in the **Villa des Brillants**, which was renovated in 2010; he was buried there in the park together with his partner Rose Beuret. In the museum you can admire Rodin's busts of Balzac and Hugo as well as studies for the *Gates of Hell*.

❶ www.ville-meudon.fr; **Fondation Arp**: 21, Rue des Châtaigners, Clamart, Fri– Sun 2pm–6pm, adults €6, www.fondationarp.org
Villa des Brillants: 19, Ave Auguste Rodin, RER Line C to Meudon Val Fleury, then bus 169 to the Paul Bert stop, May– Sept Fri– Sun 1pm–6pm, adults €6, garden €1, www.musee-rodin.fr

* Sèvres
– Cité de la céramique

In the neighbouring town, the museum of the famous **china manufactory**, established in Vincennes in 1738 and transferred to **Sèvres** in 1756, displays the finest porcelain, Middle Eastern ceramics and faïences.

❶ 2, Place de la Manufacture, Métro Line 9 to Pont de Sèvres; daily except Tue 10am–5pm, adults €6, guided tours 1.30pm, 2pm and 3pm; pottery courses take place once a month, www.sevresciteceramique.fr.

* Château de Malmaison

Renovated in 2012, this small palace where **Napoleon** and his first wife, **Joséphine de Beauharnais**, spent their happiest years, is situated 16km/10mi west of Paris and has been a national museum since 1906. Malmaison was built in 1620 in the in early Baroque style; Joséphine having acquired the property in 1799. After their divorce the empress led a secluded life here until her death in 1814. Each year on the anniversary of her death on 29 May a concert is held to commemorate the empress. Napoleon III purchased the palace of his grandmother and had it restored in Empire style. On the ground floor are the Golden Drawing Room, the music room dating from 1812, the study and the library; on the first floor are the chambers of the emperor and his spouse. Visitors can also see the collections in the Osiris Pavilion.

❶ Avenue du Château de Malmaison, RER Line A to Grande Arche de la Défense, then bus 258 to the palace; Mon, Wed–Fri 10am–12.30m and 1.30pm–5.15pm, Sat and Sun 10am–12.30pm and 1.30–5.45pm, April–Sept 30 min. longer, adults €6, April–Oct park additional €1,50, www.chateau-malmaison.fr.

With the RER A train this old royal residence can be reached in 25 minutes from Charles de Gaulle-Etoile. Even on a Sunday morning it is possible to go shopping in the boutiques and antique shops of this pleasant provincial town 20km/12mi west of Paris. All that remains of the 12th-century castle are the fortified tower and the high Gothic Ste-Chapelle. Louis XIV was born in the Renaissance palace in 1638; the building has been the **National Archaeological Museum** since the time of Napoleon. In the **studio of the Symbolist Maurice Denis** works by Paul Gauguin and Pierre Bonnard are also exhibited. In 2012, St-Germain-en-Laye celebrated the 150th birthday of the composer **Claude Debussy** (1862–1918) who was born at 38, Rue du Pain.

St-Germain-en-Laye

❶ www.saintgermainenlaye.fr; **Musée d'Archéologie Nationale:** daily except Tue 9am–5.15pm, May–Sept Sat and Sun 10am–6.15pm, adults €6, www.musee-antiquitesnationales.fr.
Maison Natale Claude Debussy: 38, Rue du Pain, Tue–Fri 2.30pm–5.45pm, Sat 10.30am–12.30pm and 2.30pm–5.30pm, admission free
Musée Maurice Denis: 2 bis, Rue Maurice Denis, Tue–Fri 10am–5.30pm, Sat and Sun 10am–6.30pm, adults €4.50, www.musee-mauricedenis.fr.

The **Rococo château** in Champs-sur-Marne 18km/11mi east of Paris, which was furnished by Madame de Pompadour, the favourite of Louis XV, is a wonderful example of a »Louis Quinze« interior. The film *Dangerous Liaisons* starring John Malkovich and Glenn Close and directed by Stephen Frears was shot here.

Champs-sur-Marne

❶ RER Line A in the direction of Chessy Marne la Vallée to Noisiel, then bus 220 to the palace: Jan weekends only 10am to 12.15pm and 1.30pm to 5pm, Feb–May and Oct–Dec daily except Tue 10am to 12.15pm and 1.30pm to 5pm, June–Sept Mon and Wed–Fri 10am to 12.15pm and 1.30pm to 6pm, Sat and Sun 10am–6pm, park closes 30 min after the château; adults €7.50, under 18s free, http://champs-sur-marne.monuments-nationaux.fr

SIGHTS FROM A TO Z

Paris combines luxury, sensational museums and stately pomp, promises elegant shopping arcades, romantic squares and atmospheric bistros. It is exciting, forward-looking and enchantingly nostalgic at the same time – it is the very heart of the Grande Nation.

** Arc de Triomphe · Place de l'Etoile

✦ **D 4**

Location: Place Charles de Gaulle (8th arr.)
Métro station: Charles-de-Gaulle–Etoile
Internet: http://arc-de-triomphe.monuments-nationaux.fr

The end of the Champs-Elysées is marked by the mighty triumphal arch on Place de l'Etoile. The Arc de Triomphe was built in honour of the French Revolutionary Army. In 1806, Napoleon commissioned the architect Chalgrin with its construction but never lived to see its completion in 1836.

Arc de Triomphe
The reliefs on the east and west façades of the 50m/164ft-high and 45m/147ft-wide arch tell of the departure and glorious return of the victorious French armies. The side facing the Champs-Elysées bears a relief by François Rude of the departure of the volunteers to fight against Prussia in 1792, commonly called the »Marseillaise«. The inside walls of the monument are decorated with the names of more than 660 generals and over 100 battles.

The platform at the top provides fantastic views of Paris and the twelve avenues radiating from Place de l'Etoile. A museum beneath the platform documents the construction history of the arch and the Napoleonic era. Every year at the end of July the turn around the Arc de Triomphe onto the Champs-Elysées marks the final sprint in the Tour de France.

❶ Oct–March: 10am–10.30pm
April–Sept: 10am–11pm; Adults €9.50,
tours €13–16, under 18s and EU
ciitzens 18-25 free

The first **Tomb of the Unknown Soldier** was dedicated beneath the Arc de Triomphe in 1921 as a memorial to the First World War – the flame is re-ignited every evening at 6.30pm. The fallen of both world wars are commemorated each year on 11 November, the anniversary of the armistice of 1918.

? MARCO POLO INSIGHT

Aerial acrobatics

For the victory parade on the Champs-Elysées on 14 July 1919, the military command had ordered the airmen to march, like the infantry. The »heroes of the skies« took this as an affront and decided that one of them should fly through the Arc de Triomphe during the parade. It didn't happen because the chosen pilot was killed in a practice flight, but the young fighter aviator Charles Godefroy volunteered to perform the feat after the event. On 7 August he duly flew his »Nieuport 11« biplane through the great arch. The width of the arch is 14.60 m, so there wasn't much clearance. The stunt was filmed and appeared in all the newspapers, and in the end Godefroy got away with just a warning.

Napoleons triumphal arch is the is the centre of Place de l'Etoile

Officially, the traffic-congested **Place de l'Etoile** (star square) has born the name of the former French president Charles de Gaulle since 1970. The twelve distinctive buildings that surround the square are the work of the architect Hittorff; the twelve streets are named after illustrious men of the Empire period.

Place Charles de Gaulle (Place de l'Etoile)

In the 17th century the Dutch humanist Olfert Dapper was one of the first people to become interested in the **art of Africa**. The museum named after him at 35, Rue Paul Valéry presents the hitherto little appreciated, but incredibly expressive culture of sub-Saharan Africa and the Caribbean in all its forms, including sculptures, paintings and photographs, dance, theatre and music.

Musée Dapper

❶ Mon, Wed, Fri–Sun 11am–7pm, www.dapper.com.fr, adults €6, under 26s and last Wed in month free

✶ Bastille

✈ J/K 6

Location: City centre east (3rd arr.)
Métro station: Bastille

»Is that a revolt?« the naïve, procrastinating King Louis XVI is supposed to have asked when news was brought to him of the storming of the Bastille. »No, sire,« replied one of his dukes, »that is a revolution!«

Liberté, Egalité, Fraternité

In 1789 world history was written in Paris. The French Revolution paved the way for a modern nation state founded on the principles of democracy. Napoleon Bonaparte exported the ideals of the Revolution to the European countries he conquered, where they are still recognizable in the constitutions and legislation.

▶ Symbols of the revolution

Marianne
Since the Revolution the »Marianne« has been a national emblem of the French Republic. Her bust is on display in every town hall in the country. Every four years a jury of mayors decides which French woman should be the model for a new sculpture. Famous sitters have included Brigitte Bardot, Catherine Deneuve and Sophie Marceau.

14 July 1789:
the storming of the Bastille ...
... was at least as much about getting hold of weapons as freeing prisoners. It is considered mark the beginning of the Revolution and today remains France's most important national holiday.

▶ The most important events

1789
States General

- Summoning of the States General (Nobility, Clergy and Third Estate/commoners) to Versailles
- Third Estate declares itself to be the National Assembly with constitutional powers and swears »*not to separate until the constitution of the kingdom is established*« (Tennis Court Oath)

1790 New Constitution
1792 Republic

- France becomes a constitutional monarchy, oath to the constitution by Louis XVI

Human Rights

- Election of the National Convention
- Proclamation of the First Republic

1793
Revolutionary
Tribunal

- Execution of Louis XVI
- Establishment of the R Revolutionary Tribunal
- Founding of the Committee of Public safety by Danton, Saint-Just and Robespierre

| ▶ Timeline | 1789 | 1790 | 1791 | 1792 | 1793 | 1794 | 1 |

Republic

Absolutism

▶ **Guillotine – »The National Razor«**

The National Assembly issued a decree that the guillotine should be the only instrument of execution. In the 49 days of the Great Terror of 1794 alone, 1376 condemned were beheaded on the Place de la Revolution, the present-day Place de la Concorde.

▶ **Prominent victims**

21 January 1793
Louis XVI,
King

16 October 1793
Marie-Antoinette,
Queen

12 November 1793
Jean-Sylvain Bailly,
Mayor of Paris

5 April 1794
Georges Jacques Danton,
President of the Committee of
Public Safety

28 July 1794
Maximilien de Robespierre,
Leader of the Jacobins and
Revolutionary Tribunal

It is estimated that 10,000 people died by the guillotine between 1793 and 1794. The death penalty in France was only abolished in 1981, and has been forbidden by the constitution since 2007.

10,000

©BAEDEKER

— Jacobin hat

1795 Dissolution of the National Convention and new constitution

• Government by the Directory
• Increasing influence from generals like Napoleon

New Constitution

1799 Coup d'État

• Napoleon Bonaparte becomes first consul
• Revolution is declared as finished

1804 Reign of Napoleon begins

• Napoleon crowns himself Emperor

Great Terror

n of terror by acobins led by spierre

| 1797 | 1798 | 1799 | 1800 | 1801 | 1802 | 1803 | 1804 |

The state prison of absolutism

Today, the name of the square is all that remains of the notorious state prison and hated symbol of absolutist power. After being stormed on 14 July 1789, the Bastille was completely demolished within a few months. The stones were used for part of the bridge on ▶Place de la Concorde. The giant mosaic in the Bastille métro station is a free interpretation of the flag of the Revolution in the national colours of blue, white and red that Odile Jacquot created in 1988. The ▶Musée Carnavalet has a model of the former Bastille.

History of construction

The »little bastion« was begun in 1370 under Charles V, who wanted to strengthen the walls of the new city by adding a fortress. His successors expanded the bulwark until by 1382 it was a massive defensive ring, which, despite its more than 20m/66ft-high fortified towers, offered little protection – the city was captured on six of the seven occasions when it was besieged during the French Wars of Religion. Cardinal Richelieu, minister under Louis XIII, declared the building to be a **state prison**. The number of prisoners was always very low, however – there were 40 under Louis XIV and just 19 persons were imprisoned under Louis XVI; most of them were high-ranking personages, few of whom had been jailed for a crime. Most were considered to be malcontents, free-thinkers and liberals, who were often incarcerated simply by royal decree (lettre de cachet) without trial The imprisonment was not always unpleasant. A number of the »guests« had their own servants and were allowed to receive visitors – the prisoner Cardinal Rohan even arranged to have

»Les Grandes Marches« near Opéra Bastille is a gourmet's place

a banquet for 20 guests. Voltaire, who had infuriated the government with his satirical attacks on politics and religion, also served time there (in 1717) and wrote his *Oedipus* during his detention. Other prisoners were Mirabeau, Fouquet and and the Marquis de Sade, who had to be transferred to an insane asylum. When the French Revolution began on 14 July 1789, with the storming of the Bastille, the liberators found only seven prisoners whom they could free from their cells: five were petty criminals, the two others mentally deranged. But the triumphant mob celebrated them anyway.

François René, Vicomte de **Châteaubriand** described the storming of the Bastille in his *Mémoires d'Outre-Tombe* published in 1848: »As a spectator, I witnessed this attack on a few cripples and a timid governor; if the gates had been kept closed, the crowd could never have entered the fortress. I saw two or three cannon shots fired, not by the cripples, but by the Gardes Françaises, who had climbed up to the towers. De Launay, the governor, was dragged from his hiding place, and after suffering a thousand outrages was butchered on the steps of the Hôtel de Ville; Flesselles, the provost of the merchants of Paris, had his brains blown out: this is the spectacle that the heartless onlookers enjoyed so much. In the midst of these murders, they indulged in wild orgies, as in the street battles in Rome under Otho and Vitellius. Happily drunk and proclaimed the conquerors of the Bastille in the taverns, they were driven about in carriages, escorted by prostitutes and sans-culottes, who were just beginning their reign« *The storming of the Bastille*

Like no other event, the annual celebration on **14 July** commemorates the independence of the French state. Dances and street festivals are held in every quarter of Paris with parades and firework displays (▶p. 119). *National holiday*

At the middle of Place de la Bastille is the 51m/167ft-high **Colonne de Juillet** with a gilded **statue of the spirit of liberty** by Dumont (▶picture p. 10). The graciously balancing figure is in memory of the republicans killed during the July Revolution of 1830 that brought the Citizen King, Louis-Philippe, to power. Four French cockerels and a relief of a lion on the pedestal symbolize the free people. There is a good view of the opera house from the observation platform. *Colonne de Juillet (July Column)*

✱ OPÉRA BASTILLE

President Mitterrand inaugurated the opera house on Place de la Bastille on 14 July 1989. It was designed by the Uruguay-born Canadian architect **Carlos Ott**. The prestigious building with its curves and right angles covers an area of almost 16ha/40 acres. The design of its glass façade with its stepped, latticed square structure has a cool and functional appearance. The bright foyer forms a semi-circle around the main auditorium, whose tent-like illuminated ceiling harmonizes with rows of white seats. At the base of the steps visitors are greeted by a colourful statue of the female Genius by Niki de St-Phalle. The opera house auditorium seats 2,700 and its stage is surrounded by five auxiliary stages. The view of the stage and the acoustics are excellent. The complex also boasts an amphitheatre, a studio, a rehearsal stage and a boutique.

❶ Viewing daily 10am–5pm, adults €9; tickets in France tel. 08 92 89 90 90 or online at www.operadeparis.fr. Tickets at €5 for the standing-room only section behind the orchestra, from where one can see and hear everything very well, are available only at the box office.

Les Grandes Marches   In the €€/ €€€ brasserie next to the opera house Jacky Ribault spoils his guests with traditional French cuisine.

❶ Tel. 01 43 42 90 32; www.groupe-bertrand.com/grandes_marche.php.

✳ BASTILLE QUARTER

Dance halls and designers   The building of the new opera also heralded the transformation of the Bastille quarter into a desirable »quartier branché«. **Rue du Faubourg St-Antoine**, where the French elite school for furniture making, the Ecole Boulle, has been based since 1886, was once the heart of the Parisian furniture industry. Traditional trades now mix with the latest chic, and numerous traditional workshops have been converted into elegant lofts, designer boutiques and exhibition spaces for art galleries. Star architect and designer Jean-Michel Wilmotte has his head office at No. 68, while at No. 30 design guru **Jean-Paul Gaultier** has installed a temple of fashion, and at No. 28 up and coming designers display their work in the **»Ateliers de Paris«**. Typical for the street are its arcades and courtyards with evocative names like Cour Bel-Air (No. 56) or Cour de l'Etoile d'Or (No. 75). The old craft centre at No. 74 is now the **»Le Lieu du Design«**, a showcase for design from the Île-de-France, where exhibitions are supported by the government.

Le Lieu du Design: Tue– Fri 1pm–6pm, Sat 11am–6pm, documentation centre Mon–Thur 2.30pm–6pm, Fri 10am–1pm, Sat nV, admission free, www.lelieududesign.com

Maison Rouge and designers   Another good place to go is the Maison Rouge belonging to the Fondation Antoine de Galbert, which puts on **exhibitions of contemporary art** in its four rooms at 10, Boulevard de la Bastille.

❶ Wed–Sun 11am–7pm, Thur until 9pm, tel. 01 40 01 08 81, www.lamaisonrouge.org, adults €7

Artisan courtyards also characterize the surrounding streets. **Cour Delépine** is today a studio village among bamboo and ivy at 37, Rue de Charonne., while **Cour St-Joseph** at 5, Rue de Charenton was once home to a pottery. The once typical craft workshops in the leafy backyard at 12, Rue Popincourt look like a village in the middle of the city. Behind a pretty Art Nouveau facade at 1, Rue Jules Vallès hides Cyril Lignac's **Bistro Chardenoux**, a listed building, serving fine French cuisine (tel. 01 43 71 49 52). The oldest bistro in the Bastoche is the delightful Art Nouveau style **Bistrot du Peintre** (▶MARCO POLO Insight p. 104).

One of the best fashion houses in the busy Rue de Charonne is **Isabel Marant** (No. 16), who has established an international reputation with her urban ethnic fashion. **French Trotters** (Nr. 30) has its own collection designed and produced exclusively in Paris.

At 76, Rue de la Roquette the small **Théâtre de la Bastille** experiments with avant-garde works. In **Rue de Lappe** too, where scrap metal dealing once flourished and the musette waltz rang out from the ballrooms, galleries for abstract art, cafés, and antiques dealers have established themselves. At the **Balajo** (No. 9), frequented in the 1930s by stars such as Arletty and Edith Piaf – you can enjoy yourself today with the musette waltz at lunchtime and salsa and rock 'n' roll in the evening. (▶MARCO POLO Insight p. 84).

Studios, bistros and boutiques

What has always been special about the Bastille quarter is its mix of immigrants. Migrants from the Auvergne were followed by Bretons, and later by Italians, Spaniards, Russians, Jews, Arabs and immigrants from the former colonies. Each population group brought its own culture that made its mark with taverns, dance halls and shops. The lively **market at the Place d'Aligre** with its (listed) 19th-century hall reflects the colourful atmosphere that has evolved. The mixture of chic and shabby is still exactly right in the newly fashionable district. For the moment, the blend of chic and shabby works in this

*Around Place d'Aligre

hip district, the narrow lanes of the »Bastoche« still have idiosyncratic shops and traditional workshops, simple restaurants and sleepy courtyards alongside the trendy places – though modernisation is clearly advancing. This is also evident in the most beautiful cinematic homage to the neighbourhood: »Chacun cherche son chat« (*When the Cat's Away*, 1996) directed by Cédric Klapisch.

Batignolles

✴ E / F 1 – 3

Location: 17th arr.
Métro station: Villiers

The once independent rural community in the 17th arrondissement is one of the fashionable trendy districts of the Seine metropolis and today finds itself in a state of transition. The district was made famous by the chanteuse Barbara (1930–1997), who has raved about her home in her song »Perlimpinpin«.

Artists' quarter

Batignolles, incorporated into Paris in 1860 by Napoleon III, was a popular artists' district in the 19th century. The poet **Stéphane Mallarmé** lived here and the painter **Edouard Manet** had his studio in Rue de la Condamine. Other artists belonging to the »Groupe des Batignolles« included Edgar Degas, Camille Pissarro, Alfred Sisley and Henri-Fantin, who in 1870 immortalized Manet together with his artist friends in the group portrait »Un atelier de Batignolles«. In those days they met up at the Café Guerbois at Avenue Clichy 9. Legendary too is the **music café L'Européen** at rue Biot 5, in which singers like Charles Trenet thrilled their audiences – today it has an alternating programme of concerts and theatre (www. europeen. info).

Cimetière de Batignolles

Many artists have found their final resting place in Batignolles Cemetery, which was laid out in 1933. Beneath the tall trees you will find the graves of the poet **Paul Verlaine** (1844–1896) and the painter Edouard Vuillard (1868–1940), and that of **André Breton** (1896–1966) – »Je cherche l'or du temps« (I'm searching for the gold of time) is inscribed on the gravestone of the author of the first Surrealist Manifesto.

Cité Lemercier

On his arrival in Paris in 1958, **Jacques Brel** lived at the Hôtel du Chalet in the Cité Lemercier, a workers' settlement just 142 m long that was built along Rue Lemercier in the 19th century. It was here that he wrote one of his most beautiful chansons: *Ne me quitte pas.*

In the heart of the district rises the church of Ste-Marie des Batignolles, whose construction in 1826–1829 was mainly financed by donations from Marie-Thérèse. The church, which resembles a Greek temple with its columned portico and pediment, plays a central roll in the novella »The Legend of the Holy Drinker« by Joseph Roth, published in 1939.

Ste-Marie des Batignolles

Right behind the church begins the Square des Batignolles. It has been a park for more than 100 years and is set to be extended further. On the former SNCF railway yards northwest of Gare de Lazare, alongside new residential and office buildings and the new Paris police headquarters, the new **Parc Clichy Batignolles–Martin Luther King** is being created over an area of 11ha. In 2008 the first, 4.3-ha section of the park with its various sports activities was opened to the public. Also very green is the organic **Marché de Batignolles**: every Saturday morning from 9am–2pm exclusively organic fruit and vegetables as well as meat, sausage and cheese are sold along the Boulevard des Batignolles between Rue des Batignolles and Rue Puteaux.

Square des Batignolles

Belleville

✦ K–M 4–6

Location: 20th arr.
Métro stations: Belleville, Couronnes, Ménilmontant

Edith Piaf, the »Little Sparrow«, is said to have been born in this multicultural district, on the steps of house No. 72 in Rue de Belleville.

It is a fact that she grew up in the quarter and was already singing on the streets as a child. The museum at 5, Rue Crespin du Gast tells of the eventful life of the petite **Grande Dame of Chanson** (▶ MARCO POLO Insight, p. 64)

*Musée Edith Piaf

❶ Mon–Thu 1pm–6pm; door code on calling the attendant, tel. 01 43 55 52 72, admission free but donations welcome

The special atmosphere of the east side of Paris, personified in the 1930s by Piaf and the likes of Maurice Chevalier, is long gone. Several waves of immigrants have made the quarter, which was incorporated into Paris around 1900, into the most exotic in the French capital. Armenians came to this **workers' stronghold** after the First World War, Russians after the victory of the Bolsheviks and opponents of Franco after the Spanish Civil War. Innumerable

Multicultural district

> **MARCO⊕POLO TIP**
>
> *Colourful market* **Insider Tip**
>
> Immigrants from all over the world meet every Tuesday and Friday morning at the exotic weekly market on Boulevard de Belleville. People come from all over Paris to buy plantains, yam roots and chayotes. Mix among the women wearing boubous, and try a savoury couscous or tajine in one of the restaurants.

Sephardic Jews and Arabs followed after the end of colonial rule in Tunisia and the war in Algeria, mixing in with those for whom the west side of Paris was still too expensive: workers in the automobile factories in Pantin, proprietors of junk shops, hot food stalls and workshops. Urban renewal began in Belleville at the end of the 20th century. Many of the old tenement houses have already been pulled down and replaced by modern blocks of flats. The result is rising rents. So it is only a matter of time before this working-class, multi-cultural quarter becomes an expensive middle-class district.

Vibrant art   **Le Plateau** serves as exhibition space for the Fonds Régional d'Art Contemporain d'Île-de-France, which together with guest exhibitors has been displaying works of new and experimental contemporary art since 2009.

❶ Wed–Fri 2–7pm, Sat–Sun noon–8pm, www.fracidf-leplateau.com, admission free, concerts and events adults €5

Maison de Metallos   **Modern Art** can also be enjoyed in an old metal factory at 94, Rue Jean-Pierre Timbaud, which offers artists workshops, performing and exhibition spaces and promotes human as well as cultural exchange – with dance, theatre, debates and dialogues, concerts, workshops and a very nice café.

❶ daily except Sun 9am–7pm, Sat from 2pm, www.maisondesmetallos.org

Open doors   In May, the artists from Belleville give kick off the **season of open doors** by inviting people into their 250 studios (www.ateliers-artistes-belleville.org). They include the four creators of Beau Travail – Delphine Dunoyer, Céline Saby, Rachel Péloquin and Hélène Georget – who every two or three months also exhibit the work of colleagues in their studio.

❶ Rue de la Mare 67, Sat 2pm–7pm, www.beautravail.fr

Maison de l'Air   Belleville derives its name from belle vue, beautiful view – the open pavilion of the Maison de l'Air above the terraced Parc de Belleville at the end of Rue Piat provides what is indisputably one of the best **panoramic views** of Paris. In addition, you can learn in an entertaining way all about the Paris air quality and the dangers of air pollution.

❶ Tue–Fri and Sun 1.30pm–5pm or 6.30pm, admission free

There are always fresh flowers on the grave of Edith Piaf at Cimetière du Père Lachaise

The main attraction of the 20th arrondissement is the **most beautiful cemetery in Paris**; with its 44ha/100 acres, it is also the largest. The cemetery was laid out in 1804 and named after Louis XIV's father confessor, Père La Chaise. The map of the grounds, obtainable at the main entrance on Boulevard de Ménilmontant, shows the way to all the celebrities' graves.

*Cimetière du Père Lachaise

Inscribed on Alfred de Musset's gravestone is »Dear friends, when I die, Plant a willow in the graveyard. I love its weeping foliage, Making the light subdued and sweet. Its shadow lightens the earth, in which I eternally rest«. Literary buffs can visit the graves of Molière (Jean-Baptiste Poquelin), La Fontaine, Balzac, Nerval, Apollinaire, Marcel Proust, Oscar Wilde, Colette and Gertrude Stein, whilst music fans will want to see the graves of Chopin, Rossini, Bizet and Maria Callas. The oldest »inhabitants« of the necropolis are considered to be Abélard and Héloise, the tragic lovers of the 12th century (►Sorbonne). The most visited graves are those of Edith Piaf (Edith Gassion) and Jim Morrison, lead singer of the group »The Doors«. Among the most famous painters are Delacroix, David, Corot, Modigliani and Max Ernst. The actresses Sarah Bernhardt and Simone Signoret – together with Yves Montand – are also buried here, as is the dancer Isadora Duncan, the inventor of the guillotine, Dr Guillotin, and the redeveloper of Paris, Baron Haussmann (▶MARCO POLO Insight p.28). To the east of Avenue Principale lies the **Jewish part of the cemetery** with the graves of Pissaro, Rothschild and Singer. The victims of the Nazi concentration camps are also remembered here. The Mur des Fédérés, the Communards' Wall, recalls the tragic end of the **Paris Commune**. The 147 survivors of the last battle were shot here on the morning of 2 May 1871. President Adolphe Thiers, who was responsible for the massacre, also lies buried in the cemetery.

❶ Nov–15 March daily 8am–5.30pm, 16 March–Oct till 6pm, www.pere-lachaise.com

Bercy

—————————————— ✳ **K/L 8/9**

Location: 12th arr.
Métro station: Bercy, Cour St-Émilion

Right on time for the third millennium, this quarter in the 12th arrondissement shed its image of stagnation, poverty and decay. The former wine village has gained a completely new appearance through new housing blocks, office complexes and parks.

Quarter for the future
The »Projet de l'Est Parisien«, a redevelopment plan dating from the time of President Giscard d'Estaing, set things in motion well over 30 years ago. Conceived on the drawing board, a quarter of the future was created with a sports arena, amusement park and the first Club Med World – easily reached by the computer-controlled Métro line 14, the »Météor«.

Ministère des Finances
In order to make space for the arts, the **Finance Ministry**, after occupying the north wing of the ▶Louvre for more than one hundred years, moved upstream into a new building in 1989. The architects responsible for the huge complex anchored in the riverbed were Paul Chemetov and Borjo Huidobro.

Palais Omnisport de Bercy
The futuristic stadium for sports and music events at Boulevard de Bercy 8 was officially opened in 1984. The grass-covered pyramid with glass and steel lattice roof has a seating capacity of 17,000.
❶ Tel. 01 40 02 60 60, www.bercy.fr.

*Parc de Bercy
To the south of the sports arena, occupying the site of the former royal wine warehouse and wine wholesale market of Paris since 1997,

the 14-ha/35-acre Parc de Bercy stretches along the banks of the Seine. It consists of three gardens: the water features and open lawns of the Grandes Prairies, the geometrically laid-out parterre complete with box hedges, and the idyllic Jardins Romantique with the Maison du Lac. From the middle of the park the wave-like **Passerelle Simone de Beauvoir**, a pedestrian and cyclist-only bridge designed by Dietmar Feichtinger and completed in 2006, crosses the Seine to Tolbiac, home to National Library and the guinguettes on the Rive Gauche.

At the northern edge of the park at 51, Rue de Bercy are the boldly interlocking concrete boxes of the former **American Centre** that was designed by Frank Gehry. Since 2006 it has housed the National Film Library and the Cinémathèque française; in the latter the **Musée du Cinéma** explains the development of from the first pantoscope to Fritz Lang, Charlie Chaplin and Alfred Hitchcock and contemporary cult movies of the present day. Creator of this cabinet of rarities was Henri Langlois, who collected everything to do with film, including cinema posters, film sets, scripts and costumes from the 1930s onwards.

*Cinéma-thèque française

❶ Mon–Sat noon–7pm, Thur till 10pm, Sun 10am–8pm, www.cinemateque.fr, adults €5, discount film and museum ticket €7.

Sidewalk cafés in the old wine storehouses of Bercy Village

Café-restaurant »Le 51«	Inside and outside crispy grilled chicken, sausages and steaks are served up on the giant picnic tables, and picnic hampers can be made up on request. In the summer you can dance in the open-air at Bal Pop, in the winter there are salsa classes. ❶ Tel. 01 58 51 10 91, www.restaurant51.com
*Musée des Arts Forains	For half his life, Jean-Paul Favand, an antique dealer with a passion, collected fairground attractions. His **fairground museum** in the old wine warehouses at 53, Avenue des Terroirs de Franc covers the years 1850–1950 and includes a fairground organ, shooting gallery figures, fortune-telling machines and carousels. ❶ Sat–Sun 2–7pm, www.art-forain.com, guided tour €14.
Bercy Village	In the south Park de Bercy finishes at the Bercy Village **shopping complex** by the Cour St-Emilion Métro, where the old wine warehouses (called »chais«) are now home to restaurants, cafés, boutiques and the UGC cinema (www.bercyvillage.com).
Immeuble Lumière	Behind the glass façade of the »Building of Light« escalators lead up to commercial offices and service providers, and a café-restaurant. The building got its name from the illuminations that take place there every evening, when a display of colours lights up the façade from 8pm.
Cité Nationale de l'Historie de l'immigration	In the Palais du Porte Dorée, which was designed by Albert Labrade for the Paris Colonial Exhibition of 1931, the **Museum of Immigration** documents the story of immigration to France in a very objective way with charts, films, photos and memorabilia of refugees. The cultural programme includes cinema, music and theatre from the migrants' home countries. ❶ Avenue Daumesnil 293, Tue–Sun 10am–5.30pm, Sat 10am–7pm, www.histoire-immigration.fr, aduts €5, free admission first Sun in month

* Bois de Boulogne

✳ **A/B 3–6**

Location: On the western outskirts of the city (16th arr.)
Métro stations: Sablons, Porte Maillot, Porte Dauphine, Porte d'Auteuil

Besides the exclusive 16th arrondissement, the 865ha/2140 acres of the Bois de Boulogne offer an oasis of peace and quiet with lakes, gardens and labyrinth of footpaths.

Green oasis	It derives its name from Notre Dame de Boulogne le Petit, a church that pilgrims on their return journey from Boulogne sur Mer in the

14th century erected to honour the Virgin Mary. In 1556, during the reign of Henri II, the holm oak woods, – long the hunting reserve of the kings as well as a hideout for layabouts and infamous bandits – were enclosed by a wall with eight gates. Louis XIV commanded his first minister Colbert to run roads through the woods. In 1852, Napoleon III had the walls pulled down and commissioned Haussmann to landscape the park along the lines of Hyde Park in London. It became fashionable in the mid-19th century to ride through the woods, not least because of the new Longchamp and Auteuil race tracks. During the day you will meet joggers, cyclists and boule players; at night the forest becomes the city's busiest area for prostitution.

On the Route de Sèvres to Neuilly in the northwest stands the château of Count d'Artois in Parc de Bagatelle. In 1720, the Duchess of Estrées had a country estate built here that went into disrepair after repeatedly changing hands. When the young Count d'Artois, the future Charles X, acquired the property in 1772, he wagered the tidy sum of 100,000 livres with his sister-in-law, Marie Antoinette, that he could have a new **château** with an English park built within 64 days. He hired 900 workers, who finished the building designed by François Alexandre Bélanger on time – although the name bagatelle means trifle, the price was not. At the same time, the Scottish landscape gardener Blakie laid out the park. Alongside the **orangery**, planted with evergreens, where the attraction in the early summer is the »Les Musicales de la Bagatelle« series of concerts (tel. 01 42 29 07 83), the most northern of the four

*Parc de Bagatelle

> **Insider Tip**
>
> *Helmet on and away we go!*
>
> Start the day with a bike ride through the Bois de Boulogne. On Sunday mornings hundreds of cyclists take to the well-marked routes that allow you to explore the vast forest. You can rent out mountain and city bikes at the roundabout in the Jardin d'Acclimatation. Helmets, locks and child seats can also be rented. Your tour can include cycling around the lakes and taking a break at the big waterfall. (May–Sept daily, Oct–April Wed, Sat and Sun 10am–7pm, www.pariscycles. fr, bike rentals from A5/hr and A12/day).

ponds with its glorious display of water lilies entices visitors. Between June and October the scent of 10,000 roses fills the grounds; the climax in June is when the park annually hosts the International Rose Competition.

❶ Mon–Fri 8am–8pm, Sat and Sun from 9am, winter until 5.30pm

This artificial waterfall that dominates the Carrefour de Longchamp is almost 10m/33ft high. If you can afford it, have a meal at La Grande Cascade gourmet restaurant in Allée de Longchamp (▶p. 113).

La Grande Cascade

Watching horseraces at Longchamp

A pavilion in the style of the Second French Empire provides the setting for the exclusive **Pré Catalan restaurant** on Route Suresnes (€€ €/€€ €€ tel. 01 44 14 41 14, www.precatelanparis.com) in the park of the same name. The park is named after the troubadour Armand Catelan, who is said to have been murdered by a jealous husband in around 1300. A giant, 200-year-old beech gives shade to almost 500 sq m/5,500 sq ft of lawn. All of the plants in **Jardin Shakespeare** (the Shakespeare Garden) are mentioned in the poet's works. From May to September the **Théâtre de Verdure** performs plays by the bard on the open-air stage.

The upper and lower lakes are a popular weekend destination for Parisians. They take a motorboat or rowing boat to the islands in the lower lake or enjoy creative market cuisine by Filipe da Assunçaõ either inside or on the terrace of the **Chalet des Îles** restaurant (www.chalet-des-iles.com).

Hippodrome d' Auteuil, Stade Roland Garros	Only steeplechases are held at the Auteuil **racetrack**, which opened in 1850. On the clay courts beyond the Carrefour des Anciens Combattants the international tennis championships of the ** **French Open** have been held between late May and early June since 1891 – the only clay court tournament of the Grand Slam series. Outside this period guided tours of the tennis centre and the player area are available Tue–Sun. Because the Roland Garros complex is so much smaller than other Grand Slam venues, it has been decided to expand the venue, increasing its capacity by 60% (www.rolandgarros.com) by the completion date of 2018.
Hippodrome de Longchamp	With seating for 10,000 spectators, **Longchamp racecourse** has guaranteed excitement and glamour ever since 1857. The latest fashion and the most sensational hats are worn every year at the Grand Prix meeting – the restaurant is open only on race days. Just to the south the 15-ha/37-acre **Parc de Boulogne Edmond de Rothschild** surrounds the dilapidated palace of the Rothschild family

at 3, Rue des Victoires. The first Parc des Princes stadium was erected in 1867 on the former royal hunting grounds and served as the French national stadium until the construction of the Stade de France in ►Saint-Denis in 1998. The first **football matches** were played at the **Parc des Princes** as long ago as 1899, and in 1924 it was the main venue for the Olympic Games. Today the arena, which can accommodate almost 50,000 spectators, is used for the home games of Paris-St-Germain, as well as for rugby matches and mega concerts (www.leparcdesprinces. fr). At one time the ***Jardin d'Acclimatation** in the north of the Bois de Boulogne was a zoo, which features in several chapters of Marcel Proust's *In Search of Lost Time*. Young visitors can still look forward to the petting zoo, go-kart circuit, carousel and the **Musée en Herbe** (►p. 106), and you can eat well and quite reasonably at the €€ **La Grande Verriere** bistro operated by Christian Le Squer.

> **MARCO POLO INSIGHT**
>
> ### New course record
>
> With a princely €4 million in prize money, the Qatar Prix de l'Arc de Triomphe is one of the world's most prestigious horse races. Run on the first Sunday in October at Longchamp Racecourse over a distance of 2400m (about 1.5 mi), it counts as the unofficial world championship for thoroughbreds. Many highly acclaimed horses have won the race. The fastest ever time for the »Arc« was achieved in 2011 when the three-year-old »Danedream« ridden by Andrasch Starke from the Burg Eberstein stables in Germany won it in just 2:24.49 minutes.

Fondation Louis Vuitton

At 8, Avenue du Mahatma Gandhi the Fondation Louis Vuitton has erected a new **contemporary art centre**, completed in 2013 at a cost of 100 million euros. Frank O. Gehry designed the building as a transparent chrysalis for modern art, surrounded by shady trees.

*Musée Marmottan Monet

Insider Tip

A must for lovers of Impressionism is the exhibition at the 2, Rue Louis Boilly, created by Jules Marmottan and his son Paul. In 1934, she bequeathed her villa with late-Gothic sculptures, Burgundian Renaissance tapestries and precious Empire furniture to the Institut de France. In 1948 Donop de Monchy donated the first of the paintings by Claude Monet and in 1966 Monet's son Michel bequeathed 65 of his father's works to the museum, including studies on the »water lilies«. Other highlights include Monet's »**Impression, soleil levant**« from 1872, from which the art movement gets its name, his »La Cathédrale de Rouen« a composition of colour and light dating from 1895, and the Parisian bridge »Pont de l'Europe« from 1877. Also on display are paintings by Renoir, Sisley and Pissarro.

❶ daily except Mon 10am–6pm, Thu until 8pm www.marmottan.com, adults €10

✳ Canal Saint-Martin

✦ J/K 3/4

Location: 10th arr.
Métro stations: Jaurès, Jacques-Bonsergent

Writers and filmmakers have made it famous: the Canal Saint-Martin, today exclusively the preserve of cruise boats rather than barges. And the paths along its banks make some of the most popular walking trails in the city.

Romantic waterway
With its nine locks between the Port de l'Arsenal by the ►Bastille and the basin of ►La Villette, the Canal St-Martin overcomes a height difference of 25m/82ft in 4.5 km/2.8 mi. The canal was built from 1806–25 by order of Napoleon, to connect the Seine with the 108 km/67 mi-long Canal de l'Ourq (►La Villette). Together with the Canal Saint-Denis, it offered boatmen a 12 km/7 mi shortcut between the loops of the Seine. The shaded towpaths inspired filmmakers and writers to produce timeless classics: in 1938 Marcel Carné filmed the cult movie *Hôtel du Nord* here; in 1956 Leo Malet chose the quarter as the setting for his thriller *Nestor Burma: M'as-tu vu en cadavre?*; and in 2001, the canal was used as a setting for *Le Fabuleux Destin d'Amélie Poulain*. When the waterway became too narrow for modern freighters, the stretch between Rue du Faubourg du Temple and Bastille was covered over.

The banks of the open waterway are now firmly in the hands of the strollers. Yet few tourists have discovered its tranquil charm. It is mostly Parisians who go for walks on Sundays along the embankments that are closed to cars, have brunch in the small bistros and browse the young trendy stores that have opened up – especially west of the canal. In the trendy ethno boutique **»Antoine et Lili«** at Quai de Valmy 95, in addition to the clothes by Martine Senac and Alexandre Gattegno, 20 different varieties of kir are served (www.antoineetlili.com).

> ! **MARCO ⊕ POLO** TIP
>
> *Welcome aboard!*   **Insider Tip**
>
> The cruise along the Canal Saint-Martin is romantic and unusual. You will discover the old Paris, cruise through the mysterious tunnel of the Bastille, negotiate four double locks, two swing bridges and the more than 100-year-old lift bridge Pont de Crimée before reaching the park of ►La Villette.
> **Canauxrama** boats depart from the Paris-Arsenal leisure harbour (www.canauxrama.com, adults from A16), while passengers embark on **Paris-canal** vessels at Musée d'Orsay and thus have the added bonus of being able to admire the Louvre, Pont Neuf and Notre-Dame from the water at the beginning of the trip (www.pariscanal.com, adults from €12).

»**Artazart**« at the Quai de Valmy 83 is a treasure trove of photography, graphics and design, which also organises exhibitions by young artists (www.artazart.com). The nearby Rue Beaurepaire is considered a hub of fashion: fashion rebel **Liza Korn** likes to embellish her eccentric outfits with a dash of rock 'n' roll and presents her fashion shows as raucous happenings (No. 19, www.liza-korn.com). Also in house No. 19, the design boutique **Idéco** sells sells a colourful range of household fittings and accessories (www.idecoparis.com). Absolutely politically correct are the clothing fashion and cosmetics found at **Bazar Éthique** (No. 25), which only sells sustainably produced organic, Fairtrade products. Showcase for local creative types is the **Espace Beaurepaire**, in which the artists themselves design the spaces for their exhibitions, readings, concerts and fashion shows (No. 21; www.espacebeaurepaire.com).

Up the canal in the direction of ▶La Villette, the Péniche Opera is moored by the Quai de Loire. For more than 30 years the old barge has staged musicals and operas from the baroque to the present day. **❶** Tel. 01 53 35 07 77, www.penicheopera.com

Péniche Opéra

A trip on Canal Saint-Martin takes about two hours

Maison de l'Architecture

The **Couvent des Récollets** at 148, Rue du Faubourg St-Martin, post 1870 a military hospital for wounded soldiers from the front, has been given a new lease of life as a centre for researchers and artists, as well housing the Île-de-France Chamber of Architects. There are also cultural events and lectures. Well known for its Sunday brunch, **Café A** puts its tables outside under the trees in the summer.

❶ Mon–Fri 2–6pm, café: 10am www.maisonarchitecture-idf.org, admission free

Parc des buttes Chaumont

The Hills of Chaumont were not only gypsum and limestone quarries or centuries, but also the location of the **Gibet de Montfaucon**. It was at this solid stone-built gallows that enemies of the state and the king were hanged between 1278 and 1629. They included Enguerrand de Marigny, the faithful chamberlain and treasurer of Philip IV, who met his end here in 1315 having been convicted of sorcery just a few months after the king's own death. In 1863 the area was transformed into a **landscaped park** and officially opened in 1867 for the Paris World Exhibition. With its cliffs and grottoes, winding paths and waterfalls, temples, islets and suspension bridge, the park chimed with the tastes of the time and became a worldwide role model. For the young there is not only a playground but also **puppet shows and pony rides** Wed and Fri 3–6pm. The park is also popular for the fact that its lawns can be used for picnics, games and sports – a major exception in his town!

*Artistic melting pot

Since 2008, the enormous halls at 104, Rue d'Aubervilliers, in which the municipal undertakers once made coffins, have been home to the **CentQuatre** (104) Arts Centre with studios for 200 artists of all persuasions from around the world, who provide insights into their work with performances, concerts, festivals and exhibitions.

CentQuatre: Tue–Sun 11am–8pm, www.104.fr; admission price according to event. Sat from 11am organic market in the Halle Aubervilliers

✶✶ Centre Pompidou · Beaubourg

————————————— ✦ H 5/6

Location: Rue Rambuteau / Rue St-Martin (4th arr.)
Métro stations: Rambuteau, Hôtel de Ville, Châtelet Les Halles
❶ Tel. 01 44 78 12 33
www.centrepompidou.fr

The Centre National d'Art et de Culture Georges Pompidou, rising between ▶Châtelet-Les Halles and ▶Le Marais, has been a major attraction ever since its opening in 1977 and was given a €90-million facelift at the turn of the millennium.

The young architectural team, British architect Richard Rogers and Italian Renzo Piano, who won the international competition to design the building, which attracted almost 700 entries from 50 countries, also supervised the restoration work. In less than five **Fascinating »culture factory«**

years, a structure emerged under their supervision that immediately triggered a lively discussion. Critics called it a »monstrosity« and an »oil refinery in the centre of the city«. Supporters saw the Centre Beaubourg – Beaubourg is the name of the city district – as an important contribution to help Paris regain its position of »world capital of the arts« The 166m/545ft-long and 42m/138ft-high **steel and glass structure** certainly does bring to mind a refinery. All of the service systems, installation shafts and conveyance systems are located in ducts outside the building. As a result, the interior space is free to be arranged as required – ideal for changing exhibitions. The renovated Centre Pompidou has become more practical and sober-looking. Gone are the garish greens and flashy orange colours of the 1970s; black, white and plum blue are the defining colours

Niki de St-Phalle's *Firebird* in the Strawinsky fountain

today. The museum, library and restaurant now each have their own entrances. The four event halls for concerts, dance and theatre in Level -1 can be entered from the square. Anyone wanting simply to go up the caterpillar-like glass-encased escalator for the panoramic view on the 6th floor requires a »Billet Panorama« (€3). Due to the centre's popularity it's worth getting this or museum tickets online.

The main purpose of the gigantic cultural machine was not to function as a museum but to promote artistic production. Even though the originally conceived close, interactive relationship with conservatories, artists and the public has now waned, and artists today appear more as exhibitors while the public simply comes to look at their work, the Centre Pompidou still sees itself as a **contemporary cultural centre**. Part of the government's innovative cultural policy is that exhibitions and events from the French regions are to be presented in the Centre Beaubourg, while exhibitions conceived in Beaubourg are to be displayed in provincial museums. **Innovative model**

**Musée National d'Art Moderne (MNAM)
The escalator now services exclusively the collections and exhibition rooms in the sixth floor. Visitors to the **Museum of Modern Art** have to take it to the fourth floor and then climb the stairs or take the lift to the fifth floor. A visual dialogue is the basic pattern of the world-class museum that now extends over two floors with 14,000 sq m/150,700 sq ft of space. The fifth floor, simply titled »Modern«, holds works from 1905 to 1960; the fourth floor, titled »Contemporary« has everything after that. The exhibition of the classic modern art is changed around every 18 months; recent art is rearranged once a year. The museum aims not for completeness but rather affinity. Thus you might find Hyperrealism paintings next to video projections, Matisse in dialogue with wire cocoons by Calder, Picasso confronting Surrealists, Bacon together with Giacometti and the large-format pictures by Miró hanging opposite works by Pollock and de Kooning.
❶ daily except Tue 11am–9pm, till 11pm for big exhibitions, adults €12, under 18s free, billet panorama €3; 1st Sun in the month free admission.

Bibliothèque Publique d'Information (BPI)
Up to 2,000 visitors a day can use the reference library on the first, second and third floors free of charge. There are more than 50,000 books, newspapers and periodicals, as well as DVDs, learning software and Internet access.
❶ Mon–Fri noon–10pm, Sat and Sun 11am–10pm, www.bpi.fr

Galerie d'Exposition
The sixth floor is reserved for changing exhibitions of contemporary art and artists' retrospectives. It is also the location of **Le Georges**, the museum's panoramic French-fusion restaurant, which was styled by Dominique Jacob and Brendan McFarlane, architects of the Docks en Seine. Open from 11am–2am, its terrace provides stunning views over the city, especially with a sundowner (tel. 01 44 78 47 99, closed Tuesday).

Theatre, cinema, conferences
Contemporary theatre with music, dance and pictures is given the space it's due in the large room in Level -1. Feature films, documentaries and experimental films are shown on two cinema screens. screened in two cinema halls. Furthermore, the Cultural Development Department (DDC) regularly organizes seminars on current topics.

*Atelier Brancusi
Located on the forecourt in Rue Rambuteau, this building is a stage on which performing artists are constantly in action. It also houses the studio of the Romanian sculptor **Constantin Brancusi** (1876–1957) which has a retrospective of his work.
❶ Wed–Mon 2pm–6pm, admission free

IRCAM
The Institut de Recherche et de Coordination Acoustique-Musique in Rue St-Merri is dedicated to serving scientists and musicians from

all over the world in the research and development of **contemporary music**. Composers such as Pierre Boulez and Karlheinz Stockhausen have created pioneering works at the IRCAM, which are presented at the Agora Festival in June as well as at concerts (tel. 01 44 78 48 43).

In the pool on Place Strawinsky the colourful sculptures by the Parisian artist **Niki de Saint-Phalle** and the black metal creations of her life-long companion, the Swiss kinetic artist **Jean Tinguely**, provide an imaginative interpretation of the work of the great Russian composer (▶picture p. 197)

*Fontaine Strawinsky

✶✶ Champs-Elysées

✦ **D/E 4/5**

Location: between Arc de Triomphe and Place de la Concorde (8th arr.)

Métro stations: George V, Franklin D. Roosevelt, Champs-Elysées-Clemenceau

Even seasoned travellers can hardly resist the fascination of a stroll down the brightly-lit Champs-Elysées, the city's most prestigious boulevard. The »most beautiful avenue in the world« is close to 2 km/1.2 mi long. The military marches along it each year on the French national holiday, and it's also where the Tour de France starts and finishes.

A stroll down the »Champs«, as the Parisians call their »most beautiful avenue in the world«, is a must

While its lower part is still bordered by expansive parks, the upper part of the Champs-Elysées with a view of the ►Arc de Triomphe is lined by the shop windows of fashion boutiques, the offices of major airlines and banks, luxury hotels, street cafés, cinemas and theatres. On the street that the Joe Dassin immortalized in his song Les Champs-Elysées (1969) is where »La France« presents itself; this is where the world meets and a cacophony of languages can be heard from the passers-by.

Elysian Fields Until the end of the 16th century, the **Elysian Fields** were uncultivated land. It was not until 1667 that the court landscape architect Le Nôtre, who planned the Tuileries, built a wide, shady avenue up to the hill where the Arc de Triomphe stands today. At the beginning of the 18th century, this avenue was given a name – Champs-Elysées (the Elysian Fields) – but its development had to wait until after 1828. The 1910-m long and 70-m wide Champs-Elysées form part of the »voie triomphale«, a triumphal way that was completed during the reign of Napoleon III. It led from the Arc de Triomphe via Place de la Concorde to the Arc de Triomphe du Carrousel. This great **historic axis of Paris** stretches from the pyramid of the ►Louvre to the Grande Arche of ►La Défense.

After fast food and discount stores had established themselves on the boulevard, a renaissance began in the mid 1990s under Jacques Chirac. New avenues of plane trees, designer benches and polished granite paving for pedestrians made the avenue attractive once again for luxury shops: the perfume-maker **Guerlain** (No. 68) has its headquarters here and **Lacoste** (No. 95), a flagship store. Above its shop at No. 101 **Louis Vuitton** has an Espace Culturelle for temporary exhibitions of fashion and art spread over three floors; there is a magnificent view of Paris from the seventh floor. Everyone congregates in the nightclubs around the boulevard or takes in a show at the **Lido** revue theatre (No. 166, ►p. 91). At the Atelier Renault (No. 53), which was newly done out in 2011, you can eat oysters, burgers or Angus steaks with views of the electric cars from Twizy to Zoe.

Atelier Renault: open daily http://fr.atelier.renault.com

This elegant avenue runs straight as an arrow from Rond Point on the Champs-Elysées down to Place de l'Alma on the banks of the Seine. The street is now the home of **Haute Couture** having established itself in the magnificent old buildings, and a well-heeled clientele gathers at Lacroix (No. 26) Dior (No. 30), Louis Vuitton (No. 22) and Chanel (Nr. 42). You can acquire Italian chic at Prada (No. 8), Valentino (No. 17) or Dolce & Gabbana (No. 24), and the jewellery to go with it at Bulgari (No. 45). Carita at 3, Rue Boccador (www.carita.com) is where the film stars like to go for cares and styling before enjoying the three-star cuisine of Alain Ducasse at the Plaza Athénée (▶p. 103).

Avenue Montaigne

Châtelet · Les Halles

⟶ ✦ H 6

Location: Place du Châtelet (4. arr.)
Métro station: Châtelet-Les Halles

By 2016 this district around the former wholesale market halls and the present day transport hub of Châtelet-Les Halles will shine in new splendour. The scheme to make the »belly of Paris« the new »heart of Paris« will have cost around 800 million euros.

This area has been full of life ever since the Middle Ages. The first **market halls** were erected in 1183. On the orders of Napoleon III in the 19th century, Victor Baltard had huge iron pavilions constructed, which became the hallmark of Les Halles – and it was here in the early morning that many a foray into Parisian nightlife ended. Emile Zola coined the famous name for the halls, »the belly of Paris«, with his novel of the same name (*Le Ventre de Paris*) in 1874. In 1969 the wholesale market was moved out to Rungis, the iron halls were torn down and replaced by a huge public transport hub, above whose tunnels and underground car parks the **shopping and leisure complex** designed by Claude Vasoni and Georges Pencreach was created, with over 300 shops, cinemas, restaurants and cafés.

Forum des Halles

The somewhat dated Forum des Halles has been in the process of being modernized since 2008, while all the time remaining open. The highlight of the **»canopy«** project, designed by Patrick Berger and Jacques Anziutti, will be a 15m/50ft-high, light and airy, green-tinted glass canopy (canopée) spanning the new halls and the area in between. In addition, there will be a 4-ha/10-acre park for outdoor relaxation. The football pitch sized shopping hangar is due to be completed in 2016. The mammoth scheme also includes the renovation of the Châtelet-Les Halles station, which with its 800,000 daily passengers,

Canopée des Halles

three RER lines and five Métro lines is one of the biggest public transport hubs in Europe (http://projetdeshalles.wordpress.com).

Forum des Images

The Forum des Images is a **film archive and cinema with four screens**. Here aficionados can see not only daily changing movies on the big screen, but choose their favourite film. The repertoire includes more than 6500 films from 1895 to the present day.

❶ Entrance: Porte St-Eustache, Tue–Fri 12.30pm–11.30pm, Sat, and Sun 2pm–11.30pm; Salles of Collections: Tue–Fri 1pm–10pm, Sat and Sun 2pm–10pm, www.forumdesimages.net, discovery ticket €9, collection €5, movies €4–5

Fontaine des Innocents

This fountain has stood between Rue St-Denis and Rue Berger since 1549. Its architect was Pierre Lescot, who also created the façade of the ►Louvre that bears his name. It was remodelled in the 18th century in the shape of a temple. The three reliefs – the originals are now in the Louvre – are the work of the master of French Renaissance sculpture, Jean Goujon. The figures of nymphs embellishing the fourth side of the fountain were the work of Augustin Pajou in 1788.

Châtelet

The Fortress of the Grand Châtelet was founded here in the 12th century to secure the Île de la Cité. After first being transformed into a prison, the fortification served until 1789 as seat of the court of the Prévôt des Marchands, the mayor of Paris and merchant provost (►Hôtel de Ville). Napoleon had the fortress torn down in 1802. During the Second Empire, the Théâtre du Châtelet was built on the west side and the Théâtre Sarah Bernhardt on the east side. In 1980 as the **Théâtre Musical de Paris**, the former was elevated to the national theatre for operas, musicals and concerts. The **Théâtre de la Ville** opposite was acquired in 1899 by the actress Sarah Bernhardt, who had sensational triumphs here as »La Dame aux Camélias« and »Tosca«. On the programme today are classic modern plays and guest ballet performances by contemporary choreographers.

!

MARCO ⊕ POLO TIP

Just the place ... **Insider Tip**

... for a stopover is **Rue Montorgueil** to the north of Les Halles. This pedestrian street is lined by small restaurants, delicatessens and traditional establishments, most notably the »Patisserie Stohrer« at No. 51. When Louis XV married the daughter of the Polish king Stanislas, Marie Leszczynska, her father's gifted pastry chef came with her. In 1730, Nicolas Stohrer opened Paris's first patisserie here (www.stohrer.fr).

Between Place du Châtelet and Rue de Rivoli stands the **Tour Saint-Jacques**, a tower erected in 1522 as part of the parish church of Saint-Jacques-la-Boucherie. Pilgrims gathered here in the Middle Ages as they travelled by way of Paris to Santiago de Compostela on their pilgrimage to the shrine of St James.

Chinatown

✦ **H/J 9/10**

Location: 13th arr.
Métro station: Place d'Italie, Olympiades

It isn't London but Paris that has the honour of being home to the largest Asian community in Europe, with almost 450,000 inhabitants. The heart of the community is the 13th arrondissement.

From 1969–74, **Les Olympiades** social housing scheme was created on an old factory site. In the 1970s and 1980s the satellite settlement provided cheap accommodation for refugees from the former French colonies of **Vietnam, Laos and Cambodia** (Indochina). Between Avenue d'Ivry, Avenue de Choisy and Boulevard Masséna they created the largest Chinatown in the continent   most of the inhabitants coming from the former Indochina and only around 25% from China itself.

One attraction of the district is **Tang Frères** at 48, Avenue d'Ivry, in which Laos-Chinese sell exotic ingredients for Asian cuisine – and at unbeatable prices (closed Mon but open Sun). The district is at its liveliest during **Chinese New Year** when on a parade huge paper dragons are carried through the streets to the accompaniment of deafening music.

Largest Chinatown in Europe

Originally, Place d'Italie was intended as a counterpart to the Place de l'Etoile. But instead of a magnificent triumphal arch, high-rise buildings from the 1960s »decorate« the square – the result of the ambitious construction project known as **Italie 13**. Its landmark building, designed by Maurice Novarina, is the 112m/367ft-high residential tower called **Tour Super-Italie** at 121–127, Avenue d'Italie. On the roof there is a pool with sun terrace! Right on Place d'Italie a centre commercial provides space for 130 shops and the **Grand Ecran d'Italie** cinema with the largest screen in the city. On Friday morning an open-air market is held along the Boulevard Auguste Blanqui.

Place d'Italie

This only 63m/207ft-high »mountain« south of the Place d'Italie is an idyll amongst the high-rise jungle of the 13th arr. and has developed into the neighbourhood of the »Bourgeois Bohêmes«. It was named after Pierre Caille, who in 1540 planted the first vines between the **windmills** that ground the grain from Gentilly into flour. The thermals surrounding the hill were exploited by the physicist François Pilâtre de Rozie, who on 21 October 1783, together with the Marquis d'Arlandes, ventured the first manned hot-air balloon ride

*Butte aux Cailles

– and having flown for 9km/6mi landed safely back on the butte with his **Montgolfière** made of wallpaper. In 1860, the area became the centre of the insurgents of the **Paris Commune**. At 46, **Rue des Cinq Diamants** is the Association Les Amis de la Commune de Paris, which organises guided tours through Paris and has published a booklet of songs from those troubled days of 1871. The **Rue de la Butte aux Cailles** is the gastro-strip of the district with local cuisine with restaurants such as Le Temps des Cerises (No. 18) serving hearty fare. At the junction of Rue Bobillot and Rue Tolbiac rises with white facade of the neo-Byzantine **Église Sainte Anne de la Butte-aux-Cailles**, which was consecrated in 1912 and whose foundations rest on 71 pillars.

✶ Conciergerie

✶ H 7

Location: 1, Quai de l'Horloge (1st arr.)
Métro station: Cité
❶ daily 9.30am–6pm, adults €8.50, under 18s and EU citizens under 26 free, combination ticket with ▶Ste-Chapelle €12,50

If you enjoy a spine-chilling experience, tour the Conciergerie, which gained morbid fame during the French Revolution as the »waiting room for the guillotine«.

Capetian palace and state prison

King Philippe le Bel (Philip the Fair) had the three High Gothic halls of the Capetian palace built around 1300. The castellan and majordomo was known in France as »concierge«, and acted as head of the palace household in the king's absence. The building was made a **royal prison** in the 14th century. Between January 1793 and July 1794 some 2600 prisoners awaited execution here, among them Marie-Antoinette and Madame du Barry, the long-time favourite of Louis XV, Charlotte Corday, who stabbed Marat to death, and leaders of the revolution such as Danton and Robespierre. The best view of the Conciergerie and its 19th-century façade is from the Quai de la Mégisserie. It is distinctive for its three round towers and the Tour de l'Horloge (clock tower), on which the first public clock in Paris was mounted around 1370. The Conciergerie is now part of the »Banks of the Seine« **UNESCO World Heritage Site**.

Tour

The entrance to the 14th-century Gothic vaults of the **Hall of the Guards** is on the Quai de l'Horloge. The capitals of the massive pillars are richly decorated, many with scenes of animal fights. The adjacent **Salle des Gens d'Armes** of Philip the Fair is considered a gem of Gothic secular architecture. The »Hall of the Soldiers«, which was

Pont Neuf and the Conciergerie, »guillotine's waiting room« during the French Revolution

used as a dining hall by the palace staff, is 70m/230ft long, with three rows of pillars separating it into four aisles, and has a cross-rib vault. The Revolutionary Tribunal held court here from 1793 to 1795. The **kitchen** was equipped for banquets of 2000–3000 guests – whole oxen could be roasted in the open fireplaces. The condemned were turned over to the executioner, »Monsieur de Paris«, in the corridor called the **Rue de Paris**. During the Revolution the former **chapel** of the Conciergerie, the **Salle des Girondins**, served as a prison for opponents of the Jacobin dictatorship. A guillotine blade, prison regulations and a facsimile of Marie-Antoinette's last letter are displayed as mementoes of the reign of terror of the revolutionary courts. Rue de Paris leads to the cell in which **Marie-Antoinette** was held from 2 to 16 October 1793 after her failed attempt to flee. Following her twenty-hour trial, she awaited her execution here. Danton then later Robespierre were both led to the scaffold from the neighbouring cell.

* La Défense

✳ A 2/3

Location: Western outskirts
Métro station: Esplanade de la Défense
❶ www.ladefense.fr

The ultra modern high-rise district in the west of the city is an important financial centre and a showpiece of modern architecture. Glass, steel and concrete dominate the skyline of the futuristic metropolis. The name commemorates the heroic defence of the city against the Prussians in 1871.

Dizzying dimensions – the Grande Arche on the
Esplanade de la Défense

Europe's largest business district

To make way for the construction of this **satellite city** more than 50 years ago, close to 9000 flats and 1000 small businesses were demolished, and motor and rail traffic banished to tunnels below the concrete platform of the Esplanade de la Défense. Over100,000 people now commute daily to work in La Défense. Despite the presence of many restaurants, theatres, cinemas and hotels, the district appears almost deserted after close of business. The effects of the 2009 financial crisis have been felt in La Défense – with companies such as the insurance giant AXA going in search of cheaper office rents in outlying towns. Nevertheless, the **glittering high-rise world** is an experience, and not just because of the monumental Grande Arche. In June, the district swings for a week at **La Défense Jazz Festival**.

CNIT

Located at 2, Place de la Défense, the Centre for Industry and Technology, Espace Benjamin Franklin, inaugurated by Charles de Gaulle in 1958, is considered an architectural masterpiece of the new epoch. The structural marvel of the unsupported double-shelled vault with a width of 284m/932ft still impresses (www.cnit.com).

*La Grande Arche

The 110m/361ft high **»Triumphal Arc to Human Rights«** clad in Carrara marble was inaugurated as part of the 200-year anniversary celebrations for the French Revolution in 1989 – a symbol of brotherhood and a personal triumph for ex-president Mitterand, who realized one of his »grands projets« here. The construction designed by Johan Otto von Spreckelsen rests on twelve 30m/98ft concrete piles. The »Toit de la Grande Arche« roof terrace was closed in 2010 and transformed into offices (www.grandearche.com).

Renovation rather than demolition was the name of the game when, from 2007–11 **Tour First** was mounted atop the erstwhile Tour AXA. The 297m/974ft-high **Tour Phare**, designed by Thom Mayne, is due to be finished by 2017, complete with panoramic restaurant. Behind the Grande Arche the multifunctional **Arena 92** stadium by Christian de Portzamparc is projected to open by the end of 2016.

Further structures

** Disneyland Paris

——————————————— ✦ Excursion

Location: Marne-la-Vallée, 32 km/20 mi east

Since it was opened in 1992, more than 250 million visitors have been wowed by Disneyland Paris. The wonderland includes magical fairytale worlds, the Walt Disney Studios and lots of other attractions, lively shows, firework displays and colourful parades.

Experience Disneyland

INFORMATION AND GETTING THERE
www.disneylandparis.co.uk/
www.disneylandparis.com
1 and 3-day passes (1-day/1 park adults €69, children €59) can be obtained online, at the main entrance, at the Paris Tourist Offices and Welcome Centres and at the Paris airports; seasonal special offers and all-inclusive packages are available. Queues have to be expected. Disney's fairy tale park can also be explored online with a virtual flight in Google Earth. More than 85,000 pictures were taken.

Reservations
From the UK: tel. 08448 008 898
From the US: tel. 33 1 60 30 60 53

Opening hours
daily from 10am on

Getting there
RER: Marne-la-Vallée–Chessy (Line A)
Shuttle buses from Orly and Roissy airports and Gare du Nord station

ACCOMMODATION, FOOD AND RECREATION
Eight hotels from the Disneyland Hotel with pointed turrets to trapper-style log cabins are located directly in the Magic Kingdom. Fitness fans are catered for with pools, bike hire, pony rides, tennis courts and a 27-hole golf course. The 71 eateries range from the exclusive Victorian-style Walt's Restaurant to the snack cart with popcorn, hot dogs, and bagels. Those exhausted from all the activities can float in the hot air balloon above Lake Disney or opt for beauty treatment in the Celestial Spa at the Disneyland Hotels.

DISNEYLAND PARK

Turn-of-the-century charm There are Percheron horse-drawn trams to take you along the bustling, Victorian-style **Main Street**. In Liberty Court you can relive the inauguration of the Statue of Liberty in 1886, whilst the pioneering inventions of the 20th century are presented in the form of models in Discovery Arcade. A razor shave like in the good old days can be had in the Harmony Barber Shop and general stores offer temping assorted flavours of ice cream and other delicacies.

Disneyland railroad An old-time **steam engine** puffs past a diorama of the Grand Canyon to Frontierland and Fantasyland stations before returning by way of Discoveryland to Main Street.

Frontierland Frontierland is entered through the wooden gates of Fort Comstock. The ghoulish masters of the spooky **Phantom Manor** will show visitors its eerie rooms. Then it's along the Rivers of the Far West on a steamboat, in an Indian canoe or in a flat-bottomed boat. Youngsters can play around and climb in the Pocohontas Indian Village. Or take a dizzying ride through the canyons of **Big Thunder Mountain**.

Adventurelnd Among the attractions offered in Adventureland are an exploration of the labyrinth of caves of the **Pirates of the Caribbean**, a skull fortress, a precariously swaying suspension bridge over a rushing waterfall, **Captain Hook's Pirate Ship**, a runaway train on the trail of **Indiana Jones** through the ruins of the Temple of Peril, and a pirate playground for the young pirate. Refreshments can be had in the Oriental market – African cooking and Caribbean seafood.

Fantasyland The main attraction of Fantasyland is the Château de la Belle au Bois Dormant. On the first floor of **Sleeping Beauty's Castle** colourful stained glass windows and tapestries recount the age-old fairy tale and there is even a fire-breathing dragon in the cellar. Afterwards, follow in the footsteps of Snow White, take a ride on Lancelot's carousel, accompany Pinocchio on his travels and fly to Never-Never-Land with Peter Pan. Or get lost in Alice's Wonderland, take a flight on Dumbo the Flying Elephant, stroll through Fairy Tale Land or take a musical cruise through »**It's a Small World**« before trying some English sandwiches or a sweet-smelling Viennese strudel.

Discovery-land Here you will be impressed the **inventions** of Leonardo da Vinci, Jules Verne and HG Wells. At the **Buzz Lightyear Laser Blast**, with a laser sword you can help a space ranger in the fight against the evil Zurg. In **Space Mountain** you are fired into space with a turbo laser cannon and have to dodge the screaming meteorites and black holes. In **Star Tours**, you can encounter the R2D2 before beginning the journey to the Moon of Endor. **Captain EO** has returned – in a show with songs by Michael Jackson and special effects. Not too much for you? Then take control of one of the twelve rockets of the **Orbitron**, dive into the world of Jules Verne with **Les Mystères du Nautilus** or test your driving skills in **Autopia** in speedsters from the 1950s.

The glittering America for night owls equals **nonstop action** from 7.30am to 4am. The entertainment area features bars, restaurants, cinemas, the world's largest helium passenger balloon PanoraMagique, Disney boutiques and the Hurricanes club. The Planet Hollywood restaurant has lots of cinema décor on display and in Annette's Diner, waitresses on roller-skates serve brownies and burgers like they did in the 1950s – to Songs by Elvis and Chuck Berry.

Disney Village

The **Dinner Show** is on daily except Wed and Thur at 6 and 9 pm, and with chili con carne, barbecue chicken and warm apple pie it delivers the real thrill of the Wild West. Featuring intrepid cowboys, sharpshooter Annie Oakley, Chief Sitting Bull, bisons and wild longhorns the show is based on the famous Wild West shows with which Buffalo Bill toured North America and Europe at the end of the 19th century.

Buffalo Bill's Wild West Show

WALT DISNEY STUDIOS

Four film studios to tell the history of animation and special effects. In the **Front Lot** you will be sitting in the first row for a film production. Daring stunts are rehearsed outdoors on the **Back Lot**. The **Toon Studio** reveals how the animator's masterpieces are created, and the **Production Courtyard** tells you all about the worlds of TV and cinema. In **Crush's Coaster** you'll swim through coral reefs with Nemo, in **Cars Race Rally** you will whiz along Route 66 in a racing car with Flash McQueen. In the **Twilight Zone Tower of Terror** you can plunge into the fourth dimension when the mystery of the stormy night of 31 October 1939 is revealed. Or slide with the alien **Stitch** from one chat disaster to another and experience a feel-good show like **High School Musical**, with romantic ballads and groovy rock songs.

Animation or action?

! MARCO POLO TIP

Ultimate shopping   **Insider Tip**

A shuttle bus runs between Disneyland Paris and Place des Pyramides in Paris daily from 10am–8pm. It stops at »La Vallée Village«, just 35 minutes from Paris and 5 minutes from Disneyland. Also open on Sunday in summer, the village's 90 fashion and lifestyle outlets include: Armani, Diane v. Fürstenberg and Paul Smith (3, Cours de la Garonne, Serris, www.lavalleevillage.com).

In **Animagic**, Disney classics are brought to life by Mickey, Donald and their friends. Milestones in the history of film are shown at the **Ciné-Magique**.

Faubourg Saint-Honoré
✳ E/F 4/5

Location: 8th arr.
Métro stations: St-Philippe-du-Roule, Madeleine, Palais Royal, Louvre
❶ www.faubourgsainthonoreguide.com

Faubourg Saint-Honoré is the name of both a street and a district, bounded by Rue Royale, the Malesherbes and Haussmann boulevards and the ▶Champs-Elysées.

Posh shopping district

The main attraction of the quarter are the breathtakingly expensive shops on the elegant ** **Rue du Faubourg St-Honoré** with jewellers, art galleries and fashion houses such as Chanel (No. 21), Lanvin (No. 22), Hermès (No. 24), Guy Laroche (No. 24), Chloé (No. 54–56), Pierre Cardin (No. 59) and Christian Lacroix (No. 73). Stars, models and millionaires are regular guests at the luxury **Hôtel Le Bristol**, where chef Erich Fréchon is at the helm in the three-star restaurant. Woody Allen immortalized the establishment owned by German Oetker family (of baking powder fame) in 2011 with his nostalgic film *Midnight in Paris*.

*Palais de l'Elysée

Every morning at 8 o'clock the changing of the guard takes place in front of house number 55–57, which has been the **official residence of the president of France** since 1873. The president's office gleams with the opulent gold of the 18th century and when the head of state has ended a television address, recorded in the building's own TV studio, the image that appears is the floodlit façade of the palais – also jokingly referred to as »Le Château«. The Comte d'Evreux's country manor built in 1718 just outside the city gates already had a chequered history when Charles de Gaulle moved in as first president of the Fifth Republic in 1959. The second owner, the Marquise de Pompadour, Louis XV's mistress and grande dame of the Rococo period, was the subject of gossip in Paris society. Later, tongues wagged about an exclusive brothel established in the building. Napoleon I signed his second abdication here in 1815 after his defeat at Waterloo. Napoleon III installed the military headquarters of the Second Empire here. In 2008, former President Sarkozy and Carla Bruni tied the knot in the Elysée. Today »Jupiter«, a bunker to serve as the presidential command centre in case of a nuclear emergency, is in the cellar. The Council of Ministers meets every Wednesday in the Salon Murat. And every 14 July, around 5000 invited guests enjoy a garden party here – the national holiday could hardly be celebrated in a more respectable manner.

** Fontainebleau

⚡ **Excursion**

Location: 65 km south
Train: Transilien suburban train from Gare de Lyon to Fontainebleau Avon
❶ www.musee-chateau-fontainebleau.fr

It takes about 40 minutes by train from the Gare de Lyon to the unspoiled Forêt de Fontainebleau with its magnificent woodland, deep gorges and climbing boulders. The French kings lived here in the Château de Fontainebleau for 800 years. Today, it is a UNESCO World Heritage Site.

Black woodpecker, spotted salamander and squirrels abound in the forests of Fontainebleau – with 150 km of hiking trails and 160 climbing spots a must for nature lovers. From Fontainebleau the **long-distance hiking trail GR1** leads via the summit of Mont Chauvet and the Apremont Gorge to **Barbizon**. Here at the **Auberge Ganne**, a museum recalls how, in the mid-19th century, Corot, Rousseau and Millet painted their canvases of the light-filled forest »en plein air«. Jean-François Millet lived for 26 years at Grande Rue No. 27, where today a museum preserves the flair of his creative years.

Hiking paradise

Auberge Ganne: 92, Grande Rue, daily except Tue 10am–12.30pm and 2pm–5.30pm, July and Aug till 6pm, adults €3, under 18s free admission
Atelier Millet: daily 9.30am–12.30pm and 2–5pm, www.atelier-millet.fr, adults €4

The Capetian king Robert the Pious built the first hunting lodge at Fontainebleau in 998, Louis VII had a second lodge built together with monastery in 1169. In 1528 Francis I commissioned the architects Gilles le Breton, Pierre Chambiges and Pierre Girard as well as the Italian artists Le Rosso, Le Primatice and Niccolo Dell'Abate to create a splendid new **** Renaissance Château,** which was subsequently enlarged by Henry II, Henry IV and Louis XV and restored by Napoleon as his first imperial residence. A lot of history has been written at Fontainebleau: on 18 October 1685, Louis XIV revoked the Edict of Nantes here, on 6 April 1814 Napoleon signed his abdication here, and between 1949 and 1966 the palace was a

Historic palace

Fontainebleau castle is UNESCO World Heritage Site

headquarters of NATO. Highlights of the palace include the Gallery of François I, the ballroom, the royal apartments and the »Golden Door« in the Cour de Fontainebleau. The Baroque garden was laid out by André Le Nôtre in 1663–88 and the Jardin Anglais was created during the time of Napoleon.

Château de Fontainebleau: April–Sept daily except Tue 9.30am–6pm, Nov–March until 5pm; www.musee-chateau-fontainebleau.fr
Grands Appartements adults €11, Petits Appartements adults €6,50; tickets are reduced to 50% one hour before closing

∗ Grand Palais

✳ E 5

Location: 31, Avenue du Général Eisenhower (8th arr.)
Métro station: Champs-Elysées – Clemenceau
❶ www.grandpalais.fr

The Art Nouveau iron and glass structures known as the Grand Palais and ▶Petit Palais were both constructed for the World Expo of 1900. Important art exhibitions, live concerts and corporate presentations are staged beneath the 43m/141ft-high glass dome of the Grand Palais – as well as the annual Chanel fashion show. In the fine »Mini Palais« restaurant, star chef Eric Fréchon has been conjuring up his mini works of art since 2010 (www.minipalais.com).

∗Le Nef The space beneath the glorious Art Nouveau steel and glass dome of the Grand Palais is used for staging contemporary art. For the

Monumenta art show in May/June each year, a world-famous artist is asked to create a unique work: Anselm Kiefer in 2007, Richard Serra in 2008, Christian Boltanski in 2010, Anish Kapoor in 2011, Daniel Buren in 2012 (2013 was cancelled) and Ilya and Emilie Kabakov in 2014.

Insider Tip

❶ Entrance: Avenue Winston-Churchill; Mon and Wed 10am–7pm, Thur–Sun 10am 10pm, www.monumenta.com, adults from €5

Major exhibitions are mounted in the National Galleries, which are being expanded to include a café, shop and library (completion 2017).

Galéries Nationales

❶ 3 Avenue du Général-Eisenhower; opening times and admission prices depending on the popularity/ of the exhibition, www.fmn, adults from €13

On the initiative of Jean Perrin, winner of the Nobel Prize for Physics, the »**Palace of Discovery**« was established in the west wing in 1937, where it is now possible to learn about the laws of nature through interactive experiments. Highlights here are the rat school, the journey inside a cell, a presentation of static electricity and the canopy of stars in the planetarium.

*Palais de la Découverte

❶ Entrance: Avenue Franklin D. Roosevelt, Tue–Sat 9.30am 6pm, Sun 10am–7pm, tours of the electrostatic exhibition Sat 10am, Sun 10.30am, 1pm, 3pm and 5pm, www.palais-decouverte.fr, adults €8, supplement for Planetarium: €3

* Grands Boulevards · Opéra Garnier

✦ G 4

Location: Place de l'Opéra (9th arr.)
Métro station: Opéra

»If the good Lord gets bored up in heaven, he simply opens the window and looks out over the boulevards of Paris« raved the German poet Heinrich Heine about his »beautiful magic city«, which was his home for more than 20 years. A good 170 years later, the Grands Boulevards still form the axes of his chosen city, with plenty of glamour, luxury and Art Nouveau.

The Grands Boulevards, which are so typical of the Parisian cityscape, were created in 1668–1705 as the Cours Nouveau following the line of the old city walls built by Louis XIII and once connecting the Porte Saint-Antoine at today's Place de la Bastille to the Porte Sainte-Honoré, the city gate that stood where the ▶Madeleine now is. And

Grands Boulevards

just as Maupassant once described them in his »Bel Ami«, the Grands Boulevards remain today **promenades and fashionable boulevards** of the Parisians. On **Boulevard Haussmann** are two of the most beautiful Parisian department stores from the Art Nouveau period: the **Galeries Lafayette** (▶p. 144) and **Le Printemps** (▶p. 145).

**Opéra Garnier

What was at the time the largest opera house in the world was created in 1862–75 according to the plans of **Charles Garnier** in the opulent

With his Neo-baroque opera house, Garnier not only honoured the emperor but he also provided the strengthened bourgeoisie with a venue for self-expression

style of the Second Empire, with a floor area of 11,237m2/120,954 sq ft but only 1900 seats. Since the opening of the ►Opéra Bastille in 1990, it has remained a venue for **guest performances and ballet**. The seven arches at the base of the front facade are flanked by allegorical figures of poetry, music, speech, singing, drama and dance. The last one is a masterpiece by Carpeaux – the original is on display in the ►Musée d' Orsay. Above the statues are medallions of Cimarosa, Haydn, Pergolesi and Bach. The loggia resting on Corinthian columns is adorned with busts of Halévy, Meyerbeer, Rossini, Auber, Spontini, Beethoven and Mozart, the attica bears the gilded genii of Fame, Poetry and Choreography. After an assassination attempt in 1858, the Emperor had the Pavillon d' Honneur built on to the east side, enabling him to have direct access to his box. Today it houses the **Library Museum** (daily 10am–6pm), which has displays of old scores, manuscripts and opera props. In 1964 Marc Chagall took over the creation of the large **dome fresco** with famous opera and ballet scenes. Magnificent candelabras line the **grand marble staircase**. The allegorical paintings in the foyer date from the 19th century and were done by Paul Baudry. Since summer 2011, the two-starred chef Christophe Aribert has been spoiling diners at the new ***Opéra restaurant** guests with pata negra ham and lamb in herb crust (www.opera-restaurant. fr). The **Galerie de l' Opéra de Paris** bookshop on the Rue Halévy has all there is pertaining to the world of opera and ballet.

❶ daily 10am–5pm, mid-July–Aug till 6pm; adults €10. . Except during rehearsals and performances tickets are also valid for tours of the opera house: Wed, Sat, Sun 11.30am, 3.30pm (French), 11.30am, 2.30pm (English), www.operadeparis.fr.

Musée de la Parfumerie

The secrets of **perfume making** are revealed in a charming 19th century mansion at 9, Rue Scribe. With its precious vials and distilling apparatus, the **Fragonard Museum** tells a fragrant story. Founded in Grasse in 1926, the company's perfumes are sold at factory prices.

❶ daily 9am–6pm, Sun till 5pm, www.fragonard.com, free admission.

Paris Story This 50-minute multimedia show at 11b, Rue Scribe recalls the 2000-year history of the capital on a 12-m wide panoramic screen. Photos, famous paintings and portraits depict the passions of the rulers of France. Everything is narrated in 14 languages by your virtual guide Victor Hugo, whose verses are a love letter to Paris.

❶ An interactive model of Paris enables you to study each one of the capital's attractions. There's also a DVD of the show to take home (daily on the hour from 10am–6pm, www.paris-story.com; adults €10.50, family ticket for 2 adults + 2 children €26).

✴ Hôtel de Ville

✴ H 6

Location: Place de l'Hôtel de Ville (4th arr.)
Métro station: Hôtel de Ville
❶ groups only by appointment, tel. 01 42 76 54 04, security check!

Paris, long a »capital without a head«, has only had an elected mayor since 1977, with his/her official seat in the Hôtel de Ville. In 2014 Anne Hidalgo, member of the socialist party, became the first female mayor of the city.

Grand neo-Renaissance building In the Middle Ages, the city administration was headed by a **prévôt** (provost), who also was head of the Marchands de l'Eau, the company of merchant shippers of Paris. Their guild insignia, the ship, was the coat-of-arms of the city. The last prévôt was executed as a royal official by the revolutionary mob in 1789. After the Revolution, Paris had its own **mayor** (maire) only briefly from 1789 to 1794, in 1848 and in 1970–71; otherwise the city was administrated by representatives of the government, i.e. by a prefect or police prefect.

Nothing remains of the medieval town hall. The present neo-Renaissance building dates from 1882. The richly decorated façade is adorned with 136 statues and medallions of famous Parisian artists, poets and philosophers. The clock tower is crowned by the city's patron goddess. Among the decorations in the elegant state rooms are Rodin's bronze bust of the Republic and murals by Puvis de Chavannes.

Place de l'Hôtel de Ville In winter there is a floodlit ice skating rink on the **town hall square** and on the third Sunday in June it is the starting and finishing point of the annual Waiters' Race, in which the competitors must balance a tray with a full bottle and three empty glasses for a distance of 8km/5mi. At 14, Rue du Temple, the **Bazar de l'Hôtel de Ville** (www.bhv.fr), called simply »BHV« by Parisians, is an enormous

The city of Paris is run from the magnificent Hôtel de Ville

department store where you can buy everything for daily needs, fashion and household and garden items.

** Île de la Cité

 H 6

Location: Centre (1st/4th arr.)
Métro station: Cité

Île de la Cité is the historical as well as geographical centre of Paris. A Celtic tribe, the Parisii, settled on the island in the Seine in the 3rd century BC. The Romans founded the Gallo-Roman city of Lutetia here.

It was not until the High Middle Ages that the city was able to spread out on both banks of the Seine. From the 6th to the 14th centuries, the ruling monarch resided on the island with the royal palace (▶Palais de Justice) and its religious counterpart, the »Cathedral of France«, ▶Notre-Dame. When the royal residence was moved, spacious squares and wide streets were no longer required for the festivities of the court and a dense maze of narrow lanes and cramped rows of houses sprang up beneath the Gothic towers of Notre Dame.

Island for romantics

Paris was founded on the ship shaded Île de la Cité

In the 19th century, Prefect Haussmann radically transformed the face of the Cité. In a massive redevelopment campaign involving the relocation of over 25,000 people, space was created for the broad north-south axis of the city, the Préfecture de Police, the Tribunal de Commerce, the expansion of the Palais de Justice, the reconstruction of Hôtel Dieu and an unobstructed view of the cathedral. Any stroll around the island should naturally include a visit to ▶Notre-Dame, ▶Sainte-Chapelle, ▶Conciergerie and ▶Palais de Justice, but also a look at some less well-known places.

Square du Vert Galant Strollers on the prow of the ship-shaped island are greeted by an equestrian statue of **Henri IV** – the term »Vert Galant« (the gallant green), highly suggestive in French, is a reference to the countless love affairs of the womanizing monarch. His widow, Marie de Medici, had statue erected after the king's assassination.

Place Dauphin In 1607, Henry IV gave the plot of land on Pont Neuf to a wealthy court magistrate, Achille de Harlay, on the condition that he built a block of houses with uniform façades. De Harlay commissioned a triangular square with 65 buildings of light-coloured natural stone and red brick, which was named after the anticipated and longed-for dauphin, Louis XIII's successor. Today only nos. 14 and 26 of the original square remain.

There is a touch of romance about Rue des Ursins, which remained unaffected by Haussmann's urban renewal. The first harbour, **St Landry**, occupied this site until the 12th century. At the end of the street stand the remains of the Romanesque chapel of **St Aignan**. It is, together with Notre Dame and Sainte Chapelle, the last of the 23 churches formerly on the island.

Rue des Ursins

On Sundays between 8am and 7pm, canaries, myna birds, parrots and other fine feathered friends of man compete for attention at the **bird market** on the little Place Louis-Lépine. During the week, a **flower market** brightens up the banks of the Seine.

Marché aux Oiseaux

A hospital founded in the 7th century, Hôtel-Dieu, moved into the building next to Notre Dame in the mid-17th century. The original monastery stood on the small **Square Charlemagne**, where there is now an equestrian statue of Charlemagne. The **Memorial de la Déportation** on the southern tip of the island commemorates the victims of the Nazi concentration camps between 1940 and 1945.

Hôtel-Dieu

★ Île Saint-Louis

H/J 6/7

Location: Centre (4th arr.)
Métro station: Pont-Marie

At the instigation of Cardinal Richelieu in 1609, a single island was created out of the two originally separate islets, Île aux Vaches and Île Notre-Dame. The resulting island, Île Saint-Louis, was connected with the right bank of the Seine by two bridges and provided with a right-angled network of streets and uniform pattern of buildings.

The work was finished at the beginning of 1664 and the first tradesmen and merchants moved in. They were soon followed by the aristocracy, who had their elegant city palaces built along the banks. With the noble families came writers and poets like Charles Baudelaire, Théophile Gautier, Paul Claudel and Emile Zola, philosophers like Voltaire and Jean-Jacques Rousseau, as well as famous statesmen like Léon Blum and Georges Pompidou. Even today, many artists and writers are among the 6000 inhabitants of the small island. A large part of the 17th-century architecture has been retained in its original state and dignity. The harmony of the closely-packed rows of houses with small shops, refined pubs and cosy cafés, idyllic spots along the banks and the flavour of the past all contribute to its irresistible charm.

Aristocrats and artists

Saint-Louis-en-l'Île The church in Rue St-Louis-en-l'Île was begun in 1664 by Louis Le Vau and finished in 1726 by Jacques Doucet. Within its Baroque interior 17th-century paintings by Charles Coypel *(Supper at Emmaus)* and Pierre Mignard *(Flight into Egypt)* as well as *The Entombment of Christ* dating from the 16th century by Titian's brother, Francesco Vecellio, are worth seeing. There are **concerts of church music** almost every night during the summer.

Hôtel de Lauzun This hotel at 17, Quai d'Anjou, which dates from 1657 and is also attributed to the royal architect Le Vau, is used by the city as a guesthouse for state visits. For a while in the mid-19th century, Baudelaire, Gautier and the painter Beauvoir, all members of the legendary Club de Hachichins, lived here. It is no longer possible to tour the magnificent palace.

Berthillon
Insider Tip As long ago as the 1960s, Raymond **Berthillon** was being showered with awards by Gault-Millau for his fabulous ice cream. Today his daughter Marie-José Chauvin and grandchildren Muriel and Lionel run the business, which now offers up to 30 flavours. Truly sensational are the almond-chestnut ice cream and the ice cream bombe made from wild raspberries and vanilla parfait.

❶ 31, Rue Île Saint-Louis, Mon–Sun 10am–8pm, www.berthillon.fr

✳ Institut du Monde Arabe
✦ J 7

Location: 1, Rue des Fossés St-Bernard (5. arr.)
Métro station: Jussieu
Internet: www.imarabe.org
❶ Tue–Sun 10am–6pm. Current issues in the Arab world are explained at the at the »Jeudi de L 'IMA«, every Thursday at 6.30pm. New fiction and scientific publications are presented at the Café Littéraire every Wednesday from 7pm.

The task of this Islamic cultural centre on the left bank of the Seine is to mediate between the Occident and the Orient. It was designed by Jean Nouvel and completed in 1988.

Aspects of Islamic culture The filigree building with book tower, library, lecture hall, museum and documentation centre is decorated on its southern front by square glass windowpanes rising a full floor in height covered by an ornamental metallic screen with motor-controlled apertures that vary the amount of light filtered into the interior. The seven floors with calligraphy, printed books, coins and astrolabes, valuable tapestries and contemporary works provide a comprehensive insight in the art and cultural history of twenty **Islamic countries**.

Music, exhibitions and language courses are all part of the cultural programme. From the roof terrace of the **Ziryab Lebanese restaurant** there are great views of ▶Notre Dame and the ▶Île Saint-Louis. Ever since 1759, the levels of the Seine have been measured at the **Pont de la Tournelle**, which leads across to Île St-Louis.

MARCO ⊕ POLO TIP

Insider Tip

Dancing the tango

Tango dancers congregate every evening during the summer on the Quai Saint Bernard in order to practice their steps in the open air on the banks of the Seine. The accordion sounds usually come from speakers, but occasionally a small tango orchestra shows up and plays.

East of Pont de Suilly, the Quai Saint-Bernard constitutes the **Musée de la sculpture en plein air** all the way to Pont d'Austerlitz. Since 1945, more than 50 sculptures by Alexander Archipenko, Jean Arp, Constantin Brancusi, and two dozen more renowned sculptors have been placed along this bank of the Seine.

Art in the open-air

★ Invalides · Hôtel des Invalides

⎯⎯⎯⎯⎯⎯⎯⎯⎯⎯⎯⎯⎯⎯⎯⎯ ✦ E/F 6

Location: Esplanade des Invalides (7th arr.)
Métro stations: La Tour-Maubourg, Varenne (Métro), Invalides (RER)
❶ April–Sept daily 10am–6pm, Oct–March daily 10m–5pm, adults €9,50
www.invalides.org

The Sun King founded the Hôtel des Invalides as a home for 6000 of his army veterans – prior to this, the war invalids were given medical care, if any, and then left in the hands of charitable monasteries.

Today some 100 veterans live in the complex for war veterans that Libéral Bruant had constructed between 1671 and 1676 with a residential wing, hospital and the church St-Louis-des-Invalides. Most of the rooms are occupied by the military administration and the museum. The eye is immediately drawn to the main gate, whose gable displays Louis XIV clothed in Roman garb. Since the

The Dôme des Invalides, highlight of sacral French Baroque

Eglise du Dôme des Invalides

Eglise Saint-Louis-des-Invalides

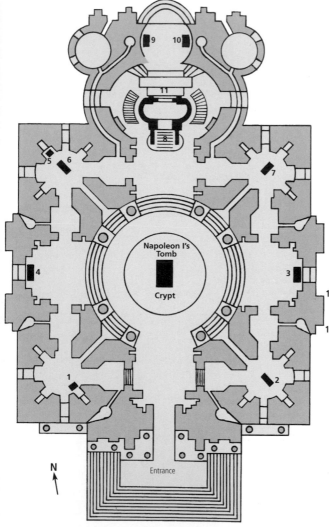

N

Entrance

Cour du Dôme/Place Vauban

1 Tomb of Napoleon's br
   Jérôme Bonaparte († 18
   in the Chapel of St-Jér

2 Tomb of Napoleon's br
   Joseph Bonaparte († 18

3 Memorial for the milita
   engineer Sébastien Le F
   de Vauban († 1707)
   with his heart

4 Tomb of Marshal Henri
   de La Tour d'Auvergne,
   Vicomte de Turenne (†

5 Heart of »First Grenadie
   France« Théophile Malc
   Corret de La Tour
   d'Auvergne († 1800)

6 Tomb of Marshal Louis
   Hubert Lyautey († 1934

7 Tomb of Marshal Ferdin
   Foch († 1929)

8 Altar with twisted colu
   and baldachin

9 Tomb of General
   Henri Bertrand († 1844)

10 Tomb of General Gérau
   Christophe Michel Durc
   († 1813)

11 Entrance to the Crypt:
   two large bronze statu
   at the entrance; inside
   Napoleon's tomb are tv
   colossal figures symoliz
   the emperor's victories
   in the background is th
   of Napoleon's son,
   François Charles
   Joseph Bonaparte († 18

10 m
33 ft
©BAEDEKER

plain soldiers' church was not to the king's liking, he commissioned Jules Hardouin-Mansart to build the Eglise du Dôme des Invalides, which he completed in 1706. Like the main façade, the roof windows facing the **Cour d'Honneur** of the Hôtel des Invalides are decorated with symbols of war. A bronze statue of Napoleon I as the »Little Corporal« in contemporary costume can be seen beneath the middle arch of the south pavilion. The spacious Esplanade leading down to the Seine was completed between 1704 and 1720 by Robert de Cotte.

Occupying the wings surrounding the Cour d'Honneur is the **Musée de l'Armée**, which has been displaying armour, uniforms, weapons and plans of major French campaigns since 1794. Beneath the Cour d'Honneur, **L'Historial Charles de Gaulle** documents the life of de Gaulle, in three main stages. At the heart of the retrospective is an auditorium, in which a 25-minute film about the achievements of the general and father of the nation is shown (www.charles-de gaulle. org). De Gaulle was also Grand Master of the Ordre de la Libération, whose commitment and success in the liberation of France is described in the **Musée de l'Ordre de la Libération** (www. ordredelaliberation.fr). Scale models of French castles, palaces and ports can be admired in the **Musée des Plan-Reliefs.**

Four museums

Begun in 1677 by Jules Hardouin-Mansarts and completed in 1735 by Robert de Cott, the **Dôme des Invalides** is considered to be the most significant religious building of the French Baroque period. The dome, rising over 100m/328ft high, is harmoniously complemented by the Doric and Corinthian columns decorating the façade. The nave is aflutter with flags and standards, the spoils of the victorious armies during the 19th and 20th centuries. The paintings in the area beneath the dome were done by Charles de la Fosse.

*Eglise du Dôme des Invalides

The open crypt is dominated by ****Napoleon's Tomb**. His mortal remains, which were brought back from St Helena in 1840, rest in a sarcophagus of red porphyry on a green granite base. Twelve goddesses in marble created by James Pradier recall Napoleon's triumphant military campaigns between 1797 and 1815. The only legitimate son of the emperor, Napoleon II, is buried in a small recess. He bore the titles King of Rome and Duke of Reichstadt, but died in Vienna in 1832 at the age of 21.

In the side chapels lie some of **France's great men**, among them Marshal Turenne (1611–75), Joseph Bonaparte, King of Spain (1768–1844), Napoleon's oldest brother, Jérôme Bonaparte, King of Westphalia (1784–1860) and the emperor's youngest brother, the military commander Théophile de La Tour d'Auvergne (1743–1800), General Bertrand (1773–1844), who accompanied Napoleon to St Helena as his major-domo, and Marshal Vauban (1633–1707), Louis XIV's military engineer.

The great caravan of elephants, rhinoceroses, lions and antelopes in the Gallery of Evolution

* Jardin des Plantes

———————————————— ✧ J 7/8

Location: 57, Rue Cuvier (5th arr.)
Métro stations: Jussieu, Place Monge, Gare d'Austerlitz

❶ April–Oct daily 7.30am–7.45pm, Nov–March daily 8am–5.30pm, greenhouses: 10am–6pm, menagerie 9am–6pm, free entrance (except Jardin alpin €2, Les Grandes serres €6), www.jardindesplantes.net

In accordance with his majesty's wishes, Louis XIII's personal physician planted a medicinal herb garden in 1633, which soon expanded into a large collection of plants.

Exotic flora and fauna A school of botany and pharmacy was established, and in 1650 the garden was opened to the public. The naturalist Georges Buffon (1707–88) expanded the garden into a **magnificent park**. Parisians first became acquainted with wild animals during the French Revolution, when the zoological collection was moved from the royal court at Versailles and resettled in the English Garden of the Jardin des Plantes. In 1795, they were able to marvel at elephants for the first time; in 1826 came the first giraffes, and Napoleon provided a bear pit. The iron and glass structures of the galleries for botany and mineralogy with greenhouses and an aviary were likewise constructed in the 19th century. The black locust tree planted in 1636, standing between the botany and mineralogy galleries, is thought to be the oldest tree in Paris. Over 170 species blossom in the rose garden and there are rare plants from the Pyrenees, the Alps and the Himalayas in the Jardin Alpin. In the greenhouses, which were restored between 2005 and 2010, visitors can study arid plants and mangrove swamps or walk through tropical rainforest to admire giant ferns, orchids and banana trees. In the ménagerie, which was opened in 1794, there are cheetahs, reptiles and exotic birds. Old trees line the path up to the bronze temple atop the Labyrinth Hill – a sanctuary for romantics past and present.

* MUSÉUM NATIONAL D'HISTOIRE NATURELLE

The museum complex is a treasure trove for naturalists of all ages. More than 600,000 unusual minerals and meteorites from all over the world can be admired in the **Gallery of Mineralogy, Geology and Paleobotany** at 36, Rue Geoffroy St-Hilaire, including gems from the French crown jewels. The gallery, which was restored in 2011, is also a pioneer in the study and classification of minerals as a systematic science. The story of the evolution of plants covers three thousand million years.

Galerie de Minéralogie et de Géologie

❶ Wed–Mon 10am–6pm, www.mnhn.fr adults €9, under 26s €7

A caravan of elephants, rhinoceros, zebras, lions and antelopes greets visitors to the **Gallery of Evolution** built in 1889 by Jules André. With almost 7000 species, including many that are threatened with extinction, the museum takes you on a journey through jungle, desert and steppe. Micro-organisms and the world of the oceans and the polar regions are the topics on the ground floor and first floor. Displays on the second floor focus on man's influence on the environment. The gallery of extinct plants and animals includes the Tasmanian tiger and the black-maned Cape lion. The Indian rhinoceros on the third floor once belonged to Louis XV. For 6- to 12-year-olds the **Gallery des Enfants** explains the themes of environment and sustainability in an exciting and playful way.

**Grande Galerie de l'Evolution

❶ Wed–Mon 10am–6pm, www.mnhn.fr, adults €8, under 26s €6

! *Allahu Akbar!*

Insider Tip

MARCO ⊕ POLO TIP

»God is great!« the muezzin call from the 33 m/100 ft high minaret of the Paris mosque opposite the southern entrance of Jardin des Plantes. The mosque from the 1920s includes an Islamic institute for religious studies. You can have a relaxing visit to the hammam (women: Mon, Wed, Thur, Sat 10am–9pm, Fri 2pm–9pm, men: Tue, Sun 2pm–9pm) while the souk sells silver jewellery from North Africa and the oriental restaurant in the inner courtyard serves mezzas, couscous and peppermint tea (39, Rue Ste-Hilaire, open daily, www.mosquee-de-paris.org).

Galerie d'Anatomie comparée et de Paléontologie A skeletal cavalcade of tigers, elephants and whales parades beneath the steel supports of the hall of the Department of Comparative Anatomy – the collection boasts close to a million skeletons. The first floor has fascinating displays of **models of dinosaurs**, mastodons and giant flying beasts from prehistoric times.

❶ Entrance: 2, Rue Buffon, Wed–Mon 10am–5pm, www.mnhn.fr, adults €8, under 26s €7. CHECK ADMISSION CHARGES

Arènes de Lutèce The ruins of this amphitheatre, which were discovered at 49, Rue de Navarre in 1869, give a good idea of the scale of the original structure: measuring 56 x 48 m, the oval shaped arena was almost as large as that of the Colosseum in Rome. And just like in the city on the Tiber, **gladiatorial battles and animal baiting** also took place at this venue in Roman Lutetia, which was built around 200 AD. While the amphitheatre had only 36 rows of seating, with its 15,000 seats it could accommodate almost the entire population of the town at that time. But it didn't last for long: when the barbarians invaded in 285, the arena was already being used as a quarry for erecting fortifications. Today the public open space is used by the »Arènes de Lutèce« **pétanque** club.

❶ April–Oct daily 9am–9.30pm, Nov–Mar daily 8am–5.30pm, admission free

✷✷ **Louvre**

✦ **G 5/6**

Location: between the Rive Droite and Rue de Rivoli (1st arr.)
Métro station: Palais-Royal–Musée-du-Louvre
❶ www.louvre.fr
daily except Tue 9am–6pm, Wed and Fri till 9.45pm, adults €12, Hall Napoléon €13, combination ticket €16; admission tickets cheaper Mon and Fri after 6pm. Admission free for those aged 18 and under, for EU citizens under 26 and for all every 1st Sun in month. To avoid a long queue it is highly recommended to buy tickets in advance online or at a branch of FNAC, such as at the airport, the Gare de l'Est or Gare de Montparanasse. Bon Marché, Printemps and the Galeries Lafayette also sell Louvre tickets.

The history of the Louvre spans more than eight centuries of building, destruction and rebuilding. France's monarchs, from François I to Louis XIV, expanded the medieval fortified castle into a magnificent palace. The Louvre opened as a museum in 1793.

Grand Louvre Its encyclopaedic arrangement of art became a model for the 19th and 20th century concepts of humanistic museums. The remodelling into the »Grand Louvre« took almost two decades. By the turn of the millennium, the exhibition space had almost been doubled through the addition of 61,300 sq m/ 659,828 sq ft, making the Louvre the **world's largest art museum**.

The Louvre palace stands on the site of a medieval fortress built by Philippe II Auguste in 1190 on the right bank of the Seine, which at the time was called Lupara – the source of the name Louvre. The remains of the **medieval fortress** can be viewed in the Sully Wing under the Cour Carrée. Raymond du Temple enlarged the existing stronghold for Charles V, who moved into it in 1360, although the palace on Île de la Cité remained the official residence.

From fortress to art museum

The **city palace** was only sporadically occupied by French rulers until the reign of Henri II. The Louvre served more as an arsenal in the 15th century since the kings preferred to stay in their castles on the Loire. François I in the early 16th century was the first to again take an interest in the building. He had the medieval keep demolished and commissioned the architect Pierre Lescot and the sculptor Jean

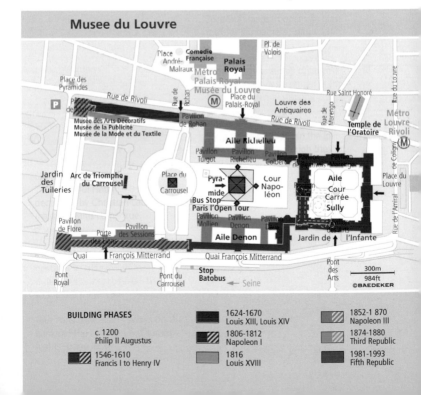

Musée du Louvre

BUILDING PHASES			
	c. 1200 Philip II Augustus	1624-1670 Louis XIII, Louis XIV	1852-1 870 Napoleon III
	1546-1610 Francis I to Henry IV	1806-1812 Napoleon I	1874-1880 Third Republic
		1816 Louis XVIII	1981-1993 Fifth Republic

©BAEDEKER

Goujon to construct the west and south wings of the old Louvre around the present day Cour Carrée following Italian models. They were completed during the reign of Henri II, and the Petite Galerie was added in 1566.

After the death of Henri II, his widow, Catherine de' Médici, had the **Palais de Tuileries** begun in 1564 as a residence for herself just 500m away from the old Louvre. During the reign of Henri IV, this palace was connected to the Petite Galerie through a long south wing along the Seine. After Henri IV was assassinated, his widow moved into the Palais du ►Luxembourg. Her son, Louis XIII, had the Cour Carrée and the Sully Wing completed. Louis XIV commissioned Le Brun and Le Vau with the remodelling of the Petite Galerie and Claude Perrault with the construction of a monumental façade on the east wing, today's Colonnade. But the Louvre and the Palais de Tuileries were only occasionally occupied, and with the transfer of the royal residence to ►Versailles the building fell into such a state of disrepair that its demolition was even considered in the mid-18th century until Louis XV ordered the first renovation work. At the same time, the idea emerged of displaying all of the royal collections together in the Louvre. In 1776, the Grande Galerie was declared a museum and on 10 August 1793, the **Musée Central des Arts** was opened in the royal chambers. Napoleon I had the Arc de Triomphe du Carrousel erected on the space in front of the Palais de Tuileries and initiated the construction of the north wing on Rue de Rivoli. The Louvre and the Tuileries were joined during the reign of Napoleon III, and the Jardin and Place du Carrousel were laid out in their present form by Visconti and Lefuel. On 23 May 1871 the Palais de Tuileries was gutted by a fire set by the Communards, but the Louvre fortunately remained unscathed. In 1981, François Mitterrand approved the renovation and expansion of the Louvre into the **Grand Louvre**, a repository of the world's cultural history.

Vieux Louvre (Aile Sully)   The buildings round the square of Cour Carrée are part of the Old Louvre (Vieux Louvre), known today as the **Sully Wing**. This was the site of Philippe II Auguste's original fortress. The Lescot façade was begun during the reign of Henri II, the other wings under Louis XIII and Louis XIV, but they were not completed until the reign of Napoleon I. The Pavillon de l'Horloge or Sully Wing was designed in the 17th century by Jacques Lemercier to match the style of the Lescot façade. In 1559–74 the architect Pierre Lescot and the sculptor Jean Goujon had created a **masterpiece of Renaissance architecture** with the south half of the west wing. The three pavilions of the *** Lescot façade** are decorated with reliefs featuring allegories, statues and garlands of fruit. The pediment reliefs by Goujon

Café Marly – a front row seat in the inner court of the Louvre

symbolize nature, war and science. On the left, Ceres (for agriculture) and Neptune (for maritime trade) and Genius with a cornucopia; in the middle is Mars, the god of war, Bellona, the goddess of war, and prisoners; on the right is Archimedes for astronomy and Euclid for geometry.

Louis XIV held a competition for the design of the east façade of the old Louvre in 1665. The winning design was a joint effort by Claude Perrault, Louis le Vau and François d'Obray. Their **colonnade** with its 36 Corinthian columns is a compromise between French Baroque and Italian models. Thanks to its exposed foundation, the colonnade now rises to a majestic height. The classical severity of this magnificent façade was meant to be relieved by a row of statues on the roof balustrade, but this part was not carried out. The Minerva figure in the tympanum and the relief of the goddess of victory above the doorway date from the early 19th century. The medallions bear the initials of Louis XIV.

Pavillon de Flore

Until 1871 the Tuileries Palace stood between the Pavillon de Flore and the Pavillon de Marsan. The Flore Wing took its name from a ballet that was staged for Louis XIV and was immortalized by Jean-Baptiste Carpeaux in 1866 in the relief *Triumph of Flora* on the side facing the Seine.

Carrousel du Louvre

Between 1989 and 1993 a spacious underground **shopping arcade** was built beneath the Place du Carrousel and the Tuileries Gardens with luxury boutiques, restaurants and four huge halls for holding exhibitions, concerts and the fashion shows of the great couturiers. During the excavations, a 130m/426ft-long section of the 16th-century city wall was uncovered. The architects, Ieoh Ming Pei and Michel Macary, skilfully integrated it into the structure of light-coloured sandstone and furrowed concrete. The inverted pyramid provides the entrance hall with daylight – Pei's counterpart to his glass pyramid that forms the main entrance to the museum.

Arc de Triomphe du Carrousel

This former **gateway to the forecourt of Tuileries Palace** is modelled on the triumphal arch of Septimius Severus in Rome. It was erected by Percier and Fontaine in 1806–08 to commemorate Napoleon's victories. F. J. Bosio created the quadriga in 1828 that crowns the Arc du Carrousel. »Carrousel« was the name given to the equestrian events and masked festivals that developed out of medieval tournaments.

** MUSÉE DU LOUVRE

Entrances

The main entrance is the **glass pyramid** in the Cour Napoléon. Those who already have a ticket can use a special entrance at the pyramid or the other entrances at the Carrousel du Louvre, 99, Rue de Rivoli, Passage Richelieu and the Porte des Lions. These entrances are also reserved for holders of a Louvre Card or Paris Museum Pass, »Friends of the Louvre« and groups and visitors to the auditorium.

❶ At the entrances Nintendo 3DS Multimedia Guides with tours and a selection of the most important works are available in seven languages (adults €5, under 18s €3). For children there is an interactive touch-screen tour with the musketier Jean de Laguarrigue, which leads through the Louvre Palace as it was at the time of Louis XIII for 90 mins. Visiting the Egyptians at the time of the Pharaohs takes the same amount of time (http://monguide.louvre.fr).

*Glass pyramid

Since 1989, the clear glass pyramid by Ieoh Ming Pei (born 1917), almost 22m/72ft high and consisting of 675 panes, has led visitors down into the **Hall Napoléon**, the vast lobby with information stands, ticket counters, bookstalls, café, an auditorium, a collection of engravings and rooms for temporary exhibitions. Corridors and

Louvre

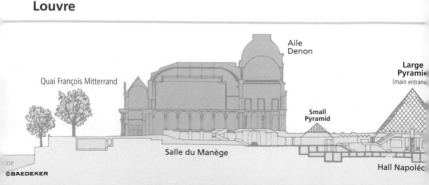

Aile Denon

Quai François Mitterrand

Large Pyrami⬤ (main entran⬤

Small Pyramid

Salle du Manège

Hall Napoléo⬤

ine

©BAEDEKER

escalators lead from there to the various art departments. In the Cour Carrée and Cour Napoléon, archaeologists uncovered the remains of Philippe II Auguste's 13th-century fortress with its fortified tower and Charles V's 14th-century palace. The exhibition on the history of the Louvre is completed by the remains of a wall of the **medieval Louvre** and a model of the stronghold.

The **Richelieu Wing**, which until 1993 housed the Ministry of Finance, now exhibits French sculpture and painting, Islamic art and Oriental antiquities, as well as handicrafts and German, Flemish and Dutch paintings.   **Aile Richelieu**

The lower ground floor of the **Sully Wing** around the Cour Carrée houses the Louvre's historical department with the excavations of the medieval fortress. On the ground floor can be seen Egyptian antiquities of the pharaohs and ancient Greek, Etruscan and Roman sculptures such as the famous *Venus de Milo,* while on the first floor visitors can admire handicrafts and works of antiquity as like the *Winged Victory of Samothrace.* The second floor is reserved for French painting from the 17th to 19th centuries and graphic arts.   **Aile Sully**

The lower ground floor of the **Denon Wing** houses Coptic, Greek and Roman antiquities and Italian, German, Dutch and Spanish sculptures. The ground floor is also home to ancient Greek, Etruscan and Roman works as well as Italian, German, Danish, Flemish and Dutch sculptures. The first floor holds the Galerie d'Apollon with the crown jewels, large-format 19th-century French paintings like David's *Coronation of Napoleon,* Spanish and British masters as well as paintings, prints and drawings from Italy from the 11th to the 18th centuries, including Leonardo da Vinci's enigmatic *Mona Lisa.* In 2012 the new exhibition of Islamic Art opened in the Cour Visconti. By 2018 all the Islamic art treasures from the ground floor of the Richelieu Wing will have been transferred here.   **Aile Denon**

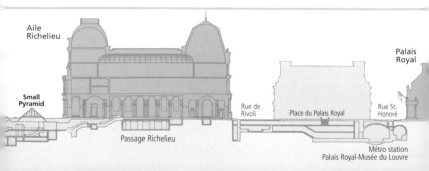

Aile Richelieu

Palais Royal

Small Pyramid

Rue de Rivoli   Place du Palais Royal   Rue St. Honoré

Passage Richelieu

Métro station Palais Royal-Musée du Louvre

Musée du Louvre

MEZZANINE

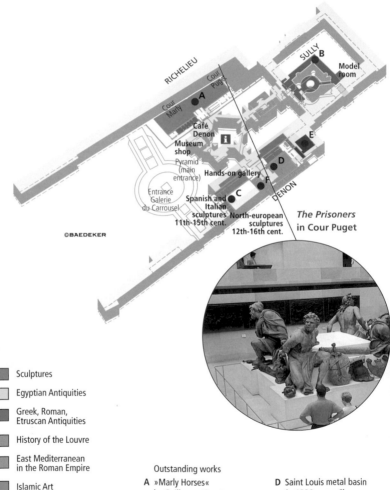

RICHELIEU

Cour Puget

Cour Marly

SULLY

B

Model room

A

Café Denon

E

Museum shop

i

Pyramid (main entrance)

Hands-on gallery

D

Entrance Galerie du Carrousel

Spanish and Italian sculptures 11th-15th cent.

C

F

North-european sculptures 12th-16th cent.

DENON

©BAEDEKER

The Prisoners in Cour Puget

Sculptures

Egyptian Antiquities

Greek, Roman, Etruscan Antiquities

History of the Louvre

East Mediterranean in the Roman Empire

Islamic Art

Medieval Louvre

Coptic Egypt

Temporary Exhibitions

Outstanding works

A »Marly Horses« by Guillaume Cousteau (c. 1743, Cour Marly)

B Medieval moat

C St Mary Magdalene by G. Erhart (c. 1515, room C/ showcase 6)

D Saint Louis metal basin (c. 1320, room 6)

E »Christ and abbot Mena« (c. AD 550)

F Portrait of a young woman (2nd cent. BC, room 1)

GROUND FLOOR

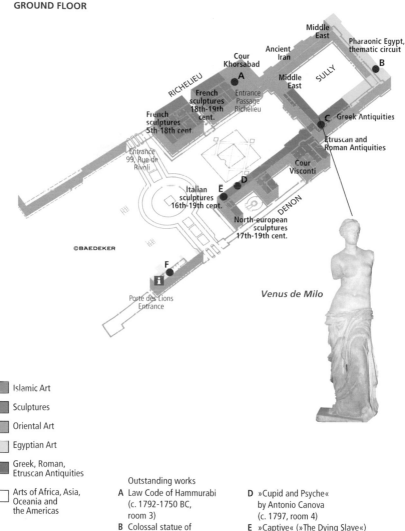

Middle East

Pharaonic Egypt, thematic circuit

Cour Khorsabad

Ancient Iran

B

RICHELIEU

A

French sculptures 18th-19th cent.

Entrance Passage Richelieu

Middle East

SULLY

French sculptures 5th-18th cent.

C Greek Antiquities

Etruscan and Roman Antiquities

Entrance 99, Rue de Rivoli

Cour Visconti

D

Italian sculptures 16th-19th cent.

E

DENON

North-european sculptures 17th-19th cent.

©BAEDEKER

F

ℹ

Porte des Lions Entrance

Venus de Milo

■ Islamic Art

■ Sculptures

■ Oriental Art

■ Egyptian Art

■ Greek, Roman, Etruscan Antiquities

☐ Arts of Africa, Asia, Oceania and the Americas

Outstanding works

A Law Code of Hammurabi (c. 1792-1750 BC, room 3)

B Colossal statue of Ramesses II (1279-1213 BC, room 12)

C Venus de Milo (c. 100 BC, room 7)

D »Cupid and Psyche« by Antonio Canova (c. 1797, room 4)

E »Captive« (»The Dying Slave«) by Michelangelo (c. 1513, room 4)

F Female sculpture from Chupicuaro (Mexico, 7.-2. cent. BC)

Musée du Louvre

FIRST FLOOR

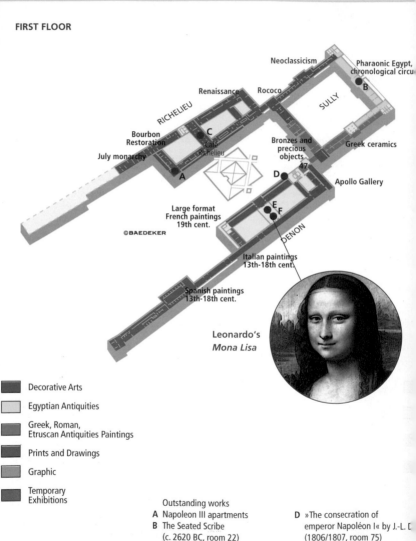

Neoclassicism

Pharaonic Egypt, chronological circu

B

Renaissance   Rococo

RICHELIEU   SULLY

Bourbon Restoration   **C**   Café Richelieu

July monarchy   Bronzes and precious objects   **Greek ceramics**

47

A   **D**

Large format French paintings 19th cent.   **E**   **F**   Apollo Gallery

©BAEDEKER   DENON

Italian paintings 13th-18th cent.

Spanish paintings 13th-18th cent.

Leonardo's *Mona Lisa*

Decorative Arts

Egyptian Antiquities

Greek, Roman, Etruscan Antiquities Paintings

Prints and Drawings

Graphic

Temporary Exhibitions

Outstanding works
A Napoleon III apartments
B The Seated Scribe (c. 2620 BC, room 22)
C Treasury of St-Denis (Suger's eagle, 12th cent., room 2)

D »The consecration of emperor Napoléon I« by J.-L. [(1806/1807, room 75)
E »Mona Lisa/La Joconde« by Le da Vinci (1503-1506, room 6)
F »The Wedding Feast at Cana« Veronese (1563, room 6)

SECOND FLOOR

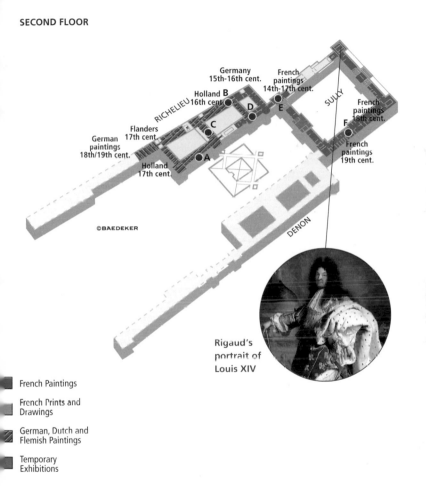

Rigaud's
portrait of
Louis XIV

German, Dutch and
Flemish Paintings

Temporary
Exhibitions

French Paintings

French Prints and
Drawings

©BAEDEKER

Outstanding works

A »The Lacemaker«by Vermeer
(1669-1670, room 38

B Dürer 's Self-portrait
at the age of 22 (1493, room 8)

C »Maria de Medici«
cycle by Rubens
(1622-1625, room 18)

D »Four Seasons« by Nicholas Poussin
(c. 1660, room 16)

E »The Cheat with the
Ace of Diamonds«
by Georges de la Tour (c. 1635, room 24)

F »The Turkish Bath«
by J.D. Ingres (1862, room 60)

ART COLLECTIONS

Origins   It was desired by the king, founded by a revolutionary nation and organized by the state – it is not only the valuable collections that make the Louvre unusual. The first of the collector kings is considered to be François I, who amassed paintings like the famous *Mona Lisa*, sculptures and reproductions in the Italian style in Fontainebleau Palace. Another monarch equally interested in art was Louis XIV, who acquired the collections of Cardinal Mazarin and the banker Jabach, which included Titian's *Entombment of Christ*. By 1683, the paintings in the royal art collection already numbered over 2,000. The **Central Museum for Arts** was opened on 10 August 1793 in the Grand Gallery and the Salon Carré, and beginning in 1794 it became the recipient of thousands of works of art, all spoils of war. The Louvre continued to add to its collections after the fall of Napoleon's empire despite being relieved of all the ill-gotten art treasures confiscated abroad – with the exception of a few works, including Veronese's massive *Wedding at Cana*. Departments for Egyptian and Oriental antiquities were established in the course of the 19th century. At the same time, the **seven major curatorial departments** have continued to develop up to the present day, having gained important additions through new acquisitions and gifts. Here it is only possible to give a general overview of the collections, their eras and directions, and the works of art displayed and highlight a few items from the museum's immense store of art.

Greek, Etruscan and Roman antiquities   The history of ancient art from its beginnings to Hellenism and the last days of the Roman Empire is uniquely illustrated in three departments by marble and bronze works, frescoes, mosaics, ivory, gold and glass objects. Among the treasures of antiquity are Greek sculptures like a fragment of the Panathenaic frieze from the Parthenon and metopes from the Temple of Zeus at Olympia dating from the 5th century BC. An undoubted highlight is the **✶✶Venus de Milo**, a statue of Aphrodite dating from the late 2nd century BC found on the island of Milos in 1820, which is considered to be one of antiquity's most perfect depictions of female beauty. Other masterpieces include the Doric **✶ Lady of Auxerre** (c630 BC), one of the oldest examples of Greek sculpture, the Ionic *Hera of Samos* (570–560 BC) and the graceful *Rampin Head* (c550 BC) from the equestrian statue whose torso is in the Acropolis Museum in Athens.

The **✶✶Winged Victory of Samothrace**, a 2.5m/8ft-high Hellenistic statue of Nike the goddess of victory (190 BC), dominating the staircase, appears to be landing on the prow of a Rhodian ship after a wild flight from Olympia. Other items particularly deserving of attention are the **✶ Borghese Wrestler** (1st century BC), the bust of

Agrippa (1st century BC) and the *Altar of Domitius Ahenobarbus* (1st century BC) from the Temple of Neptune in Rome. The *Birth of the Tiber* also dates from the first century BC. For history fans there are fragments of the Roman altar of peace, the Ara Pacis, antique bronzes like *Apollo of Piombino* (c500 BC), an engraved Etruscan mirror (3rd century BC) and Greek vases ranging from the geometric style (9th century BC) to Hellenistic pottery (2nd century BC).

Major works from the Mesopotamian, Sumerian and Akkadian cultures include the * **Stele of Naram-Sin** commemorating the victory of the king of Agade (Akkad) over the barbarians in the Zagros Mountains around 2270 BC, and 21 statues of Gudea, the Sumerian prince of Lagash (c2150 BC). Not to be missed are the decorative fragments from the palaces of Nimrud, Nineveh and ***Khorsabad**, residence of King Sargon II (721–705 BC), whose huge 4m/13ft-high Assyrian winged beasts, benevolent spirits intended to protect the palace, give an impression of its original size. The main exhibit, however, is the ** **Code of Hammurabi** (1792–1750 BC), king of the first Babylonian kingdom. Discovered in Susa in 1901 by a French archeological mission, the stele is a conical, 2.25m/7ft 5in-high basalt cylinder covered with columns of cuneiform script in the Akkadian language delineating Hammurabi's code of laws. Hammurabi is depicted on the top of the stele, standing and praying to Shamash, the god of the sun and justice.

Oriental antiquities

The Egyptian department, founded in 1826 by Jean-François Champollion, who deciphered **Egyptian hieroglyphics**, provides details about the art and culture of the Old, Middle and New Kingdoms of Egypt down to the Christian era. Among the numerous artefacts providing an insight into the life of the early inhabitants of the Nile are the Stele of King Wadj (also known as the »Serpent King«) from the First Dynasty with its capital at Thinis around 3100 BC and the Stele of Antef, a high official under Thutmosis III (c1490–1439 BC). The bas-relief with excellently preserved polychrome painting on the * **Tomb of Sethos I** from the Valley of the Kings is a splendid example of the art of the New Kingdom (c1303–1290 BC). The goddess Hathor is handing her necklace, a mark of her divinity, to the ruler.

Egyptian antiquities

The famous * **Seated Scribe**, a painted sandstone figure, was found in a fifth-dynasty tomb at Saqqara dating from around 2620 to 2350 BC. The impressive wood sculpture of an administrative official of Memphis and his wife (c2350 BC) is almost equally old. The sandstone statuette of Amenemhatankh, a worker at Crocodilopolis, dates from the time around 1850 BC. The monumental bust of King Akhenaten (first known as Amenhotep IV, c1365–1349 BC) is typical of the soft lines of the Amarna period.

Sculpture The collections from the Musée des Monuments Français, which was disestablished during the Restoration, formed the nucleus of the sculpture collection. Among the numerous works from the 12th to 19th centuries, the following are especially worth seeing: the 11th-century Romanesque capital decoration, *Daniel in the Lion's Den*, from the church of St Geneviève in Paris, the plain *Auvergne Madonna* (12th century) and the masterly Gothic column statue of the * **Queen of Sheba** (c1180). Dating from the 14th century are the Norman *Blanchelande Virgin* and the stone figure of Charles V (c1390).

The extraordinary funeral procession from the ** **Tomb of Philippe Pot**, the Grand Senechal of Burgundy (1493) is a masterpiece. Nymphs and sea monsters of heathen sensuousness adorn Jean Goujon's bas-relief from the Fountain of the Innocents (1547–49). Germain Pilon's group of the *Three Graces* (c1560) bore the urn with the heart of Henri II (c1560). The triumphal monument to Queen Anne of Austria was created by Simon Guillan in 1643. In 1670 Pierre Puget began work on his * *Milo of Croton*, a statue of the famous Greek wrestler with lions for the park of ▶Versailles. The horses in Guillaume Coustou the Elder's * *Horse Tamers* rear up with flowing manes and distended nostrils; they are two of a group of sculptures commissioned for Marly Park in 1745.

Both **Canova's** classical marble composition of * **Psyche** being awakened by a kiss from Amor (1793) and Pigalle's *Mercury Attaching his Winged Sandals* (1744) demonstrate elegant gracefulness. The animal studies by Barye, Rude's *Neapolitan Fisherman playing with a Turtle* (1833) and James Pradier's *Satyr and Bacchante* (1834), which created a scandalous sensation, all possess great power. **Michelangelo's** ** *Dying Slave* and his **Rebellious Slave** are masterpieces of international standing created for the tomb of Pope Julius II as an earthly counterpart to the apotheosis of the Holy Father.

French painting Only a few museums in the world offer such a variety and scope of genre and style as the Louvre's collection of European painting. Almost half of the exhibits are works by French painters from the Middle Ages to the 19th century. The major works of the late Middle Ages are the * **Pietà of Villeneuve-les-Avignon** (c1455), which has been ascribed to Enguerrand Quarton, and a ** *Portrait of King Jean the Good* by an unknown artist (c1360), the oldest known French panel painting and the first life-like portrait north of the Alps. The portraits of the dignitaries of the realm painted by Clouet are exemplary of the Fontainebleau School of the 16th century. Antoine Caron's Massacre under the Triumvirate (1566) is an allegorically laden reference to the horrors of the Thirty Years' War. The early 17th century brought innovative ideas from Italy, evident in **Georges de**

Michelangelo's slaves in the Aile Denon

La Tour's candle-lit night-time scenes including *Magdalen of the Night Light* and *Christ with St Joseph in the Carpenter's Shop*) and ****Cheat with the Ace of Diamonds** (1630, an encounter of deceit with the unsuspecting. Louis Le Nain's sensitive milieu study, *Peasant Family in an Interior* (c1643), is illuminated only by the light of the fireplace. Episodes from the Old Testament are the basis of the portrayals of the *Four Seasons* (c1660), mystically lyrical paintings by **Nicholas Poussin**.

Historical painting comes to the fore in the magnificent portraits by Charles Le Brun, including *The History of Alexander the Great* (1669) and a depiction by **Hyacinthe Rigaud** of the Sun King, **** *Louis XIV in Coronation Robes*** (1701). The colourist **Antoine Watteau** opened up new avenues for 18th-century French painting. His *Pierrot* (1718), with his slowly fading smile, conjures up delicate moods. **Boucher** (*Diana Leaving her Bath*, 1742) and **Fragonard** (*The Bathers*, c1770) handled subjects that some considered licentious.

Jacques-Louis David's *The Oath of the Horatii* (1784) became the manifesto of neoclassicism, but the artist's masterpiece remains his enormous canvas of **** *The Coronation of Napoleon*** (1805–07).

One of the outstanding exponents of Romanticism was **Géricault** with his dramatic scene of the *Raft of Medusa*, in which the dark greenish tones and the realism of the shipwrecked figures shocked visitors to the salons of 1819. *** Liberty Leading the People** (1830, by **Eugène Delacroix** is a revolution of passionate emotions, colours and movement. His painting of Dante and Virgil created a regular scandal, whilst his portrait of Frédéric Chopin (1838) appears rather romantic in contrast. Because of his unconventional use of light, **Camille Corot** with his *** Souvenir de Mortefontaine** (1864) is considered one of the first plein-air painters and a forerunner of the Impressionists. The landscape painter Théodore Rousseau also used a varying intensity of light in his *Edge of the Forest of Fontainebleau*. *The Valpinçon Bather* (1808) by **Jean-Dominique Ingres** reveals this neoclassical painter to be an admirer of the harmonious compositions of the Venetian and Florentine masters.

Italian painting Italian painting from the second half of the 13th to the end of the 18th century makes up the second-largest body of paintings in the Louvre. Cimabue's *Madonna with Angels* (c1270) from the church of San Francesco in Pisa is an example of the early Florentine School.

Cheat with the Ace of Diamonds by Georges de la Tour is an encounter of deceit with the unsuspecting

Giotto's *St Francis Preaching to the Birds* (c1300) from the predella of the altar of St Francis of Assisi represents an early attempt at achieving three-dimensionality. The beginning of the Renaissance of the Quattrocento is heralded by **Fra Angelico** freeing himself from Byzantine artistic restriction in his * *Coronation of the Virgin* (1434–35) from the church of San Domenico in Fiesole and his Martyrdom of St Cosmas and St Damian (1440). Andrea Mantegna also achieved a well conceived geometric depth in his *Calvary* (1459), while delicate, curving lines and translucent colours mark the transfigured faces in **Sandro Botticelli's** allegorical frescoes (c1483). The golden age of the Italian Renaissance, from the end of the 15th century to the first half of the 16th century, is represented by an outstanding collection of works by **Leonardo da Vinci**, including the *Annunciation* (1475), *Virgin and Child with St Anne* (c1506) and his ** *Mona Lisa* (*La Gioconda*, French *La Joconde*, 1503–1505). The lady known for her inscrutable smile is most probably Lisa del Gioconda, the wife of the Florentine merchant Francesco del Giocondo. The beauty of the face in the changing play of light unfortunately loses something of its effect behind the protective screen of bulletproof glass. Further treasures include the *Holy Family,* painted in 1507 by **Raphael** in Florence, the *Portrait of Balthasar Castiglione* (1516), courtier and author, also by Raphael, **Titian's** melancholy *Entombment of Christ* (c1525) and the massive ** *Wedding Feast at Cana* (1563) by Paolo Veronese. **Caravaggio's** *Death of the Virgin* (c1605) created a scandal at the time because of its realistic portrayal and was rejected, whilst Guido Reni's theatrical * *Abduction of Helen* (1631) became one of the most admired paintings of the time.

Francesco Guardi's picture cycle is an outstanding work of the 18th century; it was painted around 1770 on the occasion of the coronation of Doge Alvise Mocenigo IV in Venice.

The masterpieces of German, Flemish and Old Dutch painting span the time from late Gothic to the 17th century. Among the major Flemish works are **Jan van Eyck's** * *The Virgin of Autun* (c1435), Hans Memling's *Portrait of an Old Woman* (c1470), Quentin Metsys' genre scene, *The Moneychanger and his Wife* (1514), and **Pieter Bruegel the Elder's** *The Beggars* (1568). Collected in a room all on their own are 21 paintings of **Peter Paul Rubens'** ** *Medici Cycle* that Queen Marie de Médici commissioned for the Palais du Luxembourg in 1622. The tender feelings Rubens had for his young family are expressed in his unfinished study, *Hélène Fourment and her Children* (c1636). In addition, there is **Anthony van Dyck's** impressive portrait of * *Charles I of England* (c1635) and Jacob Jordaens's *Four Apostles.* Among the Dutch painters are Hieronymus Bosch with his seemingly surrealistic *Ship of Fools* (c1490), **Frans Hals** with his char-

German, Flemish and Dutch painting

acter study of the *Gypsy Girl* (1628–30), **Jan Vermeer van Delft** with his poetic, atmospheric ** *The Lacemaker* (1664) and Astronomer (1668) and Jacob van Ruisdael's *The Ray of Sunlight* (c1670). **Rembrandt** is represented by self portraits, his moving *Christ and the Disciples at Emmaus* (1648), his portrait of Hendrikje Stoffels, his companion in the last years of his life, and his nude ** *Bathsheba at her Bath*, holding in her hand the letter from David declaring his love (1654). Even the smaller collection of German masters holds significant works, including **Albrecht Dürer's** * *Self Portrait of the Artist Holding a Thistle* painted when he was 22 (1493), the strolling *Venus* (1529) by **Lucas Cranach the Elder** and *Anne of Cleves* (1539) and the portrait of the scholar *Erasmus of Rotterdam* (1523) by **Hans Holbein the Younger**.

English painting

English painting of the 18th and 19th centuries is represented with portraits by **Gainsborough** (Conversation in the Park, around 1746), **Reynolds's** * *Master Hare*, a child portrait from 1788–89, as well as paintings by Raeburn and Sir Thomas Lawrence, who painted portraits at all of the courts of Europe. The 19th century is reflected in the naturalistic landscapes of **John Constable** (*Weymouth Bay*, 1824) and the romantic landscapes of **William Turner** (*Landscape*, c1830).

Spanish painting

Among the masterpieces of Spanish art of the 14th to 18th centuries are **El Greco's** * *Christ on the Cross Adored by Donors* (c1585), **José Ribera's** *The Club Foot* (1642), *The Death of Saint Bonaventura* (c1630) by Francisco de Zurbarán and *The Young Beggar* (1650) by Esteban Murillo. Other fine works include the *Infanta Margarita* (c1654) attributed to **Velázquez** and a series of portraits by **Francisco Goya**, including *Don Evariste Perez de Castro* (1805), the physician and France's ambassador to Spain, *Ferdinand Guillemardet* (1798) and the *Marquesa de la Solana* (c1810).

Decorative arts

The section on medieval decorative art includes masterpieces such as the small equestrian statue of Charlemagne (9th century) from Metz Cathedral and the famous ****Harbaville Triptych** (mid-10th century), a Byzantine work in ivory. The Suger Eagle (porphyry vase with gold ornament, mid-12th century) is from the Royal Abbey of St-Denis. The portrait of Anne de Montmorency (1566) worked on copper by Leonard Limosin of Limoges stands out among the graceful works of French Renaissance enamel painting. Among the magnificent exhibits in the **tapestry collection** are ***Maximilian Hunting**, woven in 1530 in Brussels after cartoons by Bernaert van Orley, and The *Story of Scipio*, based on drawings by Jules Romain. Examples of the **goldsmith's art** of the 16th century are Charles IX's enamelled and gilded iron helmet and shield. The 17th century is impressively illustrated by the bronze sculptures of Henri IV and Maria de Médici by Barthélémy Prieur. The Duke of Bourbon's table centre-piece in luxuriant Rococo style was created in 1736, Napoleon I's Athenienne at the beginning of the 19th century for the Tuileries Palace.

The crown jewels are housed in the **Galerie d'Apollon**, which was reopened in late 2004. The highlight here is the 137-carat *** Regent Diamond**, which was found in 1698 in India, acquired by Philip of Orléans in 1717 and has adorned the coronation crown of Louis XV since 1722. | **Crown jewels**

The **Grand Salon** was decorated in the elegant style of the Second Empire between 1856 and 1861 by Hector Lufuel for Napoleon III's minister of state. Tranchant did the gold-covered stucco decorations, pilasters and column figures. The ceiling painting by Charles-Raphaël Maréchal illustrates the joining together of the Louvre and the Tuileries. | **Grand Salon**

The Louvre possesses over 120,000 drawings and engravings, including works by the court painters **Le Brun**, Pierre Mignard and Antoine Coypel, 4500 engravings by **Rembrandt**, **Leonardo da Vinci's ** Isabella d'Este** (c1490) as well as works by Pisanello, Jacopo Bellini, Veronese, Raphael, Füssli, Goya, Dürer, Corot, Delacroix and the Impressionists. The collections are shown in regularly organized temporary exhibitions. | **Graphic arts**

In 1999 in the Louvre's Pavillon de Marsan, Jean Nouvel created the **Museum of Advertising**. Visitors can see posters dating from the 18th century to the present day, signed by such masters of the profession as Toulouse-Lautrec, Mucha, Utrillo, Savignac, Bouvet and Widmer. Commercials from home and abroad dating from the 1930s to the present day tell the parallel story of cinema and TV advertising, with radio commercials and jingles highlighting the creativity of great slogans. Packaging and giveaways make it clear how much advertising has long permeated our everyday lives. ED: The museum is part of »Les Arts Decoratifs«, which also includes Decorative Arts and Fashion and Textiles. | **Musée de la Publicité**

❶ Entrance: 107, Rue de Rivoli, Tue–Sun 11am–6pm, Thur till 9pm, www.museedelapub.org, adults €9.50

The former royal parish church on Place du Louvre (No. 2) is consecrated to St Germanus, Bishop of Auxerre. From the Romanesque tower the bell called »Marie« sounded on the night of 23 August 1572, marking the beginning of the bloody St Bartholomew's Day Massacre. The Gothic choir dates from the 13th | **Saint-Germain-l'Auxerrois** century, while the nave and porch are in the flamboyant Gothic style of the 15th century. The pews for the royal family were designed in 1684 by Le Brun. Many of the artists who were in the service of the French kings during the 17th and 18th centuries are buried here, including the architect Le Vau, the painters Boucher, Chardin and Nattier and the sculptors Antoine Coysevox and Nicolas and Guillaume Coustou. The church is home to the **Choeur Grégorien de Paris**, whose twelve women inspire listeners at concerts and festivals with their medieval A capella music, and they also sing at the 7pm Sunday mass.

❶ daily 9am–7pm, Sun till 8pm, www.saintgermainauxerrois.cef.fr

Luxembourg

✦ G 7

Location: Boulevard St-Michel (6th arr.)
main entrance: Place Edmond Rostand
Métro station: Odéon

Children and students from the nearby university are regular visitors to the Luxembourg Gardens. At its heart is the straight-lined symmetry of French Baroque style, with sheltered spots in the idyllic English landscaped style at the sides.

*Jardin du Luxembourg Lovers meet under the plane trees at the Italian-style **Fontaine de Médicis**. The Renaissance fountain with 17th-century grotto architecture commemorates of its former owner, Marie de Médici. Her grandson, Louis XIV, had the grandiose perspective of the Avenue de l'Observatoire extended, guiding the eye along the line of erstwhile **Paris meridian**, up to the observatory. In 1874 the **Fontaine de l'Observatoire** by Gabriel Davioud was unveiled with four female figures symbolising the four continents known at that time; the horses in the basin around the statue were carved by Emmanuel Frémiet. In the large central pond children can sail model boats, which can be rented from the booth. Every Wednesday at 4pm, and Sat and Sun at 11am and 4pm, the Théâtre des Marionettes entertains the little ones with the **Guignol**, the French equivalent of Punch and Judy (http://guignolduluxembourg.monsite-orange.fr).

Statues of prominent French artists and politicians line the paths; French queens and famous women frame the terrace. On the Rue Vaugirard are fruit trees and the beehives of the beekeeping school that annually produces more than 100 kg of honey – in the autumn all the produce from the Jardin de Luxembourg is sold in the Orangerie. During the summer, temporary exhibitions are put on at the **Musée du Luxembourg** in the Orangerie.

Park: daily 9am till dusk, **Museum:** daily 10am–7.30pm, Fri till 10pm, www. museeduluxembourg.fr; adults €11

Marie de Médici, the wife of Henri IV, purchased the estate in 1612 from Duke Francis of Luxemburg for her residence after her husband died. She wanted a palace in the style of her family estate, Palazzo Pitti in Florence. Although Salomon de Brosse, who started construction in 1615, followed the French tradition, he imbued it with a Florentine feeling through the addition of columns, capitals and rounded arches. Rubens' Médici Cycle depicting stages in the life of the princess hangs today in the ►Louvre. Marie de Médici was hardly able to use the palace because shortly after its completion in 1630 she was forced into exile to Cologne – she had once and for all lost the game of political intrigue with her opponent Cardinal Richelieu. In 1800, the Palais du Luxembourg became the **seat of the French Senate**, with a newly designed interior by Chalgrin, and the extension of the garden side in the style of the original construction. The former library was provided with luxurious murals by Delacroix between 1845 and 1847. The President of the Senate today resides in the Petit Luxembourg.

Palais du Luxembourg

❶ 15, Rue de Vaugirard; Senate sessions can only be attended with ID, schedules: tel. 01 42 34 20 01 (answerphone), tours on one Saturday each month at 10.30am and 2.30pm given by staff of the Centre des Monuments Nationaux by appointment only, tel. 01 44 54 19 49, www.senat.fr

✴ Madeleine

—————————————— ✦ F 4

Location: Place de la Madeleine (0th arr.)
Métro station: Madeleine
Internet: www.eglise-lamadeleine.com
❶ daily 9.30am–7pm

Few churches can look back on such an eventful history as the Church of St Mary Magdalen. The foundation stone for this domed Baroque edifice was laid in 1763 during the reign of Louis XV. Louis XVI then wanted it remodelled in the neoclassical style to look like the ►Panthéon – but the Revolution put a stop to any building plans.

In 1806, Napoleon commissioned Vignon to build an army Hall of Fame in the style of the Parthenon on the Acropolis. Louis XVIII, on the other hand, wanted a church of atonement for the victims of the French Revolution. Eventually, in 1842 under the Citizen-King Louis-Philippe, it was consecrated as a parish church in the style of a

Eglise Sainte Marie Madeleine

Greek temple. Nowadays, funeral masses are held here for prominent French citizens, such as for Gilbert Bécaud, the singer. Created by Philippe Lemaire in 1833, the frieze in the pediment above the main portico depicts the Day of Judgement. The bronze doors are decorated with reliefs of the Ten Commandments. The vestibule, nave and choir receive light from three large domes. Hanging to the left in the portico is François Rude's *Baptism of Christ*. The spandrels are decorated with reliefs of the twelve apostles, and the high altar is adorned with a marble group, *The Assumption of Mary Magdalen* (1837). The **Cavaillé-Coll organ** is famous for its sound.

*Place de la Madeleine   A number of exclusive shops are clustered around this square in front of the church. Sparkling crystal vases are the trademark of **Baccarat** (No. 11) and a little further on **Fauchon** (No. 26) offers tempting delicacies from around the world. Its competitor **Hédiard** (No. 21) has been a byword for exotic fruits and fine wines ever since 1854. The **Pinacothèque de Paris** at No. 28 shows monographic and thematic exhibitions.

Pinacothèque de Paris: daily 10.30am–6pm, 1st Wed in month till 9pm, www.pinacotheque.com; adults €10, under 12s free

With ist Corinthina columns, the neo-classical church of La Madeleine, is reminiscent of a Greek temple

Linking Madeleine with ►Place de la Concorde, *** Rue Royale** is also one of the **most exclusive streets** in Paris. Luxury shops like the porcelain manufacturer Villeroy & Boch, jewellery shops like Poiray, tableware specialist Christofle and the **fashion boutiques** of Gucci, Cerruti and A.P.C. reside in the listed 18th-century buildings that line the street. The Ladurée tea salon at No. 16 is enchanting; the gourmet restaurant Maxim's legendary. The latter's museum recalls the glory days around the turn of the 20th century, today rekindled at soirées with dancing and cabaret (www.maxims-de-paris.com).

> **MARCO ⊕ POLO TIP**
>
> **Stroll, look and shop** — *Insider Tip*
>
> In the small but very elegant shopping arcade of Village Royale smart boutiques from Chanel, Dior and Anna Fontaine tempt you to part with your money. At lunchtime the fashion world from the surrounding shops congregate in »Le Village«, where delicious cakes, salads and sandwiches are served on the terrace. The chocolate truffles from Patrick Roger are simply heavenly – our tip: »Amitié« pralines with almond cream (entrance: 25, Rue Royale, www.villageroyal.com).

Chapelle expiatoire

Louis XVIII made available almost 3 million livres for the construction of this neoclassical chapel on the site of the former Madeleine cemetery in 1816. It was built as a **memorial to Louis XVI and Marie-Antoinette**, who were buried in the cemetery after their execution in 1793 before their remains were transferred to the royal tombs of the basilica of ►Saint-Denis in 1817.

❶ Thur–Sat 1–5pm, www.chapelle-expiatoire.monuments-nationaux.fr; adults €5.50, under 25s free

** Marais

✦ H/J 5/6

Location: 4th arr.
❶ www.parismarais.com, www.parislemarais.com
Métro stations: Saint-Paul, Rambuteau, Pont Marie

Elegant city palaces and winding lanes, trendy pubs and chic boutiques, kosher restaurants and the world's most amazing Picasso collection – the Marais, which is almost the same area as the 4th Arrondissement, is without doubt one of the highlights of Paris.

Quartier branché

In the 13th century, monks and Templar knights drained the **former marsh**, the »Marais«, on the old Roman road that is known today as Rue St-Antoine. The Marais, the highlight of which is the enclosed ►Place des Vosges, is considered the birthplace of the »hôtel«, the magnificent Parisian mansions of the French nobility – the term »palais« in the ancien régime was only used for the residences of the royal family. The heyday of these aristocratic city residences was the 16th and 17th centuries. The characteristic features of the **hôtels** are the cour d'honneurs, forecourts facing the street, a main building with side wings and a rear terrace with a garden. Towards the end of the 17th century, the quarter lost a lot of its cachet because the nobility and the upper crust followed the court to ▶Versailles. Tradesmen, small businesses and immigrants moved into the quarter. Following the Revolution, many hôtels became dilapidated or were torn down to make way for new housing. It wasn't until 1962 that the then Minister of Culture, André Malraux, finally undertook the restoration of the district, which was already a protected area. The Marais has long since become a fashionable and trendy „quartier branché«, which also has a lively gay scene around the Rue Ste-Croix-de-la-Bretonnerie. A small Chinese community has established itself in the Rue du Temple.

Jewish Quarter

The Jewish community is centred on the bustling **Rue des Rosiers**, with a colourful mixture of small shops, falafel stands and kosher food stores like the »yellow boutique« of **Sacha Finkelsztajn** at 27, Rue des Rosiers, where tarama, blinis and strudel have been produced ever since 1946. The **Panzer Charcuterie** at No. 26 has first-class pickelfleisch (pastrami) and schmaltz herring. Oriental-Jewish delicatessen and felafel to take away can be found opposite at **Chez Marianne** on the corner of Rue des Hospitalières-St-Gervais.

THE FINEST HÔTELS IN THE MARAIS

*Hôtel de Sens

This late Gothic hôtel at 1, Rue du Figuier is characterised by its has little corner towers and a dainty roof gable. It was commissioned in 1475 by Tristan de Salazar, the archbishop of Sens. Today its **Bibliothèque Forney** documents the history of the decorative arts.
❶ Tue–Fri, Sat. 1pm–7.30pm, Wed and Thur 10am–7.30pm.

Musée de la Magie

Right at the entrance, the »fortune teller of Pigalle« greets everyone with a »Bonjour!« She is but one of the many automata in the **Museum of Magic** at 11, Rue St-Paul, which also numbers a »sawed-in-half lady« among its treasures. The magic acts are fantastic – in 2012 David Copperfield performed here with his wonderful world of illusions.
❶ Wed, Sat, Sun 2pm–7pm, www.museedelamagie.com, adults €9

Village Saint-Paul

On Sundays those in search of antiques can find old silver, trinkets and curiosities in the winding backstreets of the Village Saint-Paul between Rue des Jardins-Saint-Paul and Rue Saint-Paul.
❶ Thur–Mon 11am–7pm, www.village-saint-paul.com

Aristocratic Place des Vosges, heart of the Marais

An elegant neoclassical façade decorates the garden front of the city palace at 7, Rue de Jouy, which was built by Le Vau between 1630 and 1650, and remodelled by Mansart in 1656. Nowadays, the Tribunal administratif de Paris, the **Paris administrative court**, sits here.

Hôtel d'Aumont

Accompanied by his father and sister, the seven-year-old Mozart stayed with the Bavarian ambassador here at 68, Rue François-Miron in this hôtel designed in 1658 by Lepautre, and gave several concerts.

Hôtel de Beauvais

This hôtel at 5, Rue de Fourcy 5 dates from the early 18th century. Here the **Maison Européenne de la Photographie** stages temporary exhibitions of work by famous photographers such as Annie Leibovitz, William Klein and Peter Knapp, as well as by up-and-coming talents and multimedia artists who incorporate photographs into their works.
❶ Wed–Sun 11am–8pm, www.mep-fr.org, adults €7

Hôtel Hénault de Cantobre

Between 1657 and 1660, Lepautre also constructed this hôtel at 47, Rue Vieille-du-Temple, where Beaumarchais later wrote *The Marriage of Figaro*. Today, it houses the **Dutch Embassy**.

Hôtel Amelot de Bisseuil

Pierre Alexis Delamaire, a pupil of Mansart, supervised the construction of this elegant hôtel at 60, Rue des Francs-Bourgeois, with the colonnade-lined cour d'honneur, for Princess Soubise from

*Hôtel de Soubise

! *Mariage Frères* **Insider Tip**

Tea drinkers swear by Mariage Frères, which was founded in 1854 at 30, Rue du Bourg-Ti-bourg. More than 500 tea varieties from around the world are served with homemade macaroons, millefeuilles and a mousse au chocolat that has a hint of Earl Grey. A small museum tells the history of tea and how to drink it properly (Tea Museum 10.30am–7.30pm, Salon de Thé 3pm–7pm, www.mariagefreres.com).

1704 until 1712. The rococo building is the headquarters of the Centre Historique des Archives Nationales. Its **Musée de l'Histoire de France** has documents pertaining to the history of France, including a papyrus roll dating from 629 signed by King Dagobert I, a letter from Joan of Arc to the citizens of Reims and Napoleon's will.

❶ daily except Tue 10am–5.30pm, Sat and Sun from 2pm, adults €3, exhibitions €6, www.archivesnationales.culture.gouv.fr/chan

Completed in 1647, the Hôtel de Saint-Aignan today houses the ***Musée d'Art et d'Histoire du Judaïsme**, which has displays of medieval gravestones, Thora rolls and documents pertaining to the history of the Jewish community in France – with over 700,000 members, one of the largest in Europe.

❶ 71, Rue du Temple Mon–Fri 11am–6pm, Sun 10am–6pm, www.mahj.org, adults €7, under 26s free

*Hôtel Guénégaud Mansart designed this elegant hôtel at 62, Rue des Archives in 1651, for François de Guénégaud, Treasurer of France. Today it houses the collection of a hunting enthusiast, industrialist François Sommer, in the **Musée de la Chasse et de la Nature**. On display are weapons and trophies, animal studies by François Desportes and hunting scenes by Lucas Cranach, Pieter Brueghel the Elder, Rubens, Chardin and Oudry.

❶ daily except Mon 11am–6pm. Free admission on the first Sunday of every month.

*Hôtel de Rohan Built by Delamaire, this fine property at 87, Rue du Vieille-du-Temple served as the residence of four cardinals of the Rohan dynasty. Among the most magnificent rooms are the Golden Salon and a small chamber with illustrations of Jean de La Fontaine's fables. The second cour d'honneur features an 18th-century alto-relievo of *The Horses of Apollo* by Robert Le Lorrain.

❶ Visits by appointment on Sun pm only, tel. 06 10 12 67 27

The **Galerie Yvon Lambert** at 108, Rue du Vieille-du-Temple is the undisputed star with artists such as Anselm Kiefer, Bertrand Lavier and Jenny Holzer (www.yvon-lambert.com). The **Galerie Xippas** in the same building exhibits paintings and photographs by Dan Walsh, David Reed and Ian Davenport (www.xippas.com). The other galleries in the Marais also promise surprises and discoveries, including **Marian Goodman** at 79, Rue du Temple, who works with renowned artists such as Jeff Wall, Annette Messager and Gabriel Orozco (www.mariangoodman.com).
Artists and galleries

The Architect Libéral Bruand had this palais at 1, Rue de la Perle constructed for his own use in around 1685. He had made a name for himself principally as the builder of the Hôtel des ▶Invalides.
Hôtel Libéral-Bruand

▶******Musée Picasso
Hôtel Salé

This hôtel at 8, Rue Elzévir, constructed for Sieur Méderic de Donon in the 16th century accommodates the *** Musée Cognacq-Jay**. The valuable collection that the department store founder, Ernest Cognacq, and his wife, Louise Jay, left to the city in 1928 include 18th-century masterpieces, among them paintings by Boucher, Watteau, Rembrandt and Ruysdael, and sculptures by Houdon, Greuze and Fragonard.
❶ Tue–Sun 10am–6pm, admission free
*Hôtel de Donon

This city palais at 31, Rue des Francs-Bourgeois was built in 1650. Used in the 19th century as a place for manufacturing light bulbs, since 1989 it has been the seat of the Municipal Cultural Office, which in the summer lays on open-air concerts in the courtyard.
❶ Mon–Fri 2pm–6pm, tel. 01 42 76 84 00
Hôtel d'Albret

▶*****Musée Carnavalet
Hôtel Carnavalet

In the 17th century, Guillaume de Lamoignon, the first president of the Parlement, received illustrious guests like Racine, Boileau and Madame de Sévigné in his hôtel at 24, Rue Pavée, which was built in 1584. The **Bibliothèque Historique de la Ville de Paris**, founded in 1763, possesses important documents on the French Revolution – it is worth taking a look at the ceiling painting in the reading room.
❶ Mon–Sat 9.30am–6pm
Hôtel Lamoignon

Barely 800 m to the northeast at 110, Rue Amelot, international circus stars perform at this beautiful *** Belle Epoque circus**, which was inaugurated by Napoleon III in 1852. The small private museum be-
Cirque d'Hiver Bouglione

longing to the Bouglione family recalls some of the acclaimed artistes.

❶ Métro: Filles-du-Calvaire, tickets from ❷26.50, www.cirque hiver.com

Place des Vosges	▶p.297, ▶picture p.249

Hôtel de Sully   This magnificent palais at 62, Rue Saint-Antoine, built in 1624 by Jean Androuet du Cerceau, was the city residence of Maximilian de **Béthune-Sully**, the minister and right-hand man of Henri IV. Decorating the cour d'honneur are allegories of the four elements and seasons. Today it is where the **Centre des Monuments Nationaux** preserves more than 100 historical monuments across the country. In addition it is a venue for **temporary exhibitions of modern photography** and video art. Also the garden, which is only accessible during the day, often serves as a stage for music, dance and modern performance art.

❶ Mon– Fri 9am–12.45pm and 2pm–6pm, www.monuments-nationaux.fr

> **! MARCO ⊕ POLO TIP**
>
> *Magical moments...*   **Insider Tip**
>
> ... waiting in the »Le Double Fond« restaurant on the charming Place du Marché Ste-Cathérine. The »Double Stage« is a café-theatre that is run with great enthusiasm and daily presents artistes from the world of magic. Get one of the waiters to tell you how the tricks work! (tel. 01 42 71 40 20, www.doublefond.com, »Formule Plaisir« with cocktail, snacks, wine and performance at 7.30pm for €65 per person).

✳ Montmartre

✦ **G/H 2/3**

Location: in the north of the city (18th arr.)
Métro stations: Place Clichy, Blanche, Pigalle, Anvers, Abbesses
❶ www.montmartre-guide.com, www.montmartre-paris-france.com

Cabarets, the cancan and risqué revue shows, Toulouse-Lautrec, Henry Miller and the myth of love for sale: that's what the famous Parisian entertainment district around Place Pigalle stands for. Montmartre itself, however, has long been regarded as »bobo«, chic and trendy, with charming restaurants, galleries and shops run by young creative types.

Artists' »colony« with two faces   And away from the beaten tracks of Boulevard de Clichy, Place du Tertre or ▶Sacré-Cœur, the former artists' colony, with the charm of an eternal village, has retained some very delightful spots. The hill even produces wine. Each year, the city bottles more than 500 litres/132 gallons of **»Clos de Montmartre«** – cause enough for a parade in October in which the wine-growing brotherhoods march past the political bigwigs of Paris in their traditional costumes. In Roman times, a temple to Mars gave the hill its name. After the martyrdom of St Dionysius, Mons Martis was renamed **Mont des Martyrs**. The massive Benedictine convent, St Pierre-de-Montmartre, crowned the Butte Montmartre from 1134 until it was razed to the ground in 1794. Today, the name Place des Abbesses recalls the convent's abbesses. In the 19th century, the hill with its vineyards, windmills and inexpensive garden cafés became one of the Parisians' favourite destinations for a day's outing. The charm and low rents of the wine village, which remained outside the city's boundaries until 1860, attracted young, mostly penniless artists and writers. The studios of artists like Picasso, Monet, van Gogh, Toulouse-Lautrec, Renoir, Utrillo and Modigliano became the birthplace of modern painting and made Montmartre famous. After the First World War, many artists moved to ▶Montparnasse and Montmartre became synonymous with Parisian nightlife.

*Swinging Montmartre

Every July the arena that the Romans once built on the Butte de Montmartre is now used as the venue for the **Montmartre Jazz Festival.** With the nightly illuminated facade of Sacre Coeur acting as a backdrop, the festival attracts legends such as John Abercrombie, Daniel Humair and Martial Solal as well as newcomers like Thomas Savy and Norma Winstone.
❶ Rue Chappe/Rue Saint-Fleuthères, tickets: www.fnac.com, www. festival jazz montmartre.com

Funiculaire

Butte Montmartre, at 129m/423ft being the only appreciable »mountain« in Paris, also has the city's only **funicular railway**, which runs between Place Saint-Pierre and Sacré-Cœur, daily 6.45am–12.45am and saves you climbing the 237 steps to the top.

*Place du Tertre

The low 18th-century houses round the square form a picturesque backdrop to the year-round tourist onslaught. The cafés and restaurants that frame the old village square are packed and expensive. Painters and quick portrait artists offer their overpriced work for sale at the market. Attention - there are even signs warning of **pickpockets around the square**.

Private art exhibitions

Just as eccentric as he was creative, the renovated **Espace Dalí** at 11, Rue Poulbot pays homage to the artist Salvador Dalí with more than 300 of his works. The life and work of undoubtedly the most famous chronicler of the district are presented by Louis Barbier in his private **Espace Toulouse-Lautrec** at 11 Rue André Antoine Further rooms

are devoted to life in Montmartre as well as artists like Van Gogh, Raoul Dufy and Maurice Utrillo, who were also active here.

Espace Dalí: daily 10am–6pm, July and Aug till 8pm, www.daliparis.com, adults €11; Espace Toulouse-Lautrec: daily 10am–8pm, adults 1€11

Amongst the most exciting contemporary art galleries is the **Kadist Art Foundation** at 19–21, Rue des Trois Frères. It supports young artists with its »Artist in Residence« programme and displays **all manner of contemporary works**, (www.kadist.org).

On Place du Tertre with Sacré-Coeur in the background

Saint Pierre de Montmartre

This simple church in Rue du Mont-Cenis is the sole reminder of the 12th-century Benedictine convent, whose last abbess died under the guillotine in 1794. Four black marble pillars in the choir and on the west side of the interior date back to the Roman temple that stood here when Paris was still called Lutetia. The choir consecrated in 1147 was given the first cross-rib vault in Paris. The vineyards and mills of Montmartre can be seen on the enamel panels of the high altar created by Froidevaux in 1977.

Art Brut and folk art

The St-Pierre market halls at 2 Rue Rosnard, constructed in the style of Baltard in 1868, have now been transformed into a cultural centre. Alongside its **Museum of Naïve Art** containing 500 paintings and 80 sculptures from the collection gathered by Mr and Mrs Fourny, it also has a gallery in which temporary exhibitions of Art Brut and contemporary works are displayed. A bookstore, auditorium and café complete the cultural complex.

Halles Saint-Pierre: Tue–Sun 10am–6pm, Mon 1pm–6pm adults €8.50, www.hallesaintpierre.org

Moulin de la Galette

The last-but-one of several windmills that once provided the dance floor for the high-spirited celebrations immortalized by Auguste Renoir (▶picture p.267) is today no longer open to the public. As for the neighbouring **Badet Mill** at 83, Rue Lepic, Roger Heerah makes use of the glorious past and in his **Le Moulin de la Galette** restaurant serves French specialities such as Brittany sea bass and braised lamb shoulder from the Gâtinais (tel. 01 46 06 84 77, www.lemoulindelagalette.fr).

A visit to 12, Rue Cortot promises a nostalgic journey back to the heyday of Montmartre. **Renoir** had his studio here in 1876. Later came Susanne Valadon and her son Utrillo, Emile Bernard, Maximilian Luce and Maurice Delcourt. **Utrillo's** favourite café, the Café de l'Abreuvoir, was recreated for the museum, which reopened in 2014 after renovations. The original Lapin Agile sign, Théophile Steinlen's designs for posters for the Le Chat Noir cabaret and studies of Montmartre's milieu by Francisque Poulbot can all be admired here.

*Musée de Montmartre

❶ Tue–Sun 11am–6pm, www.museedemontmartre.com, adults €8

The Art Nouveau Métro entrance to Paris's deepest Métro station (30m/100ft) is by **Hector Guimard**. Across from it stands **St-Jean-L'Evangeliste**, a graceful church of reinforced concrete and brick designed by Anatole de Baudot in 1904. At weekends the street trading in Rue des Abbesses has an authentic local feel about it, and on Sunday mornings the Montmartrois enjoy their coffee and pain au chocolat at the »Sancerre« (No. 35) or the neighbouring »Le vrai Paris« (No. 33). And that Paris is the city of love is demonstrated on a **blue-tiled wall** at Square Jéhan-Rictus, on which there Frédéric Baron and Claire Kito have immortalized those magic words »**Je t'aime**« in 311 languages.

*Place des Abbesses

In **Rue Cavalotti** to the north of Place de Clichy, at the instigation of two female decorators 21 shopkeepers have decorated their roller shutters with reproductions of famous paintings, so that after the shops have closed the street is transformed into an open-air art gallery including works by Vermeer, Modigliani and Toulouse-Lautrec.

Shops as works of art

On the serene Place Emile Goudeau, the rambling tenement house at No. 13 is considered to be the birthplace of modern painting and poetry. It was named after the boats used by laundry women. Many famous artists visited, lived in or had their studios in **Le Bateau-Lavoir**, including Paul Gauguin, Juan Gris, Otto Freundlich, Max Jacob, André Salmon, Brancusi, Modigliani and **Pablo Picasso**, who settled in here in 1904 and subsequently created the key work of Cubism with his *Demoiselles d'Avignon*. Back then there was no heating and no running water, not to mention electricity. The »laundry-boat« burned down in 1970, but was later rebuilt just like the original complete with studios.

Place Emile Goudeau

Drawn by André Gill, it's the sign that gave the **cabaret** at No. 22 on the steep Rue des Saules its name. Around the turn of the 20th century everyone went along to the »Agile Rabbit« to hear Aristide Bruant and his friends Frédéric Gerard and Père Frédé present their

Le Lapin Agile

Sketches of the Demimonde

At the end of the 19th century, Henri de Toulouse-Lautrec-Monfa, scion of one of the oldest noble families of France, advanced to becoming the most celebrated artist of the Parisian demimonde and its prostitutes.

Born in Albi in 1864 and descended from crusaders and counts, Henri spent his childhood at Château du Bosc. At a relatively young age his eccentric father introduced him to the Parisian art scene, where family friend René Princeteau taught the boy who couldn't stop drawing his artistic skills. In his early teens, Henri started suffering from pycnodysostosis, a rare bone disorder that curtailed his growth, and after breaking both thighs his legs stopped growing altogether. He had to use crutches to get around on his short legs that would hardly bend. His childhood dream of leading a chivalrous lifestyle like his father was over.

Cabarets and brothels

Only reluctantly did Henri's aristocratic family give in to his wish to become a painter. In 1882 he got a place to study in Paris at the studio of Léon Bonnat, a celebrated »painter of millionaires« on the edge of Montmartre. Toulouse-Lautrec no longer wanted to be the mollycoddled care case and for his subjects turned to the city's demimonde, in which depravity and the petit bourgeois collided and differences were not important. Entertainment venues such as the vaudeville Folies-Bergère, the ret Chat Noir, the newly d Elysée Montmartre, the Moulin de la Galette and the Moulin Rouge were very popular among night owls.

Chronicler of the demimonde

In between downing glasses of Absinth, from the bizarre characters and the rhythm of whirling dance moves Toulouse-Lautrec produced wonderful, often profound portraits. In search of his subjects he also visited racecourse, the circus, the suburban theatres and the maisons closes – club-like brothels. He first found recognition in 1888 at the annual exhibition of the group XX (Les Vingts) in Brussels. In the 1890s his poster designs for the singer Yvette Guilbert, for the Moulin Rouge, Aristide Bruant, Emilienne d'Alençon and May Belfort became acknowledged as great art and were to have a big influence on Art Nouveau. In addition he illustrated books and drew cartoons for newspapers. But after massive success between 1892 and 1896 his creativity waned while his alcohol consumption and depression increased. Only when intoxicated did he feel any hint of self-confidence.

By 1901 Toulouse-Lautrec was at the end of his tether and died at Castle Malromé with his parents at his bedside at the age of only 36.

witty, risqué and saucy songs to an enthusiastic audience. Chansons and poems are performed here to this day – though everything is more expensive; ►MARCO POLO Insight p. 64.

Musée de la Vie Romantique

Wild grapevines and wisteria are twined around the walls of the fashionable villa from the Restoration period at 16, Rue Chaptal. It served as a studio for the painter **Ary Scheffer** (1795–1858), who did portraits of the celebrities of the July Monarchy. Every Friday was a jour fixe, a fixed day, at the successful artist's house, when Alexandre Dumas, George Sand and Chopin, Delacroix, Franz Liszt, Ingres, Rossini, Lamartine and Turgeniev would visit. Opening hours:

❶ Tue–Sun 10am–6pm, www.paris.fr/loisirs/musees-expos/musee-de-la-vie-romantique/p5851; cultural programme from April to Aug; family tour Sun 11am; permanent exhibition free, special exhibitions adults €7

*Cimetière de Montmartre

Paris' third-largest **cemetery** which was laid out in 1795, is the final resting place of the writer Heinrich Heine, the painter Edgar Degas, the composer Jacques Offenbach, the Russian dancer and choreographer Nijinsky, the singer Dalida and the film director François Truffaut (►Famous People). The main entrance is on Avenue Rachel.

*Jardin Sauvage Saint-Vincent

Rocks smothered in ivy, stepped paths, a small pond and an amazing variety of flowers and trees: the 1.5-ha (4-acre) »wild garden« of Saint-Vincent is an enchanted **oasis of green** in the middle of the big city. The entrance is just opposite 14, Rue St-Vincent.

❶ April–Oct Sat 10am–12.30pm and 1.30pm–6pm.

GOUTTE D'OR

New trendy district

From the Bronx to in-district: the east of the Butte Montmartre, criticised by politicians only in 2009 as »dirty and loud«, is on the way to becoming a hip area with trendy bars, eateries, boutiques and rapidly skyrocketing property prices. Where in the Middle Ages they cultivated a much-prized wine, after the loss of France's colonies, Goutte d'Or (»drop of gold«) became the country's most famous multi-cultural neighbourhood. Before its rediscovery by the Bourgeois Bohêmes (bobo) it was home largely to African immigrants, a gathering ground for outcasts and workplace for prostitutes and pickpockets, immortalized by Ariste Bruant in his song *À la Goutt' d'Or*. In 2010, the locally based Institut des Cultures d'Islam commissioned the British Magnum photographer Martin Parr to explore the predominantly Muslim neighbourhood with his camera. The everyday scenes he captured are the most beautiful tribute to a district that is in the process of casting off its sleazy image and proudly revelling in its diversity.

! MARCO ⊕ POLO TIP

M'sa-Mode **Insider Tip**

Glamorous, with a touch of romance – all the leading fashion magazines have long since stood up and taken note of the feminine creations of talented designer Sakina M'sa. The likes of Ludivine Sagnier and Eva Mendes kit themselves out at her boutique in the Goutte d'Or. For her social involvement, for example in employing the skills of women with an immigrant background in putting together her garments, in 2010 this fashion designer from the Comoros was awarded the Social Entrepreneur's Award (6, Rue des Gardes; Mon–Sat 10am–noon and 2pm–7pm, www.sakinamsa.com).

Right next to the Eglise St-Bernard, the tiny **Écomusée** at 21, Rue Cave is devoted to the cultural diversity of the district.

❶ Tue–Sun 2.30–7pm, www.cargo21. org/index.php3; admission free

Gold embroidered kaftans, silk scarves, bags and talmi: **Boulevard Rochechouart** in the shadow of the Métro that here runs above ground is a Mecca for reasonably-priced fashion from around the world. The most famous textile merchant is **Tati**; opened in 1848 the department store boasts the lowest prices in Paris. Right under the elevated railway it's worth visiting the ∗ **Marché Barbès** (Wed 7am–2.30pm and Sat 7am–3pm). Once a notorious thieves' market, with its bustle, piles of goods and stallholders from the Maghreb, it is now more like a Moroccan bazaar. No less colourful is the Marché Dejean on the site of the old Château Rouge in Rue Dejean, which is open daily except Mondays.

∗ Montparnasse

 ✳ F/G 8

Location: On the border of the 6th and the 14th arr.
Métro stations: Vavin, Edgard-Quinet, Montparnasse-Bienvenue

While ▶Montmartre was the preferred meeting place for artists and writers around 1900, Montparnasse took over the lead role after the First World War.

The Centre of »Années Folles« between 1910 and 1940 Philosophers, painters and writers populated the cafés, bars and restaurants at the junction of Boulevard du Montparnasse and Boulevard Raspail. »In the evening, you only had to take a few steps around »La Coupole« to meet people like Cendrars, Aragon, Man Ray, Derain or Fernand Léger«, wrote their contemporary Claire Goll. Simone de Beauvoir and Jean-Paul Sartre, Ernest Hemingway, Henry Miller and James Joyce frequented the Dôme, Coupole, Select or Rotonde. Matisse, Kandinsky, Chagall and Picasso, Lenin and

Trotsky all lived for a while in Montparnasse. Once a week near the Vavin junction, where Rodin's bust of Balzac has stood since 1939, there was a model market, where supposedly Kiki, the »Muse of Montparnasse« whom Man Ray immortalized in his photographs, was discovered. After the Second World War, the artists moved on to ▶Saint-Germain-des-Prés. Today, Montparnasse is above all the quarter for a night out, with many cinemas and gourmet restaurants.

The most striking landmark in the district is the black-glazed, 210m/689ft-high Tour Montparnasse, which together with the Métro station was constructed at Avenue du Maine 33 between 1969 and 1972 and remained the tallest office building in Paris until 2011, when it was toppled from the No 1 spot by the Tour First in La Défense with a height of 231m/758ft. The lift takes just 38 seconds to travel the 196m/643ft to the **56th floor**, with its **panoramic café**, photo gallery, interactive terminals and multimedia exhibits that showcase the world's tallest buildings. There is also a short video about Paris. Steps lead up to the ***panoramic terrace** (ED: Panoramic terrace not glassed over!!) on the 59th floor at a height of 210m/689ft.
Tour Montparnasse

❶ April–Sept daily 9.30am–11.30pm, Oct–March 9.30am–10.30pm, Fri, Sat till 11pm, last admission 30 minutes before closing; adults €13, children under 7 free

The TGV train travels from Montparnasse station to the Atlantic. The tracks were covered over with the **Jardin de l'Atlantique**, where stone waves and undulating grassy areas symbolize the sea. At 23, Allée de la 2e DB, the **Mémorial du Maréchal Leclerc de Hauteclocque et de la Libération de Paris – Musée Jean Moulin**
Gare de Montparnasse

The most striking landmark in the district is Tour Montparnasse

MARCO ⊕ POLO TIP

! *Friday Night Fever* Insider Tip

Every Friday evening at 10pm enthusiastic skaters meet up for the skating procession that runs for just over 30 km along the illuminated boulevards through the middle of Paris. Organized by the »Pari-Roller« association, the starting and finishing point of the the three-hour skating tour is Place Raoul Dauby between the train station and Tour Montparnasse. However, night-skating is not something for beginners because you have to be able to keep up the pace. Métro station: Montparnasse-Bienvenue, www.pari-roller.com.

provides information about the Résistance fighter, Jean Moulin, who is buried in the ►Panthéon, and the French Résistance movement in general.

❶ Tue–Sun 10am–6pm, www.paris.fr, adults €4

At Boulevard Raspail 261, the **Fondation Cartier pour l'Art Contemporain** mounts temporary exhibitions of contemporary art and photography. Jean Nouvel designed the bright complex of aluminium and glass in 1994; the garden was laid out by Lothar Baumgarten.

❶ Tue–Sun 11am–8pm, Thur till 10pm, Wed 2pm–6pm, adults €9,50, www.fondation.cartier.com

*Fondation Henri Cartier-Bresson
In an artists' studio dating from 1912 you can admire some **world-famous images** by Henri Cartier-Bresson, the co-founder of the Magnum photo agency. Special exhibitions are devoted to Bresson's contemporaries in the fields of painting, photography, illustration and design, as well as the winners of the HCB Prize initiated by Bresson, which is awarded every year to a reportage photographer.

❶ entrance: 2, Impasse Lebouis, Tue–Sun 1pm–6.30pm, Sat from 11am, www.henricartierbresson.org, adults €6

Musée du Montparnasse
The collection of this museum at 21, Avenue du Maine consists exclusively of artworks provided by friends of the quarter and artists that live here.

❶ Tue–Sun 12.30pm–7pm, www.museedumontparnasse.net, adults €6

Cimetière du Montparnasse,
The second-largest cemetery in Paris has existed since 1824. To the right of the main entrance on Boulevard Edgar Quinet, where maps of the cemetery are available, lie the graves of Jean-Paul Sartre and Simone de Beauvoir (►Famous People). But Baudelaire, Guy de Maupassant, Samuel Beckett, Eugène Ionesco and Serge Gainsbourg are also buried here. The gravestone of the photographer Henry Langlois displays movie scenes.

Catacombes
Running beneath around a third of the urban area of Paris is a network of **quarries and tunnels** from which the building materials for the city were extracted from the 11th century all the way up to the 19th century. Most of the mining was done in the hills of

»Paris – A Moveable Feast«

Hemingway's last book was on the New York Times bestseller list for seven months. He had worked on this autobiographical retrospective of his happy times spent in Paris until shortly before his death in 1961 (p. 235)..

In 1921, at the age of only 22, the young foreign correspondent for two Canadian newspapers arrived in Paris. While America at the time was stuck in the mud, Paris bubbled with avant-garde ideas and trends; while prohibition reigned across the pond, in Paris the champagne was flowing freely. »If you are lucky enough to have lived in Paris as a young man, then wherever you go for the rest of your life, it stays with you« wrote Hemingway in »A Moveable Feast«.

Cafés of the Bohème

Absolute musts were the La Coupole brasserie on Boulevard du Montparnasse ("p. 85) and also La Rotonde, which Picasso and his artist friends Max Jacob and Modigliani also frequented. The nearby Closerie des Lilas was a regular haunt of the poets André Gide, Apollinaire and Dos Passos. Hemingway, who penned most of his novel »Fiesta« here, is remembered by a brass plaque at the bar and by having the pepper steak named after him. After finishing his writing Hemingway would like to treat himself to a whisky and soda, followed by a visit to a museum, a game of tennis or having a look at new publications in Sylvia Beach's bookshop Shakespeare & Company (▶p. 300). Or he would meet friends in the Dôme ("p. 92) and the Brasserie Lipp, where he would usually start by ordering a »distingué«, a half litre of beer ("p. 85). It was in the Dingo Bar at 10, Rue Delambre that Hemingway first encountered his writer colleague F. Scott Fitzgerald (»The Great Gatsby«). When in 1925 the universally popular Dingo barkeeper Jimmy opened Café Falstaff, the whole literary crowd moved with him.

Hemingway later liked to portray himself as a poor wretch who was hardly able to keep his head above water in Paris. Granted, his salary as a correspondent wasn't great, but his wife did have a respectable inheritance. Hemingway's flat at 133 Rue Notre-Dame-des-Champs, where he lived with his first wife Hadley, has long since given way to apartment buildings. The same goes for the home of his girlfriend, the art patron Gertrude Stein, who could afford a chic studio complete with art collection at 27, Rue Fleurus.

Hemingway often visited Shakespeare & Company

Montparnasse, Montrouge und Montsouris. It was here that medieval stonemasons quarried the limestone blocks for Notre-Dame, and even Haussmann's redevelopment plans would not have been possible without the extensive »Carrières«. Gypsum from Montmartre, which was especially in demand because of its fire-retardant properties, has been exported as far away as America. The last hoisting shafts were sealed in 1860.

In 1786, the abandoned quarries began to be used to hold skeletons from old cemeteries that had to make way for the construction of new city districts. Following the examples of Rome and Naples, in the galleries of the catacombs the remains were arranged according to cemetery and stacked up high along the walls in the labyrinth of winding tunnels. The Résistance took advantage of the fact that the passageways were beyond Nazi control and set up their headquarters there in 1944. Following a series of strange orgies in the underground in the 1970s, all of the entrances were either barred or walled up. The Banque de France uses one of the catacomb tracts to house the gold of the French National Bank.

Musée des Catacombes The only official entrance is to be found at the Musée des Catacombes, where a 2-km long tour begins. A narrow spiral stairway leads steeply down 120 steps to the dim passageways, many damp and just head-high, barely illuminated by an occasional light bulb. Don't forget to take a sweater and torch!

❶ entrance: 1, Avenue Colonel Henri Rol-Tanguy, Thur–Sun 10am–5pm, often queues at weekends, http://catacombes.paris.fr, adults €8

✳ **Musée Carnavalet**

————————————————— ✦ **J 6**

Location: 23, Rue de Sévigné (3rd Arr.)
Métro-Stations: Saint-Paul, Chemin-Vert
❶ www.carnavalet.paris.fr
Tue–Sun 10am–6pm, permanent exhibition free

Carnavalet is a mocking play on the name of the former owner, the widow of the Breton Sire de Kernevenoy. The distinguished, Renaissance-style Hôtel de Carnavalet was built in 1548.

The entrance portal with lions sculpted by Jean Goujon dates from that period. The other wing around the entrance court with a statue of Louis XIV (1698) by Coysevox in the middle was remodelled by Mansart in the 17th century. Madame de Sévigné lived in the palace between 1677 and 1696. She impressively described life in Paris and at the court of Versailles in over 1,500 letters sent to her daughter – one of the best contemporary documents of the time of the Sun King.

The exhibition in Hôtel Carnavalet is devoted to the history of the city from its beginnings in Gallo-Roman times to the Enlightenment. The department in the neighbouring Hôtel Le Peletier de Saint-Fargeau, which was constructed under the supervision of Pierre Bullet between 1686 and 1690, documents developments since the French Revolution. Highlights of the building are the Galerie Sévigné, the studio of the gifted jeweller, Fouquet's; Alphonse Mucha, the grand ballroom designed for Madame de Wendel in 1924 by José Maria Sert and a recreation of Marcel Proust's room with the original bed in which Proust wrote his *Remembrance of Things Past*.

*Musée de l'Histoire de Paris

** Musée d'Orsay

✈ **F/G 6**

Location: 62, Rue de Lille (7th arr.)
Métro station: Solférino
❶ www.musee-orsay.fr

Tue–Sun 9.30am–6pm, Thur till 9.45pm, adults €11, under 18s, EU citizens 18–25 and 1st Sun in month admission free. Combination tickets with the Musée de l'Orangerie and the ►Musée Rodin available. To avoid the queues tickets should be purchased in advance online or at one of the FNAC branches, such as at the airport or Gare de l'Est. Thematic tours; audio guide in nine languages, €5. Fri–Sun one-hour Seine cruises with Marina de Paris including lunch and museum entrance without queuing (www.marina-de-paris.com, ► p. 157).

Completed for the 1900 World Fair, the Gare d'Orsay was the world's first railway station conceived for electric trains. The daring iron structure was clad in stone and stucco. 40 years later, the platforms became too short and the station was closed – and became a setting for artistic works.

The gigantic deserted building served as the setting for several films, including Orson Welles's *The Trial*, based on the novel by Franz Kafka, and in 1972 the Renard-Barrault theatre ensemble installed itself here. Demolition was prevented when the building was classified as a cultural monument in 1978. Plans were already being made in 1977 to use the magnificent Belle Epoque train station designed by Victor Laloux as a museum of 19th century art. Three French architects – Pierre Colboc, Renaud Bardon and Jean-Paul Philippon – and the Milanese interior designer Gae Aulenti transformed the station into

The Musée d'Orsay exhibits 19th-century art in a magnificent belle epoque railway station

a fantastic museum, which since 1986 has displayed beneath its gigantic glass roof the **fine arts from 1848 to 1914**, that is from French Romanticism to Art Nouveau. The Impressionist and Post-Impressionist galleries on the top floor as well as the Amont Pavilion have recently been redesigned. And more spaces will follow by 2015. The Brazilian Campana brothers were responsible for the new decoration of the Café de l'Horloge, a homage to the Art Nouveau style.

GROUND FLOOR

Pre-Impres-sionists
Ingres expressed the contrast between the neoclassical and Romantic movements with *The Source* (1820–57) in the mid-19th century. »Never have more beautiful, intense colours penetrated through the channels of the eyes to the soul«, Baudelaire noted in 1855 about **Eugène Delacroix**'s passionate *Lion Hunt* (1854). **Honoré Daumier**, considered a connecting link between Romantic art and Realism, created 36 uncompromising terracotta bust caricatures of members of parliament in 1831. **Jean-François Millet** portrays the simple life of the peasant in his Evening Prayer (1858). The **Barbizon School**,

including Théodore Rousseau, Jules Dupré and Camille Corot, pioneered the painting of landscapes on the spot, working outdoors (plein air). **Gustave Courbet** was accused of creating unmitigated ugliness when his *Burial at Ornans* provoked a scandal in 1850. His *Artist's Studio* (1855) revealed the artist's ideals and aversions. The canvases of plein air painter **Camille Corot** convey a poetic concept of nature while pre-Impressionist **Eugène Boudin** made atmospheric moods and pulsating

? | MARCO POLO INSIGHT
Don't miss

- Ground floor: the Barbizon School, Courbet's »The Painter›s Studio«
- Mezzanine: »The Mature Age« by Camille Claudel, Gauguin's »Self Portrait« and Van Gogh's »Church of Auvers-sur-Oise«
- Top floor: Manet's »Breakfast in the Open Air«, Degas's »Dancers« and Renoir's »Dance at Le Moulin de la Galette«

light his first priority. Without doubt, the two most important painters of the second half of the 19th century were **Edgar Degas** (*The Bellelli Family*, c1858) and **Edouard Manet** (*Olympia*, 1863), whose early works blended the style of the old masters with new and daring painting techniques. And **Henri Toulouse-Lautrec** instantly captured the likenesses of the great Parisian Stars including Jane Avril, Loie Fuller and Aristide Bruant (►MARCO POLO Insight, p. 256). Admirers of historicism will discover in addition numerous sculptures, including *Napoleon I as a Roman Emperor* by **Louis-Antoine Barye** (1863 and *Le Masque* by **Ernest Christophe**, which inspired Baudelaire to Canto XX in his *Fleurs du Mal*. The emergence of polychrome sculpture and the Oriental fashion popular in Europe at the time can be seen in **Charles Cordier's** *Nègre du Soudan*. The cutaway scale model of the Opéra Garnier displays a regal grandeur. **Jean-Baptiste Carpeaux** earned furious criticism in 1863 with his »disgustingly degenerate« *The Dance* that Charles Garnier commissioned for the façade of his Paris opera house.

MEZZANINE

Naturalistic painting is on display on the mezzanine, including **Jules Bastien-Lepage's** *Bringing in the Hay* (1877) and **Fernand Cormon's** *Cain flying before Jehovah's Curse*, the hit painting in the Paris salons in 1880. Among the leading representatives of Symbolism are the Pre-Raphaelites **Sir Edward Burne-Jones** (*The Wheel of Fortune*, 1883) and **Winslow Homer** (*Summer Night*, 1890). A whole terrace is dedicated to **Auguste Rodin** (*The Gates of Hell*, c1880); next door is **Camille Claudel's** passionate sculpture group, *The Mature Age* (1899–1905). **Emile-Antoine Bourdelle's** bronze statue, *Hercules the Archer* (1909 is graceful and **Aristide Maillol's** *The Mediterranean* (1905) shows clarity of line in its forms.

Naturalism, Nabis and Art Nouveau

Musée d'Orsay

MEZZANINE

51 Sales des Fetes: Moreau-Néret, Fritel, Hugues
52 Vases: Baccarat and Sèvres; furniture: Diehl, Hébert, Hulbe
53 Crockery: Lambert
54 »Nabis«und Cézanne
55 Fremiet, Baffier, Roll
56 Naturalism: Dalou, Meunier
57 Greber, Hodler, Giacometti, Rodin
58 Tanner, Bloch, Pasternak, Cottet
59 Desbois, Watts, Ménard

60 Gauguin, Amiet, Maillol, Renoir, Boudin, Corot, Courbet
61 Henry van de Velde, Bonvallet, Guimard, Horta
62 - 64 Vases and crockery: Dammouse, Gallé, Sèvres
65 »Stile Liberty«: Bugatti and Zecchin
66 Dining room Art Noveau style by Charpentier

67-72 Gallery of neoimpressionists and post-impressionists Vallotton, Bonnard, Denis,
67 Vuillard, Maillol
68 Bashkirtseff, Cassatt
69 Signac, Seurat, Matisse, Pissarro
70 Gauguin

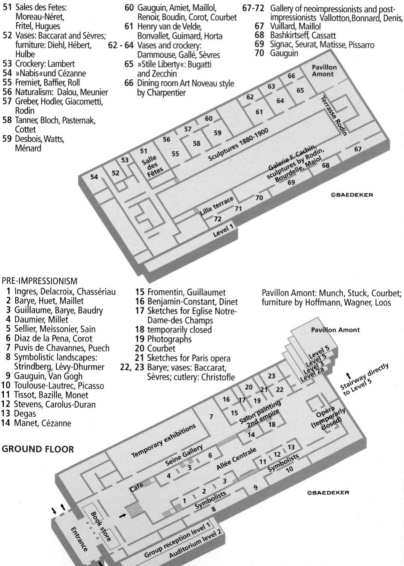

PRE-IMPRESSIONISM

1 Ingres, Delacroix, Chassériau
2 Barye, Huet, Maillet
3 Guillaume, Barye, Baudry
4 Daumier, Millet
5 Sellier, Meissonier, Sain
6 Diaz de la Pena, Corot
7 Puvis de Chavannes, Puech
8 Symbolistic landscapes: Strindberg, Lévy-Dhurmer
9 Gauguin, Van Gogh
10 Toulouse-Lautrec, Picasso
11 Tissot, Bazille, Monet
12 Stevens, Carolus-Duran
13 Degas
14 Manet, Cézanne

15 Fromentin, Guillaumet
16 Benjamin-Constant, Dinet
17 Sketches for Eglise Notre-Dame-des Champs
18 temporarily closed
19 Photographs
20 Courbet
21 Sketches for Paris opera
22, 23 Barye; vases: Baccarat, Sèvres; cutlery: Christofle

Pavillon Amont: Munch, Stuck, Courbet; furniture by Hoffmann, Wagner, Loos

GROUND FLOOR

Musée d'Orsay

UPPER FLOOR

29 Renoir, Cézanne, Monet, Degas
Fantin-Latour
30 Sisley, Monet, Manet, Pissarro
31 Degas, Sisley, Monet, Pissarro
32 Renoir, Degas, Manet, Caillebotte,
Gauguin, Manet
33 Degas

34 Monet, Pissarro, Renoir, Rodin, Sisley
35 Sisley, Pissarro, Cézanne,
Monet, Morisot
36 Monet, Renoir, Cézanne, Degas
37 Rousseau

38-47 under reconstruction

Renoir's *Moulin
de la Galette*

In the Amont Pavilion visitors can admire the large-format paintings
by Courbet, and the paintings of the Nabis together with the furniture of that epoch are also on display. The Nabis' **Pierre Bonnard**
(*The Croquet Party*, 1892) and **Edouard Vuillard** (*Still Life with Salad
Greens*, c1887) moved beyond Impressionism, whose splashes of colour were however continued in their Pointillism. Art Nouveau furniture from that time includes a music box (1903) by **Koloman Moser**,
wood panelling by **Victor Horta**, furniture by the **Thonet Brothers**,
Frank Lloyd Wright and **Charles Rennie Mackintosh**, a display
cabinet (1904) by **Emile Gallé** and an oak writing desk (1898) by
Henry van der Velde. The Post-Impressionists include **Vincent van
Gogh** with his colourful form of expression in *The Church in Auvers-*

MARCO ⊕ POLO TIP

> ! **Insider Tip**
>
> *Crystal chandeliers, gold leaf and stucco*
>
> ... decorate this stylish restaurant in the mezzanine of the Musée d'Orsay. Head chef Yann Landureau prepares French specialities that reflect the exhibitions. On Thursday evenings you can combine the enjoyment of art with a dinner. On Sunday afternoon tea is served from 3.30pm to the accompaniment of piano music (Tue–Sun 9.30am–5.45pm, Thur till 9.30pm, tea salon daily except Thur 2.45pm–5.45pm).

sur-Oise (1890). Fascinated by the exotic beauty of the South Seas, **Paul Gauguin** painted the *Women of Tahiti* in 1891. Four years later, Gauguin, whose self-portrait hangs in room 70, moved to the Marquesas Islands forever.   The tour of this floor ends with the beginnings of photography and film, from the invention of the daguerreotype (1839) up to the end of the First World War. Exhibits include the idiosyncratic portraits of the Countess de Castiglione (1837–99) done by Louis Pierson, Napoleons III's royal photographer, which were only acquired by the museum in 2008.

TOP FLOOR

**Impressionists collection
All of the great masters of Impressionism are represented in the upper gallery. Rapid brushstrokes, richly contrasting colours and striking poses are to be seen in **Edouard Manet's** famous *Luncheon on the Grass* (»Le Déjeuner sur L›Herbe«, 1863). **Alfred Sisley** combined strong lines with attenuated brushstrokes in his *Footbridge at Argenteuil* of 1872. **Auguste Renoir** immortalized the boisterous mood in the Montmartre nightclub *Moulin de la Galette* (▶picture p. 243) in 1876, while his composition *Two Girls at the Piano* (1888) is infused with soft colours and warm, golden light. Fascinated by the world of opera and ballet, **Edgar Degas** also studied life behind the scenes and underscored with intensive pastel tones the shimmering effect of artificial light in paintings such as *Dance Foyer at the Opera* (1872) and *Blue Dancers* (c1893). Degas's bronze statue *Little Dancer of Fourteen Years* (1879–81) with real hair and tulle tutu is simply enchanting. **Claude Monet** graduated from working with dabs of colour to Expressionism. In his series of *Rouen Cathedral* (c1892), the daylight reflected by the cathedral façade becomes a medium for conveying mood. Monet's influence is apparent in the lighting and texture of the *Sailboats at Argenteuil* (1888) by **Gustave Caillebotte**, who at the same time painted a realistic representation of the boats. In his emotionless, monumental still life *Woman with Coffee Pot* (around 1890), **Paul Cézanne** divides the canvas into geometric forms and areas of colour. Characteristic of the *Customs Officer* by **Henri Rousseau** are the clear lines and clear shapes, as also seen in his *Portrait of a Woman* from 1897.

★★ Musée du Quai Branly

D 5

Location: 37, Quai Branly (7th arr.)
Métro station: Alma Marceau, Pont de l'Alma (RER)
❶ www.quaibranly.fr
Tue–Sun 11am–7pm, Thur–Sat till 9pm, adults €9, under18s free

In the shadow of the Eiffel Tower on the banks of the Seine is this museum of anthropology. Created by star architect Jean Nouvel 2006, it introduces visitors to the planet's indigenous cultures.

The museum's highlights include an impressive collection of more than 8000 exotic musical instruments, some of which are displayed together in a transparent glass tower, others spread across their respective geographical areas. Perforated solar blinds create a mystical twilight in the huge space, in which objects from around the world come to ghostly life. As well as African masks and bronze sculptures from the kingdom of Benin you can admire Pre-Columbian busts, Chinese imperial robes and Polynesian headdresses and fetishes. On the **Mur Végétal**, which Patrick Blanc conceived for the museum façade, there are more than 15,000 plants from Japan, China, the USA and Central Europe covering an area of 800 sq m/8600 sq ft. Festivals and lectures, workshops for children and adults, and the museum's anniversary festival complement the collections. On the roof, with a panoramic view of the Eiffel Tower, is the **Les Ombres** restaurant where head chef Sébastien Tasset conjures up culinary delights such as suckling lamb with pistachio crust.
Les Ombres €€€: tel. 01 47 53 68 00, www.lesombres-restaurant.com,

The Musée du Quai Branly introduces to the indigenous cultures of the earth

✶ Musée Jacquemart André

✦ E 4

Location: 158, Bd Haussmann (8th arr.)
Métro station: Miromesnil
❶ www.musee-jacquemart-andre.com
daily 10am–6pm, July/Aug daily 2.30pm–5.30pm,
adults €11, free holiday programme for children

Flemish painting, Italian Renaissance artists and French 18th-century masters – the museum of the Institut de France presents its sensational art treasures in a beautiful Second Empire city palais.

Edouard André, scion of a Protestant banking family, and his wife, Nélie Jacquemart, had this magnificent residence built by the architect Parent at the end of the 19th century. United through their passion for art, the couple travelled throughout Europe and the Orient amassing one of the most beautiful private collections in France. An audio guide in six languages explains the museum's history and works that include Italian Renaissance paintings by Bellini, Uccello, Tiepolo, Botticelli and Della Robbia, Flemish masterpieces by Rembrandt, Frans Hals, Jacob Ruisdael and van Dyck, as well as French painters of the 18th century like Boucher, Chardin, Fragonard and Nattier. The rooms are decorated with embossed chests of drawers and tapestries from the Royal Beauvais Tapestry Manufacture. The ***museum café** occupies the dining room of the elegant palais, complete with with magnificent ceiling painting by Tiepolo and a terrace looking out into the cour d'honneur.

✶ Musée National du Moyen Age

✦ H 7

Location: 6, Place Paul-Painlevé (6th arr.)
Métro station: Cluny-La Sorbonne
❶ www.musee-moyenage.fr
Wed–Mon 9.15am–5.45pm, adults €8, EU citizens
under 26 free

The museum of medieval art stands in the ▶Quartier Latin on the site of the Gallo-Roman baths built in AD 200 and destroyed in AD 380.

Musée de Cluny The Benedictine Abbey of Cluny in Burgundy acquired the ruins in 1330 and, under the direction of Abbot Jacques d'Amboise, built a

Paris domicile for their abbots on it between 1485 and 1510. The Hôtel de Cluny, in the Flamboyant style of the late Gothic period, and the Hôtel de Sens (in the ►Marais) are the only late medieval residential palaces still existing in Paris – and since 1844 have made an ideal setting for collections of medieval art, including the elaborate declaration of love *L'Offrande du Cœur*, a 15th-century Dutch tapestry. The most beautiful of the sculpture fragments are the 13th-century statues of the four apostles from ►Sainte-Chapelle and a dozen Gothic heads of the kings of Judah and Israel, which were fashioned between 1210 and 1230 for the west façade of ►Notre-Dame, then lost in the French Revolution and not found again until 1977.

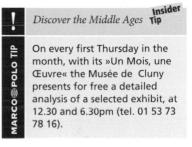

!   *Discover the Middle Ages*   **Insider Tip**

MARCO ● POLO TIP

On every first Thursday in the month, with its »Un Mois, une Œuvre« the Musée de Cluny presents for free a detailed analysis of a selected exhibit, at 12.30 and 6.30pm (tel. 01 53 73 78 16).

Room XII, with its massive ribbed vault, is the 20m/65ft-long and 15m/50ft-high **Frigidarium** (cooling room), which, thanks to the restoration, regained its subtle colours in 2009. The consoles of the pillars supporting the cross vault on the north side resemble the prow of a ship – probably indicating that wealthy ship owners, the »Nautes«, financed the construction of the baths.

*Frigidarium

The sculpture on the **Nautes Pillar** from the Temple of Jupiter, which was excavated beneath ►Notre-Dame, dates back to the 1st century, making it the oldest sculpture from Paris. The baths also had a caldarium (hot water bath), a tepidarium (tepid bath), two gymnasiums and a 10m/33ft-long swimming pool. On display on the first floor are enamels and goldsmith's work dating from the 7th to the 13th centuries, including a gilded 11th-century antependium from Basel Minster.

*Pilier des Nautes

Displayed in a circular room, the museum's greatest treasure is the series of six 15th-century tapestries known as the ****Lady and the Unicorn**, which were probably woven in a Brussels workshop. While five of the tapestries are allegories of the five senses, the sixth depicts a blue tent bearing the inscription »A mon seul désir«. In front of it, a charming young lady next to a unicorn, the symbol of purity and intelligence, is placing her jewellery in a casket – perhaps as a symbol of abstention from worldly delights. The 15th-century tapestries from the Gobelin Auxerre workshop on the walls of the late Gothic chapel, once the abbots' oratory, depict the legend of St Stephen (St-Etienne) in 23 scenes.

Traditional culinary and medicinal herbs grow in the **Jardin Médiéval**. Songs and melodies of the Middle Ages resound throughout the year at evening concerts.

** Musée National Picasso Paris
✦ J 6

Location: 5, Rue de Thorigny (3th arr.)
Métro stations: Chemin-Vert, Saint-Paul
❶ www.musee-picasso.fr
daily except Tue 9.30am–6pm, Oct–March until
5.30pm

From 2009 the curator Anne Baldassari sent up to three exhibitions a year around the world in order to finance the refurbishment of the Picasso Museum – 23 of the required €45 million had to be generated by the museum itself. By the time the museum reopened in October 2014 the exhibition space had been tripled.

Inheritance tax

Paris has to thank the Minister of Culture, André Malraux, for its Picasso Museum. It was he who initiated a law in 1968 allowing inheritance tax to be paid with works of art. Picasso's offspring paid the inheritance tax due with 250 paintings, 160 sculptures, 30 reliefs, 88 ceramics and over 3,000 graphic works.

There are few artists who have had such a lasting and profound influence on the art of the 20th century as **Pablo Picasso** (1881–1973), who lived and worked in Paris for most of his life. Whether the melancholic blue, Cubist, Surrealist, neoclassical or wildly expressive, the Spaniard always had a surprise in store. Born in Málaga and trained at art colleges in Barcelona and Madrid, Pablo Ruiz y Picasso moved to Paris at the beginning of 1904 and lived there until 1967 before retiring in Mougins near Cannes.

Picasso's painted the portrait of Dora Maar in 1937

In his Blue Period between 1901 und 1903 he painted melancholic figures in shades of blue, not least in order to come to terms with the early death of a friend. After 1904, he brightened up the colours for his circus images, which frequently appear on a pink background. His radical change of style from 1907 was triggered by African masks and his encounter with paintings by Paul Cézanne. In his preliminary studies for the first Cubist painting, the **Demoiselles d'Avignon** from 1907 (►picture p. 46), which is now exhibited in New York, fragmented shapes and colours gradually lead to the dissolution of the representational. After 1914, the cubist rigour loosened in favour of a monumental neoclassical style of painting incorporating ancient mythological motifs. From 1925, Picasso's contact with the Surrealists was reflected, amongst other things, in his »minotauromachie« – mystical peaks of psychic experiences such as Eros, death, violence and passion in encrypted form. First unveiled in the Spanish Pavilion at the Paris Fair in 1937, his large format painting **Guernica** was a memorial to the destruction of the Basque town of the same name during the Spanish Civil War. Between 1945 und 1949 Picasso discovered lithography. In addition, while in Vallauris in the South of France he created ceramics and sculptures. Bucolic themes with flowing lines run through his often wildly expressive late works. In addition, paintings by old masters such as Rembrandt and Velázquez served as a template for everything from idiosyncratic metamorphoses to cheerful burlesque drawings.

The collection is on display in the Hôtel Salé, which the salt-tax collector Albert de Fontenay – hence the nickname »salé«, meaning salted – had built in the ▶Marais by Jean Boullier. No other museum in the world has such a large Picasso collection or can document the course of his life's work so completely. The collection is rounded off by works of artists who influenced him, among them Cézanne, Renoir, Matisse, Derain, Braque, Miró and Rousseau. In May 2010, five of the museum's masterpieces were stolen in one of the biggest art thefts in recent history – estimated value: 100 million euros.

Hôtel Salé

** Musée Rodin

✦ F 6

Location: 77, Rue de Varenne (7th arr.)
Métro station: Varenne
❶ www.musee-rodin.fr
Tue–Sun 10am–5.45pm, park till 5pm, adults 7.30 €, EU citizens under 26 free; free admission to museum and park first Sun in month. Combination ticket with the ▶Musée d'Orsay.

Auguste Rodin left three gifts to the French state in 1916: his own complete collections, his personal archives and his estate in Meudon with all his work. Three years later, Rodin's former residence, Hôtel Biron, was opened as a museum.

The **garden** alone with its original-size copies of Rodin's famous sculptures merits a visit. Bending with intense concentration in front of the silhouette of the Dôme des Invalides is the figure of **The Thinker**, which was originally conceived for the top part of **The Gates of**

Delightful garden

The Thinker in front of the silhouette of the Invalides church

Hell (*La Porte de l'Enfer*). The first bronze casting of the dramatic sculptural group **Burghers of Calais**, one of a total of eleven existent copies, was dedicated in Calais in 1895. To the right of it in a covered gallery are works in marble like the large tomb figure, Ariane, which remained uncompleted because of the First World War.

Tour of the Museum Among the works in the museum are several hand studies, including *The Hand of God* modelling Adam and Eve from clay. Because of the clever juxtaposition of the hands, few observers notice that La Cathédrale is actually two identical right hands whose silhouette suggests the pointed arch of a church.

The inexhaustible subject of couples enabled Rodin to express all the nuances of sensuality and tender emotions including the pure passion of the salon dancers in *The Waltz* and the stormy devotion of *Eternal Spring*. The artistic embrace of **Le Baiser** (*The Kiss*), which was originally meant for the *Gates of Hell* to depict Paolo Malatesta's hapless passion for his sister-in-law, Francesca, is considered to be a major work of erotic art. Rodin's first full-sized female figure was the bronze *Eve*, also meant for the *Gates of Hell* after Dante's Divine Comedy.

In *Aurora* the melancholy face of the gifted sculptress **Camille Claudel** (1864–1943) emerges out of the raw marble. For ten years, Claudel was Rodin's lover, assistant and model. Rodin entered *The Call to Arms*, a sculpture of soldiers, into a competition in 1879 for a monument commemorating the defence of Paris during the Franco-Prussian War of 1870. Thanks to Zola's support, Rodin was granted the commission for the Balzac statue in 1891, which turned out to be so unflattering that it sparked a scandal. Drawings, designs, works by Camille Claudel like *The Age of Maturity* and a female nude by Renoir complete the exhibition. For a time, two other internationally renowned artists lived in the former **Hôtel Biron** without ever meeting each other. A young man by the name of **Jean Cocteau**, who rented part of the building, and a German who worked as Rodin's secretary, the poet **Rainer-Maria Rilke**.

FAUBOURG SAINT-GERMAIN

In the 18th century much of the nobility left the ▶Marias and erected their mansions in the suburb of Saint-Germain in order to be nearer the ▶Louvre and the road out to ▶Versailles. Almost 300 of these **»hôtels particuliers«** are still preserved here today and make the district of Faubourg, where Rodin resided and one of the best places to live in Paris. The **Hôtel Matignon** at 57, Rue de Varenne, is the official residence of the Prime Minister of France. The former **Hôtel de Salm**, at 64, Rue de Lille, is the residence of the French Foreign Legion. Karl Marx also liked the upper-class ambience – in 1843 the author of the Communist Manifesto took up residence at 38, Rue Vaneau. Exquisite antiques shops and art galleries have established themselves in the eastern part of the district.

Desirable properties the Museum

»Your house is the nicest in Paris«, wrote Queen Hortense, sister in law of Napoleon I., to her brother Eugène de Beauharnais in 1806. The palais that was named after him at 78, Rue de Lille was acquired by the Prussians in 1817 and today serves as the **residence of the German ambassador,** who uses the state rooms for receptions. Gilded stucco, silk tapestries and selected furniture adorn what is probably the most coveted German overseas mission.

Hôtel de Beauharnais

** Notre-Dame

H 6

Location: Île de la Cité (4th arr.)
Métro station: Cité
❶ www.notredamedeparis.fr

In 1163, the foundation stone of the massive Cathedral of Our Lady was laid on the site where the Romans had erected a temple and in the 6th century an early Christian basilica later stood.

St Louis and his canon, Maurice de Sully, wanted to build a cathedral that was worthy of the capital on ▶Île de la Cité in the recently developed Gothic style. The work on Notre-Dame lasted until 1330. The church has since experienced some structural and functional changes and even served as a council hall, a setting for opulent banquets and a stage for amateur performances. Monarchs came and went and Napo-

Gothic architecture perfected

? *Point Zero*

The bronze star set into the paving of the square in front of Notre Dame is the point from which distances from Paris to all other French cities are calculated. It follows that the marker is the zero point in terms of kilometres for all distance measurements along French roads.

leon crowned himself the first Emperor of the French here. For centuries, not much was done to maintain the cathedral, which increasingly fell into disrepair. It was Victor Hugo's **The Hunchback of Notre-Dame** that first awakened the building to new life. During the restoration from 1841 to 1864, **Viollet-le-Duc** took the original anatomy of the cathedral very much into consideration. Since then there has been a succession of renovation works. There is an unobstructed view of the wonderful main west façade from the broad square in front of the church, **Place du Parvis Notre-Dame**, which itself holds treasures below ground. The 117m/ 384ft-long Crypte Archéologique under the square contains remains of Gallo-Roman and medieval houses as well as the foundations of the Merovingian church.

** WEST FAÇADE

St Anne's Portal The monumental **main façade** has beautifully balanced proportions. To the right, the gaze falls on St Anne's Portal, which dates back to about 1220. In the lower field of its tympanum relates the story of Anne and Joachim, the parents of the Virgin Mary, from the annunciation of Mary's birth, the encounter beneath the Golden Gates and the marriage of Mary and Joseph. In the middle is Mary in the temple, Christ's Annunciation and Nativity, the shepherds, Herod and the Three Magi. The upper area shows Mary enthroned with Jesus, surrounded by heavenly hosts and the kneeling figures of a king and a bishop – presumably the two founders of the cathedral, Louis IX and Maurice de Sully. The sculptures of the upper and middle sections, fashioned between 1165 and 1175, are the cathedral's oldest. A heavenly choir decorates the arches, and a statue of St Marcellus, the 5th century bishop of Paris, the door jambs. The latter is a copy from the 19th century, as are most of the other larger statues. French rulers and saints appear on the side walls. The four modern figures of the flying buttresses are, from left to right, St Stephen, the »church triumphant«, the »vanquished synagogue« and St Dionysius.

Notre-Dame de Paris

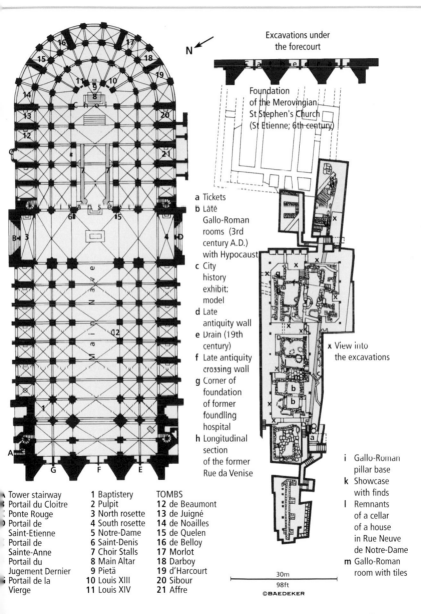

a Tickets
b Late Gallo-Roman rooms (3rd century A.D.) with Hypocaust
c City history exhibit: model
d Late antiquity wall
e Drain (19th century)
f Late antiquity crossing wall
g Corner of foundation of former foundling hospital
h Longitudinal section of the former Rue da Venise
x View into the excavations
i Gallo-Roman pillar base
k Showcase with finds
l Remnants of a cellar of a house in Rue Neuve de Notre-Dame
m Gallo-Roman room with tiles

Excavations under the forecourt

Foundation of the Merovingian St Stephen's Church (St Etienne; 6th century)

Tower stairway
Portail du Cloitre
Ponte Rouge
Portail de Saint-Etienne
Portail de Sainte-Anne
Portail du Jugement Dernier
Portail de la Vierge

1 Baptistery
2 Pulpit
3 North rosette
4 South rosette
5 Notre-Dame
6 Saint-Denis
7 Choir Stalls
8 Main Altar
9 Pietä
10 Louis XIII
11 Louis XIV

TOMBS
12 de Beaumont
13 de Juigné
14 de Noailles
15 de Quelen
16 de Belloy
17 Morlot
18 Darboy
19 d'Harcourt
20 Sibour
21 Affre

30m
98ft
©BAEDEKER

** *Gothic Masterpiece*

The world-famous cathedral on the Île de la Cité is a masterpiece of Gothic architecture. For more than 800 years, the grand old lady has accompanied the fortunes of France and its capital.

❶ Cathedral daily 8am–6.45pm, Sat and Sun till 7.15pm. South Tower: April–Sept daily 10am–6.30pm, June–Aug Sun till 11pm, Oct–Mar 10am–5.30pm. Archaeological Crypt: Tue–Sun 10am–6prn. Treasury: Mon–Fri 9.30am–6pm, Sat till 6.30pm, Sun 1.30pm–6.30pm. Organ concerts: Sun 4.30pm. Audio guides; free tours in English: Wed and Thur 2pm–3.30pm, Sat 2.30pm–4pm. Visitors should expect long queues between April and October, so it's best to get there for the early morning.

❶ Gallery of Kings
Above the portals this is a series of 28 statues of the kings of Judah and Israel. Created after 1220, the statues we see today are replicas, the originals having been decapitated during the French Revolution.

❷ Grand Gallery
The filigree arches, whose columns are just 20cm thick, conceal the lower sections of the towers and the roof of the nave. They were added in around 1230.

❸ Organ
The clangorous organ, built at the beginning of the 19th century by François Thierry and extended by Aristide Cavaillé-Coll in 1863–1868, is among the largest organs in France with its 8500 pipes and 113 stops on five keyboards. Free organ recitals are given every Sunday at 4.30pm.

❹ Notre-Dame de Paris
Since 1855, a slender statue of the Virgin created in 1330, the venerated miraculous image of the patron saint, has stood on a column next to the southeastern pillar of the crossing.

❺ Choir screens
The choir screens bear 23 stone reliefs depicting scenes from the life of Christ up to the Passion. Painted and partly gilded, they were created in 1319–51 by Jehan Ravy and his nephew Jehan de Bouteiller.

❻ Treasury
Entered to the right of the choir, the treasury contains the »Great Relics«: the crown of thorns as well as a nail from the Passion and a fragment from the True Cross. Louis IX originally had ▶Sainte-Chapelle erected as the repository for the crown of thorns, which he acquired from Constantinople in 1237. Every first Friday of the month at 3pm it is presented at the »Vénération de la Sainte Couronne d'Épines«. The treasury also houses priceless manuscripts and monstrances.

❼ South Tower
For €8.50 those not afraid of heights can climb the 387 steps past the famous bell to the top of the 70-m high South Tower. With Paris at your feet, the tower ascent also provides close-up encounters with some of the cathedral's demonic gargoyles. Entrance: Rue du Cloître Notre-Dame – there's no lift!

tympanum on three levels the life, martyrdom and resurrection of St Stephen, to whom the older church on this site had been dedicated. Eight small reliefs on either side of the portal show images from everyday and student life.

INTERIOR

The huge dimensions of the cathedral, which extends over a length of 130m/427ft and with its double aisles has a width of 48m/157ft, make a deep impression. The church can accommodate close to 9000 people, 1500 in the galleries alone. The sexpartite rib vault of the nave appears almost to float, as do the large rose windows in the transept.

Fantastic view from the south tower

In the course of his restoration work in the first bay of the nave, Viollet-le-Duc had already begun to return the High Gothic tripartite elevation back to the early Gothic quadripartite division. As he fortunately abandoned this plan, it is now possible to make the comparison and see the greater elegance of the High Gothic solution. An interesting point in the history of style is the change from the Romanesque acanthus and leaf ornamentation of the capitals in the choir to the Gothic leaf-decorated capitals in the nave. Completed in 1255, the huge *rose window in the north transept is the biggest such window to be built in the Middle Ages. The stained glass depicts 80 scenes from the Old Testament connected with the Virgin Mary. The south rose window, which dates from 1270, depicts Christ surrounded by the apostles, martyrs, the wise and foolish virgins and the story of Matthew. The original medieval furnishings of the church include the **choir screens** begun around 1300 by Pierre de Chelles (►picture p. 279). They bear 23 relief depictions of scenes from the life of Christ up to the Passion that Jehan Ravy and his nephew Jehan de Bouteiller worked in stone, painted and partly gilded between 1319 and 1351. In the southeastern choir chapel is the Burgundian-influenced tomb of Jean Juvénal des Ursins (†1431), who as »**prévôt des marchands**« established free trade for shipping on the Seine and Marne in the Middle Ages. Here too is the elaborate black and white monumental tomb of the Comte d›Harcourt (†1718) by Pigalle. Also note the finely carved choir stalls, a Pietà by Nicolas Coustou, the Baroque high altar and the mighty *organ.

Palais Bourbon · Assemblée Nationale

F 5

Location: 33, Quai d'Orsay (7th arr.)
Métro station: Assemblée Nationale
❶ www.assemblee-nationale.fr
Except Tue and Wed, free guided tour by
appointment 2.30pm–4, tel. 01 40 63 69 69

The Palais Bourbon is the seat of the French National Assembly; the second chamber, the Senate, sits in the Palais du ▶Luxembourg.

France's
parliament

Until 1946, the **Assemblée Nationale** – the legislative organ – bore the name Chambre des Députés (Chamber of Deputies). The Palais Bourbon was built between 1722 and 1728 for Duchess Louise-Françoise de Bourbon, the legitimized daughter of Louis XIV and Madame de Montespan. Seized during the French Revolution and later remodelled as a parliament building, it has been the seat of the representatives of the French people since 1827. The imposing design of the front, completed in 1806 with a ten-column portico facing the Seine, corresponds to the main front of the Madeleine Church, which was also given a classical porch with columns and a triangular gable. The monumental sculptures depict famous ministers of French kings (from left to right): Sully under Henry IV, Michel de l'Hospital under François I, Henri II d'Agnesseau under Louis XV and Colbert, minister under Louis XIV. The allegories in the tympanum representing France flanked

Palais Bourbon is the seat of France's parliament

by Freedom and Order were fashioned by Cortot in 1839–41. To left and right of the flight of stairs are Minerva symbolizing Wisdom and Themis symbolizing Justice. The semi-circular chamber of the **National Assembly**, constructed in the time of the Directoire and remodelled by Jules de Joly in 1826, can be toured by appointment even when the 577 representatives are in session. The ceiling painting in the library was completed by Delacroix between 1838 and 1847. The library's inventory includes the original records of the trial of Joan of Arc.

Next door to the west is the Hôtel de Lassy, which was built by Prince de Condé in 1722–24 and today is the **official residence of the President of the National Assembly**. A few steps away, on the Quai d'Orsay, is the Ministère des Affaires Etrangères, the French Foreign Ministry.

Hôtel de Lassy

✶ Palais de Chaillot · Trocadéro

✦ C/D 5

Location: Place du Trocadéro (16th arr.)
Métro station: Trocadéro

Skateboarders and street vendors dominate the marble terrace between the wings of the Palais de Chaillot, which was erected on the site of the former Palais du Trocadéro for the 1937 Paris World Fair.

The main terrace, flanked by gleaming bronze statues, undoubtedly offers the most spectacular view of the Eiffel Tower (▶picture p. 158). The **maritime museum** in the west wing recounts the story of seafaring from galleys to the atomic submarine with models of ships, nautical equipment and figureheads. Highlights among the models include Columbus' *Santa Maria*, the French navy's last sailing ship the *Valmy*, which was constructed of ebony, and the aircraft carrier *Charles-de-Gaulle*, launched in 1999.

*Musée de la Marine

❶ Mon, Wed and Thur 11am–6pm, Fri 11am–9pm, Sat and Sun 11am–7pm, www.musee-marine.fr; adults €7, EU citizens under 26 free

Prehistoric, anthropological and palaeontological collections are displayed in this **museum of anthropology**, including a cast of the Hottentot Venus and the Venus of Lespugue carved from a mammoth's tusk. Africa is represented with rock drawings from the Hoggar mountains, the Arctic region with Inuit art and masks from Greenland. A reconstructed temple and markets testify to the cul-

*Musée de l'Homme

tural richness of the Maya and Aztecs. The view from the terrace of the Le Totem restaurant stretches to the Eiffel Tower.

❶ closed until 2015 for renovation, www.museedelhomme.fr

*Aquarium de l'Homme
The aquarium at 2, Avenue des Nations Unies was built for the World Fair in 1878 and reopened in 2006 with a mammoth show including 15,000 fish in 43 tanks and three cinemas. Anyone eating at the **Ozu Japanese restaurant** will have a free view of the underwater world.

❶ daily 10am–7pm, www.cineaqua.com, adults €19.90.

*Cité de l'Architecture et du Patrimonie
In this collection relating to national architecture, urban development and building preservation, models of churches, palaces and tombs outline more than twelve centuries of French stylistic history.

❶ Mon, Wed, Fri–Sun 11am–7pm, Sat 11am–9pm, www.citechaillot.org, adults €8, admission free for EU citizens under 26 and 1st Sun in month.

Théâtre National de Chaillot
After the Second World War, such illustrious actors as Gérard Philippe and Maria Casarès performed at this theatre with its two stages and a seating capacity of 3000. Today, it is known for innovative dance and theatre under its director Ariel Goldenberg.

Booking: tel. 01 53 65 30 00, www.theatre-chaillot.fr.

Several prominent figures who died after 1870, including the painter Edouard Manet, the writer Jean Giraudoux and the composers Gabriel Fauré and Claude Debussy, are buried in the **Cimetière de Passy** on Avenue Paul Doumer.

> ! **Bon chic, bon genre** _Insider Tip_
>
> MARCO ⊕ POLO TIP
>
> Chanel, Christian Lacroix, Escada, Givenchy and Sonia Rykiel – Rue de Passy in the 16th arrondissement combines everything that is »BCBG« for the French – stylish and tasteful.

* Palais de Justice

✳ **H 6**

Location: 4, Boulevard du Palais (1st arr.)
Métro station: Cité
❶ www.ca-paris.justice.fr

First the Gauls, then the Romans and finally the Merovingians built their fortified settlements, forts and castles on the site where today the Palais de Justice stands on the ▶ Île de la Cité. This was the cradle of French royal power.

France's highest court
The **medieval residence** with the newly built ▶Sainte-Chapelle has its golden age during the reign of Louis IX. However, the royal court

soon moved to the ▶Louvre, and from the 16th century onwards, this was the seat of the »Parlement«, the **highest court of justice**, without whose approval royal laws were not legally binding. This purely technical privilege was abolished by a young king on his way to becoming an absolute monarch: Louis XIV. The French Revolution, for its part, not only did away with the king but also the Parlement by sending all its members to the guillotine. The new court, now a civil court, moved into the building that from then on was called the Palais de Justice. Repeatedly damaged by fire and then reconstructed, the building was given its present appearance in 1900.

The south wing houses the **civil and criminal courts**, while the Quai des Orfèvres range is occupied by the **criminal investigation department**. The **Cour de Mai**, where once a maypole was erected, is reached through a wrought-iron gate dating from the time of Louis XVI. A flight of stairs leads from there up to the **Galérie Marchande**, where until the outbreak of the French Revolution, litigants, lawyers and curious spectators were met by a gallery of merchant stalls. At the end is the **Salle des Pas Perdus**, the »Hall of Lost Steps« – a reference to the futile legal efforts of those waiting here. Opposite is the ***Salle des Gens d'Armes** of the ▶Conciergerie, the old **Grand' Salle**, the showpiece of the royal palace where the monarch signed treaties and held official receptions. The neoclassical decor, a reproduction of the original by Salomon de Brosse, was completed after the great fire of 1871. The **Vestibule de Harlay** is adorned with statues of Charlemagne, Philippe II Auguste, Louis IX and Napoleon I, rulers who had a particular connection with lawmaking.

Also open to the public is the **Chambre Dorée**, the first civil chamber, once the bedchamber of Louis IX, which was turned into the assembly room of the parliament. From 1793 this was the Salle de la Liberté, in which the Revolutionary Tribunal pronounced over 2000 death sentences, including that of Marie-Antoinette. The neo-Renaissance interior dates from the 19th century.

❶ Mon–Fri 9am–6pm; only with ID, security check!

Palais de Tokyo

✳ **D 5**

Location: 11, Av. de Présid.-Wilson (16th arr.)
Métro stations: Iéna, Alma-Marceau
❶ www.palaisdetokyo.com

The former Palais d'Art Moderne was erected for the 1937 Paris World Fair in Bauhaus style. It has recently been expanded to accommodate contemporary artistic trends.

*Musée d'Art Moderne de la Ville de Paris

To designs by Anne Lacaton and Dominique Vassal, in 2012 the Palais de Tokyo was enlarged with a further 5,500 sq m of exhibition space to cover current trends in all areas of art. The east wing displays **European classical modern art**, including post-Impressionists Paul Cézanne, Dunoyer de Segonzac and Utrillo, still lifes by Georges Braque and Picasso's *Evocation* – the first picture of his Blue Period from 1901. Highlights are the large-format *Dance* by Matisse and the monumental *Fée Electricité* by Raoul Dufy, an allegory of electricity done for the 1937 Paris World Fair. In summer, the stylish museum café places tables and chairs on the terrace, where visitors are greeted by three statues by Bourdelle: Strength, Victory and the Allegory of France dating from 1927.

❶ Tue–Sun 10am–6pm, Thur till 10pm for special exhibitions, www.mam.paris.fr; adults from €8, 1st Mon in month admission free from 6pm

*Site de Création Contemporaine

In the west wing of the **Museum of Contemporary Art**, factory aesthetics with bare concrete walls provide an exciting harmony with the extended Art Deco glass ceiling. The works of art on display, judged by the curators as being avant-garde works in the international art scene, are **no older than one year**. The exhibitions are supplemented with workshops, lectures and concerts.

❶ Tue–Sun 12pm–12am, adults 6 €, under 18s free

*Musée de la Mode et du Textile

The nearby museum in the **Palais Galliera**, which was built at the end of the 19th century in the style of the Italian Renaissance, exhibits clothing and accessoires, prints and fashion photos from the 18th century to the present. In the »Atelier des Enfants« youngsters are introduced to the world of fashion. Because only a fraction of the costumes can be shown at any one time, the temporary exhibitions are devoted to particular themes.

❶ 10, Avenue Pierre 1er de Serbie, www.galliera.paris.fr, Tue–Sun 10am–6pm, Thur till 9pm.

Palais Royal

✦ G   5

Location: Place du Palais Royal (1st arr.)
Métro station: Palais Royal-Musée du Louvre

The »royal palace« opposite the ►Louvre is the official seat of the Conseil d'Etat (Council of State) and Secrétariat (ministry) de la Culture et de la Communication.

Historic oasis

Cardinal Richelieu had this palais built for himself between 1634 and 1639, and later bequeathed it to the Crown. After the death of Louis

XIII, the widowed queen, Anne of Austria, moved into the palais, named thereafter Palais Royal. Her son, Louis XIV, moved back into the ►Louvre in 1652, only to transfer his court to ►Versailles after a brief stay in the palace of ►Vincennes. Thereafter, the palace was given to the House of Orléans. Louis Philip of Orléans – who was called Philippe-Egalité because he supported the principle of the Revolution (which did not save him from being sent to the guillotine) – had it remodelled to its present form, including the little garden with colonnades, shops and rented flats. On 13 July 1789, the lawyer and journalist Camille Desmoulins led a revolutionary assembly under these colonnades that was followed the next day by the storm-

The Buren sculptures provide a playground for inline skaters

ing of the ►Bastille. Before and during the Revolution and in the First Empire, the palais was a public gathering place with restaurants, cafés, gambling halls and brothels. During the occupation of Paris by the Allies in 1814, Field Marshal Blücher reportedly lost six million francs in the gambling halls of the Palais Royal. They, along with the brothels, were closed in 1830. Among the distinguished residents of the flats were Colette and Jean Cocteau. Napoleon and Victor Hugo dined in the **Le Grand Vefour** restaurant, opened in 1784.

Open day

Every year during the »Journées du Patrimoine« on a weekend in September many of the city's cultural monuments can be visited free of charge or at reduced prices. And that includes otherwise inaccessible buildings such as the Palais Royal, the Elysée Palace and the Hôtel de Matignon (www.journeesdupatrimoine.culture.fr).

Colonnes

Dominating the inner courtyard are **Daniel Buren's** 260 black-and-white striped columns, which were restored in 2010. The geometrically placed columns of varying heights sprout from the ground like mushrooms, and skateboarders and inline skaters use the works of art as an obstacle course.

In the Cour d'Orléans stand the **Sphérades**, two fountains by Pol Bury (1922–2005), where the pressure of water once set the ten polished steel balls in motion on their base.

Arcades

Under the arcades of the Palais Royal there are some very **elegant boutiques**: the New York fashion designers Marc Jacob and Rick Owens have their shops here. At Po Nayar you can buy hand-knitted children's clothes, and encounter refined scents at Parfums de Rosine. Anyone who is hungry can dine at the »Macéo« like Colette and Eisenhower once did, or enjoy a fine glass of wine at the famous **»Willi's«** wine bar.

Place des Victoires

Barely 200m/220yd east of Jardin du Palais Royal is the circular royal Place des Victoires with the **equestrian statue of Louis XIV**. The elegant houses surrounding are an appropriate setting for expensive fashion boutiques such as Kenzo, Cacharel and Thierry Mugler. In 1685, the Sun King was so thrilled by Mansart's square that he immediately commissioned him to do another one close-by: ▶Place Vendôme.

Théâtre Français

France's oldest national theatre is the home of the famous state theatre company, Comédie Française. It was founded in 1680 by Louis XIV, originating in a troupe of actors that Molière led until his death in 1673. Napoleon issued a decree in 1812 making the members of the ensemble state actors, whose director is to this day appointed by the government. The works performed here are principally classical French plays, including the dramas and comedies of Corneille, Racine, Molière, Marivaux and Beaumarchais, but also modern classics by Paul Claudel, Jean Giraudoux, Jean Anouilh, Alfred Jarry and Samuel Beckett. In 1799 the building burned down but was rebuilt by 1807. The present façade dates from 1867 and the interior from the turn of the 20th century. Molière's chair, in which he died after suffering a haemorrhage, can be seen in the foyer, along with Jean-Antoine Houdon's bust of the ageing Voltaire from 1781.

❶ 2, Rue de Richelieu, box office: tel. 08 25 10 16 80
www.comedie-francaise.fr.

** **Panthéon**

✦ **H 7**

Location: Place du Panthéon (5. arr.)
RER station: Luxembourg

»Columns like oaks, walls like smoothed rocks«, wrote Friedrich Hebbel in 1843, deeply impressed by his visit to the building. Having recovered from a severe illness, Louis XI fulfilled his vow to the patron saint of Paris and in the year 1758 charged his master builder, Jacques-Germain Soufflot, with the construction of a church to replace the Abbey of St Geneviève that had fallen into ruin.

The Pantheon is France's national temple of glory

The domed church was completed on the Montagne Sainte-Geneviève in 1789, ten years after Soufflot's death. In 1791, the National
Assembly resolved to convert it into a **Panthéon** for the »mortal remains of the great men of the era of France's liberty«, which, as in
antiquity, was to be dedicated to all the deities. Puvis de Chavannes
depicted the life of the saint in several frescoes on the side walls.
Other wall paintings show Charlemagne, Louis IX and Joan of Arc.
The Panthéon was the first building in Paris in neoclassical style and
set the standard for structures like the ►Arc de Triomphe and the
►Madeleine.

The first prominent French personality to be ceremoniously laid to
rest in the Panthéon was the revolutionary leader Mirabeau, in 1791.
However, when he fell from grace his bones were removed from the
national shrine, in 1793. The mortal remains of Voltaire were also
transferred to the Panthéon in 1791, where they remain to this day.
The mathematician Monge, the physicist Marie Curie, the inventor
of the system of reading and writing used by the blind, Louis Braille,
and the résistance fighter Jean Moulin have also found their final
resting place here. In a solemn ceremony on 30th November 2002 the
coffin containing the mortal remains of Alexandre Dumas, the creator of the novels *The Count of Monte Christo* and *The Three Musketeers*
was transferred to the shrine. He is the 70th personage, and the sixth
writer after Voltaire, Jean-Jacques Rousseau, Victor Hugo, Emil Zola
and André Malraux to be admitted to the French »Holy of Holies«.

Léon Foucault demonstrated the diurnal motion of the earth from
the gallery of the dome – thrillingly described in Umberto Eco's best-
selling novel, *Foucault's Pendulum* (Vintage Books, 2001).

Memorial for great French-men and one woman

Foucault's Pendulum

** *France's National Temple of Glory*

Perched on the Montagne Sainte-Geneviève, the mighty domed build-ing is visible from afar. Even shortly after the French Revolution, the re-mains of great Frenchmen like Voltaire, Rousseau and Zola were buried here. Alexandre Dumas, whose coffin was interred here in 2002, was the 70th French personality to be transferred to the national shrine.

❶ April–Sept 10am–6.30pm, Nov–March 10am–6pm, last admission 45 mins before closing, adults €7,50
http://pantheon.monuments-nationaux.fr

❶ Portico and pediment

Soufflot sought to distance himself from his model, Sir Christopher Wren, builder of St Paul's Cathedral in London. He therefore designed a portico projecting far out in front of the main façade, blocking the view of the dome so that it seems to float above its base. The triangular pediment supported by 18 Corinthian columns bears the inscription »To great men, their grate-ful fatherland« and a relief by David d'Anger on the history of France with Mirabeau, Voltaire and Rousseau ap-pearing to the left and Napoleon and his generals to the right.

❷ Supporting columns

Designed by Soufflot the interior was organised entirely around clarity. In or-der to maximize space, instead of the massive supporting pillars that usually chracterise such a structure, he used a continuous line of thinner supporting columns, behind which he placed a second colonnade of columns against the wall.

❸ Barrel vault with lunettes

Each dome takes up a square out of whose edges a barrel vault is created.

The barrel vaults are equipped with openings ("lunettes"), a design that allowed an optimal transfer of the shear forces to specific intersections supported by columns.

❹ Windows

Because the windows were walled up during the French Revolution, the only source of natural light in the building today, apart from the windows in the central dome, are the semi-circular clerestory windows at the top of the aisles. Just like the flying buttresses they can't be seen from the outside.

❺ Tambour

The special feature of the cylindrical base to the dome is its double row of columns separated by wide openings.

❻ Central dome

The three spherical segments, which are stacked on top of each other and built entirely of stone, were a bold in-novation for the time. The Panthéon temporarily served as a church during Napoleon I's reign, and in 1811 he had the dome decorated with a fresco of the Assumption of St Genevieve. Climb up into the dome – there are beautiful views out over Paris from the columned gallery.

Marie Cu
physicist
winner i
nterred
national

front o
ands in

*Saint-Etienne-du-Mont The remains of Racine and Blaise Pascale rest opposite the Panthéon in the The church of the Benedictine monastery that formerly occupied this site, Saint-Etienne-du-Mont, that was begun in 1492. The church is consecrated to **St Stephen** but **St Geneviève** is also venerated here. She is the patron saint of Paris and is said to have saved the city from destruction by Attila the Hun in the 5th century. The district around the church and the Panthéon is called the Montagne-Ste-Geneviève after her. The richly decorated, Renaissance-style façade was created by Claude Guérin between 1610 and 1618. The little tower on the right is a remnant from the 13th century. An unusual architectural feature found normally only in Gothic churches is the triforium, which, halfway up the nave, encircles it like a gallery. The church is famous for its **choir screen** created between 1530 and 1541 according to the design of Philibert de l'Orme, with a spiral staircase on each side. The graves of the philosopher Blaise Pascal (1623–62) and dramatist Jean Baptiste Racine (1639–99) are at the entrance tot he Lady Chapel. The sarcophagus in front of the next side chapel but one is said to contain a stone from the tomb of St Geneviève. The mighty **organ** was made famous by the composer Maurice Durufle (1902–86). First built in 1630, it was enlarged by Aristide Cavaillé-Coll in the 19th century. Durufle worked as organist of the church for 50 years and in 1947 created his famous Requiem for organ and orchestra. Today his place is occupied by Thierry Escaich, who has made the church and organ the highlight of the new »Paris of the Orgues« festival held in May (www.orguesparis.fr).

* Petit Palais

✦ F 5

Location: Avenue W.-Churchill (8th arr.)
Métro station: Champs-Elysées-Clemenceau
❶ www.petitpalais.paris.fr
Tue–Sun 10am–6pm; Sun till 8pm for special exhibitions, permanent exhibition free admission, special exhibitions adults €5–11

Built together with the ►Grand Palais for the World Fair of 1900, the »small palais« exhibits the same architectural features as its larger counterpart. The dome rises majestically above the main entrance, impressively complemented with rich sculptural decoration.

Artistically-minded patrons In addition to excellent exhibitions on cultural history, the Petit Palais has been home since 1902 to the valuable **art collections of the city of Paris**, which are based to a great extent on private donations. The Dutuit brothers contributed works of ancient, medieval and Renaissance art, including paintings by Rembrandt and Rubens, valuable books, majolica, enamels and ceramics. The Tuck collection primarily consists of 18th-century furniture, tapestries and sculpture. The Zoubaloff Gallery exhibits sculptures by Jean-Baptiste Carpeaux and paintings from the neoclassical period to the Impressionists, including works by Géricault, Ingres, Delacroix, Corot, Courbet, Cézanne, Monet and Pissarro.

Pigalle

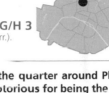

✦ **G/H 3**

Location: in the north of the city (9th/18th arr.).
Métro station: Pigalle

Sex shops and street prostitution: the quarter around Place Pigalle and Boulevard de Clichy is notorious for being the red light area – but that is only one aspect of the ►Montmartre district, which Picasso and Piaf immortalised with their art.

The dubious reputation of the district goes back to the 19th century, when Toulouse-Lautrec designed his iconic posters for the daring can-can shows at the Moulin Rouge. Even in those days, Clichy was a byword for the thrill of depravity, with easy girls cavorting on Place Pigalle. In the 1930s Maurice Chevalier made hearts melt with his *Pigalle Pigalle*, Edith Piaf named one of her albums *La Rue Pigalle* and in 1961 Bill Ramsey stormed the German charts with *Pigalle, Pigalle, das ist die große Mausefalle mitten in Paris* (Pigalle, Pigalle, that's the big mousetrap in Paris). **Adult entertainment** still predominates around Place de Clichy, Place Pigalle and Boulevard de Clichy, with sex shops, porn shows, revealing cabarets and revues, bars, hourly hotels and prostitution. But the wave of »yuppification« doesn't stop for anything, and former cabarets have been transformed into such trendy nightclubs as **Les Folie's Pigalle** at 11, Place Pigalle (www.lefoliespigalle.com).

Artistically-minded patrons

The **Musée de l'Erotisme** at 72, Boulevard de Clichy is the only such establishment in Paris, displaying displays its treasures until late at night: 2,000 objects of erotic art and practice from the 2nd century AD to the present day, across various cultures and continents.

❶ daily 10am–2am, www.musee-erotisme.com, adults €10

*Varieté at the Moulin Rouge The art of erotic suggestion has been presented at the Moulin Rouge since 1889. This is the cradle of the **French Cancan** and marked a stage in the careers of Edith Piaf, Josephine Baker, Yves Montand, Frank Sinatra and Liza Minelli. Feathers, tulle, sequins, rhinestones and leather also feature in the current variety show, »Féerie", which every evening juggles with the tried and tested mix of Paris myth, exotic scenes and the bird of paradise-like Doriss Girls. For dinner in the Belle Epoque dining room they serve lobster, foie gras and champagne.

❶ 82, Boulevard de Clichy, www.moulinrouge.fr, ▶picture p.72

*SoPi »**South of Pigalle**« known as SoPi, is a small district with the atmosphere of New York's Lower East Side or that corner of Brussels between Les Marolles and Les Sablons, with independent boutiques, galleries and restaurants. Among the hottest newcomers is **Andrea Crews** (10, Rue Frochot), whose fashion is beyond conventions and flirts with Pop Art. The **Pigalle** boutique (7, Rue Henri Monnier), has funky T-shirts and bags, **Chloe's Cupcakes** (40, Rue Jean-Baptiste Pigalle) seduces with cake art by Chloé S. On Sunday morning queues form in front of Arnaud Delmontel's bakery, which doesn't only have crispy bread rolls but also irresistible macaroons (39, Rue des Martyrs).

✷✷ Place de la Concorde

——————————————— ✦ F 5

Location: 8th arr.
Métro station: Concorde

The expansive Place de la Concorde, at the intersection of the two main axes, Louvre–Arc de Triomphe and Madeleine–Palais Bourbon, is the largest square in Paris (8.6ha/21.3 acres) and one of the most beautiful squares in the world.

Magnificent buildings and an impressive panorama Jacques-Ange Gabriel supplied the design and built the two similar, magnificent buildings on Rue Royale on the north side of the square between 1755 and 1775; the one on the right is the Ministère de la Marine (Ministry of the Navy), the one to the left the elegant Hotel Crillon, one of the city's most prestigious places to stay (▶ p. 150). In 1793 the guillotine was set up on the square, which was given the name **Place de la Révolution** at the time. Among the enemies of the Revolution beheaded here were Louis XVI, Marie-Antoinette, Danton and Robespierre. It received its present name, meaning »square of harmony«, in 1795 during the rule of the Directory.

Obélisque The main eye-catcher in the centre of the square is a 22m/72ft-high obelisk hewn from pink granite originating from the Temple of

Monumental Place de la Concorde

Ramses in Luxor. The monument dating from the 13th century BC was a gift from the Viceroy of Egypt, Mehmet Ali, to the Citizen King, Louis-Philippe, in 1833. In the winter months the square is also home to the 60-m high *** ferris wheel**, which offers fantastic views; at other times of year it is packed up and sent to other cities around Europe.

Roue de Paris: daily 10.30am–midnight, www.rouedeparis.com adults €10, children €5 – after dark the wheel is illuminated by 30,000 lightbulbs.

Between 1836 and 1854 Jacob Ignaz Hittorff from Cologne completed the square with two fountains, which were renovated in 2002. The Fontaine des Fleuves to the north is decorated with allegories of the Rhine and Rhône rivers and agriculture and industry, while the Fontaine des Mers to the south has allegorical figures representing the Mediterranean and Atlantic, seafaring and fishing. In the corners of the octagonal square, Hittorf also added eight statues of females symbolizing, in clockwise direction, France's eight largest cities after Paris: Marseille, Bordeaux, Nantes, Brest, Rouen, Lille, Strasbourg and Lyons.

*Fountains and sculptures

Contemporary photography and video art is exhibited in the Jeu de Paume in the Jardin des ▶Tuileries. Nearby, at 12, Rue Boissy d'Anglas, the work of young artists is presented by the **Fondation d'Entreprise Ricard** at eight annual exhibitions. The foundation also lays on concerts and workshops about contemporary art.

Modern art

❶ Tue–Sat 11am–7pm, tours Wed and Sat 12.30pm, Sat also 4pm, www.fondation-entreprise-ricard.com, admission free

Place de la République
✳ **H 5**

Location: 11th arr.
Métro station: République

In his radical rearrangement of Paris, in 1854 Baron Haussmann laid out a vast parade ground for Napoleon III's soldiers. Had he ever imagined the Place de La République would soon enough become synonymous with the biggest demonstrations in France, he may well have made it smaller.

Freedom, equality and fraternity
In order to create the Place de la République, Haussmann had the theatre district of the Boulevard du Temple demolished. The only survivor is the Théâtre Déjazet dating from 1851, and today theatre and concertgoers can still enjoy performances from the splendid setting of the red and gold auditorium (www.dejazet.com).

In the middle of the square, between the allegories of Freedom, Equality and Fraternity and the 12 bronze reliefs depicting French history, the almost 10-m high statue of **Marianne** stands on 15-m high plinth. The embodiment of the French Republic is dressed in a Roman toga and she holds aloft a laurel wreath (►MARCO POLO Insight p. 178). Four great boulevards and three main roads still converge at the square. However, with a new scheme for the square designed by Pierre-Alain Trévelo, Antoine Viger-Kohler and landscape architect Martha Schwartz, by 2014 the large amount of traffic should be channeled so as to enable Parisians to enjoy the space as an **outdoor oasis** with a densely planted city garden and a central open space around the statue of the Republic.

Musée des Arts et Métiers
More than 200 years ago Abbot Henri Grégoire established the Conservatoire National des Arts et Métiers as a repository for all inventions of trade and industry.

Visitors today to the former Benedictine abbey of Saint-Martin-des-Champs can marvel at **milestones of technical progress** from Lavoisier's laboratory to Daguerre's darkroom, from Pascal's calculating machine to Vaucanson's mechanical loom, from Gallé's artistic works in glass to Watt's steam engine, from Bell's telephone to Volta's battery and from Clément Ader's first aeroplane to the early high-performance computers like the Cray 2.

Three times a month at the attached **Théâtre des Automates** mechanical slot machines from the 18th to the 20th centuries are set in motion for three quarters of an hour, demonstrated and explained.

❶ 60, Rue Réaumur, Tue–Sun 10am–6pm, Thur till 9.30pm, www.arts-et-metiers.net, adults €6.50, under 26s free.

** # Place des Vosges

✦ J 6

Location: Centre east (4th arr.)
Métro stations: Saint-Paul, Bastille

Place des Vosges is the oldest and, for many, the most beautiful square in Paris. It was officially opened as Place Royale with a festive tournament in 1612 on the occasion of the double wedding of Louis XIII to Anne of Austria and the king's sister, Elizabeth, to the future King Philip IV of Spain – confirming the ▶Marais as an elegant aristocratic residential quarter.

Louis Métezeau designed the festive setting for tournaments, state receptions and court weddings in line with the concepts of the Renaissance. In spite of Cardinal Richelieu's ban on the practice, **Place Royale** was also a favourite spot for duelling. The Parisian literati gathered at No. 11 in Marion Delorme's salon. Madame de Sévigné, an eloquent witness to her era in her letters to her daughter, was born at No. 1 in 1626. The enclosed square (▶ picture p. 249), each of whose sides has a length of 108m/354ft, is surrounded by 38 houses with two-storey façades in light-coloured natural stone and brick over open arcades. The royal residences – to the north the **Pavillon de la Reine**, to the south the **Pavillon du Roi** bearing the initials of Henri IV – were built higher and statelier than the other houses and

Enchanting square in the heart of the Marais

»Ma Bourgogne«, the favourite restaurant of inspector Maigret at Place des Vosges

MARCO ⊕ POLO TIP

!

Crime Scene Paris **Insider Tip**

With wit and intuition he solved all his 75 cases: the grumpy but lovably human Parisian Inspector Maigret. Georges Simenon created not only the most successful investigator of all time, but in his crime novels he demonstrated a profound knowledge of the indigenous bistro cuisine. Robert Courtine, long-time food writer at »Le Monde« and a good friend Simenon, wrote an amusing guide to the Paris bistros in which Maigret used to dine, and also compiled Madame Maigret's favourite recipes – from bouillabaisse to profiteroles au chocolat. Bon apetit! (»Madame Maigret's Recipes«).

function at the same time as entrance gates. The remaining residences on the square were privately owned. Place Royale lost prestige during the reign of Louis XIV and in 1800 was renamed »Place des Vosges« – the département of the Vosges had been the first to pay its taxes to the new Republic of France. Now, once again, the smart set meets in the antique shops, galleries and restaurants under the arcades, including Maigret's favourite place **Ma Bourgogne** (No. 19, tel. 01 42 78 44 64, www. ma-bourgogne.fr, €€) and the **L'Ambroisie** gourmet restaurant (▶ p. 86). In summer, children play on the grass around the **equestrian statue of Louis XIII** that Dupaty and Cortot created in marble in 1829.

*Maison Victor Hugo Victor Hugo was 30 years old, when in 1832, together with his wife and four children, he moved into this 280 sq m apartment on the second floor of the **Hôtel de Rohan-Guéménée** at 6, Place des Vosges. The author lived here for 16 years. Among the treasures of the museum are the original manuscript of *Les Miserables*, the decoration of the Chinese salon designed by Hugo himself, as well as paintings and drawings that prove Hugo knew how to handle a pencil and brush.

● Tue–Sun 10am–6pm, www.musee-hugo.paris.fr, permanent collections free

** **Place Vendôme**

──────────────── ✳ G 5

Location: Centre west (1st arr.)
Métro stations: Madeleine, Opéra, Concorde

Extremely expensive jewellery, Parisian chic and the legendary Ritz Grand Hotel are the trademarks of the charming Place Vendôme, one of Paris's most prestigious squares.

Royal square Jules Hardouin-Mansart, architect of the ▶Palace of Versailles, designed the elegant square in 1685 with its harmonious appearance and proportions. Originally, the royal academy, the mint and the royal library were meant to be housed behind these façades. The Sun King's financial difficulties, however, brought the rights of use into the hands of the city, which sold them to aristocrats and wealthy citizens. These new owners built city palaces and courtyards behind the existing façades, successfully combining the prestigious regal style with middle class simplicity. The square was restored to its former glory at the end of the 1990s. On Place Vendôme the finest jewellery by Boucheron (No. 26), Cartier (No. 23), Van Cleef & Arpels (No. 22) and Bulgari (No. 25) can be found. Ernest Hemingway once voiced the wish that heaven would be as inviting as the Bar Américain in the **Ritz Hotel** (▶ p. 71). He was a regular guest here, as were Scott Fitzgerald and Gertrude Stein. The luxury hotel gained sad notoriety in 1997 as the last stopover of Princess Diana, who died a short while later in an automobile accident near Pont de l'Alma. In 1849 the composer Frédéric Chopin died in No. 12 at the age of only 39.

Napoleon's victory column

The centre of the square is occupied by a 44m/144ft-high column based on Trajan's Column in Rome and cast from 1200 captured enemy cannon. The upward spiralling bronze reliefs recount the glorious deeds of the French army. On the top is Napoleon dressed as a Roman emperor. The **victory column** replaced an equestrian statue of Louis XIV, which had fallen victim to the turmoil of the French Revolution in 1792.

Colonne de la Grande Armée

✳ Quartier Latin

✦ **G/H 6/7**

Location: Centre (5th arr.)
Métro stations: St-Michel, Cluny-La Sorbonne

Schools and universities, libraries and bookshops still dominate everyday life where once, in the Middle Ages, the academic centre of Paris was located and Latin was the official local language.

Lively student quarter
Today almost every language can be heard in and around Boulevard St-Michel, with the exception of Latin. In addition to the ▶Sorbonne University (Université de Paris IV), most of the »**Grandes Ecoles**« are located in this quarter. These famous elite schools include the Ecole Polytechnique, Ecole Normale Supérieure and the universities of Censier / Université de Paris-III and Jussieu / Universités de Paris-VI, which Jean Nouvel renovated from the ground up. Paris VII's 20,000 students moved in 2005 to the Tolbiac district. The scholastic spectrum is completed by the Collège de France (▶p.318) and grammar schools steeped in tradition like the Lycée Henri IV and the Lycée Louis-le-Grand.

The student quarter is teeming with cinemas, pubs and restaurants, cheap shops, cafés, boutiques, jazz clubs and bars. Students from all over the world dominate the street scene during term time from October to June. In the summer months, on the other hand, it is mostly tourists who populate the **Boul' Mich'**, (Boulevard St-Michel) and they sometimes appear disappointed that they only meet other tourists, especially along the pedestrianized restaurant alley, Rue St-Séverin.

With works by everyone from William Shakespeare to James Joyce, George Whiteman's original **Shakespeare & Company** at 37, Rue de la Bûcherie is a delightful place to browse and buy classic English-language tomes. A literature festival is held here on every even year (www.festivalandco.com).

Shakespeare & Company: daily noon–midnight, Readings Mon 8pm, www.shakespeareandcompany.com

St-Julien-le-Pauvre
The little 12th-century Romanesque church of **St-Julien-le-Pauvre** on leafy Square Viviani belongs to the Greek Orthodox community. The elections of the rectors of the ▶Sorbonne were held here in the 15th and 16th centuries, and until it was plundered in 1524 it served as a site for the university's School of Theology and Arts – the beginning of lectures was signalled by the church bell.

St-Séverin
Begun in 1230 and finished in the late Gothic Flamboyant style in 1520, the parish church of **St-Séverin** in Rue des Prêtres-St-Séverin is famous for its mighty **organ** and the intricate fan vaulting in its 15th-century choir ambulatory.

* Rue de Rivoli

✦ F 5–J 6

Location: Between Place de la Concorde and Marais
(1st and 4th arr.)
Métro stations: Concorde, Palais-Royal, Tuileries, Châtelet

**The always busy Rue de Rivoli was created on the orders of
Napoleon from 1802. Following the right bank past the Louvre
it connects Place de la Concorde with the ▶Marais.**

The street, which runs alongside the Tuileries and the north wing of
the ▶Louvre, was given its name after Napoleon's defeat of the Austrian army at Rivoli during his Italian campaign in 1797. But it was
only in 1833, 12 years after Napoleon's death, that work on the street
was completed, combining traditional, uniform façades and round-
arched arcades with modern, multi-storey buildings and iron roof
structures. Twenty years later, Baron Haussmann continued Rue de
Rivoli by running Rue St-Antoine all the way to Place de la ▶Bastille.
The First French Republic was proclaimed in house No. 230 in 1792.
Ivan Turgenev wrote his novel *Fathers and Sons* in 1862 in No. 210,
and No. 194 was the residence of the writer René de Chateaubriand
from 1812 to 1814. The stretch of Rue de Rivoli opposite the Tuileries
Gardens, with jewellers, art galleries, antique shops, cafés, boutiques
and souvenir shops under the **arcades**, is a great place for a stroll.
Between the Louvre and the ▶Hôtel de Ville are two of the largest
department stores in Paris, Belle Jardinière and Bazar de l'Hôtel de
Ville. The protected Art Nouveau department store La Samaritaine,
closed since 2005, was reborn at the end of 2014 as the classy **Hôtel
Cheval Blanc**, with 80 rooms and roof garden.

**Shopping for
tourists**

Decorative art from the Middle Ages to the present is on display in
the Musée des Arts Décoratifs at 107, Rue de Rivoli.
❶ Tue–Sun 11am–6pm, Thur till 9pm for special exhibitions,
www.lesartsdecoratifs.fr; adults €9.50, EU citizens under 26 free

**Musée des
Arts
Décoratifs**

A gilded equestrian statue of the French national heroine, Joan of Arc
(Jeanne d'Arc; c1410–31), by Emmanuel Frémiet, stands triumphant-
ly on **Place des Pyramides**. Joan, the pious daughter of simple country folk from Lorraine, believed she had been called by »voices« to
liberate France from England during the Hundred Years' War. Her
victory in 1429 at Orléans was the turning point of the course of the
war. A short while later she fell into English-Burgundian captivity
and was burned at the stake in Rouen in 1431. Ever since 1920, when
she was canonized, the »Maid of Orléans« has been France's second
patron saint.

***Joan of Arc
Monument**

✳ Sacré-Cœur

H 3

Location: 35, Rue du Chevalier de la Barre (18th arr.)
Métro station: Anvers
❶ www.sacre-coeur-montmartre.com
Basilica: daily 7am–10pm, dome and crypt: daily 9.15am–5.15pm. Those
wanting to attend a service in the church can take part on Fridays and
Saturdays in a »Nuit d'Adoration« from 8.30pm–8.30am with Holy
Communion in the evening and early morning and accommodation with
breakfast in the guest house of the basilica, booking on tel. 01 53 41 89 03.

**At twilight, the gleaming white Basilique du Sacré-Coeur de
Montmartre almost looks like an Oriental mosque, its neo-
Byzantine dome and small towers rising high above the city
and visible from afar.**

Oriental-
looking
landmark

After defeat in the Franco-Prussian War of 1870–71 and the bloody
suppression of the Paris Commune of 1871, French Catholics vowed
to erect a **church of atonement** consecrated to the Sacred Heart on
the hill of ►Montmartre. The work begun in 1876 by Paul Abadie
lasted almost 40 years. The massive gold mosaic in the choir shows
Christ with a flaming heart, the Archangel Michael and the Maid of
Orléans to his right and Louis XVI with his family to his left. But the
high point of a visit, in the truest sense of the word, is the view from
the huge dome.

The gleaming white basilica Sacré-Cœur

** Saint-Denis

———————————————————— ✦ **Excursion**

Location: 10km/6mi to the north (A1)
Métro station: Saint-Denis-Basilique
❶ www.ville-saint-denis.fr, http://saint-denis.monuments-nationaux.fr
April–Sept daily 10am–6.15pm, Sun from noon, Oct–Mar 10am–5.15pm,
Sun from noon; adults €7.50, EU citizens under 26 free

There are two reasons to go to the suburb of Saint-Denis: sport and one of the most venerable churches in France. In addition, from March every year the »Banlieues Bleus« offer five weeks of jazz, blues and funk (www.banlieuesbleues.org).

With a capacity of 80,000, France's largest **football and rugby stadium** was completed in 1998 for the World Cup. Today it is also used for other sporting events and rock concerts.(www.stadedefrance.com).

Stade de France

** BASILIQUE SAINT-DENIS

The Romanesque and Gothic basilica, burial place of **St Dionysius**, the first bishop of Paris, and almost all French kings, was declared a **UNESCO World Heritage site**. According to legend, St Dionysius, who was beheaded sometime around 250, supposedly carried his own severed head to the place where he wanted to be buried. A chapel was erected over his grave in the 5th century, which under King Dagobert in the 7th century gained the status of an abbey. Starting with Hugh Capet in 996, it subsequently became the burial site for royalty; with the exception of Louis VII, Philippe I and Louis XI, all French monarchs and their queens were interred here: 42 kings, 32 queens, 63 princes and princesses as well as ten further outstanding personages of the realm.
Under Abbot Suger (1081–1151), who was a close confidant of Louis VI and Louis VII, the links between the abbey and royalty led to the conversion of church into a grand basilica. The »royal necropolis« also became the repository of the fleur-de-lis banner and the crown. During the Revolution in 1789 the tombs were destroyed and the bones buried in a mass grave. Louis XVIII then had them reburied in a charnel house in the cathedral. In the mid-19th century began the restoration of the abbey following historical documents.

Burial place of royalty

The transition from the massive **late Romanesque style** to delicately structured **early Gothic architecture** can be seen in the west façade: three large rounded portals flanked by figures, the larger central doorway surmounted by round and pointed arches, and a rose win-

West façade

Saint-Denis

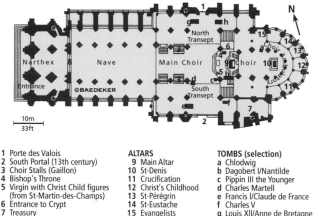

1 Porte des Valois	**ALTARS**	**TOMBS (selection)**
2 South Portal (13th century)	**9** Main Altar	**a** Chlodwig
3 Choir Stalls (Gaillon)	**10** St-Denis	**b** Dagobert I/Nantilde
4 Bishop's Throne	**11** Crucification	**c** Pippin III the Younger
5 Virgin with Christ Child figures	**12** Christ's Childhood	**d** Charles Martell
(from St-Martin-des-Champs)	**13** St-Pérégrin	**e** Francis I/Claude de France
6 Entrance to Crypt	**14** St-Eustache	**f** Charles V
7 Treasury	**15** Evangelists	**g** Louis XII/Anne de Bretagne
8 Cavaillé-Coll Organ	(mosaic remnants)	**h** Henry II/Catharine d'Medici

dow. It originally had two towers, weighty and slightly set back, until the north tower was hit by lightening in 1837 and pulled down. None of the original doorway sculptures have survived except for the figures in the central one portraying the wise and the foolish virgins and the months and the signs of the zodiac. The restored tympanum of the central doorway portrays Judgement Day while the tympanums of the side doors are copies; the right one shows the communion of St Dionysius, the left one the martyrdom of his companions, Rusticus and Eleutherius.

Birthplace of Gothic architecture   The impressive 108m/354ft-long and almost 30m/98ft-high interior has towering composite pillars and 37 windows, each 10m/33ft high. The church is a **Gothic pillared basilica** divided into narthex, nave, crossing, main choir, north and south transepts and choir with ambulatory. The choir – consecrated in 1144 by Abbot Suger – is considered to be the »birthplace of the Gothic style«, which spread from here via the cathedrals of the crown›s domains, like Paris, Chartres, Laon, Amiens and Reims, to much of Europe. Abbot Suger had the choir suffused in light from the radiating chapels. Then during the 13th century, the whole church was transformed into an »architecture of light« through the slender composite pillars, delicate quadripartite rib vaulting, huge **stained-glass windows** and external flying buttresses supporting the walls of glass and the roof. This allowed not only the celestial light to flood into the interior through the expansive clerestory fenestration, but also brought the interior space to life, throwing its height and depth into sharp relief at different times of day.

There are two communal graves in the **crypt**, one for the royal house of Bourbon, to which Louis XVI and Marie-Antoinette belonged, the other for members of the royal Merovingian, Capetian, Orléans and Valois dynasties. There are over 70 tombs, some of them masterpieces of French mortuary sculpturing of the 12th to the 16th centuries, including the marble and bronze Renaissance mausoleum of Louis XII († 1515) and his queen, Anne de Bretagne († 1514), in the north transept. Next to it stands the tomb finished in 1573 by Germain Pilon for Henri II († 1559) and Catherine de' Medici († 1589), who are depicted in an attitude of prayer and as giants, i.e. sculptures of the dead in a recumbent position. The 13th-century sarcophagus of Dagobert I to the right beside the high altar is decorated with a statue of Queen Nantilde and her son Clovis II. Philibert de l'Orme designed the magnificent tomb in the form of a triumphal arch for François I (1494–1547) and Claude de France in the south transept.

**Royal tombs

! Classical soundscapes

MARCO❖POLO TIP

Insider Tip

Lully's Te deum, Verdi's Requiem and Mahler's Second Symphony – at the Festival de Saint-Denis each June big names and an extraordinary repertoire inspire fans of classical music in the choir of the basilica and at the Maison d'éducation de la Légion d'Honneur (www.festival-saint-denis.com).

** Sainte-Chapelle

✦ H 6

Location: 4, Boulevard du Palais (1st arr.)
Métro station: Cité
❶ http://sainte-chapelle.monuments-nationaux.fr
Nov–Feb 10am–5pm, March–Oct 9.30am–6pm, weekdays 1pm–2pm closed for lunch. Tours 11am–3pm, adults €8.50. Regular classical concerts at 7pm and 8.30pm. Because Sainte-Chapelle is situated next to the ▶Palais de Justice there are security checks – no metal objects!

It took ten years to finally complete the renovation of the two-storey palace chapel in the courtyard of the ▶Palais de Justice in 2009. Yet this marvel of Gothic architecture was originally completed in 1248 in a space of less than 33 months, probably by Pierre de Montreuil.

Louis IX, commonly called Saint Louis, built the Sainte-Chapelle as a repository for the precious relics from the Holy Land that he had

Gothic jewel

Sainte-Chapelle

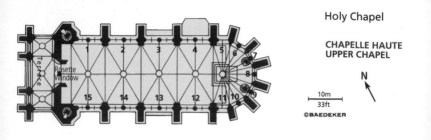

Holy Chapel

**CHAPELLE HAUTE
UPPER CHAPEL**

N

10m
33ft

©BAEDEKER

STAINED GLASS SCENES IN SEQUENCE (total area c. 615 sqm/6,620sqft, partially supplemented)

1 Story of Creation,
Adam and Eve, Noah, Jacob
2 Exodus from Egypt; Joseph
3 Pentateuch Levi,
Law of Moses
4 Deuteronomy Joshua,
Ruth and Boas
5 Judges: Gideon, Samson

6 Isaiah, Tree of Jesse
7 John the Evangelist
Life of Mary Childhood
of Jesus
8 Passion of Christ
9 John the Baptist; Daniel
10 Prophecies of Ezekiel
11 Jeremiah; Tobias

12 Judith; Job
13 Esther
14 King Samuel, David, Salomon
15 Legend of the True Cross
Discovery of the True Cross
Procurement of the Relics
by Louis IX and delivery
Consecration of the Holy Chap

acquired from the Byzantine emperor – the purchase price of 1.3 million francs was three times as much as the building costs. The chapel in the former royal palace was neglected during the Revolution and later served as a storehouse and to archive records before it was carefully restored in the mid-19th century.

Chapelle Sainte-Chapelle is entered through the **lower chapel (Chapelle Basse), which was used by the lower nobility and was therefore smaller and darker. A spiral staircase leads to the **upper chapel** (Chapelle Haute), which was for the relics and the royal family. The relics – a fragment of the True Cross and a branch of the Crown of Thorns – are today in the treasury of ►Notre-Dame. Only the French king held the keys to the reliquary, the contents of which he displayed to the assembled court on Good Friday. The quadripartite rib vault, studded with stars, is supported by 14 slender buttresses. Apart from a low blind arcade displaying scenes of martyrdom in the base zone, there are no walls as such: just lots of colourful glass. The 15m/49ft-high windows hold the oldest and most significant **stained glass** in Paris, with over 1100 biblical scenes in radiant colours – from the 13th-century depiction of the Creation to the late 15th-century Gothic rose window at the western end with 86 scenes from the Apocalypse. The overwhelming play of colours shining through the stained glass is especially impressive on sunny days.

Saint-Eustache

✦ H 5

Location: Rue Rambuteau (1st arr.)
Métro station: Les-Halles
❶ www.saint-eustache.org
daily 9.30am–7pm, Sat from 10am, Sun from 9am

The parish church of the Les Halles district is dedicated to the early Christian martyr Eustace, patron saint of hunters. It was the last church in Paris to be built in the Gothic style and it shows signs of the emerging Renaissance.

The foundation stone was laid during the reign of François I in 1532 but it took until 1640 to complete the church of the ►Les Halles quarter. Like ►Notre-Dame, the cruciform plan, double aisles, triforium and net vaulting followed the Gothic model. However, Renaissance columns were added to the Gothic-style pillars. The impressive church with a vault measuring 88m/289ft in length, 44m/144ft in width and 34m/112ft in height fittingly reflects the size and importance of its parish. The choir windows fashioned in 1631 from drawings by Philippe de Champaigne show the apostles, the the fathers of the church and St Eustache, who is also to be seen above the left door arch in a painting by Simon Vouet from around 1635. In a niche to the left of the apse is the tomb of Jean-Baptiste Colbert, Louis XIV's minister of finance, fashioned by Coysevox according to the design of Le Brun. Created in 1969, Raymond Mason's colourful sculpture entitled the *Departure of Fruit and Vegetables from the Heart of Paris* recalls the market halls (►Les Halles) that once stood next door. Every Sunday from 5.30pm to 6pm, Saint-Eustache is filled with the truly heavenly sounds produced by organist Jean Guillou on the famous **Ducroquet-Gonzalès organ**, which Jan van den Heuvel replaced with a newly-built organ in the old casing in 1989. All of the »auditions de l'orgue« are free. The annual mass marking the opening of hunting season is also an experience; information.

Saint-Eustache

** Saint-Germain-des-Prés

✦ F/G 6

Location: 6th arr.
Métro stations: Saint-Germain-des-Prés, Mabillon, Odéon
❶ www.saint-germain-des-pres.com

The Saint-Germain-des-Prés quarter is a cosmos of many smaller worlds. Top managers, leading politicians and film stars stay here and it is quite possible to stroll around for days indulging in that popular Parisian sport of seeing and being seen.

Best quarter to stroll and rummage

Saint-Germain-des-Prés has excellent jazz bars, imaginative designer shops and extremely cosy bistros. Galleries and antique shops are lined up back-to-back in Rue des Saints Pères, Rue du Bac and Rue de Seine. Shoe fans must visit Rue du Cherche Midi; high-end boutiques like Armani, Ralph Lauren and Sonia Rykiel prefer Boulevard Saint-Germain and Rue de Grenelle. At the latter the perfect Parisian host will find the best cheeses at Barthélémy (No. 51) and the most divine cakes and macaroons for dessert in Dallayou (No. 63). Rue de Buci promises not only a market with fresh fruit and vegetables, but also charming cafés with Parisian flair.

Literary café Les Deux Magots

Collectors of antiquarian books go into raptures about Rue de l'Odéon, where at No. 7 Adrienne Monnier was once in charge. In 1929 she published the French translation of James Joyce's Ulysses, helping to make the author world famous. One in three Paris publishers has its offices in the 6th arrondissement – the Espace des Femmes with feminist bookstore and gallery at 35, Rue Jacob belongs to the popular Editions des Femmes publishing house and regularly organizes author evenings. The La Hune art bookstore at 170, Boulevard Saint-Germain, which specializes in film, architecture and design, is open Mon–Sat until midnight, Sun from 11am–7.45pm.

In 1783 the treaty by which Great Britain recognized the independence of the United States was signed at 56, Rue Jacob. And it was at 28, Rue Mazarine that Jean François Champollion first succeeded in deciphering the Egyptian hieroglyphs in 1822.

Centre of Existentialist Bohème

The literary and artistic centre of Paris gained notoriety in the 1940s and 1950s through the Existentialist group led by **Jean-Paul Sartre** and **Simone de Beauvoir** (▶Famous People). A multitude of small art galleries, the Paris School of Fine Arts in Rue Bonaparte and a series of legendary cafés and restaurants still provide a taste of the artistic and intellectual milieu that was still a cheap quarter back then – and not chic and expensive. Sartre and his life companion, Simone de Beauvoir, were always to be found in **Café de Flore** on Boulevard Saint-Germain, where they read, worked and debated with other Existentialists (▶ p. 116). Opposite are two other literary cafés – **Café Les Deux Magots**, once frequented by Albert Camus, André Gide and André Breton, and **Brasserie Lipp**, where Picasso, Hemingway and Joan Miró drank their »p'tit noir« and ate sauerkraut with their beer (▶ p. 105). Henry Miller loved the »La Palettre« café-bar at 43, Rue du Seine, which was also frequented by Cézanne und Braque. Richard Wagner completed his Flying Dutchman at 14, Rue Jacob, and Mata Hari, the famous First World War spy, once danced at No. 20 for the guests at Nathalie Clifford Barney's lavish receptions. Macabre, biting ridicule was the trademark of the multi-talented **Boris Vian**. The uncrowned »Prince of Saint-Germain« was a trained engineer, played jazz trumpet and wrote seven novels and more than 450 chansons. Together with his wife Michelle, Jacques Prévert, Raymond Queneau and Juliette Gréco, Boris Vian spent his nights in the over-crowded jazz cellars of the district, such as Tabou in Rue Dauphine or Club Saint-Germain. His scandalous writing aroused the censors – and made him a bestselling author. Vian died in 1959 at the age of only 39 during the filming of his controversial novel, *I Shall Spit On Your Graves*.

Place de Furstemberg

This little square under the plane trees was named after the German Wilhelm Egon, Count of Furstemberg (1629–1704), who was first Cardinal-Archbishop of Strasbourg and later abbot of the Abbey of Saint-Germain-des-Prés. There were stables for the horses and a coach house for the carriages in the courtyard.

Musée Delacroix

The author of *Antigone*, **Jean Anouilh**, lived at 5, Rue de Furstemberg. The play was first performed in 1944 with the permission of the German occupying forces in Paris – although it was clearly a call for resistance, cleverly disguised as a story from antiquity. The Romantic painter **Eugène Delacroix** lived opposite at No. 6 from 1861 until his death in 1863, while working on the frescoes for Saint-Sulpice. Today his apartment is a national museum.

❶ Wed–Mon 9.30am–5pm, www.musee-delacroix.fr Adults €5, EU citizens under 26 free

*Eglise Saint-Germain-des-Prés

A church stood on the meadow (prés) as early as the 6th century. It was the burial site of the Merovingian kings Childeric I, Chlothar II and Childeric II. When the bishop of Paris, Germanus, was canonized in 754, the **Benedictine abbey** took his name. Repeatedly destroyed by the Normans, the nave was rebuilt around the year 1000 in Romanesque style and the choir in early Gothic style in 1163. Of the once vast Benedictine monastery only the late 16th-century abbot's palace, the priory and some remains of the destroyed Lady Chapel have survived. In the right-hand transept are the tomb designed by Caspar Marsy for the Polish king and honorary abbot, John II Casimir Vasa († 1672) and a marble statue of St Francis Xavier by Guillaume Coustou. The gravestones of the philosopher René Descartes († 1650) and the scholars Jean Mabillon († 1707) and Bernard de Montfaucon († 1719) can be seen in the side chapel of the choir dedicated to St Benedict. Next to the old abbey church a tiny park surrounded by hazelnut trees is home to the sculpture **Hommage à Apollinaire** by **Picasso**, whose house and studio at Rue des Grands Augustin 7 was nearby. He lived there from 1937–55 and in the summer of 1937 painted his famous picture *Guernica* there, which today hangs in the Museo Reina Sofía in Madrid.

Insider Tip

! MARCO ⊕ POLO TIP

The oldest coffee house in Paris ...

... is the elegant **Procope** in Rue de l'Ancienne Comédie 13. A Sicilian named Francesco Procopio dei Coltelli founded it in 1686, and Procope was soon a meeting place of the Parisian intellectuals, frequented by the philosophers of the Enlightenment and later the hotheads of the Revolution and the poets of the Romantic era. Today it is an excellent place to dine try the Brittany oysters or the coq au vin, marinated in Beaujolais and twice braised, tel. 01 40 46 79 00, www.procope.com, €€€ / €€).

Magnum Gallery

In 1937 Henri Cartier-Bresson, Robert Capa, David Seymour and George Rodger founded the **Magnum photo agency**, but only since 2009 has the legendary organization had its own shop window in the city: the Magnum Gallery at 13, Rue de l'Abbaye, which in the purist ambience annually puts on four shows featuring works by its 80 contract photographers, including Martin Parr, Lisa Sarfati, Marc Riboud and Antoine d'Agata.

❶ Tue–Sat 11am–7pm, www.magnumgallery.fr, admission free

*Saint-Sulpice

No less than six architects were involved in the building of Saint-Sulpice. Work on the choir was begun in 1646, but the classical façade

Queen of Bakers

Rustic bread rather than baguette? For many people, the best bread in Paris is produced by Apollonia Poilâne. As soon as her hearty rustic bread leaves the ovens, the Parisians are queuing up for it.

Apollonia Poilâne was 18 years old when in 2002, after the death of her parents in a road accident, she inherited the most famous bakery in Paris. Twelve years later she runs a bakery empire with 160 employees and a turnover of 15 million euros. Since her father, Lionel Poilâne, took over the family business at 8, Rue du Cherche Midi in 1970, no baguette has been produced in the 200-year-old bakery. Instead and in ever-increasing numbers, they have the 2 kg sourdough **boules**, which are, after all, what gave this profession its name: »boulanger«.

Made with yeast, the lightweight **baguette** only began its triumphant advance onto French tables after the First World War. It was in the mid-19th century that Viennese bakers brought the recipe for the elongated bread rolls to the French capital, and by 1870 there were more than 400 Austrian and German bakers busy meeting the demands of the upper classes in particular. With the introduction of the ban on night time baking in 1920, the time consuming sourdough process became a real luxury while the yeast dough completely did away with the need to bake before the early morning.

The ban has long since been lifted, and so Poilâne today operates three shifts preparing **sourdough** in the basement of the former monastery, kneading the dough and sliding the flour-dusted loafs into the great wood-fired ovens where the wort of wheat from the Marne valley and sea salt encounters the aroma of burning logs of oak and poplar. A new batch of loaves is ready every two hours, and will also be delivered to regular customers like Catherine Deneuve and the star chefs Alain Ducasse and Joël Robuchon. There are now additional bakeries, at 49, Boulevard de Grenelle and, since 2011, 38, Rue Debelleyme. In the suburb of Bièvres a factory with 24 wood-burning ovens dispatches more than 5,000 loaves daily to brown bread aficionados around the world, including Johnny Depp, Steven Spielberg and Sean Connery. Apollonia's success story is encouraging and proves that bread can be sold profitably without ready-made dough (www.poilane.fr).

by Jean-Nicolas Servandoni was not completed until 120 years later. Chalgrin erected the 73m/240ft-high north tower in 1777, whereas the 68m/223ft-high south tower remained uncompleted. Louis Visconti created the Fountain of the Four Bishops for Place St-Sulpice in the mid-19th century with the figures of Bossuet, Fénélon, Massillon and Fléchier. Christophe Gamard and Louis Le Vau were responsible for the further work on the church nave in the mid-17th century. The two stoups at the entrance were originally a gift from the Republic of Venice to François I. In the first chapel on the south side are three 19th-century frescoes by Delacroix portraying Archangel Michael's battle with the dragon, the expulsion of Heliodorus from the temple and Jacob wrestling with the angel. The ten statues on the choir pillars that Bouchardon produced in 1734 depict Christ, Mary and eight of the apostles. A dome painting by Lemoyne and a marble statue of the Queen of Heaven by Jean-Baptiste Pigalle from the 18th century are worth noting in the Lady Chapel. On Sundays at 4pm there are recitals on the **powerful organ**, which was rebuilt by Cavaillé-Coll in 1860. **Victor Hugo** and Adèle Foucher exchanged wedding vows in this church in 1822, and in 1841 the German poet **Heinrich Heine** married his Mathilde, actually a simple shoe salesgirl named Crescencia Eugénie Mirat. St-Sulpice has been a very popular place to visit ever since the bestselling author **Dan Brown** published *The Da Vinci Code* in 2004: the trail of the esoteric murder story leads right through the church, which is said to hide the key to the Holy Grail.

❶ daily 7.30am–7.30pm, www.paroisse-saint-sulpice-paris.org (church), www.stsulpice.com (organ)

*Musée Maillol   Art lovers can gain an insight into the life and works of **Aristide Maillol** (1861–1944), whose sculptures, drawings and engravings from the private collection of his muse and model Dina Vierny are displayed at 61, Rue de Grenelle. The museum also has works by Matisse, Degas, Picasso, Ingres, Cézanne, Rodin, Poliakoff, Kandinsky and Raoul Dufy.

❶ Wed–Mon 10.30am–7pm, Fri till 9.30pm, www.museemaillol.com, adults €11.

** Seine

A10 – M10

Course: the Seine rises in Burgundy and empties into the English Channel. It divides Paris into the northern Rive Droite (right bank) and the southern Rive Gauche (left bank)

The Parisians love their river. Whether by boat or walking along its banks, whether cycling, jogging or sunbathing, the Seine stands for rest, relaxation and pure enjoyment.

Anyone crossing Paris via the Seine can breathe in the city and experience any number of little adventures, on the river, along its banks, on the bridges and islands, day and night. Even if the days when the Seine was the city's most important transport artery are long gone, Paris is always rediscovering its river. In 1991 the banks between Pont de Sully und Pont d'Iéna were declared a **UNESCO World Heritage Site**.

Some are reminiscent of a cat's arched back, others weigh on the water like a ton of bricks and others are delicately crocheted as if fashioned by fairy hands. Once threatened by high water, today they appear to be planted in the riverbed for eternity: Paris's bridges. The majority of them had been subjected to extensive restoration work by the end of the last millennium. Within the city, the Seine is spanned

Bridges of the Seine

►MARCO POLO Insight p. 315

A summer night at the Seine

The Capital's Lifeline

It's always worth taking a stroll along the banks of the Seine. Some of Paris's finest buildings line the swiftly flowing river. But there are other ways of enjoying the river than »just« on foot.

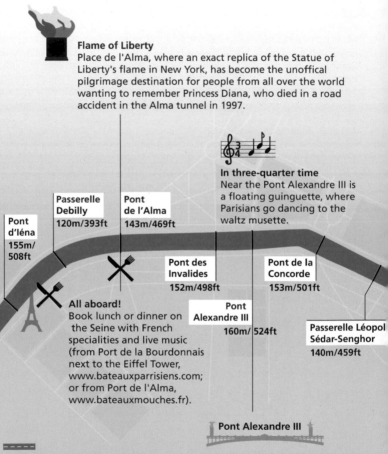

Flame of Liberty
Place de l'Alma, where an exact replica of the Statue of Liberty's flame in New York, has become the unoffical pilgrimage destination for people from all over the world wanting to remember Princess Diana, who died in a road accident in the Alma tunnel in 1997.

In three-quarter time
Near the Pont Alexandre III is a floating guinguette, where Parisians go dancing to the waltz musette.

Passerelle Debilly
120m/393ft

Pont de l'Alma
143m/469ft

Pont d'Iéna
155m/508ft

Pont des Invalides
152m/498ft

Pont de la Concorde
153m/501ft

All aboard!
Book lunch or dinner on the Seine with French specialities and live music (from Port de la Bourdonnais next to the Eiffel Tower, www.bateauxparrisiens.com; or from Port de l'Alma, www.bateauxmouches.fr).

Pont Alexandre III
160m/ 524ft

Passerelle Léopol Sédar-Senghor
140m/459ft

Pont Alexandre III

Batobus
The Batobus plies between the Eiffel Tower and the Jardin des Plantes every 15–30 minutes. With a day ticket you can get on and off at the eight stops as often as you like (www.batobus.com).

Named after Tsar Alexander III, this arched bridge is adorned with four gile statues representing the four great epochs of French history: the time of Charlemagne, the Renaissance, the Sur King Louis XIV and the modern era.

Reclaiming the river banks

In recent years Paris has made increasing efforts to divert main roads away from the riverbanks and reclaim them as recreation areas. In 2012 there began the 40 million euro *Berges de Seine* scheme intended to provide new pedestrian promenades, cycle paths, cultural areas, floating gardens and island cafés between the Pont de l'Alma and Pont de Sully.

Pont Neuf

»Which is Paris's oldest bridge?« »The New Bridge!« (Pont Neuf). It was built between 1578 and 1607 and restored in the 19th century. Often celebrated in song, paintings and a popular film location, it is the most beautiful, and with its 330m also the longest, of the old bridges across the Seine. It spans both arms of the river at the western tip of Île de la Cité.

Pont au Change

During the French Revolution the condemned were taken by cart from the Conciergerie across the Pont au Change to the Place de la Concorde, where the guillotine awaited.

©BAEDEKER

Les Vedettes du Pont Neuf
Discover Paris with a one-hour cruise on the Seine!

Urban beaches

Under the *Paris Plages* scheme, for a period of four weeks from 20 July roadways along the banks of the Seine between the Louvre and Pont de Sully are blocked off to make way for beaches, palm trees and deckchairs and a host of summer activities.

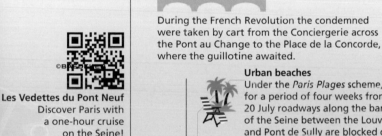

Bouquinistes
Independent booksellers along the banks of the Seine are one of the features of Paris. Their books, maps and prints are almost exclusively antiquarian. Very often the wooden bookstalls have been in the same family for generations.

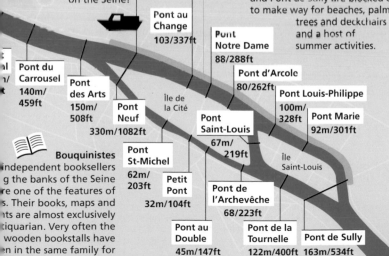

Pont au Change 103/337ft

Pont Notre Dame 88/288ft

Pont d'Arcole 80/262ft

Pont Louis-Philippe 100m/328ft

Pont Marie 92m/301ft

Pont du Carrousel 140m/459ft

Pont des Arts 150m/508ft

Pont Neuf 330m/1082ft

Île de la Cité

Pont Saint-Louis 67m/219ft

Île Saint-Louis

Pont St-Michel 62m/203ft

Petit Pont 32m/104ft

Pont de l'Archevêché 68/223ft

Pont au Double 45m/147ft

Pont de la Tournelle 122m/400ft

Pont de Sully 163m/534ft

by 37 bridges, three of which are for pedestrians and cyclists only. In medieval Paris, the bridges served as promenades with the shops and residences of the merchants built directly on them. One year after the flood disaster of 1740 a decree was passed to banning the building of new houses on the Seine's bridges. With the development of traffic routes the old houses were gradually pulled down.

The most beautiful bridges are **Pont Neuf** at the western tip of der ▶Île de la Cité and ***Pont Alexandre III** which was named after Tsar Alexander III in honour of the Franco-Russian Alliance of 1892 and links the ▶Grand Palais with the Esplanade of the ▶Invalides. It's little wonder that Woody Allen chose the latter for the last scene of his 2011 film *Midnight in Paris*, where Gil bumps into the beautiful Gabrielle as he strolls across the bridge and, walking with her in the warm summer rain, realizes that Paris is still most beautiful and romantic place in the world.

Paris Plage From 20 July those who have stayed at home can enjoy a beach holiday under the palm trees on the banks of the Seine, when the deck chairs are put out for four weeks between the ▶Louvre and Pont de Sully, at the foot of the National Library (Port de la Gare) and in the Bassin de La ▶Villette from the Rotonde de Ledoux to the former Magasins Généraux in Rue de Crimée. On the free beach you can get some sunshine, saunter around, play beach volleyball, enjoy a picnic or see an open-air concert. In front of the National Library, the open-air **Piscine Josephine Baker** offers swimming with a view of the Seine.

Piscine Josephine Baker: 8, Quai François-Mauriac, Tue and Thur till 11pm, www.piscines.paris.fr

Egouts de Paris Next to the Pont de la Concorde it's worth taking a detour into the »city beneath the city«, the labyrinth of Paris's sewers (Les Egouts). In several of the underground passageways the history of the sewers is revealed with the help of maps, documents and an audiovisual show – from ancient Lutetia to the siphons (Siphon del'Alma), which were installed by the engineer Eugène Belgrand during the reign of Napoleon III, to present-day Paris.

❶ Entrance opposite 93, Quai d'Orsay, Sat–Wed 11am–5pm, in winter till 4pm, www.egouts.tenebres.eu, adults €4.30

*Bouquinistes The bouquinistes (bouquiner: colloquial for book browsing) provide a mecca for antiquarian book lovers, selling French classics, old prints, postcards, art books, mysteries or posters from their traditional wooden stalls along the banks of the river in the ▶Quartier Latin. Until the middle of the 19th century, the bouquinistes usually carted their bookstalls home every evening, but now most of them lock up at nightfall and open up around noon.

At the end of the reign of Louis XV, in 1771, work began on the for- **Monnaie de**
mer royal and present-day **state mint** on the left bank of the Seine **Paris**
near Pont Neuf, according to designs of Jacques Denis Antoine. The
portal of the 117m/384ft-long main façade features allegorical figures
representing trade and agriculture. Since 1973 the coins (monnaie)
have been minted in Pessac/Gironde, but the ateliers (workshops),
which can be visited, still have the privilege of producing special gold
or silver coins. The **museum** in the cour d'honneur recounts the history of money from 300 BC to the present day.

Ateliers: 11, Quai de Conti, Mon–Sat 10am–6pm. Museum newly
renovated and equipped with café, shops and a Zen garden, www.
monnaiedeparis.fr.

Sorbonne

 H 7

Location: 47, Rue des Ecoles (5th arr.)
Métro station: Cluny-la-Sorbonne
❶ www.sorbonne.fr

**On the initiative of Robert de Sorbon, Canon of Paris and
Louis IX's confessor, a college for 20 penniless theology students was founded in 1257 with the financial support of the
king.**

The Sorbonne soon developed into a leading university, where Alber- **Venerable**
tus Magnus, Thomas Aquinas and **Abélard** taught. The latter fell in **university**
love with his student, **Héloïse**, who bore him a child. Separated and **buildings**
exiled to monasteries, the two were only reunited in death – the famous grave of the two lovers is in Père Lachaise (▶Belleville) cemetery. As rector of the university, Cardinal Richelieu saved its buildings from falling into ruin and had it rebuilt by Lemercier between
1624 and 1642. Substantial enlargements followed in 1806 under
Napoleon, who raised the Sorbonne to the status of a state university.

Language and literature scholars earn their academic degrees in
the present buildings, designed by Néno and erected between 1885
and 1901. The Sorbonne was one of the hotbeds of the student unrest
of May 1968. A fundamental university reform eventually split the
Sorbonne into 13 autonomous universities of the **Université de
Paris** that are today scattered throughout the city. To soak in a little
of the atmosphere of the Sorbonne, sit down in the courtyard or in
one of the student cafés ringing the square. The main façade is decorated with allegories of the sciences. Literature, the natural sciences
and art are the themes of the neo-classical mural, The Sacred Grove,

by Puvis de Chavannes in the Grand Amphithéâtre, the largest lecture hall. The final resting place of **Cardinal Richelieu** († 1642) is the chapel in the courtyard of the Sorbonne. The magnificent Baroque tomb is the work of François Girardon as designed by Charles Le Brun.

Collège de France

With the establishment of the **Collège des Trois Langues** on Place Marcelin-Berthelot in 1530, Francis I wanted to create a scientific college independent of the church, in which the three languages of classical antiquity – Hebrew, Greek and Latin – could once more be studied using original texts. The scholars were paid by the king and not, as was usual, by the students. The Collège de France, which emerged from the »College of the Three Languages« is one of the most famous academic teaching and research institutes in France. According to the old rules, there are still no exams and the lectures are free to all. Illustrious Professors have taught here: the physicist André Ampère, the historian Jules Michelet, the poet Paul Valéry, the philosopher Michel Foucault and the literature critic Roland Barthes.

❶ visits by appointment at the porter's lodge, www.college-de-france.fr

The book towers of the National Library dominate Rive Gauche

★ Tolbiac · Bibliothèque
Nationale de France

 ✦ D 6

Location: 11, Quai F. Mauriac (13. Arr.)
Métro station: Bibliothèque François Mitterrand
❶ www.parisrivegauche.com

With the spectacular »Grands Travaux«, the prestige architectural schemes of the Mitterrand era, it was intended to restore some balance to the long-disadvantaged east of Paris.

Tolbiac in the east of the city is well known only among French schoolchildren as the place where Clovis defeated the Alemanni in 496, as well as to readers of detective stories by Georges Simenon und Léo Malet. The Belgian Simenon like to have his taciturn, pipe-smoking **Inspector Maigret**, played by Jean Gabin, Charles Laughton or Rupert Davies, solve his tricky cases in Paris's 13th Arrondissement. And in his *Fog Over Tolbiac Bridge* the author Malet also sent his private detective **Nestor Burma** among the cops, demimonde ladies and crooks of the district.

Simenon and Malet

Since the 1990s the new **»Paris Rive Gauche«** neighbourhood has been developed on the site of the old port and industrial facilities around Gare d'Austerlitz. The 130-ha/320-acre plot incorporates 8 ha/20 acres of green spaces, office buildings employing 60,000 people and apartments for 15,000. By the turn of the millennium the three-storey metro station Bibliothèque François Mitterrand was ready, the tracks that remained above ground covered by the largest concrete slab in Paris. From the metro station the Météor Métro line 14 takes just a few minutes to the centre.

Developments in Paris's East

The symbol of the new Parisian East is the ***Bibliothèque Nationale de France François Mitterrand**, which was inaugurated in 1995. Designed by Dominique Perrault, this Babel of books is a building of superlatives. Four 78m/256ft-high glass towers in the shape of an opened book delineate a courtyard planted with pine trees and surrounded by reading rooms on two floors with space

! *Dancing on the water*

Insider Tip

MARCO POLO TIP

In summer, the guinguettes bob up and down at the quayside in front of the National Library – floating music bars with dance floors. Most popular is the bright red lightship Batofar where tout Paris boogies to hip-hop, house and electropop, meets for brunch on Sun 11.30am–4pm and from May to September casually chills on terrace on shore (11, Quai François-Mauriac, www.batofar.org).

for 3600 students. A copy of every French book published since 1945 can be found on the 430km/267mi of shelving. The most precious texts are contained within the concrete plinth. The contents of the towers are kept at constant temperature and humidity in rooms with multiple glazing – the high cost of air-conditioning has become a political issue.

❶ Tue–Sat 9am–7pm, Mon 2pm–7pm, www.bnf.fr

Docks en Seine

The customs and warehouse complex **Magasins Generaux**, which was erected on the banks of the Seine in 1907, was given a neon green steel »plug-over« by Dominique Jakob und Bren dan MacFarlane which has become the optical symbol of the revitalized harbour area. Opened in 2012 at Quai d'Austerlitz 34 as the **Cité de la Mode et du Design**, the complex is intended to be a training and exhibition centre for the creative industries with the Institut Français de la Mode, the fashion school of the Institut de la Mode (IFM), fashion boutiques, cafés and restaurants (www.paris-docks-en-seine.fr).

Renowned architects

Built in 1917–21 by Georges Wybo, with its high arcades and slate roof, the **Grands Moulins** de Paris have been integrated into the campus of the Université Paris VII: Denis Didérot, as has the nearby Halle aux Farines built in 2004–6 by **Rudy Riciotti**. Also, the only two buildings that **Le Corbusier** created in Paris are to be found here: the Cubist influenced Maison Planeix (26, Boulevard Masséna) dating from 1927 and the Salvation Army Hostel dating from 1933 (12, Rue Cantagruel). Made up of cubes, the Cité du Refuge reception centre is considered the prototype for all those Parisian housing schemes that later sprang up on a huge scale all over the city. **Jean Nouvel** was responsible for the conversion of the Gare d'Austerlitz.

*Bétonsalon

At the heart of the Université Paris VII, the Halle aux Farines provides **up and coming artists** with space to exhibit their work. Exhibition space: artists, choreographers and musicians, scientists and philosophers.

❶ Entrance: 9, Esplanade Pierre Vidal-Naquet, Tue–Sat noon–7pm, www. betonsalon.net

Les Frigos

Erected in 1921, the cold store for produce destined for Paris markets is now the domain of almost 200 painters, sculptors, musicians, actors and other artists, who organize exhibitions and performances here and open up their studios for the »Portes Ouvertes«.

❶ 19, Rue des Frigos, http://les-frigos.com

Louise 132

A bastion for contemporary art is Rue Louise Weiss, whose 15 gallery owners join forces as »Louise 132« to stage a preview on one Saturday evening each month. (www.louise13.fr).

** Tour Eiffel

✦ **D 6**

Location: Quai Branly (7th arr.)
Métro station: Bir Hakeim, Trocadero
❶ www.tour-eiffel.fr
end Aug–mid June daily 9.30am–11pm, mid
June– end Aug daily 9am–midnight; lift to the top €15, second platform on
foot €5, with the lift €9. In order to avoid the long queues, it is highly
recmmended to book tickets in advance online at http://ticket.toureiffel.fr.
The free children's tour on the first level has 12 topics to discover.

**Doomsayers prophesied that the steel structure would last at
most 20 years when the Eiffel tower was first completed – in
the meantime the famous Paris landmark, which celebrated
its 125th anniversary in 2014, is visited by more than 7 million
people every year.**

Even during the two years it took to build, Gustave Eiffel's iron construction was considered the very pinnacle of progress. However, the
structural engineer who was born in Dijon in 1832 also had to thank
two of his staff for the concept and design, the engineers Maurice
Koechlin und Emile Nougier. And Eiffel only got fired up for the project
when the architect Stephen Sauvestre devised the scheme for the tripar
tite division and arches at the base of the building, which imbued it with
greater transparency. Eiffel took over management and execution of the
plan with success: as a contemporary symbol for the freedom of thought
of the Revolution, as a victory over matter par excellence, the idiosyncratic iron construction won the official tender in 1887.

A bronze bust at the foot of the tower commemorates its builder

MARCO ⊕ POLO INSIGHT

The Iron Lady

Only once you've seen it have you really arrived in Paris: the Eiffel Tower, one of the tallest, strangest and most beautiful buildings in the world.

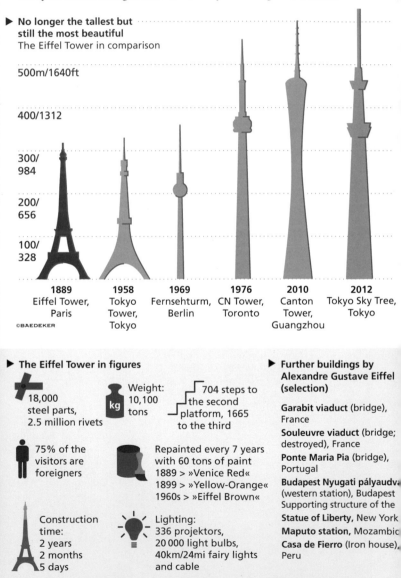

▶ No longer the tallest but still the most beautiful
The Eiffel Tower in comparison

500m/1640ft

400/1312

300/984

200/656

100/328

1889	1958	1969	1976	2010	2012
Eiffel Tower, Paris	Tokyo Tower, Tokyo	Fernsehturm, Berlin	CN Tower, Toronto	Canton Tower, Guangzhou	Tokyo Sky Tree, Tokyo

©BAEDEKER

▶ The Eiffel Tower in figures

18,000 steel parts, 2.5 million rivets

Weight: 10,100 tons

704 steps to the second platform, 1665 to the third

75% of the visitors are foreigners

Repainted every 7 years with 60 tons of paint
1889 > »Venice Red«
1899 > »Yellow-Orange«
1960s > »Eiffel Brown«

Construction time:
2 years
2 months
5 days

Lighting:
336 projektors,
20 000 light bulbs,
40km/24mi fairy lights and cable

▶ Further buildings by Alexandre Gustave Eiffel (selection)

Garabit viaduct (bridge), France

Souleuvre viaduct (bridge; destroyed), France

Ponte Maria Pia (bridge), Portugal

Budapest Nyugati pályaudvar (western station), Budapest Supporting structure of the

Statue of Liberty, New York

Maputo station, Mozambic

Casa de Fierro (Iron house), Peru

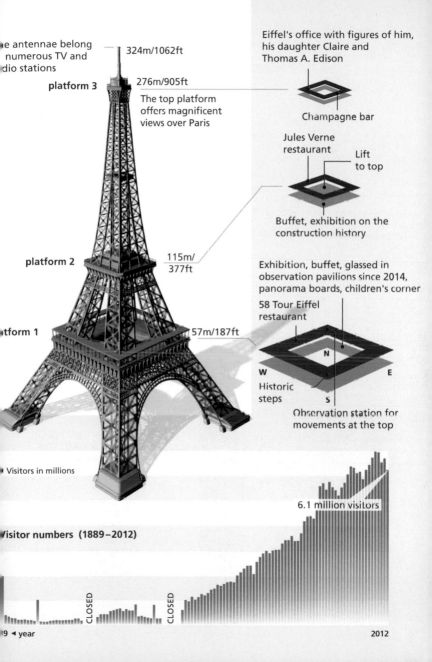

e antennae belong
numerous TV and
dio stations

324m/1062ft

Eiffel's office with figures of him,
his daughter Claire and
Thomas A. Edison

platform 3

276m/905ft

The top platform
offers magnificent
views over Paris

Champagne bar

Jules Verne
restaurant

Lift
to top

platform 2

115m/
377ft

Buffet, exhibition on the
construction history

Exhibition, buffet, glassed in
observation pavilions since 2014,
panorama boards, children's corner

58 Tour Eiffel
restaurant

tform 1

57m/187ft

N

W   E

Historic
steps

S

Observation station for
movements at the top

Visitors in millions

6.1 million visitors

Visitor numbers (1889–2012)

CLOSED

CLOSED

9 ◄ year

2012

The perfect steel structure »**La dame de fer**« stood at a height of 300m/984ft – almost 324m/1,063ft to the tip of its antenna – at the time of the World Fair of 1889. But the Eiffel Tower lost its status as the world's tallest structure to the 319m/1047ft-high Chrysler Building in New York in 1930. Eiffel designed the tower so that even under extreme wind pressure its structural weight of 7,300t alone was sufficient to prevent it from being blown over. Furthermore, the lattice construction reduced the pressure on the structure by about half compared with a closed surface, providing a double safeguard.

The tower's golden **illumination** is provided by 336 high-pressure sodium-vapour lamps, and 20,000 bulbs generate the 5-minute glimmer that takes place at the start of each hour from dusk to 1am (2am in summer). In clear conditions the beacon on the top can be seen from a distance of 80 km. You get up there by lift or by climbing 1665 steps. The **panoramic views** from the two platforms and the top, where 180° images show bird's eye views of Paris, are unforgettable. In the shops on the first level, which has been recently equipped with glazed pavilions, all sizes of souvenir towers can be purchased.

In the trendy **58 Tour Eiffel** restaurant you can enjoy lunch and dinner with a sensational view over Paris.

Anyone wanting to spend an unforgettable evening at a height of 125 m in the **Jules Verne gourmet restaurant** needs to book well in advance (▶ p. 107). Bubbly is served in the champagne bar on the top platform until 10pm. Opposite is a faithful reconstruction of **Eiffel's office**, complete with wax figures.

One of the few places in Paris where it is possible to stroll along the Seine amid greenery is the tree-lined **Allée des Cygnes** (swan promenade) to the southwest of the Eiffel Tower. Since 1889, the **Statue of Liberty** has stood at the southern point of the island. This

Showtime at Eiffel Tower

smaller version of the New York original is a reminder that the Statue of Liberty was a gift from France to the USA in 1886 and was made in Paris by the Alsatian sculptor Frédéric Auguste Bartholdi.

Laid out in 1765, this former military drill and parade ground stretches between the Eiffel Tower and the École Militaire. Today it is an extensive public open space that received a makeover in 2010. Paris's first horse race took place here in 1780, between and English and a French jockey, and in 1783 and 1784 the **Field of Mars** was the setting for two spectacular, unmanned balloon take-offs. During the **French Revolution**, on 14 July 1790 they celebrated the »Fête de la Fédération« here, by which the Marquis de La Fayette on behalf of the National Assembly and King Louis XVI, and representatives of all French *départements*, took the oath to uphold the new constitution, which established a British-style constitutional monarchy. After the royal family's unsuccessful »Flight to Varennes«, the masses demanded that they should be killed at the same spot. In 1794 the painter Jacques-Louis David organized a festival for »Cult of Supreme Being« (Etre suprême), proclaimed by Robespierre and which was intended to become the new state religion. In the years 1867, 1878, 1889, 1900 and 1937 the legendary **World Fairs** were held on the Field of Mars, which also incorporated long stretches along the banks of the Seine. At the turn of the millennium the **Mur pour la Paix** by Clara Halter und Jean-Michel Wilmotte was erected at the eastern end of the Field of Mars in front of the École Militaire: inspired by the Wailing Wall in Jerusalem, it is a pavilion made of glass, wood and steel and surrounded by 32 inox columns, on which the word »peace« is written in 32 languages. But there could be no question of peace: since it was erected the monument has been repeatedly vandalized, daubed with racist graffiti. And it also remains the subject of heated political debate.

Champ de Mars

! *Did you know* Insider Tip

MARCO POLO TIP

... that it is possible to go ice-skating on the Eiffel Tower? From mid-December until the end of January, the first platform is transformed into a 200 sq m/2,153 sq ft »Patinoire«, open from 9.30am to 11pm for ice-skating at the lofty elevation of 57m/164ft (free admission for ticket holders, skate hire).

The former elite school for officers of the royal army at the far end of the Champ de Mars is today a **French military academy**. The building, with the clean lines of the early neoclassical period, was erected in 1759–82 according to plans by Jacques-Ange Gabriel. In 1785 a young lieutenant graduated from the officers' school, whose superiors suggested had the potential to go far: it was the future **Napoleon**, the first Emperor of the French (▶Famous People). Fronting the

Ecole Militaire

north facade of the main building is Place Joffre with the statue of Marshal Joffre; behind the façade two rows of Doric columns define the main courtyard. Among the masterpieces by Jacques-Ange Gabriel is the **Chapel of St Louis**, built in the style of Louis XVI; the white interior is decorated with reliefs by Pajou and paintings depicting scenes from the life of the saint done by Vien, van Loo, Durameau, Lagrenée the Elder and Beaufort.

❶ Viewing only during services, concerts and on the Journées du Patrimoine; virtual visit: www.aumonerie-ecole-militaire.fr

UNESCO   »Peace must therefore be founded, if it is not to fail, upon the intellectual and moral solidarity of mankind«. These word are written in the constitution of UNESCO, which 37 nations jointly founded in 1945 in London. Today, the independent United Nations Educational, Scientific and Cultural Organization with its seat in Paris has 192 member states.

The Y-shaped complex by Marcel Breuer (USA), Pier Luigi Nervi (Italy) and Bernard Zehrfuss (France) dates from the 1950s. The hall of the trapezoid-shaped conference building is decorated by Pablo Picasso›s *Victory of the Forces of Light and Peace over those of Evil and Death*. Two walls bear ceramics designed by Joan Miró, *Sun Wall* and *Moon Wall*. In addition, bronze reliefs by Hans Arp and tapestries by Le Corbusier, a *Recumbent Figure* by Henry Moore and a black steel mobile by Alexander Calder are there to be admired. An angel's head in the Japanese garden commemorates the church in Nagasaki destroyed by the atom bomb.

❶ 7, Place de Fontenoy, Mon–Fri 9.30am–12.30pm and 2.30pm–5pm, www.unesco.org

* Tuileries ·

Jardin des Tuileries

————————————————— ✳ **F/G 5**

Location: Between the Louvre and Place de la Concorde (1st arr.)
Métro stations: Tuileries, Concorde

The largest and oldest park in Paris stretches across the site of the former tile kilns – »tuileries« – where later Catherine de Médici had the Tuileries Palace erected in 1593 facing the present-day Avenue du Général Lemonnier.

Tuileries   In 1664 Colbert, Louis XIV's minister of finance, commissioned for
Gardens   the park **André Le Nôtre**, the royal landscape architect and the gar-

dener who later also created the park of ▶Versailles. In the 18th century, **Tuileries Palace** was the city residence of the French monarchs. Later, during the French Revolution, the National Convention met here. Napoleon planned his campaigns here before the palace went up in flames during the revolt of the Paris Commune in May 1871 and the remains of its walls were razed in 1882. After the ▶Louvre at one end and Jeu de Paume at the other had been expanded into museum showpieces at the end of the 20th century, it became clear that a restoration of the gardens was urgently needed. The upper part radiating from the Arc du Carrousel was redesigned by the Belgian Jacques Wirtz. In the main part of the park, a French team of architects, Benech, Cribier and Roubeaud, developed Le Nôtre's original layout with geometric carpets of lawns and trees, pushing the flowerbeds that were so popular in the 19th century to the borders. Modern sculptures by Calder, Picasso, Moore, Maillol and Roy Lichtenstein as well as contemporary artists such as Tony Cragg and Lawrence Weiner are scattered about the gardens. Terraces, ramps and Baroque statues by Coustou and Coysevox are arranged around the large octagonal pond next to ▶Place de la Concorde, where some visitors like to relax in the easy chairs. Children will enjoy the carousel and trampolines.

🕐 daily 7.30am–7pm

The treasures in the Orangery, which was reopened in 2006 after extensive renovations, range from Impressionism to the 1930s, including works by Renoir und Cézanne, Utrillo, Matisse, Derain and Picasso. The eight canvases with **Claude Monet's Water Lilies** (Les Grandes Nymphéas), were assigned, as directed by the artist, two oval rooms on the ground floor. From 1918 until his death, Monet painted many variations of the water lilies in Giverny, Normandy, which he had planted himself.

*Musée Nationale de l'Orangerie

🕐 Wed–Mon 9am–6pm, www.musee-orangerie.fr, adults €7.50, free admission 1st Sun in month; combination ticket with Musée d'Orsay

A copy of a bust of Le Nôtre stands at the foot of the stairway of the former tennis court building (paume means palm – originally, the hand was used to hit the ball) that was built during Napoleon III's reign and radically remodelled in 1931. The National Gallery, remodeled by Antoine Stinco in 1991, presents temporary exhibitions of photography and video art. It isn't just well known visual artists such as Robert Frank, Jean-Luc Moulène and Richard Avedon that are displayed here, but also up and coming talents such as Cyprien Gaillard, Denis Savary and Agathe Snow. They have more exhibition space at the Hôtel de Sully in the Marais (▶ p. 252).

*Galerie Nationale du Jeu de Paume

🕐 Wed–Fri noon–7pm, Sat and Sun 10am–7pm, Tue noon–9pm, www.jeudepaume.org, adults €8.50

** **Versailles**

🔶 **Excursion**

Among the absolute highlights in the immediate area surrounding Paris is the magnificent residence of the French kings, Louis XIV's dream realized in stone, the Château de Versailles. The splendid palace of the Sun King became the model for royal palaces throughout Europe.

Capital of the Département Yvelines

The main artery of Versailles is the broad Avenue de Paris that leads to Place d'Armes. To the south lie the 18th-century **Cathedral of Saint-Louis** (www.cathedrale-versailles.org) and the **Salle du Jeu de Paume**, built in 1686 as a place for the court to play an early version of tennis, and the place in which the National Assembly convened in 1789. Sites worth visiting in the north part of the town are the church built by Jules Hardouin-Mansart between 1684 and 1686, **Notre-Dame**, the market halls and the **Musée Lambinet** in Boulevard de la Reine 54 with furniture, paintings and weaponry.

Musée Lambinet: Sat–Thur 2–6pm, adults €4, free admission 1st Sun in month

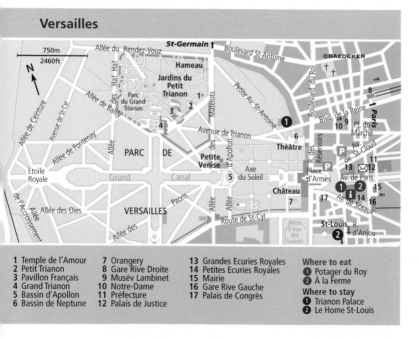

Versailles

1 Temple de l'Amour	7 Orangery	13 Grandes Ecuries Royales	**Where to eat**
2 Petit Trianon	8 Gare Rive Droite	14 Petites Ecuries Royales	❶ Potager du Roy
3 Pavillon Français	9 Muséu Lambinet	15 Mairie	❷ À la Ferme
4 Grand Trianon	10 Notre-Dame	16 Gare Rive Gauche	**Where to stay**
5 Bassin d'Apollon	11 Préfecture	17 Palais de Congrès	❶ Trianon Palace
6 Bassin de Neptune	12 Palais de Justice		❷ Le Home St-Louis

Versailles

INFORMATION
Office du tourisme
2 bis Avenue de Paris
F-78000 Versailles
Tel. 01 39 24 88 88
www.versailles-tourisme.com
http://chateauversailles.fr

ARRIVAL FROM PARIS
20km/12mi southwest (A 13, N 10)
SNCF: trains from Montparnasse and St-
Lazare. RER: Line C 5 to Versailles-Rive
Gauche, C 8 to Versailles-Chantier
(1.3km/0.8mi from the palace). RATP-Bus
171 from Pont de Sevres to the palace.

EVENTS
Le Mois Molière in June, open-air thea-
tre on the city's streets and squares;
Promenades Contées, June to Aug in
several districts of the city; Les Grandes
Eaux Musicales and Les Grandes Eaux
Nocturnes ►p. 336

PALACE TOURS
Allow a whole day for visiting the palace
and book all tickets online in advance,
otherwise you'll have to cope with long
queues in the summer that can take
hours. Main entrance A is for visitors
with tickets, entrance B for groups; the
entrance for guided tours is opposite the
ticket office.
On the banks of the Grand Canal you
can find sustenance at La Petite Venise
restaurant and/or rent a bicycle for the
park. Le Petit Train shuttles between the
palace and the Trianon.

*Opening times and entrance fees for
the palace: ►MARCO POLO
Insight p. 332*

WHERE TO EAT
❶ *Potager du Roy* €€
1, Rue du Maréchal Joffre
Tel. 01 39 50 35 34
Closed Sun evening/Mon
Fine food including delicious vegetarian
dishes

❷ *À la Ferme* €
3 Rue du Maréchal Joffre
Tel. 39 53 10 81, www.restaurant-cui-
sine-traditionnelle-versailles.com
The »farm« serves grilled food and specialities from the Southwest.

WHERE TO STAY
❶ *Trianon Palace* €€€€
1, Boulevard de la Reine
Tel. 01 30 84 50 00, 166 rooms.
www.trianonpalace.com
Truly regal accommodation in an elegant
early 20th-century palais on the edge of
Trianon Park. Gourmets are spoiled in
the Gordon Ramsay restaurant, massages at the Spa Guerlain promise pure relaxation.

❷ *Le Home St-Louis* €€
28, Rue St-Louis
Tel. 01 39 50 23 55, 25 rooms.
Well-kept establishment in the charming
Saint-Louis quarter south of the palace

THE WORLD OF PERFUME
In the workshops of the Osmothèque
des Conservatoire International des Parfums you will learn about the importance of the rose in creating scents, plus
get to know the secrets of royal perfumes (36, Rue du Parc de Clagny,
www.osmotheque.fr).

✱✱ CHÂTEAU DE VERSAILLES

UNESCO World Heritage Site   A black and gold gate on the spacious Place d'Armes, bordered in the east by the royal stables built between 1679 and 1685 by Mansart, leads to the main attraction: the Palace of Versailles. Beginning in 1661, a small hunting château built by Philibert Le Roy from 1631 to 1634 for Louis XIII was expanded and converted over a period of almost 50 years into a residential palace for **Louis XIV**. The main architect was **Le Vau**. The interior decoration was created by **Le Brun** and the gardens designed by **Le Nôtre**. The invoices, all of which have survived, reveal just how expensive the building was: 25,386 livres, almost 100 million euros. 36,000 people and 6000 horses were employed simultaneously in its construction.

Louis XIV's successors changed very little. The Rococo chambers and the neoclassical Petit Trianon were commissioned by Louis XV; the enlargement of the park was ordered by Louis XV and Louis XVI, who in 1789 was forced back to Paris by the Revolution. Versailles then lost its significance – until Franco-German history was written there. The palace was the headquarters of the German army from 5 Oct 1870 to 6 March 1871 during the Franco-Prussian War. The German Empire was proclaimed in the Hall of Mirrors on 18 Jan 1871, and on 28 June 1919, the Treaty of Versailles was signed there as well. Versailles, long since a **UNESCO World Heritage site**, has been undergoing a programme of restoration that will be completed by 2020.

From hunting lodge to palace   Behind the gate is the forecourt with an equestrian statue of Louis XIV dating from 1835. The Cour Royale behind it with access to the palace and park was once reserved for the royal family. The smaller marble courtyard, which was paved with coloured marble until 1830, is enclosed by the U-shaped erstwhile **hunting lodge of Louis XIII** with the royal apartments on the first floor. **Le Vau** built another ring of buildings around the two sides of the former hunting lodge with large state apartments on the first floor and the living quarters of the heirs and heiresses to the throne on the ground floor. **Mansart** connected this complex by building the Hall of Mirrors along the front of the building facing the park and expanded the palace with the north and south wings. The garden front, now 580m/635yd in length, has 375 windows with 2,000 rooms inside. The palace was given its present form through the addition of the Chapel Royal, designed by Mansart and **de Cotte**, and the Opera House by **Jacques-Ange Gabriel**.

*Galeries des Batailles   The 120m/394ft-long and 13m/43ft-wide **Battles Gallery** in the south wing illustrates France's greatest victories with paintings and busts of famous generals. David's painting, *Coronation of Napoleon and Josephine*, gave the **Coronation Room** its name.

The palace of Versailles, magnificent residence of the »Sun King«

The staircase leading to the **State Apartments of the Queen** is decorated with multi-coloured marble and gold leaf bronze reliefs. The paintings in the Guards' Room (Salle des Gardes de la Reine) were all themed on the Jupiter legend by Noël Coypel. The Queen's visitors once waited in the antechamber (Antichambre de la Reine) decorated with tapestries, before being admitted either to the Audience Room or the Bedroom. The ceiling paintings (1673) are by Claude Vignon and show heroines from Antiquity. The famous painting of *Marie-Antoinette with her Three Children* (1787) by Madame Vigée-Le Brun is hung in the antechamber.

*Apparte-
ments
de la Reine

In the Salon de la Reine, Michel Corneille decorated the ceiling with a depiction of Mercury accompanied by Poetry and the Sciences, in 1671. The Audience Room received its present interior under Marie-Antoinette, in 1785. Three French queens and two crown princesses inhabited the ****Chambre de la Reine**; 19 princes and princesses were born in the Queen's Bedroom, which was furnished for Louis XIV's wife, Maria Theresia of Austria, from 1671 to 1680. A Rococo ceiling themed on the four virtues of a queen – charity, generosity, wisdom and loyalty – was created between 1729 and 1735, according to designs by de Cotte. Later, Marie-Antoinette had tapestry portraits added, with the images of the Empress Maria Theresia, Emperor Joseph II, as well as of her husband, Louis XVI. The Queen's Private Chambers (Petits Appartements de la Reine, 1770 – 1781) are accessible from the Queen's Bedroom.

** *The Sun King's Residence*

Nowhere else have the ideals of a reign been implemented so consistently and impressively, and at the same time so tastefully and harmoniously, as in the enormous fairy-tale castle of the Sun King.

Palace: Tue–Sun 9am–6.30pm, Nov–March till 5.30pm.
Park: 7am–8.30pm, Nov–March 8am–6pm
Trianon palaces: daily noon–6.30pm, Nov–March till 5.30pm

Passeport (Palace, Gardens, Trianon): adults €18, €25 including Grandes Eaux show in the gardens; palace: €15, Trianon palaces and Hameau €10, guided tours €7 on top; security checks! Reduced admission fee from 3.30pm, free admission for EU citizens under 26; audio guides in eleven languages included.

❶ Chambre du Roi
In the centre of the palace is the bedroom of the Sun King, with its opulent decorative sculptures – the setting for the »lever (or coucher) du roi«. Close confidantes brought him the latest news, while the king got up, was examined by the court physician and then shaved and powdered. This was followed by the »Grand Lever« in front of dozens of »spectators«, during which he took his chocolate and finished dressing. A balustrade divided the »private« from the »public« part of the room.

❷ Water parterre
River gods, nymphs and putti inhabit the pools in front of the main facade. The large picture on the flap features »Le Rhône«.

❸ Boskette
On both sides of the main axis, romantic, variously designed little »woods« of beech hedges provide intimate spaces for courtly festivities and amusement.

❹ Orangerie
Hardouin-Mansart hid the orangery below the South Parterre, between the »Stairs of 100 steps«. Thanks to the double-glazing the temperature has never sank below 5° C. More than 1000 exotic trees planted in tubs reach down towards the almost 700-m long »Swiss Pond«.

❺ Opéra Royale
The splendid opera house at the end of the north wing, furnished in gilded bronze, marble and mirrored walls to match the rest of the palace, was completed in 1770 under Ange-Jacques Gabriel, and inaugurated on the day of the Dauphin's marriage to Marie-Antoinette. Made entirely of wood, it has excellent acoustics. Through ingenious engineering, the auditorium with seating for more than 700 guests could also be transformed into a ballroom. The royal opera house was restored in 2007–9 for around €12 million; apart from for performances – which are really worth seeing – it can only be visited as part of a guided tour in August, Tue–Sun at 9.45am by appointment, tel. 01 30 83 78 00, www.chateauversaillesspectacles.fr

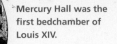

Mercury Hall was the first bedchamber of Louis XIV.

An allegory to Louis XIV: »Apollo and the Sun Chariot«

©BAEDEKER

Balls were held in the Hall of Mirrors, the German Empire was proclaimed here in 1871 and the Treaty of Versailles signed in 1919

A jewellery cupboard belonging to Marie-Antoinette, made in the workshop of J. C. Schwerdtfeger in 1787

Salon de la Paix	The **Salon of Peace** was created between 1680 and 1686 as a counterpart to the Salon de la Guerre at the other end of the Hall of Mirrors. The ceiling painting by Le Brun depicts France as Bringer of Peace. The painting of Louis XVI as a 17-year-old above the fireplace is by Lemoyne.
**Galerie des Glaces	In 1678 Louis XIV decided to build a gallery to connect the Salon de la Guerre (war) and the Salon de la Paix (peace). The large paintings on the ceiling were to document the first 17 years of the king's reign from his ascent to power in 1661 to the Treaty of Nijmegen in 1678. The number 17 divides up the world famous **Hall of Mirrors**: 17 windows open into the garden, their light reflecting in 17 arched mirrors opposite the windows. The 73m/240ft long, 10m/33ft wide and 12m/40ft high gallery with 357 mirrors was built according to plans by Mansart, the interior design is by Le Brun, the director of the state tapestry manufacturer. Festivities were rarely held in the extravagant hall – the gallery was mostly used as a corridor between the king's and queen's private rooms, where the courtiers paid their respects.
**Chambre du Roi	The former main hall of Louis XIII's hunting château was remodelled in 1701 to be **Louis XIV's bedchamber**, where the king died on 1 September 1715. It was here that the king held his famous audiences in the morning (»Lever du Roi«) and in the evening (»Coucher du Roi«). The focus of political life in old France was the **Cabinet du Conseil**. During the reign of Louis XVI important matters of state were decided in this »council chamber«. The decoration carried out by Gabriel for Louis XV in 1755 is considered a masterpiece of French Rococo. The private chambers of the king (Petits Appartements du Roi) are accessible from the Council Chamber and were also decorated in Rococo style by Gabriel at the same time. Louis XV died on 10 May 1774, in his bedchamber.
**Grands Appartements	Louis XIV's **Throne Room** is dedicated to the god Apollo. The dramatic ceiling painting, *Chariot of Apollo* by Charles de la Fosse symbolizes Louis XIV's additional title, »Roi Soleil« (Sun King). Above the fireplace in the **Apollo Salon** hangs a copy of the well-known picture of Louis XIV in an ermine robe (▶picture p. 235). Today the gold-threaded Gobelin arras displaying an allegory of Fire hangs where the 3m/10ft-high silver throne once stood. Gabriel Blanchard created the ceiling painting of *Diana guiding Hunters and Seafarers* for the **Salon de Diane** (1675–80). In the **Salon de Vénus**, there are imitations of classical statuary depicting model rulers, both ancient and contemporary, with Louis XIV as a Roman Caesar, as well as ceiling paintings showing Anthony and Cleopatra, Europa and Jupiter, Amphitrite and Poseidon. In the **Salon d'Abondance** (c1680),

Houasse has the goddess pouring out her horn of plenty on the ceiling. The ceiling painting in the **Salon d'Hercule** with the *Apotheosis of Hercules* (1733–36) is by Lemoyne.

The Baroque **palace chapel** (▶ picture p. 334) in white and gold was the last major work by Jules Hardouin-Mansart, completed by Robert de Cotte in 1710. The gallery once reserved for the royal family with its raised Corinthian colonnade is on the same level as the royal chambers. It is well worth attending one of he church concerts played on the clangorous **Cliquot organ** dating from 1710.

**Chapelle Royale

Jean Baptiste La Quintinie needed all of five years up to 1683 to transform heavy marshland into the 9-ha/22-acre **kitchen gardens** of the Sun King. 20 of the gardens, which were surrounded by lines of fruit trees, have been preserved. Over 300 varieties of fruit are harvested here every year along with more than 30 tons of vegetables.

Potager du Roi

❶ 10, Rue du Maréchal Joffre, April–Sept Tue–Sun 10am–6pm, Oct–Dec Tue and Thur 10am–6pm, Sat 10am–1pm, Jan–March Tue and Thur 10am–1pm; www.potager-du-roi.fr, adults Mon–Fri €4.50, Sat and Sun €6.50

Truly regal are also the horse shows in the Manège de la Grande Ecurie, put on by the trainer Barabas in the Académie du Spectacle Equestre de Versailles in the afternoon and evening.

Académie du Spectacle Equestre de Versailles

www.bartabas.fr/Academie-du-spectacle-equestre

** PARC DE VERSAILLES

The park, covering more than 800ha/2000 acres, is the most complete example of 17th-century French landscape gardening. Its architect was the gardener's son **André Le Nôtre** (1613–1700), who, after the ▶Tuileries and the palace park of Vaux-le-Vicomte, produced his masterpiece here. The essential features of French gardening of the time, symmetry and the taming of nature through geometric forms, correspond to the concepts of absolutism, which saw in such creations the expression of man's domination over nature. The monumental palace symbolizes the monarch's absolute power over men, while the park symbolizes the Sun King as conqueror of nature. English gardens next to the Petit Trianon were added in the 18th century to the French gardens laid out by Le Nôtre – parks of »unspoiled« nature that made it possible to mimic »real« country life in the **Hameau de Marie-Antoinette** miniature village. The Trianon châteaux with their gardens were the only places of privacy the French kings had in Versailles. Everywhere elsethey were subject to the rules of etiquette and ceremony like all members of the court.

Masterpiece of French landscape gardening

❶ April–Oct daily 7am–8.30pm, Nov–Mar 8am–6pm

*Bassin de Neptune   This pond was designed by Le Nôtre and constructed between 1679 and 1684. The fountain sculptures, done in 1740 by Adam, Bouchardon and Lemoyne, feature Neptune in the middle with his trident and his wife Amphitrite with a sceptre, flanked by Oceanus on a unicorn and Proteus with sea creatures.

*Parterres   Standing on the **open terraces** that extend in front of the stone terrace are four bronze statues of Bacchus, Apollo, Antonius and a Silenus and two marble vases with reliefs by Antoine Coysevox depicting the wars with Turkey and the peace treaties of Aix-la-Chapelle and Nijmegen. On the **Parterre du Nord** are 24 statues symbolizing the cosmic forces. The two pools on the central **Parterre d'Eau** are decorated with 24 bronze figures, allegories of the rivers of France. The **Parterre du Midi** is richly adorned with floral ornamentation. Below are the **Orangery** (1684–86) and the lake created by the Royal Swiss Guard, Pièces d'Eau des Suisses. Atop the fountain in the central pool of the **Parterre de Latone** stands the goddess Letona with her children Artemis and Apollo.

> **! MARCO POLO TIP**
>
> *Symphonie visuelle*   **Insider Tip**
>
> A sense of what it would have been like to attend a garden party given by the Sun King can be gained at the Fêtes de Nuit, Les Grandes Eaux Musicales and Les Grandes Eaux Nocturnes held on weekend evenings from April through October. Baroque music accompanies the spectacular water displays, operas, theatre and ballet performances that end with a fireworks display (www.chateauversailles-spectacles.fr, from €25)

Bassin d'Apollon, Grand Canal   The figure of Apollo on his sun chariot produced in 1670 by Jean-Baptiste Tuby is an allegorical reference to Louis XIV (▶ picture p. 333). In Louis XIV's day, golden gondolas glided along the »Grand Canal«, a present from the Republic of Venice.

*Grand and Petit Trianon   Louis XIV had Mansart's and Robert de Cotte's design for a small château, the Grand Trianon, built between 1678 and 1688. Here he could live in complete privacy, free of court etiquette. One of the château's two wings was reserved for him, the other for his mistress, Madame de Maintenon. Napoleon had the Grand Trianon, which had fallen into disrepair, restored, leaving the interior decoration partly in Baroque and partly in Empire style. The Petit Trianon château was built between 1763 and 1767 by Gabriel for Madame de Barry, Louis XV's favourite. Louis XVI later made a gift of it to Queen Marie-Antoinette.
   ❶ Nov–March daily noon–5.30pm, April–Oct daily noon–6.30pm

*L'Hameau de la Reine   An »English garden«, complete with a **miniature village** with a farm, dairy, mill and dovecote, was laid out for Marie-Antoinette on the site of Louis XV's botanical gardens.

✶✶ La Villette

✦ **L 2**

Location: Northeast (19th arr.)
Métro stations: Porte de Pantin, Porte de la Villette
❶ daily except Mon 10am–5.30pm, Sun till 6.30pm,
www.villette.com, www.cite-sciences.fr

In the mid-1980s, a 55-ha/85-acre cultural and recreation park was created under the direction of Bernard Tschumi and Adrian Fainsilber on the site of the city's main abbatoir, which was moved to Rungis together with the wholesale market halls.

Park of culture and recreation

The museum of science and technology in the centre is surrounded by ten themed gardens and two dozen bright red »follies« which act as cafés and information booths. By 1995 a spherical cinema, theatre, music centre and events hall had been added to La Villette. The new Philharmonie de Paris opened at La Villette in early 2015. Hip-Hop, dance and theatre: for two weeks in April La Villette rocks to new beats for the **Rencontres de la Villette** (www.rencontresvillette.com).

✶✶Cité des Sciences et de l'Industrie

Adrian Fainsilber designed the 270m/886ft long, glass-covered »**city of sciences and industry**«. Given a face-lift in 2012, it seeks to make science and technology accessible to everyone through lots of creativ-

The red »Folies« are landmarks at La Villette

Parc de la Villette

la Villette

━━━━ Elevated walkway

ity and fun. Ponds surround the futuristic building of stone and iron. A greenhouse with different climatic zones connects the interior with the outside of the park. Arching over the central area are circular domes that let in sunlight through a system of movable mirrors. Escalators lead to the permanent exhibition, »**Explora**«, which explores on five levels the subjects of communication, energy, medicine, transportation, aeronautics and aerospace, and the earth's oceans, environment and resources. Children between the ages of 2 and 7 can sing, feel and discover in the **Cité des Enfants**. Special projectors in the **planetarium** simulate a world of 10,000 stars. La **Cité de la Santé** serves as an information and research centre on matters related to health and **La Cité des Métiers** is a vocational training centre. An

aquarium, a **media library** and the Louis Lumière **cinema** with 3D films round off the attractions.

❶ Tue–Sun 10–30am–4.30pm, film screenings: Tue–Sun every 30 min 11am–noon, 2pm–5pm, Sun till 6pm

Close the hatche, take a look through the periscope and check the radar of this 1957 **submarine** that logged over 250,000 nautical miles underwater.

Argonaute

This futuristic spherical structure with a diameter of 36m/118ft is covered with a sheet of polished chromium-nickel steel. At night, the metal sphere is illuminated from below, creating its own star-studded heavens. Comfortably reclining in bucket seats, the audience experiences a 1000 sq m/11,000 sq ft, 172-degree screen with 12-channel stereo sound. The images of the **documentary films** shown are ten times as large as the standard 35mm format.

*La Géode

Showtimes: Tue–Sun 10.30am–8.30pm, Mon till 4.30pm, www.lageode.fr Adults €10.50, 3D film €12.50, combination ticket with Cité de la Science €18.50. Those who haven't had enough can get tossed about for 15 minutes in the **Cinaxe cinema**, which uses the technology employed in flight simulators used to train pilots, Tue–Sun 11am–1pm and 2pm–5pm.

Since 2010, **WIP Villette** has been a laboratory for young urban art (www.wip-villette.com). Art objects from all over the world are on display in the **Pavillon Paul Delouvrier** designed by the Catalan Oskar Tusquets

Young art

Barbara, Brel, Brassens, Edith Piaf, Léo Ferré, Mireille and Serge Gainsbourg – anyone interested in the history and the performers of French **chansons** should check out the Centre National du Patrimoine de la Chanson (www.lehall.com).

*Hall de la Chanson

Red velvet and a thousand mirrors surround the diners – when suddenly a trapeze artist floats down to the ground and … but then we don't want to give away the surprises.

Cabaret Sauvage

❶ Info/reservations: tel. 01 42 09 01 09, www.cabaretsauvage.com.

► p. 89

Zénith

Designed by Kristian Gavoille with seating for 650, this a popular venue for jazz, blues, funk and world music.

Trabendo

❶ Tel. 01 42 01 12 12, www.trabendo.fr

The former cattle hall has an impressive cast-iron structure dating from 1867. The multifunctional hall was modified in 2007 for exhibitions, concerts, theatre and events of all kinds.

*La Grande Halle

Théâtre Paris-Villette	Under the direction of Patrick Gufflet, this municipal theatre designed by Bernard Guillaumot with seating 300 is seen as a springboard for young writing talent ❶ Tel. 01 40 03 72 23, www.theatre-paris-villette.com
Le Tarmac de la Villette	Theatre productions from Quebec, the Congo and Algeria bring to life the great variety of francophone dramatic arts under the direction of Valérie Baran ❶ Tel. 01 40 03 93 95, www.letarmac.fr
***Cité de la Musique**	The building complex designed by Christian de Portzamparc coils like a snake around its oval-shaped central core, the **concert hall** opened in 1995 with seating for about 1200 people. In June each year the venue plays host to the Biennale d'art vocal. In the western part of the building are the classrooms of the Conservatoire Nationale Supérieur de Musique et de Danse du Paris, while the eastern part houses a media library and rooms for events. The ***Musée de la Musique** displays over 4500 music instruments including six violins made by Antonio Stradivari. Many of them can be heard during afternoon concerts. Tasty crêpes, sandwiches and crisp salads are served in the **Café de la Musique**, which has views of the Grande Halle. ❶ Tue–Sat noon–6pm, Sun 10am–6pm, www.cite-musique.fr Museum: adults €6.40, concerts: €8–41
Themed gardens	Walls of movable sails, waves of air-cushions and the hulls of ships – the **Jardin des Dunes** is one of ten themed gardens that provide La Villette with fanciful, natural and avant-garde greenery – and plenty of surprises. For example, in the **Jardin des Miroirs**, a look back at the 28 concrete monoliths suddenly becomes a view of a landscape with pine and beech trees reflected in 28 mirrors. Contemporary music concerts are performed at the adjacent **Centre de Documentation de la Musique Contemporaine**. ❶ Tue–Thur 2–6pm, Fri 11am–5pm, www.cdmc.asso.fr

Jean Nouvel, whose schemes in Paris include the ▶Institut du Monde Arabe and the ▶Musée du Quai Branly, was awarded the Pritzker Prize – the architectural »Nobel Prize« in 2008. His latest project in metropolis on the Seine is the new home of the **Philharmonie de Paris**, constructed adjacent to the Cité de la Musique and now opened, after several delays, in early 2015. With space for 2400 con-

certgoers, the new venue will also play host to guest symphony orchestras and provide space for other musical genres.
❶ www.philharmoniedeparis.com

The 108km/67m-long Canal de l'Ourcq finishes at the Bassin de la Villette, where properties bordering the waterfront, restored in 2008, have become desirable places to live. One institution near the quayside is **Le Bar Ourcq**, where you can sit outside for coffee and cocktails and rent pétanque balls. During the **Été du Canal** festival in July and August, excursion boats ply between here and ►Saint-Denis – children under 10 go free and adults pay just €1!

Canal de l'Ourq

* Vincennes

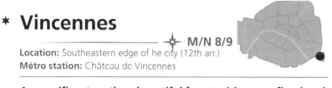

✳ **M/N 8/9**

Location: Southeastern edge of he city (12th arr.)
Métro station: Château de Vincennes

A magnificent castle, a beautiful forest with a zoo, floral park and harness racing track make Vincennes a popular excursion destination for Parisians.

CHÂTEAU DE VINCENNES

Medieval castle design and baroque palace architecture combine in the **nine-towered fortress** on the Avenue de Paris. The story of Vincennes begins in the 11th century when the crown acquired the monastery woodlands of St Maur. From then on the Bois de Vincennes belonged to the French kings. Their 11th-century hunting lodge was expanded into a stronghold in the 14th century, and by the 15th century it became the preferred residence of their Majesties. With the defeat of the Fronde in 1652, the castle was the state prison for opponents of absolute monarchy, including Cardinal Retz, finance minister Fouquet, Diderot, Mirabeau and the Marquis de Sade. In the 17th century, Cardinal Mazarin commissioned Louis Le Vau to design new royal housing in the grounds, the symmetrical Pavillon du Roi and Pavillon de la Reine, where in 1660 the 22-year-old King Louis XIV and his wife Maria Theresa of Austria spent their honeymoon. At the beginning of the 18th century, a porcelain manufactory was established on the east side of the castle, which moved to Sèvres in 1759. Napoleon used the castle as an arsenal. In the 19th century Viollet-le-Duc began with the restoration of the building, which continues to this day. In 1917, Mata Hari, the most prominent German spy of World War I, was executed in the castle.

Nine-towered fortress

Château de Vincennes, royal residence and state prison

Walls up to 3m/10ft thick, four round towers, a battlement and a moat secured the 52m/171ft-high castle keep, which was reopened in 2007 after ten years of renovation. On the ground floor is the kitchen and larders, on the first floor the audience hall and on the second floor the **royal bedchambers**, where in 1422 Henry V of England died. The third floor houses the bedchambers of the royal family, the fourth the rooms of the retinue, and the fifth the armoury. The **views** from the roof terrace are fantastic.

Begun in the 14th century in the style of ▶Sainte-Chapelle, the Gothic character of the **Royal Chapel** was preserved, despite the fact that it was only completed in the 16th century – the magnificent renaissance windows of the Apocalypse in the choir date from that time.

Pavillons Royales	The two **royal pavilions** are the last castle buildings to be completed by Le Vau, in 1654–61. Here resided Queen Anne of Austria, the mother of Louis XIV, and on 9 March 1661 Cardinal Mazarin, who had commissioned the buildings, died in the Pavillon du Roi.

ⓘ daily 10am–noon and 1.15pm–5pm, May–Aug till 6pm, visits only as part of a guided tour €8, under 18s free, www.chateau-vincennes.fr

BOIS DE VINCENNES

During the reign of Philipp II Augustus the woods of Vincennes were surrounded by a 12km/7mi-long wall, so the king could go hunting with his guests undisturbed. From the 17th century the walled forest attracted more and more walkers, access being provided through six gateways. Louis XV had the area reforested and in 1798 a training ground for the artillery was established. Napoleon III commissioned Baron Haussmann to adapt the woods to the English style, had Lac de Gravelle as well as a bridle path created, and transferred the grounds to the ownership of the city. Now on Sundays Parisian families like to congregate at one of the three lakes where in summer they can rent out boats or bicycles. On the shore of Lac Daumnesnil stands the Maison

Cameroon, built for the Colonial Exhibition of 1931 by Louis-Hippolyte Boileau and in 1977 converted into a **pagoda** – complete with the largest Buddha statue in Europe. The Tibetan **Kagyu-Dzong Temple** has stood in front of the pagoda since 1985 (http://kagyudzong.org).

On a Sunday you should arrange to have brunch at the **Les Magnolias** restaurant (Route de la Pyramide, www.restaurant-lesmagnolias-paris.com) in the Parc Floral, which was created in 1969 over an area of 35ha/86 acres. The rhododendron blossom in May and the water lilies from July and September are well worth seeing. The »Vallée des Fleurs« is replanted every season. In the summer the Théâtre Astral and the Théâtre Guignol perform adventurous stories for children. Alternatives include boat rides, horse-riding or riding around on the »White Train«.

Parc Floral

❶ June–Sept. Lespectacles youth festival with literature, dance, theatre and music (www.lespectacles.fr)

The zoo at Lac Daumesnil on Avenue de Saint-Maurice was created for the Colonial Exhibition of 1931, and it has recently been extended and renovated. A good 900 animals, including 80 species of bird, are dispersed across the 17-ha/42-acre site. A new highlight is the panoramic restaurant perched on the 72m/236ft-high artificial cliffs inhabited by mouflon and ibex.

Parc Zoologique

Ever since 1920, the winner of the Prix d'Amérique has been crowned at this harness racing track, which dates back to 1863. In the Summer the track is used as a concert venue – Bruce Springsteen, Michael Jackson, AC/DC and U2 are among the megastars to have performed here.

Hippodrome

❶ 2, Route de la Ferme, www.hippodrome-vincennes.com

Opposite the harness racing track a rural environment awaits: on the 5-ha/12-acre Ferme Georges-Ville, you can experience country life live every weekend, stroking the animals, helping to milk the cow, pulling up turnips or getting involved in the harvest.

Ferme de Paris

❶ Route du Pesage, April–Oct Sat and Sun 1.30pm–6.30pm, Oct–Mar till 5pm, July and Aug Tue–Sun, www.boisdevincennes.com, adults €2, under 26s €1, children under 7 free

In 1970, the Cartoucherie de Vincennes, in which gunpowder and munitions were once produced, was taken over by Ariane Mnouchkine as the domicile for her **Théâtre du Soleil**, which would soon become world famous. Later further acting troupes discovered the area – the Théâtre de la Tempête, the Théâtre de l'Aquarium, the Théâtre Epée de Bois and the Théâtre du Chaudron. Geared to performances, a shuttle bus runs between the bus station at the castle in Avenue de Nogent and the Cartoucherie (www.cartoucherie.fr)

Cartoucherie de Vincennes

litres of wine per person). During random inspections customs officers must be convinced that the wares are actually intended for private use.

For travellers from outside the EU, the following duty-free quantities apply: 200 cigarettes or 100 cigarillos or 50 cigars or 250g of tobacco; also 2 litres of wine and 2 litres of sparkling wine or 1 litre of spirits with an alcohol content of more than 22% vol.; 500g of coffee or 200g of coffee extracts, 100g of tea or 40g of tea extract, 50ml of perfume or 0.25 litres of eau de toilette. Gifts up to a value of €175 are also duty-free.

Customs regulations for non-EU citizens

TRAVEL INSURANCE

Citizens of EU countries are entitled to treatment in France under the local regulations in case of illness on production of their **European health insurance card**. Even with this card, in most cases some of the costs for medical care and prescribed medication must be paid by the patient. Upon presentation of receipts the health insurance at home covers the costs – but not for all treatments. Citizens of non-EU countries must pay for medical treatment and medicine themselves and should take out private health insurance. **Private travel insurance** Since some of the costs for medical treatment and medication typically have to be covered by the patient, and the costs for return transportation may not be covered by the normal health insurance, additional travel insurance is recommended.

Health insurance

Electricity

Most sockets in Paris are for 220 V; visitors from the English- speaking world should take an adapter for the standard continental European sockets and for the older types that are still sometimes found in Paris.

Emergency

IMPORTANT TELEPHONE NUMBERS
Police
Tel. 17

Fire brigade
Tel. 18

Emergency doctor, ambulance
Tel. 15

Etiquette and Customs

Restraint, politeness and good manners

The French attach importance to good manners. Politeness, an appropriate demeanour and appearance, and rhetorical subtleties are everyday standards of behaviour. People are expected to hold the door open for those following them and to say »pardon« or »excusez-moi« when they want to pass someone. In **religious places** it is particularly important to behave with restraint. Sleeveless T-shirts, shorts and short skirts, and noisy behaviour, are not considered acceptable. When friends **greet** each other, men shake hands and women kiss each other on the left and right cheek. Habits differ in the evening compared with daytime. At lunch casual clothes are accepted in **restaurants**, but not in the evening. For a stylish evening meal with several courses that could last for some hours, customers are expected to book a table in advance. Except in places of a very simple standard, the waiter or manager will show guests to their tables, bring the menu and take orders while aperitifs are being drunk. Bread and a jug of tap water are provided free of charge. To call out »garçon« is a faux pas! The polite way of addressing a waiter or waitress is »Monsieur« or »Madame«. When you want to pay, ask for »l'addition, s'il vous plaît«. For **smokers** there are separate tables. Smoking is banned in public buildings such as airports, railway stations and the Métro. As of 2008 smoking is strictly forbidden in hotels, cafes and discotheques. It is normal, even when drinking just a cup of coffee, to give a **tip**, which is placed on the empty plate or in the folder for the bill.

Language

»La Grande Nation« is proud of its culture, history and its language – which means a certain reluctance to speak foreign languages. Visitors who can handle the basics such as greetings, room reservations and orders in a restaurant in French will be made to feel all the more welcome.

Health

PHARMACIES WITH A
NIGHT SERVICE
Pharmacie Dhéry/
Galeries des Champs-Elysées
84, Avenue des Champs-Elysées (8th arr.)
Tel. 0145620241, Métro: George V

Pharmacie Européenne
6, Place de Clichy (9th arr.) Tel.
0148746518
Métro: Place de Clichy
►health insurance
►Arrival, health insurance

Information

BEFORE YOU LEAVE
Maison de la France for Australia and New Zealand (French tourist office)
Level 13, 25 Bligh Street
2000 NSW, Sydney
Tel. 02 9231 5244
Fax 02 9221 8682
www.franceguide.com

Maison de la France in Canada (French tourist office)
1800 Avenue McGill College, Suite 1010
Montreal, Quebec, H3A 3J6
Tel. 514 288 2026
Fax 514 845 48 68
www.franceguide.com

Maison de la France in Ireland (French tourist office)
Infoline only: tel. 15 60 235 235
www.franceguide.com

Maison de la France in UK (French tourist office)
Lincoln House 300
High Holborn, London WC1V 7JH
Tel. 09068/24 41 23
www.franceguide.com

Maison de la France in USA (French tourist office)
825 Third Avenue, 29th floor
(entrance on 50th street)
New York, NY 10022
Tel. 514 288 1904
Fax 212 838 7855
www.franceguide.com
Office in Chicago: tel. 312 327 0290
Office in Los Angeles: tel. 310 271 6665

INFORMATION IN PARIS
Office de Tourisme de Paris
25, Rue des Pyramides (1st arr.), Paris,
Tel. 08 92 68 30 00
Fax 01 49 52 53 00
www.parisinfo.com

Tourist information offices
Gare du Nord, Gare de Lyon, Pyramides, Carrousel du Louvre, Paris Expo/Porte de Versailles, Clémenceau Montmartre, Auvers

INTERNET
www.parisinfo.com
Accommodation, restaurants, reservations, excursions etc.

www.paris-tourism.com
Information on hotels, museums, travel

www.paris.fr
The official homepage of the city in English. Culture, education, politics, sport, business, hotels, restaurants, city tours and much more

www.paris-on-line.com
Hotel reservations, including last-minute offers

www.paris.org
Every imaginable aspect of tourist information from museums, hotels and cafés to the weather in Paris and the latest events

www.timeout.com/paris
Hotels, restaurants, events and ticket service

www.parispuces.com
Flea markets

Hotel websites
▶ Accommodation

CONSULATES AND
EMBASSIES
Australian Embassy
4 Rue Jean Rey (15th arr.)
Métro: Bir Hakeim
Tel. 01 40 59 33 00

Canadian Embassy
35 Avenue Montaigne (8th arr.)
Métro: Franklin D. Roosevelt
Tel. 01 44 43 29 00)

Irish Embassy
4 Rue Rude (16th arr.)
Métro: Argentine
Tel. 01 44 17 67 00

New Zealand Embassy
7 Rue Léonard de Vinci (16th arr.)
Métro: Victor Hugo
Tel. 01 45 01 43 43

UK Consulate
18bis Rue d'Anjou (8th arr.)
Métro: Concorde
Tel. 01 44 51 31 02

United States Consulate
2 Rue St-Florentin (1st arr.)
Métro: Concorde
Tel. 08 10 26 46 26

Language

French words and phrases

Basics

Yes./No.	Oui./Non.
Please.	S'il vous plaît (s.v.p.).
Thank you.	Merci.
You're welcome.	De rien.
Excuse me!	Excusez-moi!
Pardon?	Comment?
I can't understand you.	Je ne comprends pas.
I can only speak a little French.	Je parle un tout petit peu français
Could you help me, please?	Vous pouvez m'aider, s'il vous plaît?
Do you speak English?	Vous parlez anglais?
I would like ...	J'aimerais ...
I don't like it.	Ça ne me plaît pas.
Do you have ...?	Vous avez ...?
How much does it cost?	Ça coûte combien?
What time is it?	Quelle heure est-il?

Numbers

0	zéro	19	dix-neuf
1	un	20	vingt
2	deux	21	vingt et un
3	trois	22	vingt-deux
4	quatre	23	vingt-trois
5	cinq	30	trente
6	six	40	quarante
7	sept	50	cinquante
8	huit	60	soixante
9	neuf	70	soixante-dix
10	dix	80	quatre-vingt
11	onze	90	quatre-vingt-dix
12	douze	100	cent
13	treize	200	deux cents
14	quatorze	1000	mille
15	quinze	2000	deux mille
16	seize	10 000	dix mille
17	dix-sept	1/2	un demi
18	dix-huit	1/4	un quart

Greetings

Good morning/good day!	Bonjour!
Good evening!	Bonsoir!
Hello/Hi!	Salut!
What is your name, please?	Comment appellez-vous, s'il vous plaît?
How are you?	Comment allez-vous / vas-tu?
Good bye/See you!	Au revoir!

Travelling/Getting Around

left / right	à gauche / à droite
straight ahead	tout droit
near / far	près / loin
Excuse me, where is ...?	Pardon, où se trouve ..., s.v.p.?
How far is it?	C'est à combien de kilomètres d'ici?

Petrol station

Where is the nearest petrol station?	Pardon Mme / Mlle / M, où est la station-service la plus proche?
I would like ... litres of	Je voudrais ... litres, s.v.p.
... five-star	... du super
... diesel	... du diesel
... unleaded / at ... octane	... du sans-plomb / ... octanes.
Fill her up, please.	Le plein, s'il vous plaît.

Accident

Help!	Au secours!
Watch out!	Attention!
Please call ...	Appelez vite ...
... an ambulance.	... une ambulance.
... the police.	... la police.
... the fire brigade.	... les pompiers.
... a breakdown service.	... le service de dépannage.

Meal time

Where can I find ...	Pourriez-vous m'indiquer ...
... a good restaurant?	... un bon restaurant?
... a good café / bistro?	... un bon café / bistro?
I would like to book ...	Je voudrais réserver une table ...
... a table for four for this evening.	... pour ce soir pour quatre personnes.
Where are the toilets, please?	Où sont les toilettes, s'il vous plaît?
Cheers / Good health!	A votre santé / A la vôtre!
The bill, please.	L'addition, s'il vous plaît.

Accommodation

Excuse me, could you recommend ...?	Pardon, Mme / Mlle / M, vous pourriez recommander ...?
... a good hotel?	... un bon hotel?
Have you ...?	Est-ce que vous avez encore ...?
... a single room	... une chambre pour une personne
... a twin room	... une chambre pour deux personnes
... with bathroom	... avec salle de bains
... for one night	... pour une nuit
... for a week	... pour une semaine
How much is a room with ...	Quel est le prix de la chambre, ...
... breakfast?	... petit déjeuner compris?
... half board?	... en demi-pension?

Doctor

Can you recommend a good doctor?	Pourriez-vous me recommander un bon médecin s'il vous plaît?
I have a pain here.	J'ai mal ici.
Medicine	médecine / médicament

Post

How much is ...	Quel est le tarif pour ...
... a letter?	... une lettre?
... a postcard?	... une carte postale?
... to England?	... en Angleterre?

Carte / Menu
café noir	black coffee
café au lait	coffee with milk
décaféiné (un déca)	decaffeinated coffee

Petit déjeuner / breakfast
thé au lait / au citron	tea with milk / lemon
chocolat	chocolate
jus de fruit	fruit juice
œuf à la coque	soft-boiled egg
œufs brouillés	scrambled egg
pain / petits pains / toasts	bread / rolls / toast
beurre	butter
fromage	cheese
charcuterie	cold meat and sausage
jambon	ham
miel	honey
confiture	jam
yaourt	yoghurt

Soupes et Hors-d'œuvres
pâté de foie	liver pâté
saumon fumé	smoked salmon
soupe de poisson	fish soup

Viande / Meat
agneau	lamb
bifteck	steak
bœuf	beef
escalope de veau	escalope of veal
foie	liver
porc	pork
rôti	roast

Volailles et gibier / Poultry and game
canard à l'orange	duck with orange
coq au vin	chicken in red wine
lapin	rabbit
poulet rôti	roast chicken

Poisson, crustaces et coquillages / Fish, crustaceans and shellfish
calmar frit	fried squid
sole au gratin	baked sole
truite	trout

coquilles Saint-Jacques	scallops
crevettes	shrimps, prawns
homard	lobster
huîtres	oysters
moules	mussels
plateau de fruits de mer	seafood platter

Légumes, pâtes et riz / Vegetables, pasta and rice dishes

choucroute	sauerkraut
haricots (verts)	(green) beans
pâtes	pasta
poivrons	peppers
pommes de terre	potatoes

Desserts et fromages / Dessert and cheese

crème brûlée	creme caramel
gâteau	cake
tarte aux pommes	apple tart

Fruits

cerises	cherries
fraises	strawberries
framboises	raspberries
pêches	peaches
poires	pears
pommes	apples
raisins	grapes

Liste de Consommations / Drinks menu

vin	wine
un (verre de vin) rouge	a glass of red wine
un quart de vin blanc	a quarter-litre of red wine
bière	beer
eau minérale	mineral water (still)
eau gazeuse	mineral water (sparkling)

Literature

Fiction **Dan Brown**: The Da Vinci Code. Corgi Books, 2004. A best-selling thriller about the murder of the director of the Louvre that has brought streams of tourists to the places where the book is set. The author's detailed research on the fictional plot of the book awake the reader's curiosity to learn more of the real history.

Victor Hugo: The Hunchback of Notre-Dame. Modern Library, 2002. The greatest historical novel of the Romantic period in France spread the ideals of a new age.

Léo Malet: Mayhem in the Marais; Sunrise behind the Louvre; and others. Pan Books. Malet's classic crime stories are almost all set in different arrondissements in the 1950s. They are full of action and suspense, and the wit and intelligence of detective Nestor Burma never fail to solve the case.

Henry Miller: Tropic of Cancer. Harper Perennial Classics 2005. Miller's novel, published in Paris in 1934 and banned in the English-speaking world for 30 years, is a fictionalized version of his own experiences in the low life and artistic life of 1930s Paris.

Georges Simenon: The Bar on the Seine. Penguin Classics, 2006. Simenon's pipe-smoking detective Maigret appeared in over 50 novels, which are a good source for learning about France and Paris. This is one of the classic Maigret cases.

Jules Verne: Paris in the 20th Century. Del Rey Books, 1998. The famous author of science fiction Jules Verne (1828–1905) tried to imagine how life would be in Paris in the 20th century. Among other things, he came up with electronic music and air pollution.

Emile Zola: The Belly of Paris. Oxford World's Classics, 2007. One of the best-known novels by Zola (1840–1902), about the legendary market halls of Paris.

Ernest Hemingway: A Moveable Feast. Arrow Books, 1994. Hemingway lived in Paris in the 1920s, when he was young and unknown. He describes his happy and formative years in the city, which remained with him throughout his life; hence the title.   Non-fiction

Colin Jones: Paris: Biography of a City. Penguin, 2005. A lengthy but readable introduction to the city by an academic author who succeeds in getting his themes over to the reader by relating them to what can be seen in Paris today.

Alistair Horne: The Seven Ages of Paris. Pan Books, 2002. Highly entertaining and informative personal view of the city over seven periods from the Middle Ages until the retirement of General de Gaulle.

Michael Sadler: An Englishman in Paris. Pocket Books, 2003. A funny account of an English teacher's struggle to come to terms with life in Paris – and also an instructive book about France and the French.

Jenny Lee: Paris in Mind. Vintage, 2003. A well-chosen anthology of writings by American authors from the 19th century to the present day.

Photo books **Lisa Lovatt-Smith**: Paris Interiors. Taschen 2004. A glimpse inside the apartments and houses of some Parisians, including those of Isabelle Adjani, Helena Christensen, Thierry Mugler and Christian Lacroix.

Paris, mon amour. Taschen, 2004. Scenes of Paris by great photographers from two centuries.

Secret Gardens of Paris. Thames and Hudson, 2008. The hidden oases of Kenzo, Hubert de Givenchy, Yves Saint Laurent and other passionate garden owners.

Media

Newspapers All the main French newspapers are based in Paris; 70% of the print media in the country belong to two companies, Lagadère and Dassault. The leading national papers are **Le Monde**, **Le Figaro** and **Libération**. **Le Parisien Aujourd'hui**, once a conservative organ, is now politically middle-of-the-road. The best-known tabloid is **France-Soir**. The sports paper **L'Equipe** is essential reading for many Parisians. The best guides to events in the city are **L'Officiel des Spectacles** and **Pariscope**. English-language newspapers and magazines are available at news stands all over the city.

Money

Euro The official currency in France is the euro (€). Money can be changed in banks, currency exchanges (bureau de change) and some hotels. Currency exchanges are available in airports, railway stations and even some department stores.

Banks Banks in the Paris area open Monday to Friday from 10am to 5pm. Some banks also open on Saturday until noon. On the day before a public holiday, most banks close at noon.

ATMs (cash machines), credit cards There is no shortage of ATMs (Bancomat) in Paris, at which money can be withdrawn 24 hours a day using **bank and credit cards** in combination with the PIN. Banks, most hotels, restaurants, car hire companies and many shops accept the usual credit cards. Do not fail to report loss or theft of your card to the bank immediately!

EXCHANGE RATES

1 £ = 1.95 US$	1 US$ = 0.51£
1 £ = 1.47 €	1 € = 0.68 £
1 US$ = 0.75 €	1 € = 1.30 US$

Visa
Tel. 800 7 87 08 66

American Express
Tel. 06 / 676 41

LOST CARD?
In the event of lost bank or credit cards contact the following offices:

Eurocard/MasterCard
Tel. 800 / 87 08 66

Have the bank sort code, account number and card number as well as the expiry date ready. The MasterCard and Visa Numbers are toll-free, the Amx number is the local office in Rome

Post and Telecommunications

Post offices are open from Monday to Friday from 8am to 7pm and on Saturdays from 9am to noon. Fax and internet terminals are part of the service. Letters addressed »Poste Restante« with the name of the post office in question can be collected there by the recipient. Letters not picked up in this way are returned after 15 days. The **main post office** at Rue du Louvre 52 is open every day round the clock.

Post offices

»**Timbres**« can be bought at post offices, tobacconists, bars that sell cigarettes and postcard shops. Air mail is »par avion«.

Postage stamps

French letter boxes have more than one slit, so that »lettres« can be pre-sorted: local mail, »autres destinations« in France and abroad, and express mail marked »par express«.

Letter boxes

Public telephone boxes on the streets take **telephone cards**. Coin-operated phones remain only in cafés and post offices. **Phone cards** for 50 and 120 units are available from post offices, tobacconists and the offices of France Telecom.

Telephone

The French mobile phone operators France Telecom, SFR and Bouygues use the GSM standard. When phoning abroad, the roaming tarifs can be extremely expensive. One alternative is to buy a French prepaid card – in this case your number will be a different one.

Mobile phones

Internet cafés are easy to find all over Paris. The »**Cyberposte**« service is efficient and low-priced: an internet terminal in almost every post office in Paris, accessed using a customer card for 20 or 50 € that can be purchased on the spot.

Internet

CHEAP RATES
Phone calls are cheaper every day from 10.30pm to 8am, from Saturday 2pm until Monday 8am and on public holidays. Long-distance calls within France are cheaper on weekdays from 6pm.

CODES
From France
To Australia: 0061
To Canada: 001
To Ireland: 00353
To New Zealand: 0064

To UK: 00 44
To USA: 00 1
Then leave out the 0 of the local area code.

From other countries to France
International code (00 in most countries), followed by 33, followed by the nine-digit number without the initial 0.

DIRECTORY ENQUIRIES
Tel. 12 (renseignements téléfoniques)

Prices and Discounts

In the **bistros and cafés** drinks are considerably cheaper at the bar than at a table inside or outside; at night drinks cost more than during the day.

For **children** up to the age of seven there is a discount of 50 % on most admission charges; Small children are often admitted free of charge to museums and other attractions. **Family tickets** for museums and other attractions are widely available and usually represent a substantial saving. **Students** are admitted to cinemas and museums at a reduced price when they show their international student pass.

Time

France lies within the zone of Central European Time (CET), which is one hour ahead of Greenwich Mean Time (GMT), and from the end of March until the end of October sets its clocks to Central European Summer Time (CEST=CET+1 hr)

Transport

Driving in Paris is not easy!

For many people driving in Paris means one thing only: stress. First of all, the traffic is frenetic from morning to night; secondly, parking spaces are very hard to come by. If you do not absolutely need a car, take the Métro, the RER or buses.

In built-up areas 60kmh/37mph; on main roads usually 90kmh/56mph; on four-lane major roads (routes nationales) with a central reservation 110kmh/68mph; on motorways (autoroutes), for which a toll (péage) usually has to be paid 130kmh/81mph.

Speed limit

The maximum permitted level of alcohol in the blood is **0.5 per ml**. Seat belts must be worn during the journey.

Alcohol limit, seat belts

The wide lines on the edge of the road on medium-size and large traffic routes are markings of the taxi and bus lane, which may not be used by private cars until 8pm.

Taxi and bus lanes

According to the French philosopher André Glucksmann, the Paris **underground railway** is »the true cultural centre of France«. The first line was inaugurated for the world exhibition in 1900 between Porte Maillot and Vincennes. Nine years later 70km/45mi of track were already in operation, and in 1934 the suburbs were connected to the centre. In the early 1960s the express Métro RER (Réseau Express Régional) was added. Since 1998 Métro line 14 has connected the east of Paris with the city centre. The Métro and RER are operated by the part-state, part-private RATP (Régie Autonome des Transports Parisiens). **Timetables** Bus, RER and Métro are the fastest and cheapest means of transport in Paris. Timetables are posted at all Métro stations and at the Office du Tourisme (►Information).

Métro, RER and Bus

Within the city limits, all three forms of transport can be used with a single ticket (€1,70). In the inner city zones 1 and 2 passengers can change trains in the Métro as they please; outside these zones the Métro fares are on a sliding scale. In buses the ticket is valid for any length of journey, but a new ticket is needed when changing from the bus to the RER. A book of tickets (**carnet,** €13,70)), containing ten tickets, is a cheaper way to travel than buying single tickets. The RER and Métro operate from 5.30am to 0.45am every two to seven minutes; buses run from 6.30am to 8.30pm. From 1.30am until 5.30am there is a night bus (noctambus) once every hour, starting at Châtelet; raise your hand or wave to the driver to stop it.

Tickets

The »**Mobilis**« ticket is valid for one day's unlimited travel by bus, Métro and RER in 2 or 3 zones. The »**Paris-Visite**« ticket (valid for 1, 2, 3 or 5 days) combines free travel by Métro, RER and bus (except special buses and minibuses) with discounts on admission to sights. A passport photo is needed for the weekly ticket »**Navigo semaine**«. These tickets can be purchased from Métro stations, SNCF railway stations, airports, some banks and the Office du Tourisme (►Information). For further information about the Métro, RER, buses and RATP: www.ratp.fr or tel. 08 36 35 35 35.

Tourist tickets

CAR HIRE

Avis
In Paris: Tel. 0146106060
www.avis.com

Budget
In Paris: Tel. 01 46 86 65 65
www.budget.com

Europcar
Booking in Paris: Tel. 0130438282
www.europcar.com

Hertz
Booking in Paris: Tel. 0139383838
www.hertz.com

Sixt
In Paris: Tel. 0148625766
www.sixt.com

TAXIS
G 7
Tel. 0147394739

Taxis Bleus
Tel. 08 91 70 10 10

Alpha Taxis
Tel. 0145858585

Taxi 7000
Tel. 0142700042

Artaxi
Tel. 01 42 41 50 50

Etoile
Tel. 01 42 70 41 41

Taxis   There are about 470 taxi ranks in Paris. Unoccupied taxis, which can be recognized by the lit sign on the roof, also stop to pick up passengers who wave from the pavement. The prices and supplements are posted in the taxi. The drivers expect a tip of 10% to 15%.

Travellers with Disabilities

As an old city with lots of steps and high kerbs, Paris is not very well equipped for persons with mobility problems. Tourist sites with easy access are marked with a logo »Tourisme & Handicap«(shown on the website www.parisinfo.com). This website has a list with links of organizations that provide information or help to persons with disabilities: www.parisinfo.com, then enter handicap in the search function. The »Tourisme & Handicap« association can be contacted by e-mail: tourisme.handicaps@club-internet.fr

When to Go

Paris is an attractive destination all year round. The pleasantest months are May, June, September and October. It can be very warm and humid in July and August, when many residents leave the city for their summer holidays and many shops, restaurants and theatres are closed. In winter temperatures rarely drop below freezing, but it does rain a lot..

Index

List of maps and illustrations

Photo credits

Publisher's Information

1st Edition 2015
Worldwide Distribution: Marco Polo
Travel Publishing Ltd
Pinewood, Chineham Business Park
Crockford Lane, Chineham
Basingstoke, Hampshire RG24 8AL,
United Kingdom.

Photos, illlustrations, maps::
164 photos, 27 maps and illustrattions,
one large city map
Text:
Dr. Madeleine Reincke with contribu-
tions by Achim Bourmer, Hilke Maunder
and Reinhard Strüber
Editing:
John Sykes, Rainer Eisenschmid
Translation: John Sykes,
Anthony Halliday
Cartography:
Franz Huber, Munich; MAIRDUMONT
Ostfildern (city map)
3D illustrations:
jangled nerves, Stuttgart
Infographics:
Golden Section Graphics GmbH, Berlin
Design:
independent Medien-Design, Munich
Editor-in-chief:
Rainer Eisenschmid, Mairdumont
Ostfildern

© MAIRDUMONT GmbH & Co KG

Printed in China

Despite all of our authors' thorough
research, errors can creep in. The publishers do not accept any liability for thi
Whether you want to praise, alert us to
errors or give us a personal tip Please
contact us by email or post:

MARCO POLO Travel Publishing Ltd
Pinewood, Chineham Business Park
Crockford Lane, Chineham
Basingstoke, Hampshire RG24 8AL
United Kingdom
Email: sales@marcopolouk.com

FSC
www.fsc.org
MIX
Paper from
responsible sources
FSC® C011918

MARCO ⊕ POLO

HANDBOOKS

MARCO ⊕ POLO
TRAVEL HANDBOOK
BERLIN
INFOGRAPHICS · 3D ILLUSTRATIONS · PULL-OUT MAP
Insider Tips
NEW

MARCO ⊕ POLO
TRAVEL HANDBOOK
DRESDEN
INFOGRAPHICS · 3D ILLUSTRATIONS · PULL-OUT MAP
Insider Tips
NEW

MARCO ⊕ POLO
TRAVEL HANDBOOK
ICELAND
INFOGRAPHICS · 3D ILLUSTRATIONS · PULL-OUT MAP
Insider Tips
NEW

MARCO ⊕ POLO
TRAVEL HANDBOOK
LONDON
INFOGRAPHICS · 3D ILLUSTRATIONS · PULL-OUT MAP
Insider Tips
NEW

NEW YORK
INFOGRAPHICS · 3D ILLUSTRATIONS · PULL-OUT MAP
Insider Tips
NEW

PARIS
INFOGRAPHICS · 3D ILLUSTRATIONS · PULL-OUT MAP
Insider Tips
NEW

MARCO ⊕ POLO
TRAVEL HANDBOOK
ROME
INFOGRAPHICS · 3D ILLUSTRATIONS · PULL-OUT MAP
Insider Tips
NEW

MARCO ⊕ POLO
TRAVEL HANDBOOK
VENICE
INFOGRAPHICS · 3D ILLUSTRATIONS · PULL-OUT MAP
Insider Tips
NEW

www.marco-polo.com

Paris Curiosities

*Paris is the city of love, the city of lights and of fashion, a feast for life –
and a lively metropolis that has experienced many an astonsihing and
curious fact during its varied history.*

►Tear down the Eiffel Tower!

The Eiffel Tower was intended only for the World Exposition in 1900 and was then supposed to be torn down. That made it easy in 1925 for the con-artist Victor Lustig to convince a scrap metal dealer that the tower was supposed to be scrapped. The con was exposed because Lustig claimed to be an official of the »postal ministry«.

►Mudhole

When the Romans settled on the muddy banks of the Seine they called their settlement Lutetia, from Latin lutum, which means mud. The capital city got its present name in the 5th century after the fall of the Roman Empire im memory of the Celtic Parisii, who lived on the Ile de Cité in around 250 BC.

►No dead in the cemetery

Napoleon had the cemetaries of the inner city closed in 1804 for hygienic reasons and had the hge Cimetière du Père Lachaise opened. But no one wanted to be buried there because it was too far away. So the emperor had the remains of Abélard and Héloise moved there with great pomp. In a short time the number of graves climbed to more than 30,000 and anybody who was anybody wanted to be buried there.

►Lost in Paris

Street signs only appeared in Paris in 1805: Signs made of white porcelain with red writing for streets that ran parallel to the Seine, with black writing for streets that ran away from the Seine. Baron Haussmann commissioned the first city maps in the mid 19th century. Until then people were told to climb the city monuments for orientation.

►Cinema screen star

Since the invention of the cinema Paris has inspired film-makers like no other city. In more than 7000 productions the capital has played the main role or has given the plot its unique flair. The most recent hommage came into the cinemas in 2011: Woody Allen's »Midnight in Paris«.

►Street record

the shortest street in Paris is only 5.75m/19ft long, Rue de Degrés in the 2nd Arrondissement; it connects the Rue de Cléry to the Rue Beauregard with 14 steps. The longest street in the metropolis on the Seine is Boulevard Périphérique, which circles the Ville de Paris in 35.5km/117ft.